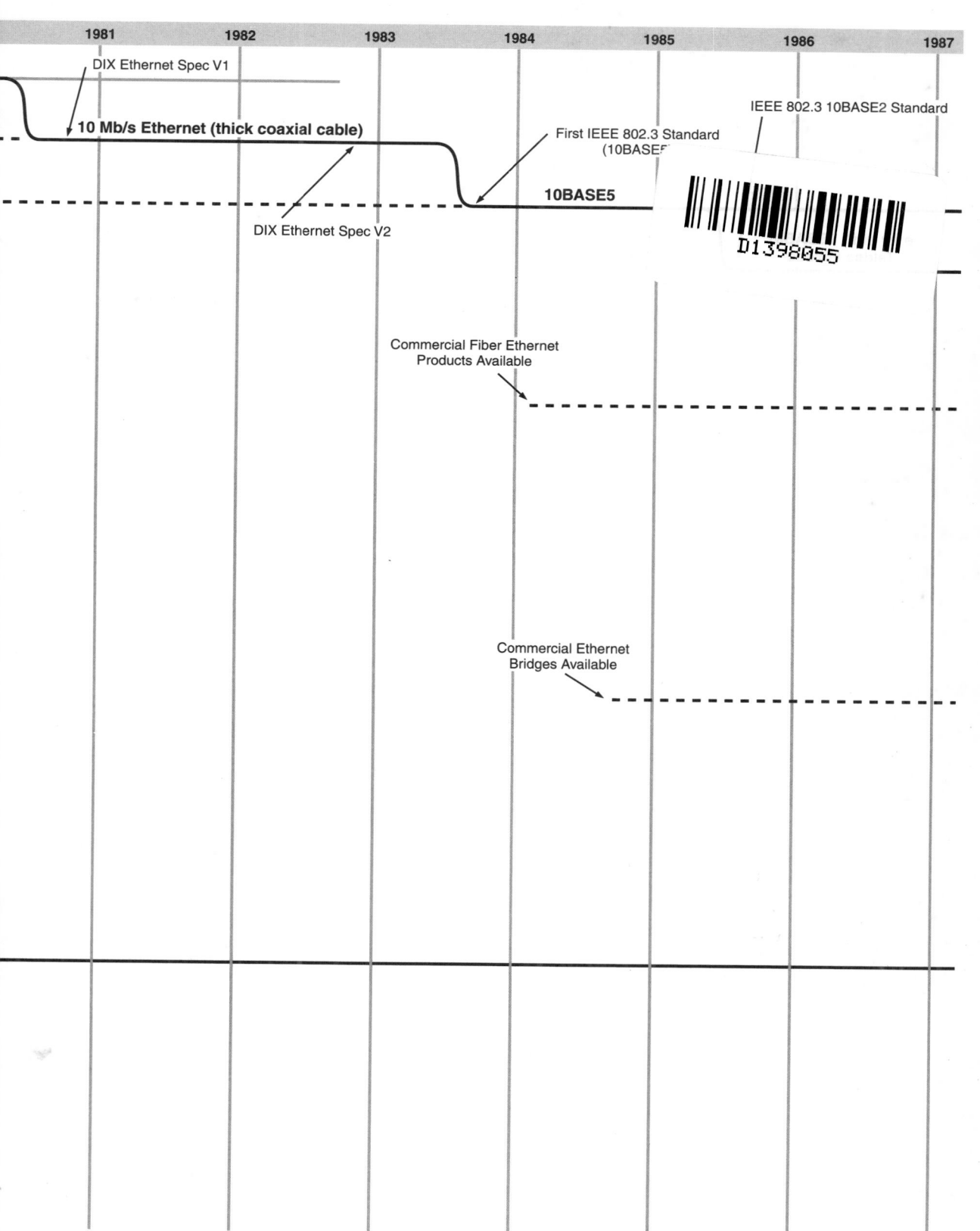

1981 | 1982 | 1983 | 1984 | 1985 | 1986 | 1987

DIX Ethernet Spec V1

10 Mb/s Ethernet (thick coaxial cable)

IEEE 802.3 10BASE2 Standard

First IEEE 802.3 Standard
(10BASE

10BASE5

DIX Ethernet Spec V2

D1398055

Commercial Fiber Ethernet
Products Available

Commercial Ethernet
Bridges Available

Gigabit Ethernet

Gigabit Ethernet

Technology and Applications for High-Speed LANs

Rich Seifert

Addison-Wesley

An imprint of Addison Wesley Longman, Inc.

Reading, Massachusetts • Harlow, England • Menlo Park, California
Berkeley, California • Don Mills, Ontario • Sydney • Bonn
Amsterdam • Tokyo • Mexico City

The publisher offers discounts on this book when ordered in quantity for special sales. For more information, please contact:

Corporate, Government, and Special Sales
Addison Wesley Longman, Inc.
One Jacob Way
Reading, Massachusetts 01867

Library of Congress Cataloging-in-Publication Data

Seifert, Rich, 1952–
    Gigabit Ethernet: technology and applications for high-speed LANs / Rich Seifert.
        p.   cm.
    Includes bibliographical references and index.
    ISBN 0-201-18553-9
    1. Ethernet (Local area network system)   I. Title.
TK5105.8.E83S45   1998
621.39'81—dc21   98–9357
                                      CIP

ISBN 0-201-18553-9
Text printed on recycled and acid-free paper.
1 2 3 4 5 6 7 8 9 10-MA-0201009998
First printing, April 1998

For Jean, to kvell,

and

for Anna, who thinks ATM is a device that

gives you small amounts of cash, rather than

taking away large amounts of it.

Contents

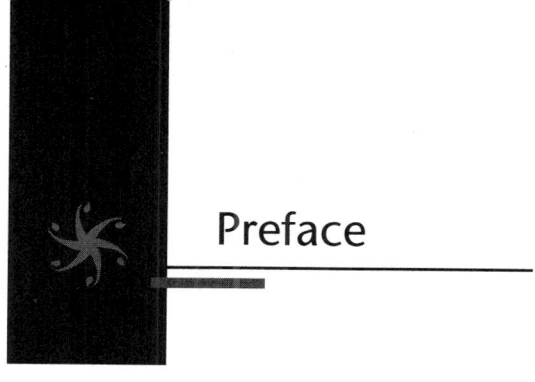

Preface

During the 1980s and 1990s, the growth in the use of computer networks has been nothing short of phenomenal. No longer do organizations consider *whether* they need a network, but only *what type* of network should be employed. The parallel growth in the capabilities of the devices connecting to the networks (personal computers, workstations, servers, and so on) and the applications using those networks have combined to transform yesterday's network technologies into a performance roadblock. Like our freeways, we constantly add lanes only to find that the traffic demand simply increases to keep the road as congested as always.

Gigabit Ethernet, conceived in 1995, is the most recent addition to the world's most popular family of local area network (LAN) technologies. The lure of riding yet another wave of successful Ethernet systems has attracted enormous interest from vendors eager to provide new products to feed bandwidth-hungry network applications. In that year, the Institute for Electronics and Electrical Engineers (IEEE) LAN/MAN Standards Committee began the process of developing an industry standard for Gigabit Ethernet. While the gestation period of an IEEE standard may exceed even that of an elephant, the IEEE 802.3z Gigabit Ethernet standard is expected to be formally approved by IEEE in mid-1998 and is already endorsed by dozens of equipment manufacturers. Even more important, products are becoming available for users to deploy in their networks.

This book guides both users and developers through the complex issues involved in designing and deploying high-speed networks.

Who Should Read this Book

This book is aimed at the needs of both:

- **Network Technologists:** This includes engineers working in companies involved in the design and manufacture of computers and communications products, academics (both instructors and students), network product marketing and sales personnel, independent consultants, and anyone else interested in understanding at a detailed level how Gigabit Ethernet works. In this context, the book is a reference work, providing technical detail without the terseness and formality of the IEEE standard.

- **Network Users:** This includes network planners, designers, installers and administrators, Management Information Services (MIS) management, Value-Added Resellers (VARs), and operations staff in any organization that selects, installs, or uses network products. This book will help these users to understand and become more comfortable with this new technology, as well as to make rational decisions in the selection and purchase of products. In many cases, these users depend primarily on equipment suppliers as their main source of information. Such information is always suspect, as suppliers have a strong motivation to sell their technology regardless of whether it is appropriate.

The reader is assumed to be at least casually familiar with LANs and Ethernet in particular. No attempt is made to provide a complete, from-the-ground-up tutorial suitable for novices. Indeed, such a work would require an encyclopedia and make it impossible to focus on Gigabit Ethernet and the related technologies on which it builds and relies. Network technologists and users grounded in the fundamentals of Ethernet will find everything they need to understand completely the workings of the new Gigabit Ethernet system. In the process, they will gain enormous insight into why things are done the way they are at 10, 100, and 1000 Mb/s, and not just the cold facts.

This book is not intended as a "standards companion." While a summary of the standard itself is provided (Chapter 13), the bulk of the book is concerned with helping the reader to understand Gigabit Ethernet technology and the ways in which it may best serve the needs of real applications. A conscious effort has been made to use practical, everyday terminology, rather than the Arcane Architectural Abstractions and Acronyms (AAAAAs) typical of standards documents.

Organization of the Book

The book is organized into three main sections:

Part I: Foundations of Gigabit Ethernet

Chapter 1 provides a historical context for Gigabit Ethernet, looks at why Ethernet is as popular as it is, and identifies the key enabling technologies that aided its development.

Chapter 2 discusses the shift from shared media (coaxial cable) to dedicated media (twisted-pair and optical fiber).

Chapter 3 introduces the principles of bridging and switching and the move from shared-bandwidth LANs to dedicated LANs with central switches.

Chapter 4 shows how full-duplex operation became possible through the use of switches, and the implications of its use.

Chapter 5 describes the subtle variations in Ethernet frame formats (and their ultimate unification) that have developed over the years.

Chapter 6 provides detailed information about the operation and use of Ethernet flow control.

Chapter 7 shows how the controller-to-transceiver interface has evolved from the original 10 Mb/s transceiver cable to the medium-independent interface used in 100 Mb/s and Gigabit Ethernet.

Chapter 8 explains the operation of the automatic link configuration mechanism (Auto-Negotiation).

Part II: Gigabit Ethernet Technology

Chapter 9 provides an overview of Gigabit Ethernet. For knowledgeable readers and experienced networkers looking for a quick summary of what's new in Gigabit Ethernet relative to its slower-speed cousins, this chapter is the place to start. (But be sure to go back and read Part I. It contains a lot of useful information and provides insights that you have never seen before!)

Chapter 10 explains the modifications made to the Ethernet Medium Access Control (MAC) algorithms to support 1000 Mb/s operation. Both half- and full-duplex operation are discussed.

Chapter 11 discusses options for the design and selection of hubs for Gigabit Ethernet use. Repeaters, switches, routers, and the concept of a "Buffered Distributor" are fully explained.

Chapter 12 delves into the details of the low-level physical signaling used with Gigabit Ethernet. Comprehensive information on encoding methods, interfaces, media specifications, and topology rules are provided, both for optical fiber and twisted-pair media. The principles of Auto-Negotiation for Gigabit Ethernet are also explained. This chapter is useful for network installers and facilities planners.

Chapter 13 is your Sherpa guide to the IEEE 802.3z Gigabit Ethernet standard itself.

Part III: Applying Gigabit Ethernet

Chapter 14 discusses the different network requirements imposed by different application environments and shows which technologies are best suited to each. It emphasizes a "top-down," application-centric approach to network design, rather than a technology-driven model.

Chapter 15 looks at the performance implications of complex networks and considers the real causes of poor network performance. Some insight is provided into the best way to measure network performance and get the most out of the network you have paid for.

Chapter 16 considers technology alternatives to Gigabit Ethernet, including switched Fast Ethernet and FDDI, Fibre Channel, HIPPI, and ATM.

My Thanks

It's a daunting task to write a book of this depth and magnitude. Fortunately, I had the help of numerous experts who reviewed material, corrected my errors, and gave excellent advice on the content and organization of this work. Thanks to: Carsten Bormann, Bob Fink, Howard Frazier, Andy Hacker, Frank Kastenholz, Dennis Miller, Rex Naden, Thomas Skibo, Joel Snyder, Rich Taborek, and Geoff Thompson, and especially to Greg Hersh, Bert Manfredi, and Mart Molle for their time and advice. Thanks also to Mary Harrington and Genevieve Rajewski for all of their help with the nuts and bolts of publishing and to Carol Long for navigating the winding roads of the Santa Cruz Mountains and getting me started on this project in the first place.

I also would like to thank all of my consulting clients, whose interesting projects continually force me to stay on top of current technologies, and my students at the University of California at Berkeley, who (unbeknownst to them) provided a testing ground for most of the figures, tables, and material in the book. Thanks also to my colleagues in the IEEE 802.3 Working Group and IEEE 802.3z Gigabit Ethernet Task Force, who consistently develop the highest-quality and most widely adopted standards in the LAN industry.

Of course, any errors contained in this work are my responsibility alone.

Technology Updates

Network technology changes quickly, especially in relation to the time required to write and publish a book such as this one. This book was written contemporaneously with the development of the Gigabit Ethernet standard; at the time of publication, the standard had not yet been formally approved. As a result, there may be minor differences between some operational parameters presented here and those of the final approved standard. Also, work on Gigabit Ethernet will not come to a halt when the first revision of the standard is approved. There are ongoing projects both to expand the usefulness of the technology, and to correct and maintain the standard.

To keep you informed with the most up-to-date information, including any corrections to this book, I will be maintaining a World Wide Web site for this purpose, at:

http://www.awl.com/cseng/titles/0-201-18553-9/

Contacting the Author

I welcome your feedback, both on the usefulness (or not) of this book, as well as any additions or corrections that should be made in future editions. While I can't guarantee a personal response to everyone, please feel free to contact me:

Rich Seifert
Networks & Communications Consulting
21885 Bear Creek Way
Los Gatos, CA 95033
(408) 395–5700
(408) 395–1966 (fax)
seifert@netcom.com

PART

I

Foundations of
Gigabit Ethernet

1   Ethernet before Gigabit

igabit Ethernet didn't appear out of nowhere, springing from the head of some networking Medusa. It was built on the lessons learned from over 20 years of Ethernet experience and incorporates the numerous advances in technology developed over that time. This chapter looks at the history of Ethernet and some of the reasons why Ethernet became the predominant Local Area Network (LAN) technology used today. Chapter 1 also identifies the technology's key building blocks—that enabled the development of Gigabit Ethernet. The remaining chapters in this section deal with each of those enabling technologies in greater detail.

On the inside covers of this book is a timeline showing the key events and milestones in the development of Ethernet (and Gigabit Ethernet in particular).

1.1   A Brief History of Ethernet

1.1.1   1973–82: The Creation of Ethernet and the DIX Consortium

Ethernet was originally conceived and implemented in a laboratory at Xerox Corporation in Palo Alto, California, in 1973. That lab prototype, developed by Dr. Robert Metcalfe (generally regarded as the "father of Ethernet") operated at 2.94 million bits per second (3 Mb/s). This experimental Ethernet (known within Xerox as the "X-Wire") was used in some early Xerox products, including the Xerox Alto, the world's first networked personal workstation with a graphical user interface.[1] Xerox never successfully commercialized either the Alto or the 3 Mb/s Ethernet network. Both remained experimental technologies used almost exclusively within Xerox.[2]

---

1. The Alto is the machine best known for inspiring the Apple Macintosh.

2. Some Altos did make their way out of the lab. During the administration of U. S. President Jimmy Carter, Xerox Altos, using 3 Mb/s Ethernet, were used for word processing at the White House.

In 1979, Xerox and Digital Equipment Corporation (DEC) joined forces to standardize, commercialize, and promote the use of network products using Ethernet technology. It was an ideal match: Xerox had the basic patents and technology, and DEC was the leading volume supplier of networked computers at that time.[3] Intel Corporation was added to the consortium (at the request of Xerox) to provide guidance to ensure that commercial Ethernet could be easily integrated in low-cost silicon. This DEC–Intel–Xerox (DIX) cartel developed and published the standard for a 10 Mb/s version of Ethernet in September 1980. [DIX80] The only physical medium supported in that document was a thick, multidrop coaxial cable. In 1982, a second revision of this standard was published that made some minor changes to the signaling and incorporated some network management features. [DIX82]

In parallel with the DIX work, the IEEE formed its now-famous Project 802 to provide a broad industry framework for the standardization of LAN technology. The first meeting was held in February 1980 in San Francisco, California. When it became clear that the IEEE 802 committee could not agree on a single standard for all LANs (its original mission), the committee subdivided into various Working Groups (WGs), each focusing on different LAN technologies. IEEE 802.3 worked on the standard for LANs based on the Ethernet technology. The IEEE 802.4 and 802.5 groups worked on Token Bus and Token Ring technology, respectively. (See Chapter 13 for a complete discussion of the IEEE 802 organization.)

1.1.2   1982–1990: 10 Mb/s Ethernet Reaches Maturity

In June 1983, the IEEE Standards Board approved the first IEEE 802.3 standard. With a few relatively unimportant differences, this was the same technology as embodied in the DIX Ethernet standard. Indeed, much of the language of the two documents is identical. During the 1980s (as the marketplace for Ethernet grew), this base standard was augmented with a set of repeater specifications and a variety of physical-medium options: thinner coaxial cable for low-cost desktop attachments, optical fibers for interbuilding connections, and so on.

The widespread adoption of structured wiring systems using unshielded twisted-pair cabling (see Chapter 2) changed the underlying physical infra-

---

3. IBM was, of course, the leading manufacturer of computers (measured by total revenue), but since DEC sold primarily smaller computers, DEC's volumes were much higher. In addition, IBM's network architecture, SNA, was very connection-oriented and so did not lend itself well to a connectionless, best-effort service, such as that provided by Ethernet.

structure of the buildings within which most Ethernets were deployed. During the 1980s, Ethernet was most commonly implemented in a physical bus topology using either thick or thin coaxial cables. These schemes were incompatible with the star-wired topology of structured wiring. Seeing an opportunity, SynOptics Communications (some of whose founders came from the same Xerox Palo Alto Research Center that originally developed Ethernet) developed a mechanism for transmitting 10 Mb/s Ethernet signals over twisted-pair cables. The commercial success of their LattisNet product led to the move to standardize this technology. The Ethernet-over-twisted-pair (10BASE-T) standard was approved by the IEEE in September 1990 and quickly became the preferred choice of Ethernet media for office automation applications.

1.1.3   1983–1997: LAN Bridging and Switching

The first transparent LAN bridges were developed by DEC during the early 1980s, with commercial products shipping by 1984. While initially low performing and relatively expensive, they were very easy to set up and use and provided a better price/performance tradeoff than the alternatives available at the time (for example, internetwork routers). Bridges became a popular tool for the interconnection of the growing number of Ethernet LANs (see Chapter 3). New start-up companies and established manufacturers alike offered a wide range of bridge products throughout the 1980s. In 1987, work began on an industry standard for vendor-interoperable interconnection of LANs using bridges. The result was the IEEE 802.1D standard in 1990 [IEEE93a].

In 1991, Kalpana Corporation was formed to develop and market a new class of Ethernet bridge, one that supported a large number of attachments and could operate at full capacity simultaneously on all ports. Sold as "LAN Switches," these devices soon became popular not only for traditional LAN interconnection, but also for high-performance dedicated computer connections. Many other companies joined the switch market, and the price of switches rapidly dropped.

The use of switches allowed LAN bandwidth to be dedicated to a single computer, rather than its being shared among multiple devices. This eliminated the need to include any access control mechanism and allowed "full-duplex Ethernet" (see Chapter 4). In 1995, the IEEE 802.3 Committee began work on a standard for full-duplex operation, producing an approved standard in 1997 [IEEE97].

1.1.4   1992–1997: Fast Ethernet

With the growth of computing capability and application needs came a con-comitant increase in the demand for network capacity. The use of switched LANs brought more bandwidth to the individual's desktop, thereby elimi-nating the need to share the pipe with other users. Of course, most networks use servers that are still shared among many users. With dedicated bandwidth for each user, the server bandwidth requirements became even greater.

In 1991–92, Grand Junction Networks recognized that for desktop switches to be really useful, a higher-speed connection was needed to shared resources such as servers and backbone connections. In response, they devel-oped a higher-speed version of Ethernet that had the same basic characteris-tics (frame format, software interface, access control dynamics) as Ethernet but that operated at 100 Mb/s. This proved to be a huge success and fostered another industry standards activity. The resulting Fast Ethernet standard [IEEE95] spawned another wave of high-volume Ethernet products. Note that this was the first data-rate increase for Ethernet since the original DIX specification 15 years earlier!

1.1.5   1996–Present: Gigabit Ethernet

Less than a year after the official standardization of Fast Ethernet, work was already underway on Gigabit Ethernet, which would operate at 1000 Mb/s. Fast Ethernet filled a pent-up demand for capacity that had been building for 15 years. It was being deployed at an amazing rate in new installations and as a LAN upgrade. However, the combination of switching and Fast Ethernet held the potential to put even greater strain on network servers and campus backbones.

Gigabit Ethernet evolved to fill that need. Numerous companies were already developing and shipping proprietary 1000 Mb/s Ethernet products. An IEEE 802.3 Task Force was formed in 1996 to develop a standard, which was completed and approved in 1998 [IEEE98]. Work continues to extend Gigabit Ethernet technology to operate over unshielded twisted-pair for desk-top applications. Figure 1–1 depicts the increase of Ethernet data rates over time.

1.2   Why Is Ethernet so Popular?

Worldwide, over 100 million Ethernet interfaces are deployed (at the time of this writing, still mostly operating at 10 Mb/s) in personal computers, servers, internetworking devices, printers, test equipment, telephone switches, cable

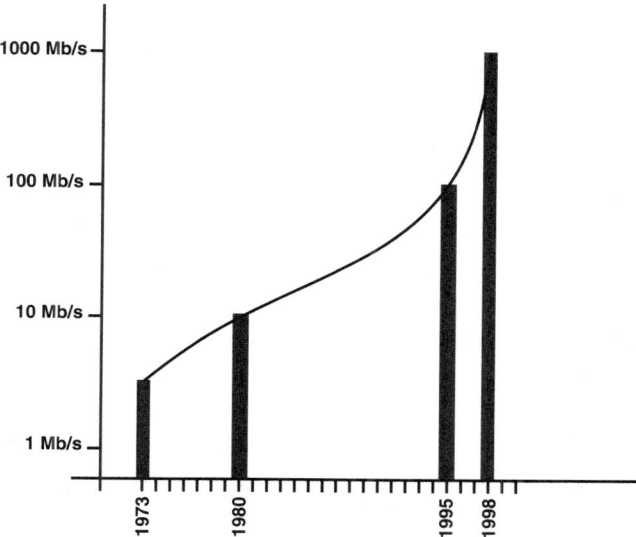

Figure 1–1 Ethernet data rate growth.

TV set-top boxes—the list is huge and increasing daily. In many products, there is no intent to connect the device to a "traditional" computer network; the Ethernet is simply a low-cost, high-speed, general-purpose interface. Ethernet has become "the RS-232 of the 90s," very much as its designers intended. [SEIF83] Why did this happen? What is it about Ethernet that makes it so popular?

1.2.1   Ethernet versus Token Ring

During the mid-1980s, when Ethernet systems were first being widely implemented and sold, IBM developed and marketed its Token Ring technology as a competitive, alternative LAN system. Many industry analysts predicted that Token Ring sales would soon equal, and then overtake, Ethernet sales. Token Ring had (at least from a cursory inspection) many features not available in Ethernet systems:

- Priority access, thereby allowing certain devices to achieve better or more reliable performance
- Automatic sensing of certain classes of physical cable and interface faults, with built-in management mechanisms for reporting errors
- The ability to support larger frame sizes
- A low-level acknowledgment mechanism which allowed receivers to report successful frame delivery to the sender.

All this, plus the support of the world's largest computer company, an approved international standard, and a long list of equipment suppliers ready, willing, and able to supply Token Ring products, made it appear that the analysts' predictions would be correct.

It never happened. While no one would reasonably argue that Token Ring was unsuccessful as a technology and product offering, it never achieved the widespread acceptance and market volumes of Ethernet. The Token Ring sales curve never crossed that of Ethernet for new shipments; neither did the installed base of products ever shift from Ethernet dominance.[4] Token Ring sales, in their heyday, captured 20–25% of the total LAN market share. In recent years, this share has steadily declined to an almost negligible percentage of the total LAN systems market. Token Ring technology provided a practical solution to the business communications problems of a lot of customers (and made a lot of money for the equipment suppliers) within its 20% market niche, but it never became the commodity that Ethernet did.

One reason for this was that even though dozens of companies were (and still are) building interface cards, hubs, routers, and so on, with Token Ring connections, IBM was the only computer *systems* manufacturer actively promoting a Token Ring-based strategy. Ultimately, the reason that we build networks is to attach the computers that support the users' applications. Network equipment vendors provide products to support the interconnection of the computers, but the network is the means, not the end. Ethernet had the necessary broad support from many computer systems manufacturers from the very beginning, including not only the original DIX consortium, but also major players like Sun Microsystems, Hewlett-Packard, and dozens of others.

1.2.2   The Price Is Right

The bottom line is cost. When there are multiple alternative solutions, all of which "solve the problem," the lowest-cost approach will usually win. End users rarely care whether the bits on the network go around a ring or use dis-

---

4. In 1995, while visiting IBM's network product development laboratories in Research Triangle Park, North Carolina, I noted a banner celebrating the shipment of the 10 millionth IBM Token Ring interface. IBM was the world's leading supplier of Token Ring interfaces, and this was a major milestone, achieved after approximately ten years of shipments. At that time, 3Com Corporation, the leading manufacturer of network interfaces overall, was shipping approximately 1 million Ethernet interfaces *each month!* That number had doubled to approximately 2 million per month by 1997, and 3Com represented "only" 40% of the Ethernet interface market.

tributed contention arbitration. What they want is to plug a cable into their computers and get their jobs done. As long as the network can support the applications running on the attached computers, the gory details of the internal network operation are largely irrelevant.

At a higher level, the organization wants the network technology that supports those desired applications at the lowest cost. There is no reason to pay more than necessary unless there is some real value to the higher-cost product—it must provide some capability that is not available otherwise and allows the users to run applications that they could not otherwise run. Ethernet is simply a lower-cost network than Token Ring.

Many people believe that if Token Ring had achieved the volumes of Ethernet, it would have reached the same low price-points; that is, Ethernet is less expensive only because it has higher volumes. This is not true. There are fundamental reasons why Ethernet is less expensive than Token Ring. Understanding this can give you a great deal of insight into what makes a network product ultimately successful. These same principles are currently at play in the deployment of Gigabit Ethernet relative to its technology alternatives, in particular Asynchronous Transfer Mode, or ATM (see Chapter 16).

Ethernet is simple. Extremely simple. The fact that it doesn't have a lot of features and options is not to its detriment. Rather, it is an advantage in that Ethernet can be built using less circuitry and therefore at a lower cost. For example:

- **Priority is complicated.** The lack of priority in Ethernet means that the access-control algorithm can be much simpler. There is no complexity (as exists in both Token Ring and Token Bus systems) for managing the current priority access level on the network. As a side advantage, network access without priority is *fair*—every station has the same probability of network access as any other. No station can impede the progress of other stations.[5]

---

5. Token Ring LANs (IEEE 802.5) use priority to give certain stations preferred access to the network upon request. Token Bus LANs (IEEE 802.4) use priority differently; they give applications preferred access within a station. This model implies even more complexity and cost, since this mechanism generally implies multiple transmit and receive queues in the stations. The result is a complicated memory interface and, most likely, the need for additional memory.

Also interesting to note is that while Token Ring supports eight levels of priority, few applications have ever used this capability. Virtually every frame ever sent on a Token Ring network has been sent at the highest user-data priority level. (Who wants lower priority?) With every station at high priority, the result is the same as if there were no priority at all, except for the cost.

- **Ethernet does not require a central control station.** Token Ring uses the concept of an *Active Monitor,* a station responsible for performing various network "housekeeping" tasks. A traditional Token Ring network cannot operate without an active monitor station. To ensure there is always at least one device on the network with this capability, virtually every Token Ring station has the active monitor features built in. Users pay for this added complexity in every station, although it is enabled in only one of them on any given LAN.
- **The Token Ring algorithms are more complicated than Ethernet's.** Simply put, there are more possible "states" (operational conditions) in a Token Ring LAN than in Ethernet. The number of exception conditions (lost Tokens, disconnected cables, stations joining and leaving the ring, and so on) is quite large and must be handled within the controller logic.

The result is that a Token Ring controller requires more circuitry to perform its tasks than does an Ethernet controller. It is possible to implement the basic Ethernet access control mechanism (CSMA/CD, see Chapter 10 for a complete explanation) using hard-coded logic (finite state machine) in less than 3000 gate-equivalents. The Token Ring access control algorithms are so complex that the most popular interface chips used an embedded microcontroller (that is, an internal computer within the controller chip on the interface card) that required software to be loaded into it from the host. This complexity made it impractical to build the controller as a simple state machine. Increased complexity equals more circuitry. More circuitry equals more cost. More cost equals fewer sales. It's that simple.

Clearly, volume sales help to bring down prices, as does improvement in silicon technology. But the underlying complexity issue cannot be avoided. By 1997, it was possible to purchase 10 Mb/s Ethernet interfaces for personal computers, in unit quantities, for under $20. A 16 Mb/s Token Ring interface cost closer to $200. The message is clear: Keep it as simple as possible.

1.2.3 And DIX So Loved the Network Business that They Gave the World Their Only LAN, Ethernet . . .

Digital Equipment, Intel, and Xerox developed the specifications for 10 Mb/s Ethernet in 1980, which became the foundation of the IEEE 802.3 standard. Unlike with most standards, when DIX published their specification they did so without any copyright restrictions.[6] It was the intent of the three compa-

---

6. This refers only to the original DIX "Blue Books." [DIX80, DIX82] The IEEE 802.3 standard developed from that base is copyrighted by IEEE and available only for a fee.

nies to make it as easy as possible for others to get access to the technology and to build Ethernet products. While this would not seem to be in the best competitive interests of the original consortium, in the long run this strategy allowed the market to grow faster than if they had "kept the keys to the castle." It is better to get a small slice of a huge pie than your own, private cupcake.

In addition, Xerox effectively relinquished its patent rights to Ethernet. [METC77, BOGG78] There is no license fee required to use Ethernet technology.[7] Ultimately, Xerox even dropped its registered trademark on the Ethernet name, thereby allowing unfettered use of the popular name for CSMA/CD LANs.[8] All of these actions tended to make it easy to incorporate Ethernet in new products.

1.3 Ethernet Swings Like a Pendulum Do

If you were using a personal computer in 1979, it was probably an Apple II, a Commodore 64, an early 8080 "kit" machine, or the equivalent. There is little practical use for any of these computers today, other than for their nostalgic value. No one would seriously consider using their core technology (for example, an 8080 processor) in a modern general-purpose PC. Similarly, disk technology from that period—low density 8-inch floppy disks and hard drives the size of washing machines—has disappeared in favor of improved versions with higher density, smaller size, and lower cost. Computer-related technology evolves quickly to obsolete current products, often before we have even finished paying for them! [BARR96]

Network technology is the exception. It is impossible to even consider running today's applications using a machine with the power of a 2 MHz 6502 (an Apple II). However, many organizations are served perfectly well by shared 10 Mb/s Ethernet, a technology that is (from a performance perspective)

---

7. Prior to the development and standardization of IEEE 802.3, Ethernet address blocks (see Chapter 5) were assigned by Xerox Corporation. For the block assignment, it charged a $1000 fee, which was structured as a one-time, worldwide, non-exclusive, royalty-free license to make, have made, or use the technology patented in [METC77] and [BOGG78]. When the address assignment authority was transferred to the IEEE, Xerox dropped even this nominal licensing arrangement. (However, IEEE still charges $1000, mostly to offset administrative costs and to make sure that every graduate student doesn't ask for his or her own block!)

8. During a ceremony celebrating the tenth anniversary of the IEEE 802 standards committee, Dr. Robert Metcalfe, the original inventor of Ethernet, addressed the issue of whether there was a difference between Ethernet and the IEEE 802.3 standard: "I invented Ethernet, and I say what Ethernet is. And I say that Ethernet is IEEE 802.3!" (to resounding cheers and applause).

unchanged since 1980. How can ancient networking technology serve us well when ancient computer technology is useful only for musuem displays?

There is a constantly changing relationship, over time, between computing and communications technology. As these two fields do not advance in lock-step synchronization, at any given time our computing capabilities may exceed that of the communications infrastructure, or vice versa. Like a pendulum swinging, the limitation on performance may be either in the communications system, or in the computing devices using those communications channels, as depicted in Figure 1–2.

Significant advances were made in computing technology during the 1970s, with the development of the microprocessor (at the low end of the scale) to super-mini and mainframe computers (at the high end). There was not, however, an equal improvement in LAN or computer communications technology. Even at the end of the 1970s, the bulk of computer communications used serial RS-232 connections, at speeds of up to 19.2 kb/s. Early low-speed (1–2.5 Mb/s) commercial LANs were available (for example, ARCnet from Datapoint and OmniNet from Corvus Systems), but they were proprietary and not widely deployed.

Ethernet swung the pendulum so far that it went through the wall and came out in the next room. A 10 Mb/s network far exceeded the needs and capabilities of the computers available at that time. Even in 1983, a VAX super-minicomputer could not saturate a 10 Mb/s network (that is, it could not transmit and receive at the full LAN data rate; see Chapter 15). Most observers (and users) thought that the Ethernet design was *too* ambitious.

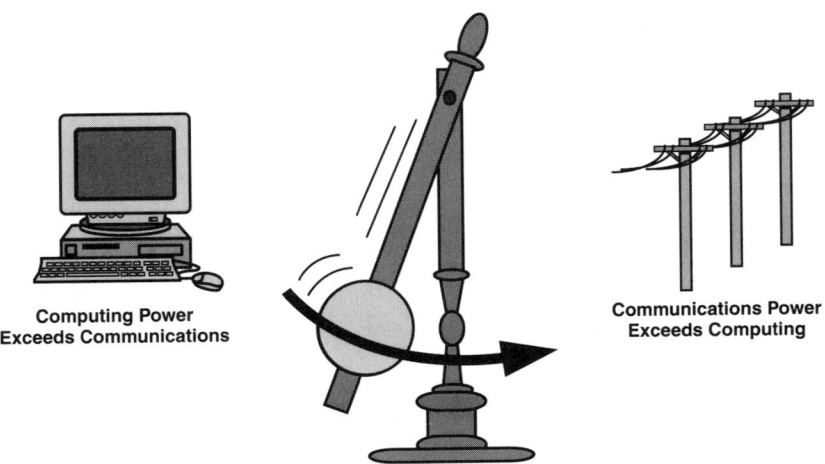

Computing Power
Exceeds Communications

Communications Power
Exceeds Computing

Figure 1–2 Computing versus communications.

The world didn't need a 10 Mb/s network; it needed a cheap, reliable 1 Mb/s network; it would take more than 10 years from the introduction of 10 Mb/s Ethernet until common desktop PCs could achieve sustained data transfers at full network speed.[9] It is not surprising that there was no driving need to upgrade the Ethernet technology during that period. A 10 Mb/s LAN was a very fat pipe indeed.[10]

By the early 1990s, the pendulum had been retrieved from the next room and was beginning to swing back across the centerpoint. Popular desktop computers could easily saturate 10 Mb/s LANs. Server computers supporting many users needed even more communications capacity. Thus Fast Ethernet (and switching; discussed in Chapter 3) evolved and became immediately popular. The Fast Ethernet market developed even faster than its proponents hoped. Within 18 months of the standardization of the technology, 100 Mb/s interfaces became low-cost commodity items. While most desktop computer applications don't really need (and cannot take advantage) of Fast Ethernet today, many new installations are using 100 Mb/s interfaces nonetheless, for the same reasons that 10 Mb/s Ethernets were installed years earlier: they are inexpensive and will support increased performance needs over time.

Of course, as desktop network capacity increases, server and backbone network requirements also increase—and at a higher absolute level. With 10 Mb/s desktop connections, 100 Mb/s backbone and server connections are appropriate. With desktops moving from 10 to 100 Mb/s, the backbone and server requirements are similarly increasing. Gigabit Ethernet provides the means to prevent the pendulum from swinging too far the other way, that is, allowing computing capability to exceed that of the communications network.

1.4   A Word on Nomenclature

When Ethernet first saw widespread commercial use, it supported only one data rate (10 Mb/s) and one physical medium (thick coaxial cable). The term "Ethernet" was therefore unambiguous in referring to this system. This clarity and simplicity was not to last, however. Ethernet was modified to operate over an increasing variety of physical media, for reasons of cost, ease of installation, and maintenance, use in electrically hostile environments, and so

---

9. A high-end 486-class PC with appropriate network interfaces and device drivers can saturate a 10 Mb/s LAN.

10. In shared LANs, a major reason for providing high-speed is not so much to provide sustained throughput at the channel data rate, but to provide low delay for a moderate-to-large number of devices. Even so, 10 Mb/s was still much more capacity than needed for its time.

on. Typically, commercial products led the market, followed by (if appropriate) standards for operation over the new medium. Later, even the data rate changed (together with even more physical media options). Hence, there are a lot of very different communications systems available today, all called "Ethernet."

In order to avoid having to say things like, "10 Mb/s Ethernet using two pairs of Category 3 unshielded twisted pair" or "Gigabit Ethernet on two optical fibers using longwave laser optics," the IEEE 802.3 standards committee developed a shorthand notation that allows us to refer to any particular standard implementation of Ethernet. Hence, a given flavor of Ethernet is referred to as

n–signal–phy

where

> **n**   is the data rate in megabits per second (that is, 1, 10, 100, or 1000).

> **signal** indicates either BASE, if the signaling used on the channel is baseband (that is, the physical medium is dedicated to the Ethernet, with no other communications system sharing the medium) or BROAD, if the signaling is broadband (that is, the physical medium can simultaneously support Ethernet and other, possibly non-Ethernet services).[11]

> **phy**   indicates the nature of the physical medium. In the first few systems to which this notation was applied, *phy* indicated the maximum length of a cable segment, in meters (rounded to the nearest 100 m). In later systems, this convention was dropped and *phy* became simply a code for the particular media type.[12]

Table 1–1 provides a complete listing of the (currently defined) Ethernet reference designations.

---

11. The only Ethernet system using broadband signaling is 10BROAD36, which allows Ethernet to operate using three channels (in each direction) of a private CATV system. Other services (broadcast television, point-to-point modems, and so on) can use the other channels simultaneously. This system is not very popular, primarily due to its high cost.

12. As part of this change in conventions, codes using the "old style" (length) convention do not use a hyphen between the signaling type and the physical medium designation (for example, 10BASE5 and 10BASE2). Later designations always have a hyphen (for example, 10BASE-T and 100BASE-FX) to show the change in meaning. In addition, the signaling designation is always capitalized. Now you can impress your coworkers and correct your boss when he or she writes "10BaseT" instead of the strictly correct "10BASE-T." Please don't call me if doing this causes your career to veer in an undesirable direction.

TABLE 1–1 ETHERNET MEDIA DESIGNATIONS

1 Mb/s Systems

1BASE5	Unshielded twisted-pair (UTP, 1 pair), 500 m maximum ("StarLAN")[1]

10 Mb/s Systems

10BASE5	Thick coaxial cable, 500 m maximum (Original Ethernet)
10BASE2	Thin coaxial cable, 185 m maximum ("Cheapernet")
10BROAD36	Broadband operation using three channels (each direction) of private CATV system, 3.6 km maximum diameter
10BASE-T	2 pairs of Category 3 (or better) UTP
10BASE-F	Generic designation for the family of 10 Mb/s optical fiber systems
10BASE-FL	2 multimode optical fibers with an asynchronous active hub, 2 km maximum
10BASE-FP	2 multimode optical fibers with passive hub, 1 km maximum
10BASE-FB	2 multimode optical fibers for synchronous active hubs, 2 km maximum

100 Mb/s Systems

100BASE-T	Generic designation for all 100 Mb/s systems[2]
100BASE-X	Generic designation for 100BASE-T systems using 4B/5B encoding
100BASE-TX	2 pairs Category 5 UTP, 100 m maximum
100BASE-FX	2 multimode optical fibers, 2 km maximum
100BASE-T4	4 pairs Category 3 (or better) UTP, 100 m maximum
100BASE-T2	2 pairs Category 3 (or better) UTP, 100 m maximum

1000 Mb/s Systems

1000BASE-X	Generic designation for 1000 Mb/s systems using 8B/10B encoding
1000BASE-CX	2 pairs 150 Ω shielded twisted-pair, 25 m maximum
1000BASE-SX	2 multimode or single-mode optical fibers using shortwave laser optics
1000BASE-LX	2 multimode or single-mode optical fibers using longwave laser optics
1000BASE-T	4 pairs Category 5 UTP, 100 m maximum

1. The 1BASE5 system was developed *after* the 10 Mb/s coaxial Ethernet but prior to 10BASE-T. It was never very successful commercially and was rendered obsolete by 10BASE-T.
2. Even though the 100 Mb/s family includes optical fiber, all are generically referred to as 100BASE-T.

1.5   Getting to Gigabit

Gigabit Ethernet is an *evolutionary,* not a revolutionary, step in the inex-
orable advance of networking technology. It was not developed in isolation
as a totally-from-scratch design or as a "solution in search of a problem."
[IEEE90a]. Rather, Gigabit Ethernet is a logical, albeit leading-edge, progression in the technology. It leverages the work that was done to date with careful consideration of those applications that require higher-speed operation.
As discussed in detail in the remaining chapters in this part of the book, Gigabit Ethernet builds upon:

■ **The shift from shared to dedicated LAN media.** While the original Ethernet used a shared coaxial medium, the benefits of a star-wired topology
with dedicated cable for every attached device became obvious with the
development of 10BASE-T. Both 100 Mb/s and Gigabit Ethernet use dedicated media exclusively, with no support for shared coaxial (or any
other) cable.

■ **The shift from shared to dedicated LAN bandwidth.** The large communications capacity of LANs was, for most of their early lives, used not so
much for sustained, high-speed data transfer between particular pairs of
devices. Rather it was a way to provide the equivalent of full-mesh connectivity among large numbers of stations, with very low delay. As the
computing and communications capacity of the attached devices has
increased and applications have been developed that can exploit the capabilities of high-speed LANs, a growing trend is to use LANs in a dedicated-bandwidth manner. This is especially true in the case of servers and
high-performance workstations. While Gigabit Ethernet allows the channel to be used in a traditional shared-bandwidth manner, optimum performance and maximum extent are achieved when it is deployed as a
dedicated bandwidth system using bridges (switches) and/or routers for
the central hub.

■ **The use of full-duplex Ethernet links.** Once the communications channel
is no longer being shared among multiple devices, it is possible to eliminate the traditional CSMA/CD[13] access control method and use each link
(station-to-station or station-to-hub) in a full-duplex (simultaneous transmit and receive) manner. This both increases channel capacity and allows

---

13. Carrier Sense, Multiple Access with Collision Detection, the traditional half-duplex
method of using an Ethernet. See Chapters 4 and 10 for a complete discussion of Ethernet
access control.

the network extent to grow beyond the limits of a CSMA/CD-controlled system. Gigabit Ethernet is expected to be deployed primarily using full-duplex, dedicated links. This will allow link lengths sufficient to support intrabuilding and campus backbone applications.

- **Ethernet flow control.** Building even further on the concepts of dedicated channels and full-duplex operation, a method that allows devices to *explicitly* control the flow of data across a full-duplex link was developed prior to Gigabit Ethernet as part of the standardization of Full Duplex Ethernet [IEEE97]. This allowed switches and other devices using full-duplex links to prevent unnecessary frame loss due to buffer overflow; the result was lower-cost products requiring less buffer memory. As the problem of buffer overflow increases linearly with the data rate of the communications channel, explicit flow control enables more cost-effective implementations of Gigabit Ethernet products. Certain new classes of Gigabit Ethernet products (for example, Buffered Distributors; discussed in Chapter 11) are not only helped by, but *require,* explicit flow control for proper operation.

- **Medium-independent interfacing.** The history of the Ethernet shows that a variety of underlying physical media need to be supported; there is no "one answer" to the question of which type of cable is "the best." Even at 10 Mb/s, Ethernets have operated over thick and thin coaxial cables, unshielded and shielded twisted pairs, and optical fibers. Depending on the particular application environment, any of these media could be the most desirable. As a result, Ethernets have always incorporated some form of medium-independent interface. Gigabit Ethernet is no exception; it supports an enhanced version of the interface developed for use at 100 Mb/s.

- **Automatic link configuration.** As device capabilities become more diverse, there is a need to ensure that interconnected devices are properly configured. Without some automatic means to determine and configure device capabilities, the burden on the human administrator becomes overwhelming. This problem was first addressed in the development of 100 Mb/s Ethernet over twisted-pair cabling in the form of an Auto-Negotiation system. Gigabit Ethernet incorporates this Auto-Negotiation system, and extends it for use over the copper cables and optical fibers used at 1000 Mb/s.

The following chapters look in detail at each of these enabling technologies for Gigabit Ethernet.

2 From Shared to Dedicated Media

As with 100 Mb/s Fast Ethernet, Gigabit Ethernet leverages off the concept that each device in the network has a dedicated media connection to a central hub. Whether the LAN bandwidth is shared among all of the stations or dedicated to each one (that is, whether shared or switched hubs are used), a given cable is allocated for use by a single device. This was not always the case for Ethernet. The original design assumed a common, shared medium: coaxial cable. This chapter explains the following:

- The driving forces behind the migration to dedicated LAN media
- The advantages (and disadvantages) of dedicated media
- The opportunities afforded by the use of dedicated media and structured wiring systems, as they relate to the design of Gigabit Ethernets

2.1 Why Coaxial Cable in the First Place?

The LAN business is one of the few fields in which, if you have been working in it for 3 years or more, you can talk about how things were "in the old days." To the thousands of people who began to learn about and use LAN technology in the 1990s, the use of structured wiring and twisted-pair cabling seems almost dogma. It is hard to understand why anyone would build a large LAN using any other wiring technology. Why didn't we design Ethernet to use twisted-pair in the first place? Why was Ethernet originally designed around coaxial cable (and a fat, expensive, hard-to-work-with cable at that)?

There are three reasons why coaxial cable was the first choice for Ethernet:

1. It is easier to design a high-speed LAN using coaxial cable than twisted-pair. While it may be easier to install or configure a LAN using twisted-pair wiring, it is much easier from the perspective of the equipment (transceiver) designer to have a coaxial cable as the underlying transmission medium. Coaxial cable has several important advantages as a medium for high-speed communications systems:

- It is much less susceptible to noise ingress (EMI susceptibility) than twisted-pairs. It is also less prone to radiate (EMI emissions) in violation of regulatory restrictions.
- The inherent bandwidth capacity of most coaxial cables far exceeds that of even the best twisted-pairs. Coaxial cable has much lower signal attenuation; thus designing a receiver is easier, since there will be more signal present than for other media. Perhaps more important, the attenuation does not degrade as much at higher frequencies. Thus the need for complex equalization circuitry at the transmitter and/or receiver is avoided.
- The impedance of a coaxial cable is controlled much better than on twisted-pairs, thereby making it easier to design transceiver circuitry.

Today 10 Mb/s Ethernet is considered the slowest of the popular LANs (remember, this is a book on *Gigabit* Ethernet!). But at the time of its introduction, 10 Mb/s Ethernet was the fastest commercial LAN ever built or sold. It was reasonable to think that we needed to use a high-grade communications medium like coaxial cable, even if it was physically inconvenient.

This may seem incongruous to the LAN newcomer, for the following reasons.

1. Coaxial cable has inherently better signal transmission characteristics than does twisted-pair, yet coaxial cable is used only for 10 Mb/s Ethernet while twisted-pair is used for 100 Mb/s systems.
2. Many sites are migrating (or have already migrated) from coaxial-based systems to newer, twisted-pair systems. This seems absurd if coaxial cable is a superior medium.

The answer lies in the fact that the advantages of the twisted-pair medium have nothing to do with its electrical or transmission characteristics. Indeed, the prime *disadvantage* of twisted-pair is its electrical characteristics. However, this is outweighed by the advantages discussed later in this chapter. Also, it is important to note that when Ethernet was being designed, 10 Mb/s was considered a very high-speed communications channel.

2. A shared medium is perfectly suitable for a shared-bandwidth LAN. When 10 Mb/s Ethernet was first designed, there was no consideration of switched LANs, hub-centric systems, bridges, and so on. A LAN was a shared-

Shared LAN Medium ⎯⎯⎯⎯

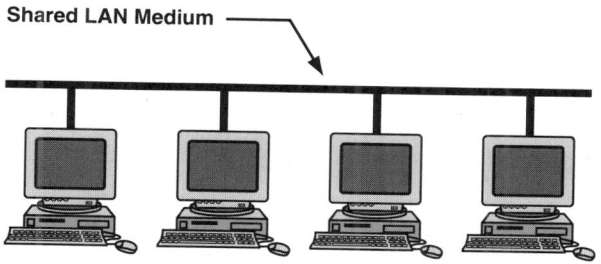

Figure 2–1   Shared LAN topology.

bandwidth communications channel, and coaxial cable in a bus topology was an appropriate means for implementing such a channel. So, given that coaxial cable was a good choice for electrical reasons, there was nothing about the topology of coaxial cabling that negated this choice. (See Figure 2–1.)

3. There was no installed base of data-grade twisted-pair to temper the decision to use coaxial cable. In the early 1980s, there was no already-installed wiring suitable for high-speed data communications in most organizations. The only wiring infrastructures were for analog telephone and for power (even today power wiring is unsuitable for high-speed LANs). The analog telephone wiring of the late 1970s was unsuitable for reliable, high-speed data communications. This wiring did not meet the requirements for even the lowest grade allowed by today's building wiring standard (that is, EIA/TIA 568 Category 3 [EIA91a]). It was inconceivable to expect that such uncontrolled, low-quality wiring would be able to reliably support even 10 Mb/s communications. Given that any practical LAN would necessitate the installation of new wire, it was perfectly reasonable to use coaxial cable as that wire, for the reasons discussed previously.

The result was a commercial LAN (Ethernet) designed around the use and installation of a specially designed coaxial cable. For years, this made perfect sense.

2.2   The Transition to Structured Wiring

Chaos theory tells us that the flutter of a butterfly's wings in Bolivia can change the weather patterns in Europe. [GLEI87] Similarly, events in one segment of the communications industry can ripple changes to seemingly unrelated disciplines. During the 1980s, the U. S. telephone industry underwent a major wave of deregulation, most easily noted by the breakup of the nationwide Bell System telephone monopoly. One element of the new regulatory environment was that customers were to be allowed to own their own telephone equipment, at least on their own premises. Formerly, all telephone equipment, right up to the desk set, was owned and controlled by the Bell monopoly. Thus deregulation created the market opportunity for Private Branch Exchange (PBX) equipment and the private ownership and control of the inside wiring.

On top of this, the 1980s ushered in the era of digital telephony, with 64 kb/s encoded signals used to communicate voice, rather than raw analog signaling. The digital telephone systems allowed numerous features and functions to be added to private telephone systems, thus further enhancing the competitive environment.

For most large (and many small-to-medium) organizations that were installing private digital telephone systems, standards and structure in the wiring system were needed. Many early wiring systems were proprietary and designed by a specific vendor (for example, AT&T's Premise Distribution System). As the industry matured, the need was recognized for wiring standards that allowed a building to be wired in a generic manner, without consideration of what equipment would be later selected and installed. Over the years, the standards have matured and been refined to accommodate the new LAN technologies, but the original driving force was the deployment of PBX equipment for digital telephony.

The important development from the perspective of LAN deployment in offices was that, for proper operation of digital telephone systems, a *higher grade of wire* was needed, higher than that traditionally used for analog telephone. Analog telephone is highly tolerant of wide variations in wire types and topologies. Such systems operate perfectly well over untwisted-pairs (for example, telephone "quad," flat modular "silver satin" wire, and so on), with their combination of uncontrolled impedances, bridged taps, and marginal connections. Digital telephone systems required a more controlled wiring environment, at least for the longer cable runs. This led to the development of "data grade" wire (later standardized as Category 3 twisted-pair). With data-grade wire and a better controlled environment, it became possible to design high-speed LANs that ran over telephone wire.

A comprehensive discussion of structured wiring systems is beyond the scope of this book, but it is important to note the key characteristics of the standard structured wiring system, especially as they relate to their use in Ethernet LANs (Figure 2–2).

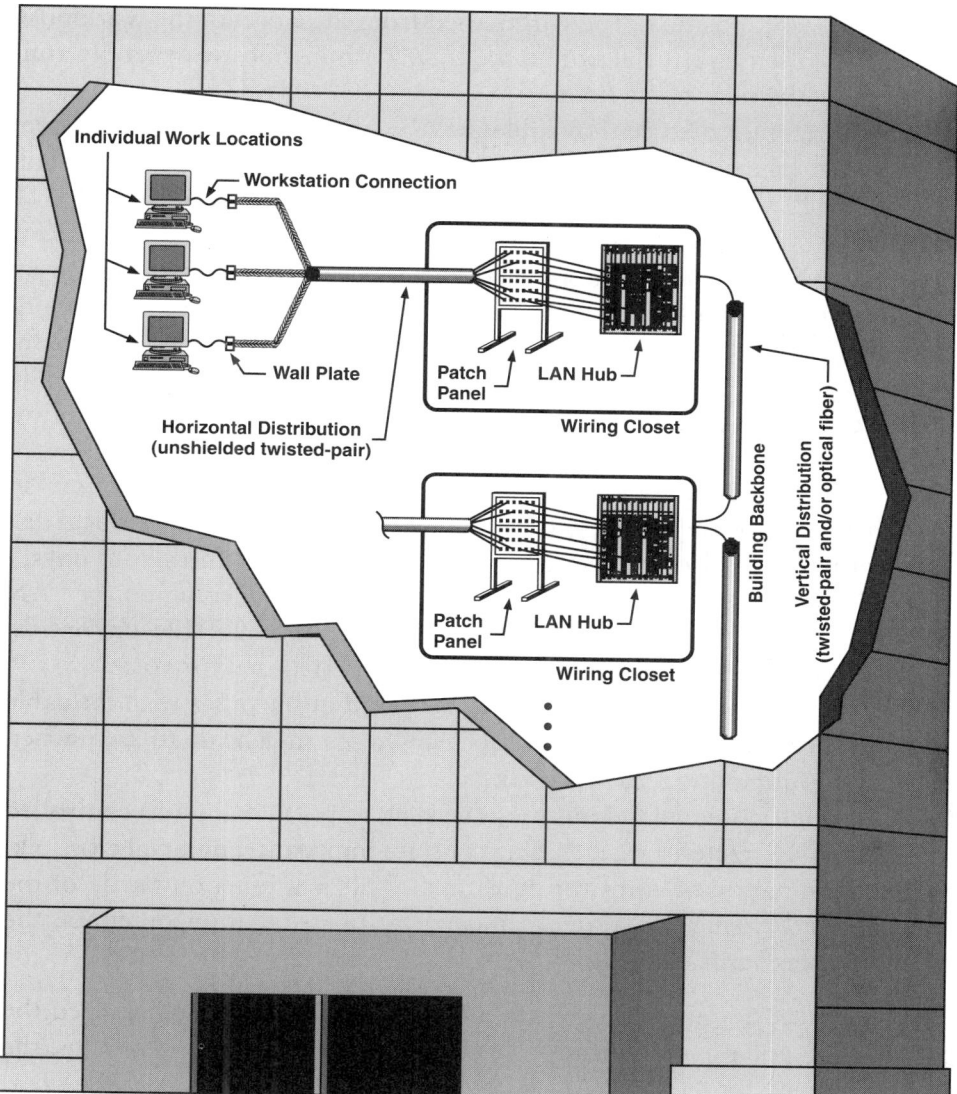

Figure 2–2 Basic structured wiring model.

■ Each work position (desktop) is provided with at least one dedicated cable that runs from the work position to a wiring closet. This cable is used exclusively by devices at that work position and is not shared or daisy-chained to any other work position. Each cable is typically 4 unshielded twisted-pairs (UTP); good practice provides two such cables to each work position. The wiring used from the closet to the work positions is often called the *horizontal distribution,* since it generally runs horizontally on a single floor.

- The horizontal distribution cable may be one of a number of different types. "In the old days," thin coaxial cable and shielded, 150 Ω, twisted-pair (STP) were common for LAN applications, with Category 3 UTP used for voice. Today, the most common cable is Category 5 UTP for both LAN and voice, with some legacy Category 3 UTP still around.

- The maximum distance for the horizontal distribution is 100 m, including allowances for patch cables, wallplate-to-computer cables, and so on.

- Structured wiring implies the presence of a *hub* device, which is typically located in the wiring closet in which the horizontal distribution terminates.[1]

- Wiring closets are interconnected through the *vertical distribution,* so named because the wiring generally runs between floors. The vertical distribution may also employ a variety of cable types. "In the old days," thick coaxial cable, 150Ω STP, and optical fiber were common for LAN usage, with Category 3 UTP used for voice. Today, 62.5/125 μm optical fiber is most commonly used for LANs, with UTP used for voice.

- The maximum distance for the vertical distribution varies with the cable type. It remains at 100 m when UTP is used but may be up to 2 km when 62.5/125 μm optical fiber is used.

- The wiring system maintains (or at least attempts to maintain) controlled electrical characteristics, including constant impedance, minimal crosstalk, and elimination of stubs (bridged taps). This is a function partly of the cable and wiring components and partly of installation practices; the wiring standards define both.

Over time, developers of wiring systems and standards recognized the need for computer communications in addition to the telephone systems, the original driving force. The EIA/TIA 568 series of standards [EIA91, EIA91a] is today generally recognized as the controlling document for building structured wiring systems. We have come full circle. That is, while the standards may originally have been driven by the needs of digital PBX systems, today

---

1. "Hub" is a generic term for a device at the center of a star-wired system. Depending on the system configuration, a hub may be performing the function of a repeater, a switch, a router, or some combination of these. See Chapter 11 for more information about hub options and architectures.

the more stringent requirements are those of high-speed LANs. Most of the current activity within the wiring standards organization focuses on supporting the needs of ever-increasing LAN speeds. Equally important, within most user organizations the LAN has become as critical a resource as the telephone system. This increased visibility has allowed the improvement of wiring systems beyond the needs of digital telephony, with LAN applications being the primary consideration. When this book discusses structured wiring systems, it refers to only their use in LAN applications and not to any use for voice/PBX.

2.3   Advantages of Structured Wiring

A structured wiring system offers something never possible when Ethernet was first developed: a stable wiring infrastructure capable of supporting high-speed LAN communications, with:

- Controlled electrical characteristics of the cables and wiring system
- A star-wired topology, with dedicated media for each device
- Every wire terminating in a wiring closet, in which LAN hub and wire interconnection equipment can be placed

Telephone systems have used star-wired topologies for more than one hundred years, with good reason. While formal specifications for structured wiring that is compatible with both high-speed LANs and digital telephone systems have emerged only recently, the advantages of a star-wiring topology are clear.

- **Ease of executing moves, adds, and changes to the configuration.** This is unquestionably the primary advantage of a structured wiring system. In most organizations, there is a constant need to add users, shift users from one location to another, and (unfortunately) sometimes even to eliminate users. With a bus or daisy-chain topology (as used in coaxial Ethernet systems), any change to the configuration could require rewiring (including climbing into ceilings or removing permanent walls to access the cables) and network disruption (while new devices are added). With a structured wiring system, every work location is prewired, thus eliminating the need for new wiring when users are added.

More important, the configuration of the network (that is, the determination of each user's physical connection to network devices, such as hubs and switches) is done at a patch panel in the wiring closet and does not require access to either the user's end of the connection or the horizontal cable itself. In this manner, reconfiguration, even as extensive as a wholesale move of an entire workgroup, can be executed quickly, in one location, without disrupting other users of the network.

- **LAN technology independence.** Using standards for structured wiring, we have designed a multitude of LAN technologies that operate over this common medium. "In the old days," a decision to use a given medium implied the network technology choice, and vice versa. Installing 50 Ω coaxial cable implied the use of Ethernet, 150 Ω STP mandated Token Ring, and so on. There was a tight interdependence between the medium and the technology.

  This is no longer true with structured wiring standards. The same infrastructure can support Ethernet (at a variety of data rates), Token Ring, LocalTalk, FDDI/CDDI, RS-232/422, ATM, and so on. We no longer have to make the technology decision at the same time that we choose the wiring system. The same system supports multiple technologies and multiple data rates within the same technology. This allows us both to use, without rewiring, different LANs in different areas of the organization that are appropriate to the needs of the individual workgroup and to migrate among technologies and data rates as those needs change.

- **Fault isolation with unitary granularity.** Since each device attached to the network has a dedicated medium connection, any fault, either with the user's device, the user's port on the network concentrator, or the wiring system itself, can be isolated to that individual user. With shared media such as coaxial cable, a single fault could disrupt multiple users, or an entire LAN.

- **Ease of network management.** With all of the user's connections and the network hub devices located in a single location (the wiring closet), network diagnosis, testing, and repair become greatly simplified. Test equipment and network monitoring tools can be either installed semi-permanently in the wiring closet or built directly into the network hub equipment. The wiring closet becomes the obvious point from which to test user devices, network devices, and the wiring system itself. Most repairs can also be made from this central location.

- **Network equipment security.** All of the network-critical equipment—patch panels, LAN hubs, switches, routers, and so on—are located in a single area that can be physically controlled. Simply put, one can lock the door and prevent unauthorized access to all of the single-points-of-failure in the LAN.

It is interesting to note that even from the beginning, the developers of Token Ring technology recognized the benefits of structured wiring. Token Ring (IEEE 802.5) systems are never wired as a physical ring, but rather as a physical star. This allows Token Ring to take advantage of many of the benefits of star-wired systems discussed previously.[2] The benefits, especially of unitary fault isolation, are especially important in Token Ring, since the logical topology permits a large class of device faults to cause total network disruption. By using star wiring and a centralized means of granting permission to join/leave the physical ring, one could minimize the impact of device faults.

Of course, there is no such thing as a free lunch. The benefits of structured wiring do not come without penalties.

- **Dedicated media is more expensive than shared media.** The cost of a structured wiring system is much more expensive than that of a shared, coaxial medium. While the cost-per-unit-length of UTP is lower than that of coaxial cable, there is much more cable required, since each device gets a dedicated "home run" cable from the work location to the wiring closet. After the costs of wire *installation* are added in (such costs can run an order-of-magnitude greater than the cost of the wire itself), the cost of a LAN based on structured wiring far exceeds that of shared-media systems.

- **A LAN based on dedicated media is more expensive than one based on shared media.** In a shared-media system, there is no need for any hub equipment. A hub of some sort (that is, repeater or switch) is always needed when using structured wiring.

- **UTP is a terrible medium for high-speed communications systems.** Most structured wiring systems use UTP for the horizontal distribution. UTP is excellent in terms of cost (per unit length), ease of installation, size and weight, availability of common tools and connectors, and so on. But when one is considering media for the foundation of high-speed communications systems, UTP is one or two steps better than barbed wire, at best. Granted, modern Category 5 UTP is vastly superior to earlier cables, especially the uncontrolled telephone wiring of the pre-1980s. However, it is still extremely difficult to design a multi–megabit-per-second communications system that operates reliably over 100 m of twisted-pair cable.

---

2. Unfortunately, the original Token Ring implementation used 150 Ω STP, which is even more expensive, unwieldy, and difficult to install than coaxial Ethernet.

Coaxial cable would make the design task (and therefore the equipment cost) much lower than that of a UTP-based system.[3]

However, the user benefits of structured wiring systems using UTP (especially in greater ease of moves/adds/changes) outweigh any cost or performance disadvantages, especially in larger, office automation environments. It is these user benefits that drove the development of 10BASE-T and, later, the 100BASE-T and 1000BASE-T systems.

2.4   The 10BASE-T/100BASE-T Revolution

Given that:

■ Structured wiring systems were being widely deployed in the late 1980s for digital telephony

■ Structured wiring offers significant advantages with respect to flexibility and network management

■ Competing LAN systems (namely, Token Ring) could use structured wiring

it should come as no surprise that Ethernet equipment manufacturers moved quickly to develop a method to use Ethernet over twisted-pair wiring. Initial products in this marketplace were proprietary in nature (for example, SynOptics LattisNet). When it became clear that Ethernet over twisted-pair was a huge potential market, the IEEE 802.3 membership took up the task of composing a standard for Ethernet operation over UTP wire, using the EIA/TIA 568 building wiring standard as the model for the cabling system. 10BASE–T rapidly became the most popular method of deploying Ethernet in large organizations. This further accelerated the move to install structured wiring systems.

Following the market success of 10BASE-T, the IEEE 802.3u (Fast Ethernet) Task Force leveraged this model of wiring and equipment interconnection and increased the channel data rate to 100 Mb/s. By the time Fast

---

3. It is always interesting to hear users discuss plans to "upgrade" their coaxial-based 10BASE2 Ethernet to UTP-based 10BASE-T. From an electrical reliability and cost standpoint, they are actually "downgrading." That is, they will get worse performance at a higher cost (although the difference in performance is more theoretical than actual and would not be noticeable by the typical user in a benign environment). Granted, 10BASE-T is more manageable and it more easily supports moves/adds/changes, but in many cases, the user does not have those benefits in mind. It is a common misconception that just because 10BASE-T was developed after the coaxial Ethernet systems, it is electrically superior.

Ethernet was being developed, the model for LAN deployment had shifted so much towards structured wiring that Fast Ethernet offered *no shared-media option*. 10BASE-T provided a means for accommodating a structured wiring system within an inherently shared-channel architecture. At 100 Mb/s, the only media supported uses the structured wiring model. The fact that these systems are so popular indicates that the advantages of the structured wiring system far outweigh the cost penalty.

One important outgrowth of the move to structured wiring is the new-found role of the LAN hub. Star-wired Ethernets require a device at the center of the star. In a shared-bandwidth LAN, this hub (a repeater) allows all of the devices to perceive the network as a common communications channel, even though each one has a dedicated media connection. The bandwidth is shared, but not the media.

Also, the requirement for a hub created the opportunity for adding value to the network by adding features to the hub. Network management, remote monitoring (RMON, [RFC1757]), and other features could be added to a single device to improve the behavior of the entire network. As discussed in later chapters, the architecture of the hub device itself could be changed (from a repeater to a bridge) to provide additional aggregate bandwidth (switching hub).

2.5   Dedicated Media and Gigabit Ethernet

You can see why and how we moved from the shared media LANs of the early 1980s to the dedicated media LANs of the 1990s. The next sections discuss the implications of this wiring infrastructure and LAN connectivity model for Gigabit Ethernet.

2.5.1   The Desktop Is Wired with UTP

Virtually every organization of significant size now uses a structured wiring system, both for voice and LAN communications. Also, virtually all new commercial buildings are prewired in this manner, even before the user has been identified, much less the specific equipment needs of that user. While the EIA/TIA building wiring standard allows the use of coaxial cables and STP wire,[4] the "industry standard" is to wire work locations (desktops) with UTP and to use optical fiber for backbone connections (both building and campus;

---

4. Future revisions of the EIA/TIA 568 wiring standard are expected to deprecate the allowance for coaxial cable and STP, at least for the horizontal distribution.

see Figure 2–2). While there is still an installed base of Category 3 UTP, virtually all new installations use Category 5 UTP for its superior ability to support high-speed communications.

Category 5 UTP can today support 100 Mb/s operation (using 100BASE-TX, -T4, or -T2) over the EIA/TIA standard horizontal distribution system, up to the maximum allowed 100 m radius from the wiring closet. Hence, installing 100 Mb/s-capable workstations throughout the organization is straightforward. As discussed earlier in the chapter, the technical challenge of operating at 100 Mb/s on UTP was daunting. But that hurdle has been overcome, and reasonably priced products are widely available for this application.

Extending UTP operation to gigabit data rates over the 100 m distance required by the building wiring standard will take considerable time, technology, and expertise—if it can be done at all. At the time of this writing, there is no demonstrated system capable of reliable operation at gigabit data rates over 100 m of 4-pair Category 5 UTP. This problem is being actively worked on by numerous manufacturers, both within and outside of the standards committee (see Chapter 12 for a complete discussion of 1000BASE-T). In the early stages of the development of Gigabit Ethernet over UTP, a number of ways to "skin this cat" were considered.

1. **Operate the system over distances shorter than 100 m.** It may not be possible to design a practical system for Gigabit Ethernet that operates over 100 m of UTP, but operation over 30–50 m seems feasible. The problem is that buildings are wired using the rule of "100 m is OK." Only a small subset of the total number of desktops in an organization may be within 50 m of a wiring closet. Worse, the lengths of each horizontal run may not have been documented during the wire installation process. Hence, it would be necessary to make physical measurements of each cable run where gigabit operation is anticipated, if the communications system did not support a 100 m extent.

2. **Use more than 4 pairs of wire.** It is possible to maintain the Gigabit Ethernet data rate while reducing the signaling (baud) rate on the channel by using more wire pairs for the link. This is done in the 100BASE-T2 system (2 pairs are used for 100 Mb/s operation, at 50 Mb/s/pair) and the 100BASE-T4 system (3 pairs are used for 100 Mb/s operation, at 33.3 Mb/s/pair). In theory, if we simply use more wire pairs, we can reduce the signaling rate to an arbitrarily low value, while still operating the system at the gigabit (aggregate) data rate.

To date, no Ethernet signaling system uses more than 4 pairs of wire. There are good reasons for this.

- Most Category 5 UTP cables have a maximum of 4 pairs per bundle. This limitation reduces the number of potential interference sources in the cable, thereby keeping the crosstalk levels (that is, interwire interference within the cable) within acceptable limits. Some short "jumper cables" are available in 25-pair bundles, but they must be used over very short lengths so as to minimize crosstalk. Category 5 UTP in 25-pair bundles is unsuitable for use in the general horizontal distribution system.

- Many buildings are not wired with multiple 4-pair cables from the wiring closet to each work location. Four pairs are sufficient to support both voice and LAN applications (for example, 1 pair for voice, 2 pairs for 10BASE-T/100BASE-T and 1 spare pair); installing additional cable increases the cost and returns little added benefit. In those sites at which two 4-pair cables are brought to each work location, typically one cable is used for voice and one for data communications. All 8 pairs are not available for the LAN.

- Even if there are multiple 4-pair cables available exclusively for LAN use, the cables will not be *precisely* the same length. Thus the absolute propagation delay of the two cables could be significantly different, especially if the cables are not routed in the same raceway or conduit.[5] A signaling system employing multiple wire pairs in separate cables would have to deal with this wide variation in cable delay. The buffering and symbol synchronization, and so on, that is required add significant complexity and cost to the communications system.

3. **Use a new type of wire.** Some have proposed the use of a new, "Category 6" UTP, which would conceivably reduce the difficulties in designing the system for gigabit operation over 100 m distances. [TIA96] While this is theoretically possible, it begs the question of how to bring Gigabit Ethernet to the desktops that are wired according to the currently accepted building wiring standard. The whole idea of standard structured wiring systems is to be able to support any technology on the same infrastructure. If we have to change the wire to support each

---

5. Even within a single cable, there will be slight differences between the propagation delays of the individual wire pairs, which must be accommodated by the signaling method used. However, these delays are a small percentage of the total delay and can be dealt with economically.

new system, then there is no real benefit to having a standard. It becomes a
standard for each different system.

Granted, if there wasn't a wiring
standard—and a large number of
EIA/TIA 568-wired buildings—then
the use of a higher-grade wire is less of
a problem (as long as it is not prohibitively expensive). At this point, if we
need to pull new cables to each work
location to support Gigabit Ethernet,

> *The only reason God
> was able to create the
> Universe in six days was
> because He didn't have
> to worry about the
> installed base.*
> —Enzo Torresi

then it makes more sense to install optical fiber rather than to design a
new type of UTP.

The bottom line is that it is currently impractical to run Gigabit Ethernet
to individual work locations over standard structured wiring systems—and it
may remain impractical for a long time. This will be a limiting factor (perhaps *the* limiting factor) in the deployment of Gigabit Ethernet at the desktop. For all practical purposes, any end-user device requiring Gigabit Ethernet
may also require that new cable be installed.

Fortunately, the number of desktop (end user) devices requiring—or even
being able to take advantage of—Gigabit Ethernet is small, at least in the
short-to-medium term. Fast Ethernet (100 Mb/s) will support the vast majority of desktop devices over the next few years, with switching employed to
increase aggregate capacity, rather than upgrading to Gigabit Ethernet at the
work location.

Gigabit Ethernet will be, at least initially, a server and backbone technology. In these applications, the limitations of the horizontal distribution system are relatively unimportant.

2.5.2   The Building and Campus Backbone Is Optical Fiber

The EIA/TIA 568 building wiring standard supports various media for use in
the building backbone (that is, the vertical distribution, between wiring closets within a building). These include twisted-pair (both UTP and STP), coaxial cable, and optical fiber.

Twisted-pair is commonly used for the vertical distribution of voice signals; in this case, the only active device may be a single, common PBX for the
entire building. The problem of catenating the lengths of the horizontal and
the vertical wiring between the end device (the telephone) and the PBX is not
a problem at voice frequencies, either for analog or digital voice.

The use of coaxial cable is an historical artifact; 10BASE5 was commonly used to interconnect wiring closets "in the old days." Unquestionably, the medium of choice for the vertical distribution today is 62.5/125 μm multi-mode optical fiber. This medium supports a wide variety of high-speed LANs, including 10BASE-F, 100BASE-FX, FDDI, and Gigabit Ethernet. Across a campus environment (for example, among buildings within a single organization or infrastructure), this same 62.5/125 μm optical fiber is the most common medium type installed.

Intrabuilding distances do not typically pose any serious problems for physical signaling over this type of fiber. Common signaling methods typically support 2 km of 62.5 μm multimode fiber at 10 Mb/s or 100 Mb/s (10BASE-FL, 100BASE-FX). It would be a rare building indeed that needed more than this for its backbone. Campus distances are more problematic, as it is not uncommon for large corporations and universities to span diameters of many kilometers. The majority of campuses are provided with a wiring system that uses multimode optical fiber over a diameter of from 2 to 4 km (radius of from 1 to 2 km from a hub device). Longer distances may employ single-mode fiber.

The important conclusion is that unlike in the desktop environment, there is an installed base of optical fiber suitable for use at gigabit data rates, at least for building backbone applications.[6] This enables the deployment of Gigabit Ethernet for wiring closet and building interconnection.

2.5.3   Dedicated Media Is the Norm

There are two elements of the structured wiring system that are important for Gigabit Ethernet deployment. First are the media themselves; UTP as it is commonly used for wiring to work locations and optical fiber for backbone connections. Equally important is the fact that regardless of the medium, the use of a structured wiring system ensures that every device has a dedicated connection. This connection connects either an end station (user device or server) to a hub or a hub to another hub (backbone connection). The use of hubs is therefore mandatory in a structured wiring environment.

When structured wiring is used, there are no shared media, even though the LAN bandwidth may be shared. The next chapter shows how this dedicated media can be used in a way that provides dedicated bandwidth through the use of switching hubs. The migration from shared to switched LANs is important for Gigabit Ethernet, as it provides a means to escape from the distance limitations of CSMA/CD.

---

6. As discussed in Chapters 9, 12, and 13, Gigabit Ethernet requires single-mode optical fiber for distances greater than 550 m.

3 | From Shared to Dedicated LANs

The previous chapter showed how users migrated from the use of shared media LANs to dedicated media LANs, with the LAN hub becoming an integral part of the network. This chapter explains how that hub-centric architecture enables the migration from shared bandwidth LANs to switched (dedicated bandwidth) LANs and how this has important implications for Gigabit Ethernet.

3.1   Shared-Bandwidth LAN Concepts

The original concept behind virtually all LANs was to provide a means to allow multiple devices to share a common communications channel (see Figure 3–1). The purpose of a high-capacity LAN was not so much to provide high sustained throughput between pairs of stations but to provide high *aggregate capacity* to be shared among all of the attached devices. During any particular exchange of data, the throughput can be extremely high (approaching the raw capacity of the channel), but it is assumed that stations do not need this capacity on a sustained basis. The high-capacity channel is available, on a time-shared basis, to all devices wishing to communicate.

A properly designed shared LAN is idle most of the time. That is, the channel should have much greater capacity than the sum of the steady-state

Figure 3–1 Shared LAN.

communications needs of the attached stations. While the channel's being idle may seem inefficient, it is the optimum approach from the perspective of the communicating stations. The probability that the channel is available when needed is extremely high; it is simply waiting for someone to use it. The channel is being used inefficiently, but the delay imposed on the communications of the attached stations is being minimized. If the cost of providing an idle channel is low (as it should be for a *local* network), this optimizes *overall system performance* at the expense of LAN utilization. Note that this would not be a reasonable approach for wide area network (WAN) communications because the cost of WAN links both recur (that is, they are charged on a monthly basis) and increase with increased capacity. LANs do not impose recurring costs; therefore there is no penalty in allowing them to be idle.

A shared LAN also effectively provides a fully connected mesh topology (that is, every station is directly connected to every other station on the LAN), without incurring the cost of hundreds of individual, point-to-point links. (Of course, the capacity is also less than it would be if there were numerous links.) For the limited number of cases in which specific devices need dedicated, high-capacity channels (for example, mainframe-to-mainframe connections), these can be provided separately from the general LAN connectivity framework.

As discussed in Chapter 1, there is a constantly swinging pendulum in the computer communications industry. At any given time, either communications technology is outpacing computing technology or vice versa. During the 1970s, computing power grew rapidly, both in the mainframe and the mini-computer/super-minicomputer worlds. There was no commensurate set of improvements in communications technology during that period. The result was that the underlying communications channel could be (and often was) the limiting factor in throughput. The development of the 10 Mb/s Ethernet in 1979–80 swung this pendulum the other way. At that time, there were very few (if any) computers in widespread commercial use that could *saturate* (that is, keep full) an Ethernet channel. The communications channel was no longer the limiting factor. Instead, the limitation was now the ability of the attached computers to process information. That made a shared LAN attractive, since no individual station could use the entire available capacity even if it wanted to.

During the 1980s, there were huge increases in computing power, especially that available at the desktop, without any change in the underlying communications. By the 1990s, the 10 Mb/s channel could easily be the limiting factor in communications. As computing power (and the number of attached stations on a LAN) increased, the channel utilization increased. At some point, the channel is said to become *congested*. This means that the communications channel, rather than the attached computers, is the limiting factor. When this happens, user performance can be improved by adding capacity to the LAN. This can be done either by increasing the LAN data rate or by *segmenting* LANs, that is, breaking single LANs with large numbers of attached devices into a number of smaller LANs with fewer devices per LAN, as indicated in Figure 3–2. This increases the aggregate capacity by the number of segments provided.[1] LAN segmentation is traditionally accomplished with bridges.

It is important to understand that the increased capacity gained by LAN segmentation is diminished by any nonlocal nature of the traffic. That is, if all of the traffic is localized within a single segment (for example, each segment is an independent workgroup, with its own local server, and both the source and

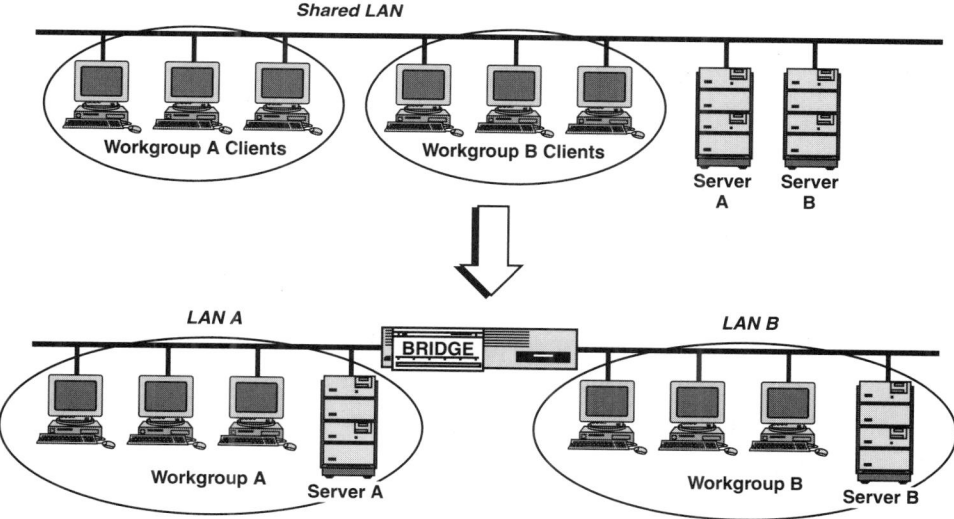

Figure 3–2   Segmenting LANs to increase capacity.

---

1. Although Figure 3–2 indicates two LAN segments connected by a bridge (as do most figures of this ilk), there is no architectural reason why it has to be two. Two segments is just the simplest case of LAN segmentation. Bridges can (and are) used to segment LANs into more than two partitions.

2. A device that generates traffic on its own behalf (as opposed to forwarding traffic generated by another device) is said to be a *source*. A device that receives frames without forwarding them (so that the data can be processed by an application within the device) is said to be a *sink*.

sink of most traffic are on the same segment[2]), then segmentation increases the overall network capacity in proportion to the number of ports on the bridge, with no loss of connectivity. If all of the traffic is nonlocal (that is, the source and destination are on different segments), then the best-case effective capacity increase is halved, since every frame must use bandwidth on at least two ports rather than just one. In the worst-case, if all of the traffic is sourced or sunk on a single segment (for example, if one segment contains a "server farm" and all other devices are user workstations accessing those servers), then there is no performance improvement gained by "classic" segmentation. This is because the capacity of the entire set of segments is limited to that of the one segment that must ultimately carry all of the traffic.[3]

3.2   LAN Bridges

Bridges, at first used primarily to segment LANs for traffic isolation and performance improvement, are the key to the development of dedicated-bandwidth LANs and switching technology (which is discussed later in this chapter). The following sections look at the operation principles of LAN bridges.

3.2.1   Data Link Addressing

Strictly speaking, link addresses (MAC addresses[4]) need only be *locally unique*. That is, achieving link-layer communications requires only the ability to distinguish among stations on a given link. The MAC address of a LAN interface must be unique among all interfaces on a given LAN, but there is no architectural requirement that it be unique among all LANs. Global uniqueness is needed at the Network Layer (to allow unambiguous internetwork-wide packet delivery), but is not a strict requirement for a Data Link.

---

3. Of course, the segment containing the server farm can be operating at a higher data rate than those segments containing the user workstations and achieve improved performance for users in this manner, but the aggregate capacity of the network is still limited to that of the single (higher data rate) server segment.

4. In this section, sometimes the term "MAC address" is used and sometimes "Link address." While "MAC address" is the more common term today, it presupposes the existence of a MAC entity. This assumption is valid on shared-bandwidth LANs (for example, Ethernets), but is not strictly correct when discussing other data link technologies (for example, SDLC). These other technologies have link addresses that are equivalent to the MAC addresses used on LANs, but they have no MAC to speak of.

"In the old days," there were two important considerations when designing a link address structure for a new link technology:

1. **Bandwidth was expensive.** Until the 1980s, multi–megabit-per-second LANs were rare. Many link technologies operated at speeds in the tens-of-kilobit-per-second range, and sometimes even lower. Saving bits on the wire was an important goal, and keeping all overhead (such as link addresses) as short as possible was an advantage.

2. **The number of stations on a given network was relatively low.** Before computers were on everyone's desks, there were many fewer computers within an organization. A computer network comprised tens of computers at most (on a single link), rather than the hundreds or thousands that are common today. Thus the address space requirements (the maximum number of addresses that must be supported by the link) were much lower.[5]

This combination of conditions leads one to design links using short link address field lengths (that is, a small local address space). This reduces the number of bits of overhead required to transmit addresses without affecting the ability to support reasonable numbers of devices on a given link, since there was no need to support thousands of devices anyway. This is why technologies such as SDLC and ARCnet (both very popular "in the old days") used 8-bit link addresses. The overhead was low, and a station limit of 256 devices per link was not a limiting factor.

This all changed with the personal computer revolution. When the 10 Mb/s Ethernet was being designed in 1979–80, we were on the cusp of the explosion in desktop computing. Fortunately (for Ethernet, that is) the designers recognized the limitations of short link addresses and designed a radically new system. Rather than requiring that the addresses be as short as practicable, they made the address space large enough to allow the use of *globally unique addresses.* [DALA81] In this scheme, a device's address is unique not only among all stations on the given link, but also among all stations on *all* LANs for all time. The address space grew from the 8 bits commonly used at the time to 48 bits. (The specific syntax and semantics of the 48-bit addresses used in Ethernet are discussed in Chapter 5.)

---

5. Readers should note that the original ARPAnet design, which is the direct ancestor of today's worldwide Internet, could address only 63 devices!

A 48-bit globally unique address is *huge* in terms of the number of devices conceivable under this scheme, no matter how you look at it. An industry producing ten million interfaces each day (about 50 times the current production of the entire LAN industry) would run out of addresses in about 40,000 *years*! Forty-eight bits allows for 50,000 network-addressable entities for every person on the planet (at the time of this writing).[6] Alternatively, you could have five uniquely addressable network entities for every square meter of Earth's inhabited surface. Clearly, we are not about to run out of 48-bit addresses soon.[7]

The use of 48-bit globally unique addresses solved the problem of increasing numbers of devices on a LAN without imposing any significant overhead burden because "bandwidth became cheap" with the development of low-cost multi-megabit-per-second LANs, such as Ethernet. The extra bits required to send such long addresses did not seriously affect the performance of the network or the applications using it.

The real benefit, though, was in the administration of addresses. With any locally unique address structure, an address administrator (usually a human being) is required to assign addresses to devices in a unique manner, since the address space is not large enough to allow globally unique address assignments. For example, it was common practice in ARCnet products to set the 8-bit address using Dual In-line Package (DIP) switches on the interface card. It was the responsibility of the address administrator to ensure that the addresses were assigned uniquely and that the switches were properly set on each interface. Also, if a device had to be moved from one LAN segment to another, its link address would have to change (in general).

As the number of networked devices grows from tens to thousands, manual administration of addresses quickly becomes an unreasonable task for a human administrator. The use of globally unique addresses eliminates this problem, since address assignment can be done once, for all time, with uniqueness ensured, regardless of where the device is used. This benefit far outweighs any penalty of overhead bits or extra controller logic and was the real driving force behind the design of the 48-bit structure in the first place.

---

6. Not counting my mother, who doesn't need (or know how to use) a computer, anyway.

7. More important, we will not run out of addresses in time for the designers of this scheme to receive any blame for it.

3.2.2   Unicast and Multicast Addresses

The 48-bit address space used in LANs today is actually divided into two orthogonal spaces:

A space of 2^{47} (47 bits) possible *unicast addresses*

A space of 2^{47} (47 bits) possible *multicast addresses*

As depicted in Figure 3–3, the first bit of the address indicates whether the address is unicast or multicast. Unicast addresses map 1:1 to LAN interfaces. That is, a unicast address denotes a single, specific interface and that interface has only that single unicast address.[8] When a frame is sent to an interface of a specific network station, the frame is addressed to the unicast address of that interface.

Multicast addresses map 1:*n* to network-addressable devices; that is, a multicast address refers to a *group* of logically related stations. Typically, multicast addresses are associated with an application or protocol common

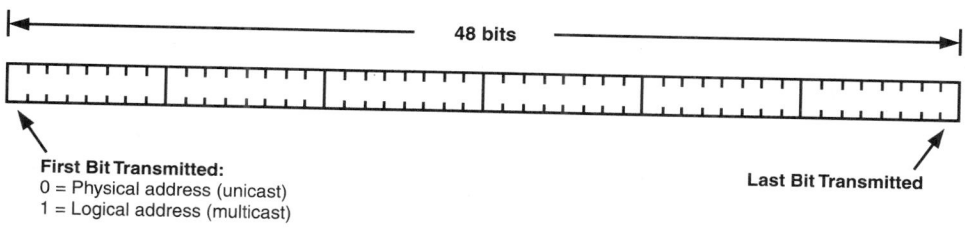

48 bits

First Bit Transmitted:
0 = Physical address (unicast)
1 = Logical address (multicast)

Last Bit Transmitted

Figure 3–3   Ethernet address format.

---

8. There are actually two philosophies for interpreting unicast addresses. One philosophy follows the premise that a unicast address identifies a *device* (for example, a workstation or server), as opposed to a network interface installed within the device. According to this philosophy, when a device has multiple interfaces, it uses the same address on all of them. This approach was used in the original Xerox Network System (XNS) and is still in use in most of Sun Microsystems' products.

The other philosophy, that an address uniquely identifies the *interface* rather than the device, is used more today and is the model assumed in this book (even though I have an affection and longing for the "architectural purity" of the single-address-per-device model). According to the *address-per-interface* philosophy, a device with multiple interfaces will have multiple unicast addresses assigned to it.

Both philosophies are "valid", in the sense that both can be made to work properly in a practical network. In neither case is there any ambiguity about the destination of a frame sent to a given unicast address.

to all of the stations in the group. For example, all devices running the AppleTalk suite of protocols will receive frames sent to the "All-AppleTalk-Stations" multicast address[9] in addition to frames sent to their unicast address. The *broadcast address* (FF-FF-FF-FF-FF-FF) is another well-known multicast address.

An address indicating the destination for a frame may be unicast or multicast; an address indicating the source of a frame must be unicast. Chapter 5 contains additional information regarding 48-bit addresses and their use. When the term "station address" is used without a unicast/multicast qualifier, it generally means the unicast address of the device or interface.

3.2.3   A Side Effect of Globally Unique Addressing

Locally unique addresses make it possible (in fact, likely) for two devices on different LAN segments to have the same link address, as shown in Figure 3–4.

The limitation of the absolute size of the address space makes this situation unavoidable. Global uniqueness is still provided at the Network Layer by adding a second hierarchy of addressing at that layer. If each link is assigned a Network Layer identifier (a "network number"), then the catenation of the globally unique network identifier and the locally unique link address constitutes a globally unique station identifier. The advantage of

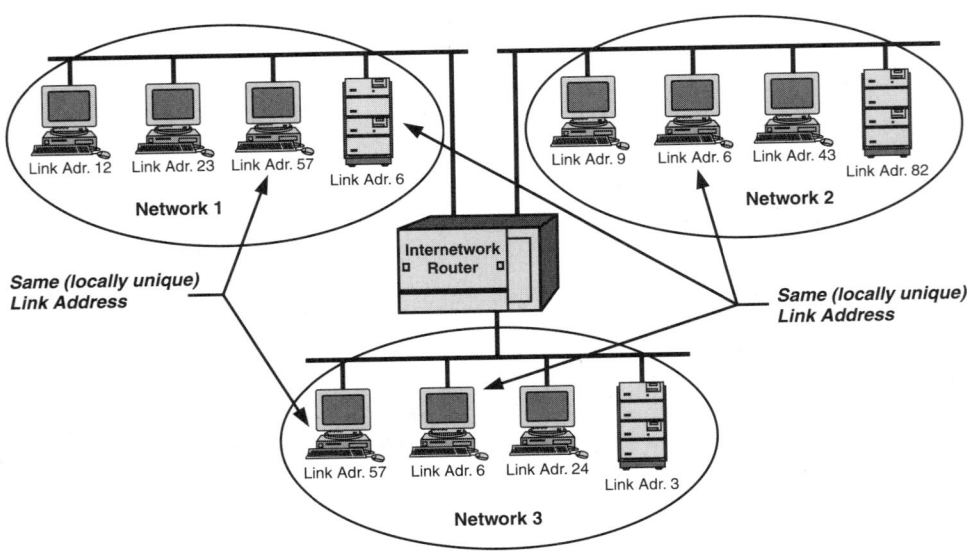

Figure 3–4   Locally unique link addressing.

---

9. 09-00-08-FF-FF-FF; see [APPL90] for more information.

doing the globally unique assignment at Network Layer is that there are many fewer networks than stations in the internetwork, thereby reducing the burden on the human administrator.

Consider now what happens if we use globally unique link addresses. It now becomes possible to uniquely identify a station in a catenation of links *solely by its link address.* This was simply not possible using locally unique addresses, since a locally unique address only identifies a station on its own link, not in a catenation of networks.

Thus it becomes possible to build a device that moves (forwards) frames among a catenation of links; forwarding decisions are made solely on the basis of the destination link address. Such a device is called a *bridge* (or MAC bridge, since it uses MAC addresses). A bridge allows Data Link Layer inter-connection of LANs without invoking any Network Layer mechanisms. Bridges did not exist "in the old days," not because LANs did not exist, but because globally unique addresses were not used. Bridges take advantage of (in fact, they require for their operation) the global uniqueness of today's LAN addresses.[10]

3.2.4 Bridge Operation

This section describes the basic operation of a bridge. It is not intended to be a treatise on the subject, but rather a means of introducing switching con-cepts, which are important for Gigabit Ethernet. The discussion focuses on the steady-state operation of the bridge and does not attempt to consider boundary conditions, initialization procedures, loop resolution (Spanning Tree operation), implementation issues, and so on. For a more complete treatment of bridges, see [IEEE93a] and [PERL92].

Figure 3–5 depicts a simplified operating scenario with a bridge. Note the following:

- There are multiple, distinct LAN segments interconnected by the bridge. (In the figure, only two LANs are shown for simplicity, but there is no architectural limit on the number of LANs that may be interconnected by a single bridge.)
- Each station has a globally unique 48-bit unicast address. This is critical; proper bridge operation depends on the use of globally unique addresses at the link layer.

---

10. If you want to sound like a real network architect, you could say, "Globally unique addressing is the only Data Link invariant upon which bridges rely." Try this at your next party. Don't blame me for what happens afterwards.

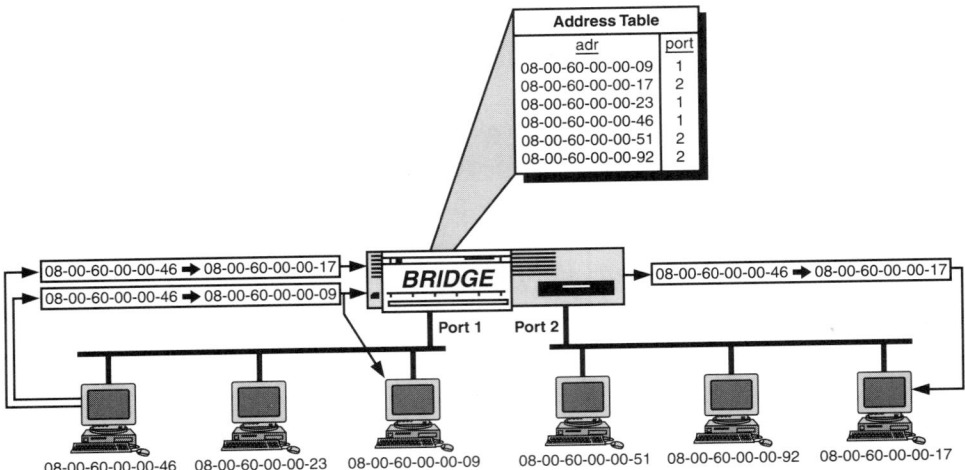

Figure 3–5 Bridge operation.

- The bridge has a *port,* or interface, on each of the LANs to which it connects.
- There is a table within the bridge that maps the station addresses to the bridge ports; that is, the bridge knows through which port each station is reachable.
- The bridge operates in *promiscuous mode.* That is, it receives (or at least attempts to receive) every frame on every port, regardless of the destination address (target) of the frame. A typical end station will attempt to receive only those frames containing a destination address that matches the station. A bridge, in contrast, receives all frames regardless of the intended destination.

When a frame is received on any port, the bridge inspects the destination address of that frame, looks it up in the table, and determines the port to which that address maps. If the port on which the frame is received is the same port on which the target destination resides, then the bridge can simply discard the frame, since it can be assumed that the target will have received the frame through the normal LAN delivery mechanisms. For example, the bridge received a frame on port 1 being sent from station 08-00-60-00-00-46 to 08-00-60-00-00-09. The bridge will discard this frame, since the address table indicates that station 08-00-60-00-00-09 is on port 1 and the frame was similarly received on port 1.

If station 08-00-60-00-00-46 next sends a frame to station 08-00-60-00-00-17, the bridge will receive this frame on port 1 (since the bridge is in promiscuous mode, it is receiving *all* frames) and look up station 08-00-60-00-00-17 in the address table. The table will indicate that the target destination is present on port 2. For the target to properly receive the frame, the bridge must *forward* the frame onto port 2. Note that in the process of forwarding the frame:

- The bridge has no "special privileges" regarding sending frames on its output ports with respect to other stations on that LAN. It must behave according to the normal access control (MAC) rules of that port. This means that the bridge must defer, detect collisions, back off, and so on, on an Ethernet port, just like any other Ethernet device.

- There can be significant delay in forwarding frames on output ports. This is called the *bridge transit delay*. If a target output port is congested, frames may queue up inside the bridge, waiting for available times to be transmitted. In the worst case, a bridge's output queue may fill, thus causing the bridge to discard frames rather than forward them due to a lack of bridge resources (buffers) in which to store frames. This is discussed further in Chapter 6.

- When the bridge forwards the frame, it uses as the Source address the address of the original sender of the frame (in this example, 08-00-60-00-00-46), rather than its own address. In fact, for the purpose of performing the forwarding operation, the bridge does not have, or need, an address of its own. It receives frames regardless of the Destination address and sends frames with the Source address of the originator. It never uses its own address as part of a retransmitted frame.

- The end stations are unaware of the presence of the bridge. The sender does not know—or need to know—that there is a bridge forwarding frames for it. The receiving station sees the frame exactly as it would have been (same addresses, same data) had the sender and receiver been on the same LAN segment. Thus the bridge is *transparent*. There is no special software or modifications to device drivers required in the end stations to use the services of the bridge.

Note that the proper operation of the bridge depends on the use of globally unique addresses. If two or more stations on connected segments ever had the same address, it would not be possible to build an unambiguous address table and the bridge could not make a correct forwarding decision.

In the case of a station's sending a frame to a destination currently unknown by the bridge (for example, station 08-00-60-00-00-46 sending a frame to 08-00-60-00-00-2C), the bridge will have a "miss" on the table lookup and will forward the frame onto all ports except the one on which it arrived. This is called *flooding*. Flooding allows communication with stations not-yet-heard-from (that is, not yet in the address table). Other than the unnecessary use of LAN bandwidth on the output ports (generally insignificant), there is no harm done in flooding such frames. If the station is really present (but unknown at this time), then it allows communications to proceed normally.

Similarly, if a station sends a frame to a multicast address, a bridge will forward that frame onto all ports except the one on which it arrived. This is because the bridge cannot tell which stations are listening to a given multicast address, so it should not restrict distribution of such frames to specific target output ports.[11]

The address table can be built dynamically by considering the Source address contained in received frames. When a frame is received, the bridge searches the table for an entry that corresponds to the station sending the frame (as indicated by the Source address). If an entry is found, the port that maps to that station is updated to reflect the port on which the latest frame arrived. This allows the bridge to properly map stations that have moved from one LAN segment to another. If an entry is not found, the bridge makes a new entry with the newly learned address and the arrival port to which it maps. Over time, as stations send frames, the bridge will learn the address-to-port mappings for all active stations.[12]

Thus a bridge:

■ Operates in promiscuous mode.
■ Has an address table that maps globally unique addresses to bridge ports.
■ Makes forwarding decisions based on the Destination address in received frames.
■ Builds and updates its address table based on the Source address in received frames.

---

11. The mechanisms used in Virtual LANs (VLANs) specifically address the issue of proper distribution of multicast traffic to only those ports necessary so as to ensure delivery to all stations desiring (and authorized) to receive a given multicast stream. [IEEE97c] This cannot be done through passive listening. Explicit protocol mechanisms (for example, the Generic Attribute Registration Protocol (GARP) and its companion, the GARP Multicast Registration Protocol (GMRP) [IEEE97b]) can be used to register multicast addresses with particular bridge ports.

12. Bridges also apply an *aging timer* to remove entries that have not been heard from over a specific period of time.

- Floods frames onto all ports (except the one on which a frame arrived) in the event of an unknown Destination address.
- Floods frames onto all ports (except the one on which the frame arrived) in the event of a multicast Destination address.
- Is transparent to end stations.

3.3   A Switch Is a Bridge

LAN bridges have been commercially available since 1984.[13] For most of their early lives, they were used for LAN segmentation and distance extension and to increase the number of devices allowed on a LAN beyond the limitations of a shared-bandwidth segment.

Early LAN bridges rarely had more than two ports. Performance of these bridges was limited by the (now viewed as) primitive hardware and software capabilities available at the time. Many bridges sold "in the old days" could not support even two ports at wire-speed.[14] Those that did support wire-speed bridging commanded a premium price. Increasing the number of ports on the bridge did not make much sense, as performance was usually limited by the internal bridging capacity and not by the bandwidth of the attached LANs. Thus it was impractical to build high port-density bridges until the semiconductor technology advanced to bring prices down to commercial feasibility.

During the 1990s, this is exactly what happened. Application-specific Integrated Circuit (ASIC), processor, and memory technology advanced to the point where it was feasible to build LAN bridges with large numbers of ports that were capable of forwarding frames at wire-speed on all ports. Bridges built this way were marketed as *switches*. It is important to note that the distinction between a bridge and a switch is a *marketing* distinction, not a technical one. The functions performed by a switch are identical to those performed by a bridge; a switch *is* a bridge. Marketers chose to call the products switches, primarily to differentiate them from the (more primitive) bridges of old.

---

13. The DEC LANBridge 100 was the first commercially available Ethernet bridge.

14. "Wire-speed" refers to the ability (or lack of ability) of a bridge to process frames at the maximum rate possible for the given technology. For example, a wire-speed 10 Mb/s Ethernet bridge port must be capable of processing 14,880.9 frames per second, while a 100 Mb/s wire-speed bridge port must be capable of processing 148,809 frames per second.

In this book, the terms "bridge" and "switch" are used interchangeably. More attention is paid to the application environment rather than the functional behavior of the device. That is, when talking about high port-density bridges used in modern applications, I generally call them switches and refer to the environment as a *switched LAN*. Similarly, in this book the term "switching hub" refers to a geographically central device that performs the function of a bridge among its ports. This is in contrast to the traditional shared LAN and is discussed shortly. This usage of the terminology is consistent with common industry practice.

3.4   Switched LAN Concepts

The original rationale for the development of LAN bridges was LAN *extension*, both of distance and in numbers of stations. With the advent of high port-density bridges capable of wire-speed operation, a new paradigm for local networking has emerged: the "switched LAN."

A switched LAN is an alternative to a traditional shared-bandwidth LAN. In terms of product deployment in a structured wiring environment, the only apparent difference is that the hub is a switching hub (bridge) rather than a shared hub (repeater). The behavior of the network changes considerably, however, between shared and switched LANs. In addition, a switched LAN offers the possibility of configurations that were not available to the shared LAN user. All of this comes at a price.

3.4.1   Separate Collision Domains

In a shared Ethernet LAN, the CSMA/CD MAC algorithm is used to arbitrate for use of the shared channel. If two or more stations have frames queued for transmission at the same time, there will be a collision among them. The set of stations contending for access to a shared LAN is called a *collision domain*. As shown in Figure 3–6, stations in the same collision domain can experience access contention, with the resulting collision and backoff. Stations in separate collision domains do not contend for access to a common channel and so do not experience collisions among themselves.

In a switched LAN, each switch port is the terminus of the collision domain of that port. If there is a shared LAN attached to a given port, then there can be collisions among the stations on that port but not between a station on that port and one on any other port of that switch. If there is only one end station per port, then there will be no collisions between any pair of end stations.

A switching hub thus separates the collision domains of each port.

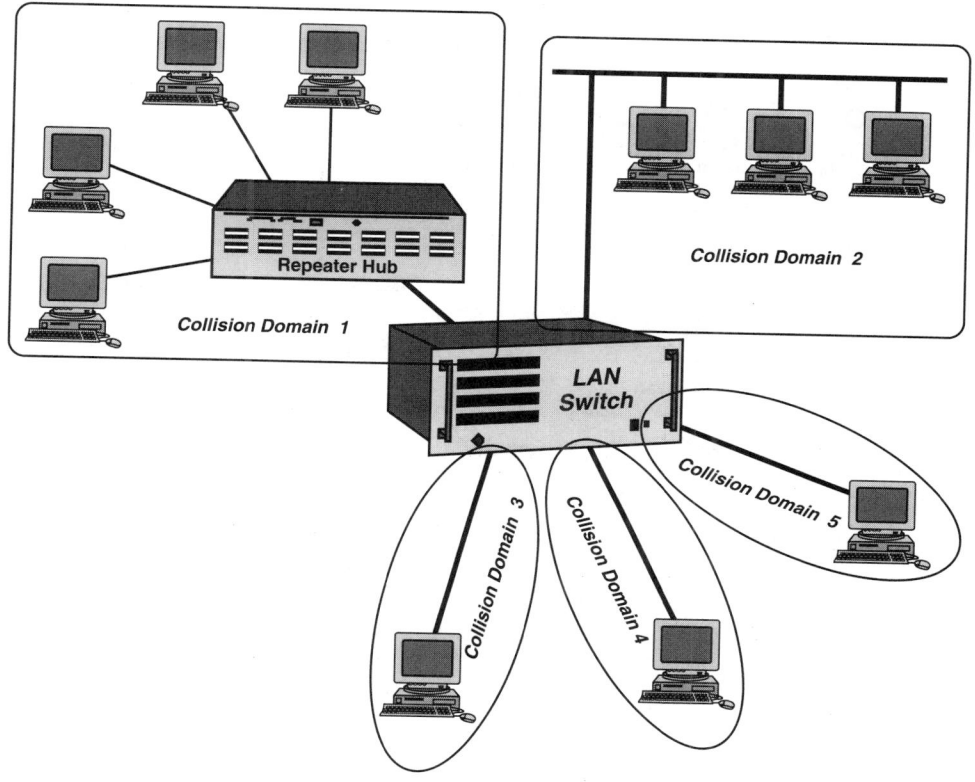

Figure 3–6   Collision domains.

3.4.2   Segmentation and Microsegmentation

A switching hub can be used to segment traditional shared LANs, as shown in Figure 3–7. A switch used in this manner is providing a *collapsed backbone*.[15] While the performance of switches used for collapsed backbone applications must be high, the model of use is really the original, traditional LAN segmentation model.

Alternatively, a switch can be used to interconnect end stations, as shown in Figure 3–8. Here LAN segmentation has been taken to the extreme, with

---

15. A backbone is a network whose primary purpose is to interconnect other networks, as opposed to interconnecting end stations. A backbone may be either *distributed* or *collapsed*. In a distributed backbone, the backbone network is brought to the internetworking devices. Geographically dispersed internetworking devices are connected to the backbone, typically at wiring closets, to provide workgroup interconnectivity. FDDI is a popular technology used for distributed LAN backbones. In a collapsed backbone, the backbone consists of a high-performance internetworking device, such as a switch. The workgroup networks must be "brought to" the backbone, often through point-to-point links.

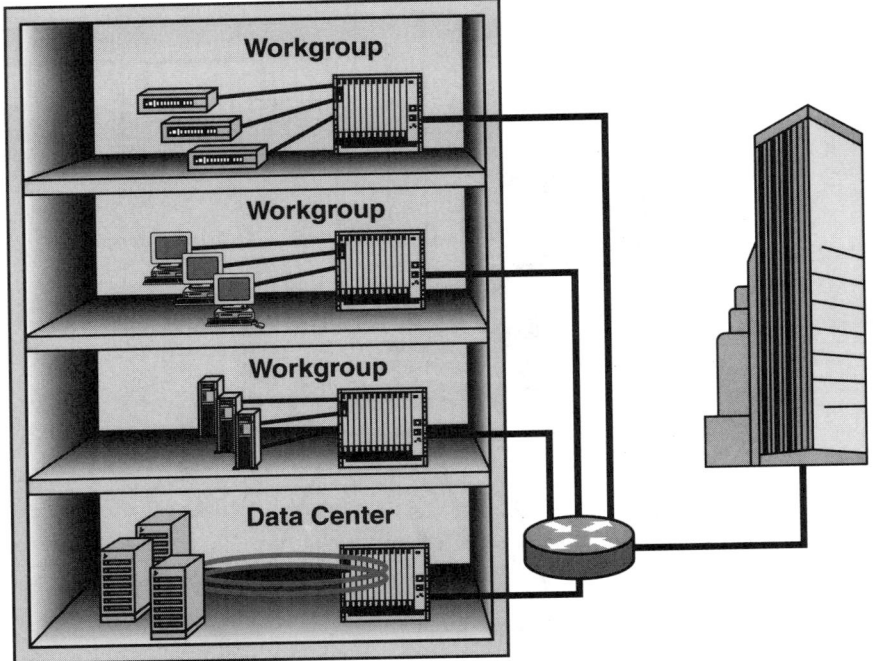

Figure 3–7 Collapsed backbone.

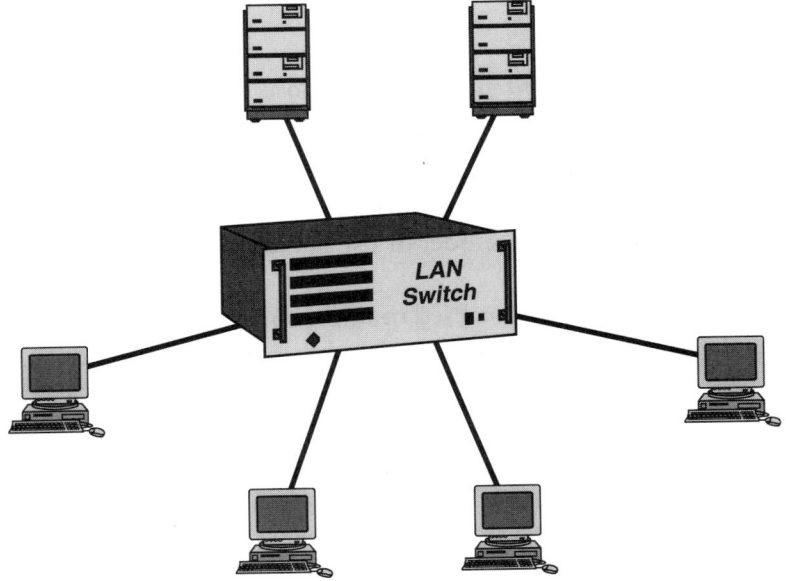

Figure 3–8 Microsegmentation.

each "segment" attaching a single end station. This is called *microsegmentation*.

A microsegmented environment has a number of interesting characteristics:

- There are no collisions between end stations. Each end station is in its own collision domain. However, it is still possible to have collisions between an end station and the MAC implemented in the switch port.[16]
- It may be possible to eliminate the collisions altogether through the use of full-duplex operation (discussed in depth in Chapter 4).
- Each end station has *dedicated bandwidth*; that is, a LAN segment is available for the exclusive use of each individual station.
- The data rate of each station can be independent of any other. There can be devices connected to the same switch operating at 10 Mb/s, 100 Mb/s, or 1000 Mb/s. This is not possible when a shared hub is used.

Of course, there can be a combination of shared LAN attachments and single-station (microsegmented attachments) on a given switching hub, as depicted in Figure 3–6. Stations connected to switch ports through shared LANs will have shared-LAN characteristics, and stations attached individually will have microsegmented capabilities.

3.4.3 Extended Distance Limitations

Switches allow an extension of the distance coverage of a LAN. Each switch port is a distinct LAN, so each port has available to it the full distance extent of the technology. Thus shared LANs attached to a switch port operating at 10 Mb/s have the full 2–3-km distance limit available, regardless of the length of LANs connected to other switch ports. This is the traditional use of a bridge to extend LAN distances.

---

16. There is a common misconception that if there is only one station connected to a port of a switch, there will be no collisions on that link. If the port is operating in half-duplex mode (that is, using normal CSMA/CD), this is simply not true. If the station has a frame queued for transmission to the switch at the same time that the switch has a frame queued for transmission to the station (a common event), then there will be a collision between the station and the switch itself. This is perfectly normal and will resolve itself via the CSMA/CD algorithm. It is important to recognize that there really are two stations on each "LAN": the station attached to the switch port and the switch itself, as depicted in Figure 3–8.

The confusion arises because in a microsegmented environment, it is possible to configure the devices to use full-duplex mode; this eliminates all collisions. This is discussed extensively in Chapter 4. Microsegmentation alone does not eliminate collisions; full-duplex operation (which requires microsegmentation as a prerequisite) does.

Chapter 4 shows that through the use of full-duplex operation, the distance constraints imposed by the MAC can be eliminated entirely on microsegmented switch ports. This is an important capability provided by the use of switching that is simply not available with shared hubs. This is especially important for Gigabit Ethernet, where the distance constraints imposed by CSMA/CD are severe, in effect excluding the use of half-duplex links for backbone applications. Full-duplex and switching provide the means to implement Gigabit Ethernet backbones over practical distances.

3.4.4   Increased Aggregate Capacity

A switch provides much greater data-carrying capacity than does a shared LAN. In a shared LAN, the LAN capacity (be it 10 Mb/s, 100 Mb/s, or 1000 Mb/s) is shared among all of the attached devices. Since a switched hub provides dedicated capacity on each switch port, the total LAN capacity increases with the number of switch ports. In the best-case, the aggregate capacity of a switched LAN will equal

$$\text{capacity}_{agg} = \sum_{port=1}^{n} \text{DataRate}_{port}$$

In practice, the total aggregate capacity will be limited by the internal capacity of the switching hub. If a hub can support full wire-speed communications on all ports simultaneously without frame loss due to switch limitations, the switch is said to be *nonblocking*.[17]

3.4.5   Data Rate Flexibility

All devices connected to a shared LAN must operate at the same data rate. Distinct LANs can operate at different data rates. Since each port of a switch is a distinct LAN, each port can operate at a different data rate. This allows complete flexibility in deploying end stations at different data rates, especially in a microsegmented environment. When a switching hub is used, each attached station can be provided with a LAN interface (NIC) at the data rate

---

17. This is a term borrowed from the telephone switch industry. In that context, it refers to a switch's ability to support connection requests (calls) without withholding resources, that is, having sufficient capacity to support calls from all attached users simultaneously. A LAN switch does not operate in a connection-oriented manner, but the same term is used to refer to a switch that will never be the limiting factor (bottleneck) for connectionless frame exchange. Output congestion may still limit aggregate throughput below that of the switch's internal capacity. See Chapter 11 for further discussion of switch architecture.

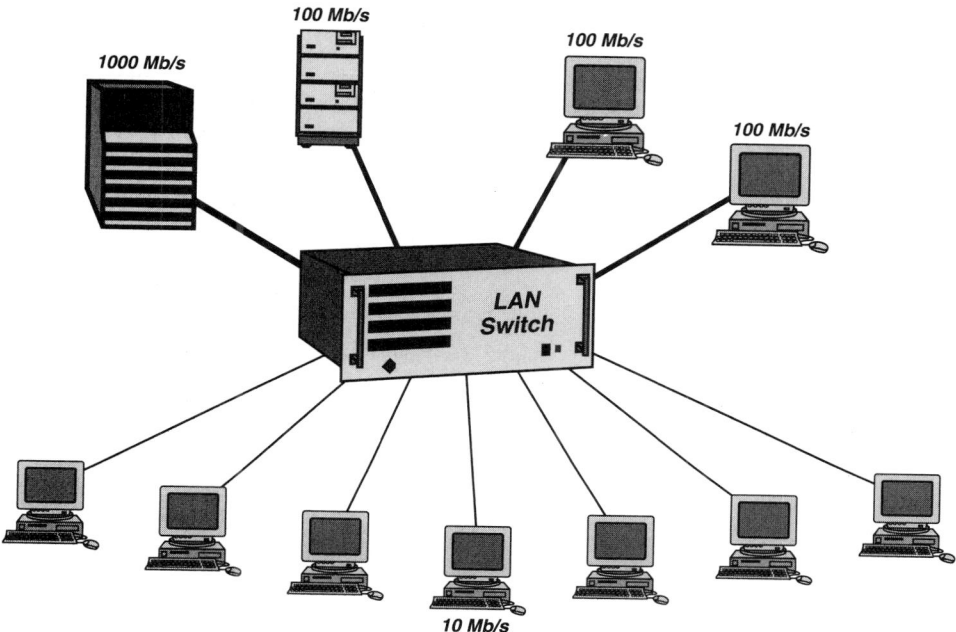

Figure 3–9 Mixing data rates on a single switch.

appropriate for the applications that are being supported on that station, as depicted in Figure 3–9.

High-performance workstations, servers, and routers can be provided with 100 Mb/s or 1000 Mb/s connections, while most end stations are provided with 10 Mb/s or 100 Mb/s connections. This provides higher performance where needed, without burdening all users with the higher associated costs.

3.5   Cost versus Performance

Clearly, a switching hub provides added capabilities beyond that of a traditional repeater hub. But there is no free lunch; the switching hub costs more than a repeater. The additional capabilities (and the cost) arise from the differences in the internal operation of the switching hub. Chapter 11 discusses the different types of hubs in detail. Meanwhile, Table 3–1 summarizes the key elements of a switching hub that cause it to cost more than a repeater:

TABLE 3–1 SWITCHING VERSUS REPEATING

Switch	Repeater
A MAC instantiation is required for each switch port.	No MAC is required.
Buffer memory is required to store complete received frames, especially in the case of output port congestion.[1]	Buffering of only a few bits is required (to allow signal retiming between ports).
Internal bandwidth must be greater than individual port capacities. (In a nonblocking switch, it must be equal to the sum of the port capacities.)	Internal bandwidth need be no greater than that of a single port.

1. This buffering requirement can be minimized through the use of flow control, discussed in Chapter 6.

The relative per-port price ratio between repeaters and switches varies, depending on the product's maturity (its place in the product life-cycle) and the particular implementation. Over time, the price difference between switched and shared hub ports shrinks, especially when low-cost commodity merchant silicon becomes available for the switching function at a given speed. In addition, the *absolute difference* in price-per-port shrinks so that the price differential between a switch and a repeater (at a given data rate) ultimately stops being the determining factor in the decision. You can get some idea of the price penalty by looking at the price history of 10 Mb/s and 100 Mb/s switches and extrapolating those prices to the Gigabit Ethernet market.

While there are always extremes in the marketplace (that is, vendors selling products at both high and low price points), Table 3–2 gives a rough indication of the per-port price ratio of shared and switched hubs at some key points in time.

As the table shows, the price penalty for the use of a switched hub rather than a shared hub decreases over time. This is also a function of the relative maturity of the competing products. When 10 Mb/s switches were first introduced, 10 Mb/s shared hubs were already fairly mature and their price had dropped quite low, so the switching penalty was rather high.

One hundred Mb/s switches were introduced at approximately the same time as 100 Mb/s shared hubs and so demanded less of a price penalty (both product families were equally immature). This phenomenon—the price penalty

TABLE 3–2 HISTORICAL TRENDS IN SHARED AND SWITCHED HUB PRICES[2]

Cost per Port	1991 (first 10 Mb/s switches are introduced)	1993 (first 100 Mb/s repeaters and switches)	1996 (mature discrete 10 Mb/s switches)	1998 [projected] (early Gigabit switches, high-integration 10 and 100 Mb/s switches)
10 Mb/s, shared	$100–200	$50–100	$20–75	$10–40
10 Mb/s, switched	$1000–1500	$250–600	$100–200	$30–70
10 Mb/s, switched/shared ratio	~8.3 : 1	~5.6 : 1	~3.1 : 1	~2.0 : 1
100 Mb/s, shared			$100–200	$40–75
100 Mb/s, switched			$500–1000	$75–150
100 Mb/s, switched/shared ratio			~5 : 1	~2.0 : 1
1000 Mb/s, shared				$500–1000[1]
1000 Mb/s, switched				$800–2000
1000 Mb/s, switched/shared ratio				~1.9 : 1

1. This is speculation, assuming that some vendor will actually build a 1000 Mb/s shared hub, which is unlikely.
2. Ratios are computed based on the average of the high-low ranges provided.

for switching is lower when shared hubs are also immature—is expected to be even more evident with Gigabit Ethernet. This is because the baseline cost of a Gigabit Ethernet product is relatively high, especially early in the life of Gigabit Ethernet. Both a shared and switched hub require many identical components for physical signaling (for example, lasers for optical fiber, one of the highest-cost components in a Gigabit Ethernet product), connectors, chassis, power supply, and so on. This baseline will be higher for Gigabit Ethernet than for 10 or 100 Mb/s systems, relative to the cost of the additional components needed for switching (processing, memory, switching fabric, and so on). This makes the switched/shared ratio lower. Said another way, the cost of admission to Gigabit Ethernet is relatively high regardless of the hub technology used. The cost of a first-class ticket (a switched hub) is not as significant a difference as it was in 10 Mb/s Ethernet (where a coach ticket was *very* cheap).

3.6   Implications of Switches for Gigabit Ethernet

There are a few obvious implications of the shared versus switched hub controversy for Gigabit Ethernet:

■ Switched hubs are typically deployed (at least initially) in backbone applications, as opposed to the desktop environment. This is because their higher cost can be more easily justified in backbones, where the quantities of equipment required are lower. Since early Gigabit Ethernets will be used primarily in backbones, it is likely that switching (or routing) will be deployed before shared hubs. This is the opposite of the evolution of 10 Mb/s Ethernet, where shared hubs were first used in desktop applications and only later did switching hubs become available and popular.

■ Gigabit Ethernets used in a backbone application will need all of the distance allowance available in order to cover the extent of a typical building or campus. A switch, by separating the collision domains of its ports, allows much greater distance coverage than a repeater. (The distance limits are further extended through the use of full-duplex operation, which is possible *only* when using switched hubs. Full-duplex operation is described in Chapter 4.)

■ Gigabit Ethernet switches will not incur as significant a price penalty over their shared LAN counterparts at lower data rates, since much of the cost of Gigabit Ethernet interfaces (especially the physical interface components) is the same for a switched or shared hub. The "switching" part is not what makes the product expensive. This implies that the relative market share for Gigabit Ethernet switches should be greater than for switches at other data rates. It is likely that the market for shared Gigabit Ethernet hubs may constitute only a small niche (or be nonexistent).

Chapter 11 considers a device—a *Buffered Distributor*—that is neither a true shared hub nor a true switched hub. A Buffered Distributor provides many of the features of a switch (for example, full-duplex operation over long distances) but at a lower price (and with lower data capacity). Chapter 4 shows how the use of a switching hub enables the possibility of full-duplex operation.

4 Full-Duplex Ethernet

This chapter looks at full-duplex operation on Ethernet. This is an important element in the deployment of Ethernet at gigabit data rates, since full-duplex operation frees the Ethernet MAC from the constraints on the diameter of a collision domain. Without this mode of operation, Gigabit Ethernet would be severely limited in its useful extent.

4.1 "Ethernet Is CSMA/CD"

The very term "Ethernet" has come to mean that class of LANs that use CSMA/CD as their MAC algorithm. The CSMA/CD MAC is considered the most important conceptual development from the original Xerox work [METC76]. It provides for the design of a communications channel that can be efficiently arbitrated among multiple devices by using an extremely simple algorithm, without requiring a central controller.[1] However, higher-layer protocols and applications operate completely unaware of the underlying MAC arbitration. They do not see, care to see, or need to see the channel access method in use. Their only concern is the ability to exchange messages across the channel in the form of Ethernet frames. That is, an application or protocol's ability to use an Ethernet has nothing to do with the CSMA/CD algorithm, only with its knowledge of the Ethernet frame format. CSMA/CD may be the "essence of Ethernet" to LAN systems designers, but to applications only the exchange of Ethernet frames is significant.

---

1. In fact, very little else was preserved in the transition from the original Xerox laboratory work from the mid-1970s to the 10 Mb/s commercial Ethernet specified in 1980 and later standardized as IEEE 802.3. The cabling system, transceiver design, signaling methods, frame formats, and even the CRC algorithm were all changed, but the CSMA/CD access method remained (although the details of the algorithm itself were not preserved!).

Many other systems can carry Ethernet frames between devices, including:

- IEEE 802.12 (100VG-AnyLAN) [IEEE95a], which can exchange Ethernet frames among stations on a LAN but which uses an alternative MAC, called Demand Priority, so it is not generally referred to as Ethernet[2]
- ATM Emulated LANs [ATM95], which can carry Ethernet frames
- Many point-to-point internetworking link technologies that simply encapsulate Ethernet frames for transmission (for example, PPP-encapsulated Ethernet over SONET)

However, without the hallowed CSMA/CD MAC algorithm, none of these systems are thought of as Ethernet. "Real Ethernets" use the CSMA/CD MAC.

4.2   Why a MAC?[3]

Why is a MAC algorithm needed at all? The purpose of the MAC is to allow multiple stations, each with data to transmit, to decide which one gets to use the channel at any given time. This is necessary when multiple stations share a common underlying physical channel and all can offer traffic simultaneously. That is, a MAC is needed *only* when there is a possibility that two or more devices may wish to use a common communications channel. The MAC algorithm provides a set of rules by which the devices negotiate access to that shared channel.

But if there is no common, shared channel, then there is no need for a MAC algorithm at all! Consider a point-to-point link that has separate paths for communicating in each direction between the endpoints (for example, RS-422 over twisted-pair, as shown in Figure 4–1).

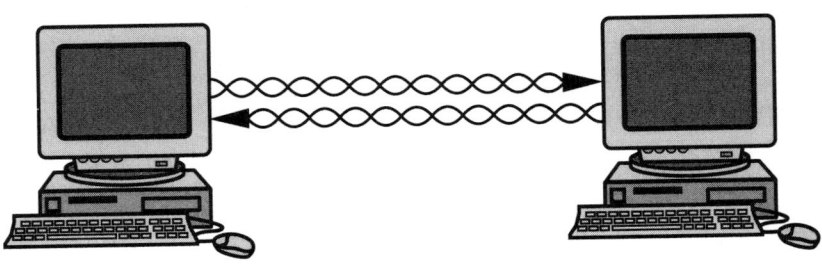

Figure 4–1 Point-to-point communications.

---

2. Indeed, it was precisely the lack of a CSMA/CD MAC that caused the 100VG-AnyLAN faction within the IEEE 802.3 High-Speed Study Group to form its own Working Group and split from IEEE 802.3 during 1993.

3. I am sure Chico Marx would have said this, had he been an expert in networking technology.

Assuming that the receiver at each end is always enabled, either device can transmit frames to the other at any time. There is no need for any sort of arbitration for use of the channel, since there is never more than one device wishing to transmit on a given wire pair. Note that there are two independent communications channels here, one in each direction between the two stations. Such a channel can simultaneously support communication in both directions and is called a *full-duplex channel*.

Historically, LAN technologies have been thought of in terms of the MAC algorithm that is used, for example, Ethernet (CSMA/CD), Token Ring, and Token Bus. The MAC algorithms differentiate these technologies based on how each one negotiates access to a common, shared channel. But if there is no shared channel, there is no reason to use any of these access methods. We may still have a LAN, but there is no MAC.

The original Ethernet specification stated explicitly:

> The following are *not* goals of the Ethernet design: *Full duplex operation:* At any given instant, the Ethernet can transfer data from one source station to one or more destination stations. Bi-directional communication is provided by rapid exchange of frames, rather than full duplex operation. [DIX80]

The underlying channel in the original Ethernet design was a shared, coaxial medium. It was incapable of supporting full-duplex operation, and the system design did not try to overcome this limitation.

4.3   Full-Duplex Enablers

Two elements (discussed in Chapters 2 and 3) evolved to enable full-duplex capability in Ethernet:

1. The shift to dedicated media, as provided by the use of structured wiring systems, and
2. The possibility of microsegmented, dedicated LANs, as provided by switches.

4.3.1   Dedicated Media

As discussed in Chapter 2, Ethernets migrated from using coaxial cable to using structured wiring with twisted-pair in the early 1990s. This is by far the most popular implementation of Ethernet used today. A structured, star-wired system, using hubs at the center of the star (as depicted in Figure 4–2),

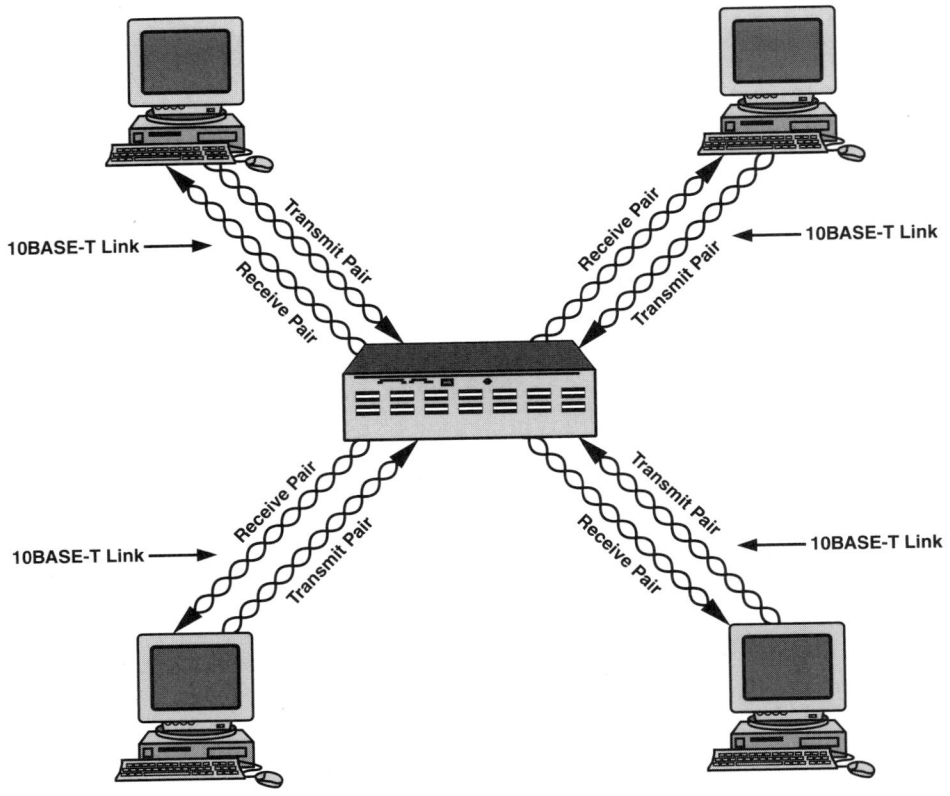

Figure 4–2 Dedicated media.

changes the fundamental assumption that the underlying medium cannot support full-duplex operation. Unlike coaxial cables, many varieties of twisted-pair Ethernet (10BASE-T, 100BASE-TX, and 100BASE-T2) can, at least in theory, support simultaneous bidirectional communications, since there are separate paths (wire pairs) for communication in each direction.

Even though the channel may be capable of supporting bidirectional communications, an Ethernet using a repeater hub uses this channel in a half-duplex mode; at any given time, only one station can transmit a frame on the LAN without interference. Multiple transmissions result in collisions, which are resolved by the Ethernet MAC in the normal way. But the migration to dedicated media at least enables the possibility of using the channel in a full-duplex fashion.

Table 4–1 indicates which of the standard Ethernet media systems are capable of supporting full-duplex operation.

TABLE 4–1   FULL-DUPLEX MEDIA SUPPORT

Standard Designation	Media Type	Full-Duplex Capable?
10BASE5	50 Ω coaxial cable	No
10BASE2	50 Ω coaxial cable	No
10BASE-T	2-pair Category 3/4/5 UTP	Yes[5]
10BASE-FL	2 optical fibers (62.5 μm)	Yes[5]
10BASE-FB	2 optical fibers (62.5 μm)	No[1]
10BASE-FP	2 optical fibers (62.5 μm)	No[2]
10BROAD36	75 Ω coaxial cable	No
100BASE-TX	2-pair Category 5 UTP, 2-pair STP	Yes
100BASE-FX	2 optical fibers (62.5 μm)	Yes
100BASE-T4	4-pair UTP 3	No[3]
100BASE-T2	2-pair Category 3/4/5 UTP	Yes
1000BASE-SX	2 optical fibers (62.5/50 μm)	Yes
1000BASE-LX	2 optical fibers (62.5/50/10 μm)	Yes
1000BASE-CX	2-pair STP	Yes
1000BASE-T	4-pair Category 5 UTP	Yes[4]

1. 10BASE-FB requires a synchronous repeater and cannot operate in full-duplex mode regardless of the media type.
2. 10BASE-FP uses a passive hub and cannot operate in full-duplex mode regardless of the media type.
3. 100BASE-T4 uses two of its pairs in an interfering, bidirectional mode and cannot support full-duplex operation.
4. 1000BASE-T is still under development, but one of the stated goals is to support full-duplex operation.
5. While the channel design supports full-duplex, the transceiver must be specifically configured for full-duplex operation. This disables the looping back of transmitted data onto the receive lines that is normally implemented in half-duplex mode.

4.3.2   Dedicated LAN

As discussed in Chapter 3, the use of dedicated media systems allowed the deployment of switching hubs (that is, bridges) rather than repeaters at the center of the star-wiring system. The use of a switch, while attractive due to its channel capacity advantages (discussed earlier), marks a fundamental architectural change to the LAN. With a repeater, all of the devices connecting to the hub shared the available channel and had to arbitrate for access. In contrast, with a switching hub each attached device has a dedicated channel (dedicated LAN) between itself and the hub.

A switching hub (unlike a repeater) has a MAC entity for each of its ports. Architecturally, each of the connections to the switching hub constitutes a distinct LAN, with access to each LAN arbitrated independently of all other LANs. A repeater with *n* ports constitutes a single LAN; a switch with *n* ports constitutes *n* LANs, one for each switch port (see Figure 4–3).

In the case of a microsegmented switched LAN, each port comprises a two-station network composed of the attached device and the switch port itself. Considering that two-station LAN in isolation, one can see that it appears *exactly* the same (architecturally) as the simple point-to-point connection shown in Figure 4–1. Each device has a private, independent channel to the other device, so there is no possibility of contention for the use of the underlying communications channel.

Unless you modify the behavior of the Ethernet interfaces in the switch and the attached device, you cannot use this connection in any manner other

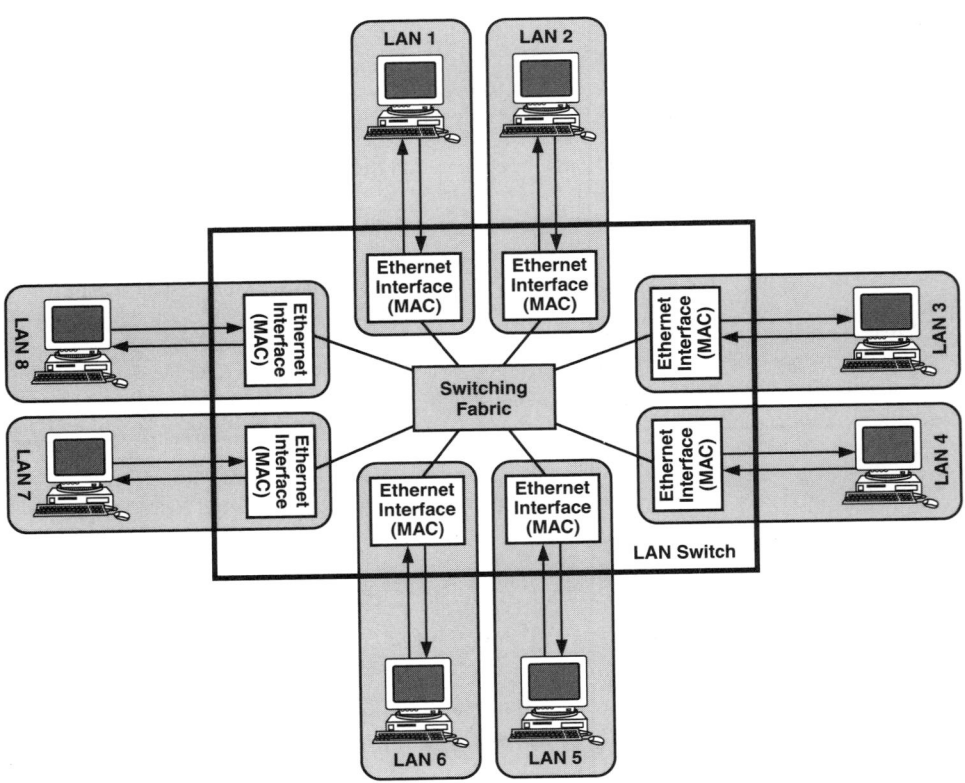

Figure 4–3 Switched LAN architecture.

than the normal, shared Ethernet mode. This is because a standard Ethernet interface in a dedicated media environment (for example, 10BASE-T) treats a "receive-while-transmitting" condition as a collision.

4.4   Full-Duplex Ethernet

In the previous scenario, you could modify the behavior of the Ethernet MAC controller in both the switch and the attached device to take advantage of their unique situation. You would need to do the following.

- Disable the *carrier sense* function as it is normally used to defer transmissions. That is, the reception of data on the "receive" channel should not cause the transmitter to defer any pending transmissions. A normal (half-duplex) Ethernet interface will use carrier sense to withhold its own transmissions, in order to avoid interfering with transmissions in progress.
- Disable the *collision detect* function, which would normally cause the transmitter to abort, jam, and reschedule its transmission if it detects reception while transmitting.
- Disable the looping back of transmitted data onto the receiver input, as is done on a half-duplex channel.

Neither end of the link needs to defer to received traffic. Nor is there any interference between transmissions and receptions. This avoids the need for collision detection, backoff, and retry. In this environment, you can operate the LAN in *full-duplex mode;* stations can both transmit and receive simultaneously. This is depicted in Figure 4–4.

4.4.1   Full-Duplex Operating Environment

There are three conditions that must be met in order to use an Ethernet in full-duplex mode:

1. **There can be only two devices on the LAN.** The entire "LAN" must comprise a single point-to-point link. A microsegmented switching hub environment meets this criterion on each of its ports. In addition, the special case of a simple, two-station interconnection with no switch (see Figure 4–5) can also support full-duplex operation.
2. **The physical medium itself must be capable of supporting simultaneous transmission and reception without interference.** Table 4–1 shows which media types can support full-duplex operation.

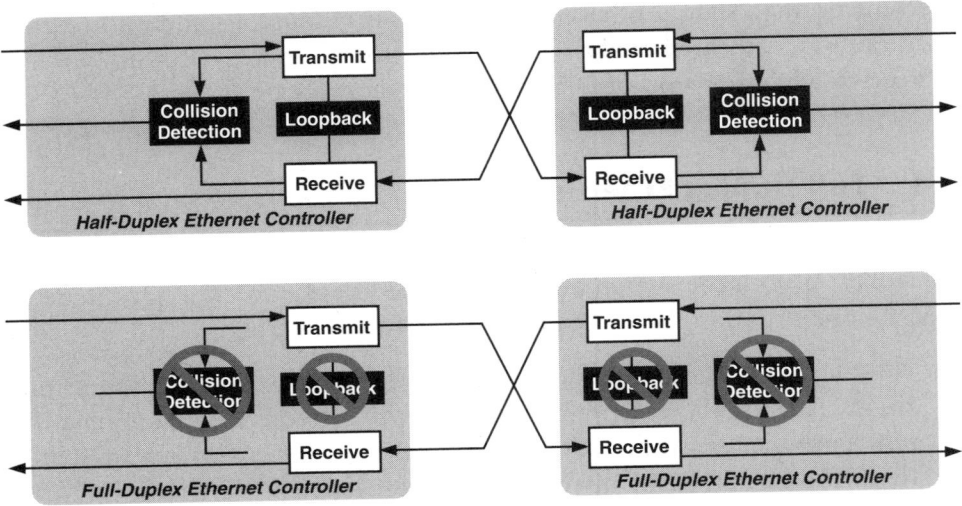

Figure 4–4 Half- and full-duplex MAC.

3. **The network interfaces must be capable of and configured to use full-duplex mode.**[1] Many legacy interfaces cannot operate in full-duplex mode; they simply were not designed with such a possibility in mind. While the modifications required to make the MAC operate in full-duplex mode are trivial, it generally is not possible to retrofit an existing, half-duplex-only device to operate in full-duplex mode.

Full-duplex operation is not possible with traditional repeater hubs, as the use of repeaters implies shared medium access. Even if a switching hub is used, there can be only one device connected to a switch port that is operating in full-duplex mode (microsegmentation). A shared hub cannot be connected to a port of a switch and still have that port operate in full-duplex mode.

Full-duplex Ethernet was standardized as part of the IEEE 802.3x supplement to the existing standard. [IEEE97] Considerable editorial changes were made to provide for two distinct operating modes in the standard, but the significant changes were to the Pascal code used for the formal definition of the Ethernet MAC. In full-duplex mode, the code disables the defer and

---

1. Chapter 8 discusses the means for automatically configuring Ethernet interfaces to use full-duplex mode where possible.

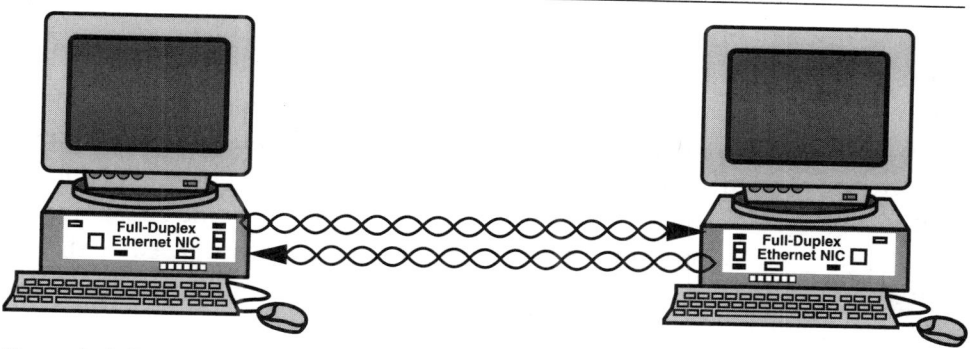

Figure 4–5 Two-station LAN.

collision detect functions and allows simultaneous transmission and reception without interference.

4.4.2   Subset of Half-Duplex Operation

A "full-duplex Ethernet MAC" is actually trivial (some would say nonexistent!). A station needs neither to "defer" to other traffic in the traditional manner (carrier sense) nor detect simultaneous transmissions (collision detect). That is, full-duplex Ethernet is CSMA/CD without the CS, the MA, or the CD! In reality, with all possibility of contention removed, we no longer have any real need for a MAC. A full-duplex Ethernet device doesn't use any MAC algorithm; a station in this mode may transmit at will, with no consideration of interference by other stations. The only properties that a full-duplex Ethernet has in common with its half-duplex counterpart are the Ethernet frame format and the encoding/signaling method used on the physical medium.

Of course, supporting the Ethernet frame format does imply some important functionality, including address decoding and checksum (Cyclic Redundancy Check, or CRC) generation and verification, which are required in both full-duplex and half-duplex mode devices. However, full-duplex Ethernet is a proper subset of half-duplex (traditional) Ethernet operation. Full-duplex operation requires no *additional* functionality to be built into an interface; it simply disables functionality needed for half-duplex operation. This implies that full-duplex capability, despite providing performance improvements and application enhancements, should not increase the cost of an Ethernet interface.

The standard [IEEE97] allows manufacturers to build conformant interfaces that can operate in half-duplex mode only, full-duplex mode only, or both. In theory, a "full-duplex mode only" interface could be built and sold for less than a half-duplex capable interface. In practice (at least at 10 Mb/s and 100 Mb/s), a "full-duplex mode only" interface would not be usable in many installations. There are tens of millions of existing legacy interfaces that operate only in half-duplex mode. Coexisting with these devices (including repeaters as well as some existing switches) requires half-duplex capability.

In practice, the portion of an Ethernet interface concerned with the shared-access MAC is insignificant relative to the portions devoted to the other functions that must be performed (for example, memory and buffer management, host bus interface, and statistics collection), so including half-duplex capability does not impact the cost of the interface in any meaningful way. Virtually all Ethernet interfaces designed today (at 10 Mb/s and 100 Mb/s) are capable of both half- and full-duplex operation. In contrast, Gigabit Ethernets will be deployed almost exclusively in full-duplex mode (for reasons discussed shortly). There will be many "full-duplex only" Ethernet interfaces available at this data rate, especially in switches used for collapsed backbone applications.[2]

4.4.3   Transmitter Operation

A full-duplex transmitter may send a frame any time there is a frame in its transmit queue, provided it follows two simple rules:

1. The station operates on one frame at a time. That is, it finishes sending one frame before beginning to send the next pending frame.
2. The transmitter enforces a minimum spacing between frames (the same as for half-duplex operation). This interframe gap allows receivers some minimum "breathing room" between frames to perform necessary housekeeping chores (posting interrupts, buffer management, updating network management statistics counters, and so on).

4.4.4   Receiver Operation

The receiver in a full-duplex Ethernet interface operates identically as one in half-duplex mode, as follows:

---

2. While the inclusion of half-duplex operation would not add significantly to the cost, doing so adds unnecessary complexity that can be avoided in a Gigabit Ethernet interface. In fact, design verification and conformance testing of the half-duplex MAC algorithm implementation is usually more work than the actual design. A full-duplex-only design thus has a shorter time-to-market.

1. When a frame begins to arrive, the receiver waits for a valid Start-of-Frame delimiter and then begins to assemble the data link encapsulation of the frame.[3]

2. The Destination address is checked to see whether it matches an address that the device has been configured to accept. Any frames not so destined are discarded.

3. The Frame Check Sequence (CRC) is checked. Any frame that is deemed invalid is discarded.

4. The frame length is checked. All frames shorter than the minimum valid length (512 bits) are discarded. In a half-duplex LAN, any fragment that is the result of a collision is guaranteed to be less than this minimum length. Thus discarding such frames ensures that collision fragments are not improperly perceived to be valid frames. In full-duplex mode, there are no collisions, so it is not possible for collision fragments to appear. Nonetheless, this step does not cause any problem or damage. Ethernet maintains the 512-bit minimum frame length constraint, even for full-duplex operation (see later in this chapter for further discussion).

5. The receiver passes up to its client (that is, higher-layer protocols or applications) all frames that have passed the previous tests. The order of executing the previous validity tests is not critical and may vary with different implementations.

4.4.5   Minimum Frame Size Constraint

Commercially available Ethernet existed in its "half-duplex only" incarnation for over 15 years before the networking environment could support (and the standards recognized and legitimized) the use of full-duplex mode. Because of this history, there is a huge installed product base (and knowledge base) surrounding half-duplex Ethernet. To allow a peaceful coexistence between the half- and full-duplex modes, a certain amount of "baggage" from half-duplex Ethernet has been retained in the full-duplex version.

In half-duplex mode, it is necessary to enforce a minimum valid frame length that is at least as long as the worst-case round-trip propagation delay of the network, plus the time to transmit the 32-bit jam signal. This ensures that a station will always be transmitting when a collision is detected on a frame. If a station were allowed to send frames shorter than this minimum,

---

3. See Chapter 5 for a discussion of frame format and the Start-of-Frame delimiter.

such frames could experience collisions without the transmitter's being aware of them. The transmitter would not reschedule these (corrupted) transmissions; thus network performance would be severely degraded.

All standard Ethernets use a minimum frame length of 512 bits from the Destination address to the Frame Check Sequence, inclusive. While there is no need for a minimum frame length in full-duplex mode, retaining this restriction allows device drivers and higher-layer software to treat identically both flavors of Ethernet (full- and half-duplex). In addition, it allows for seamless bridging between half-duplex and full-duplex Ethernets.

4.5   Implications of Full-Duplex Operation

The use of full-duplex mode on Ethernet has a number of important implications:

- It eliminates the link length restrictions of CSMA/CD.
- It increases the aggregate channel capacity.
- It increases the potential load on a switch.

These are discussed in the following sections.

4.5.1   Eliminating the Link Length Restrictions of Half-Duplex Ethernet

The use of CSMA/CD as an access control mechanism implies an intimate relationship between the minimum length of a frame and the maximum round-trip propagation delay of the network. You need to make sure that if a collision occurs on any transmission, all transmitting stations know of the collision so that they can take proper action. This implies that the minimum length of a frame must be longer than the maximum round-trip propagation time of the network, plus an allowance for the jam time, synchronization delays, and so on, so that the station will still be transmitting the frame when it is informed of the collision.

Since full-duplex operation does not use CSMA/CD, this distance restriction no longer applies. Regardless of the data rate of the LAN, the length of a full-duplex Ethernet link is limited only by the physical transmission characteristics of the medium. While twisted-pair links may be used at distances of up to approximately 100 m (at 10 Mb/s and 100 Mb/s), optical fiber may be used at distances of up to 2–3 km (multimode fiber) and 20–50 km or more (single-mode fiber).[4] With appropriate line drivers and signal regeneration,

---

4. The precise limits for physical link lengths for various types of media are given in later chapters of this book.

there is no reason why a full-duplex Ethernet link cannot be extended across national and international distances by using satellite, private fiber, SONET, or other technologies. The distance restrictions of CSMA/CD no longer apply.

This makes full duplex Ethernet especially attractive as a building and campus backbone technology. It can be used at any supported data rate (10, 100, or 1000 Mb/s) over kilometer-scale distances on switch-to-switch connections in a collapsed backbone. This is expected to be a primary application area for Gigabit Ethernet. It already is popular for 100 Mb/s switched networks today.

4.5.2   Increasing the Link Capacity

Clearly, a half-duplex channel that could previously carry a maximum of x Mb/s can carry $2x$ Mb/s in full-duplex mode, since it can carry data in both directions simultaneously. Unfortunately, this doubling of capacity occurs in a symmetrical manner. The most common bandwidth-intensive application on LANs today is bulk file transfer. File transfers move large amounts of data in one direction, but only small amounts (acknowledgments) in the other. The aggregate channel capacity may have increased, but the maximum data transfer rate from one device to another is still x Mb/s. Since no widely used, traffic-intensive LAN applications use bandwidth in a symmetrical manner, the doubling of capacity does not directly double application throughput.[5, 6]

The capacity doubling can be of benefit if there are multiple applications in use and some are intensively moving data in one direction, while others are intensively moving data in the other. This would be rare in an end user's workstation, but more common in a server.[7] Since servers typically support many users and applications simultaneously, the probability that some applications will need to move data into the server at the same time that others are moving data out of the server is much higher than for an end-user workstation. Thus full-duplex operation is commonly used in connections from a

---

5. In theory, a bidirectional video application could take advantage of symmetrical bandwidth, but this is not a common application on LANs today.

6. Some suppliers market full-duplex Ethernet as "20BASE-T" or "200BASE-T," but this is misleading, since the maximum asymmetrical application throughput is not doubled.

7. Appearances to the contrary, most desktop (PC) operating systems are single-tasking, single-processor, and single-threaded. Even though the user interface makes it appear that there are multiple tasks operating simultaneously (that is, multiple open windows into separate applications), there is little parallelism or concurrency in operation. Servers, on the other hand, are by necessity multitasking and often multiprocessor and/or multithreaded. They can receive, transmit, and process data simultaneously and thus achieve real benefits from full-duplex operation.

server to a switch port. This also makes sense from a cost perspective. It may be prohibitively expensive to dedicate a switch port to every end user (especially at 100 and 1000 Mb/s), but it is not unreasonable to dedicate switch ports to servers, since there are fewer servers. The servers can then be operated in full-duplex mode, and the end-user workstations in the traditional, half duplex mode. This is depicted in Figure 4–6.

Similar to a server, a switch used as a *collapsed backbone* can benefit from the symmetrical increase in capacity. A backbone is a network used to interconnect other networks (as opposed to interconnecting stations and servers). A collapsed backbone is a switch (or a router) used as the combining point for the interconnected networks, as shown in Figure 4–7.[8]

If the traffic distribution among groups is relatively uniform (that is, there is no one group that is either a dominant source or sink of data), then the traffic through the switch ports on the collapsed backbone will be roughly

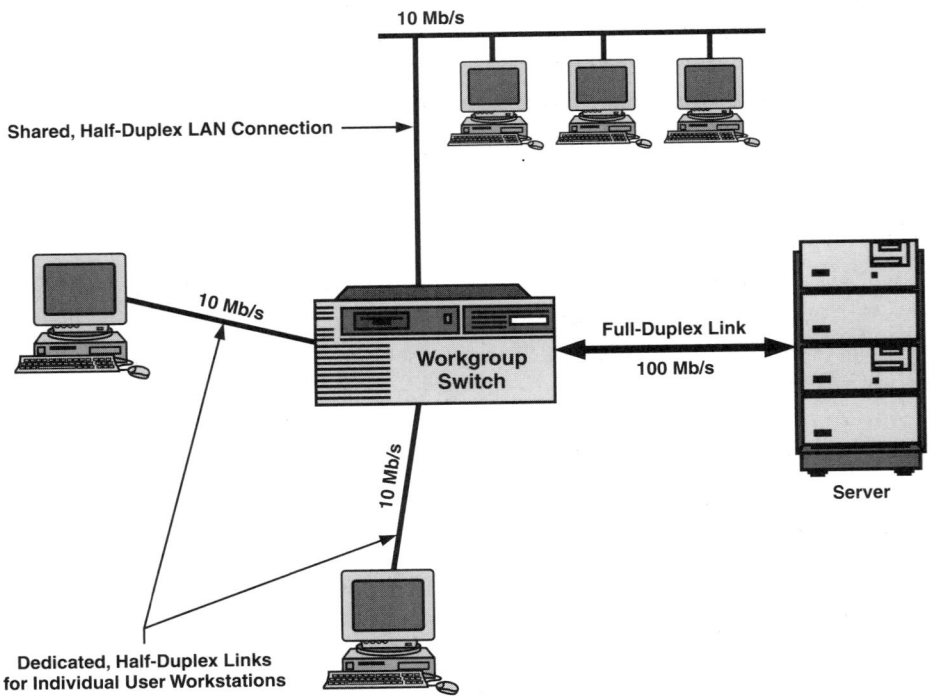

Figure 4–6 Full-duplex server connection.

---

8. The alternative to a collapsed backbone is a *distributed backbone*, such as an FDDI ring.

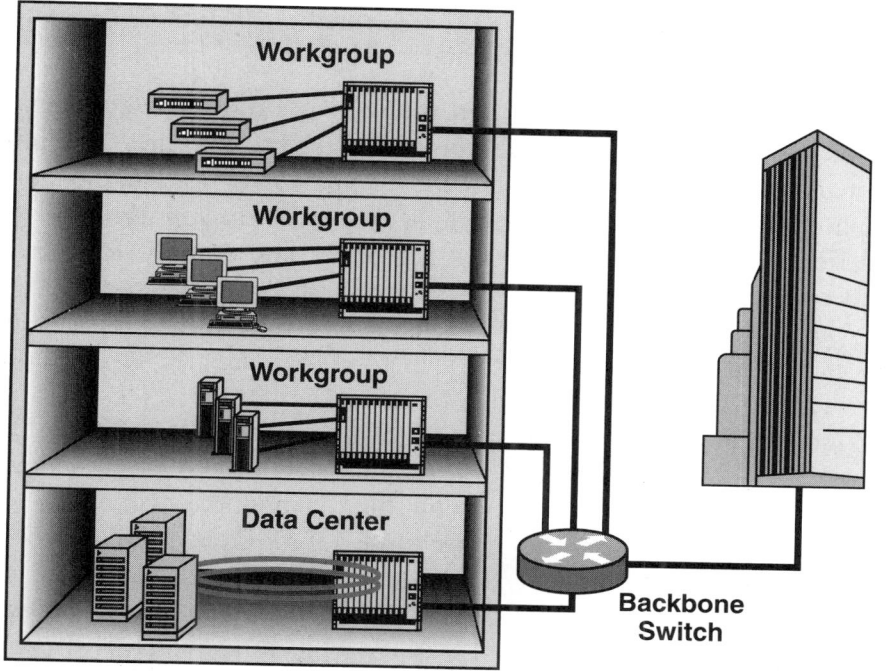

Figure 4–7 Switch used as a collapsed backbone.

symmetrical; traffic flow into and out of any given switch port will be approximately equal. Given this, the backbone switch can take advantage of full-duplex operation to increase the channel capacity, since bandwidth usage is approximately symmetrical.

4.5.3   Increasing Switch Load

A switch supporting full-duplex mode on any or all of its ports must deal with the possibility of increased data flow through the switch. The maximum aggregate capacity required of a switch with n ports all operating at x Mb/s in half-duplex mode would be

$$\text{capacity}_{agg} = \frac{n\,x}{2},$$

since:

- A port can be either transmitting or receiving at a given time, not both (half-duplex mode), and

■ All traffic flowing into the switch flows out as well (that is, the switch is neither sourcing nor sinking significant traffic).

If the ports of the switch are operating in full-duplex mode, then this maximum capacity requirement doubles, since the previous first disclaimer is no longer true. If a switch is to operate in a *nonblocking* fashion, then it must have double the internal switching capacity in order to support full-duplex operation. This can affect the cost of a product, and even the fundamental architecture required.

Nonblocking operation means that under steady-state conditions and without output port congestion, the switch can operate at wire-speed on all ports without dropping frames due to switch limitations.[9] That is, a nonblocking switch is never the limiting factor for network throughput. Other factors may limit throughput, of course, including port congestion and end station limitations, but these are beyond the control of the switch.[10]

Of course, a switch designer may choose not to provide for nonblocking operation as a legitimate cost/performance trade-off. If the steady-state loads and network traffic patterns are such that the blocking nature of the switch would not normally come into play, then a blocking switch will provide equivalent performance to a nonblocking one, and at a lower cost. Clearly, it is more likely that a switch will be a potential blocking problem if its ports can operate in full-duplex mode. The bottom line is that the use of full-duplex mode implies that a switch may have greater performance demands placed on it than if it operated only in half-duplex mode.

A similar argument can be made for end stations, particularly servers, operating in full-duplex mode. However, unlike switches, end stations rarely have large numbers of ports, and the doubling of the capacity to operate in full-duplex mode is much less of a concern with low port densities.

---

9. Port congestion is the condition in which the load offered to a given port exceeds the capacity of that port. This would typically occur if the traffic patterns were such that many flows were simultaneously directed at a given port (either instantaneously or steady-state) and the sum of the flows exceeded the data-carrying capacity of the port.

10. This use of the term "nonblocking" is somewhat different from the same term used in association with connection-oriented switches (that is, telephone switches), but its use in this way implies the same result. That is, a nonblocking switch never becomes the performance-limiting factor for the network. See Chapter 11 for a more complete discussion of nonblocking switch architecture.

4.6   Full-Duplex Application Environments

Half-duplex Ethernet has been used for over 20 years in every conceivable LAN application environment. No special conditions are required to use a traditional, CSMA/CD-based LAN. It can operate on dedicated and nonded-icated media (for example, twisted-pair and coaxial cable) and dedicated and nondedicated LANs (switched and repeated). Full-duplex Ethernet is usable only in specific LAN configurations that have both dedicated media capable of supporting simultaneous, bidirectional communications and exactly two devices on the "LAN" (microsegmentation).

While the use of dedicated media and switched LAN configurations meet-ing these requirements is rapidly increasing, there is still a huge installed base of legacy LANs that cannot support full-duplex operation. In addition, switches are more expensive than shared LAN hubs and may not be justified for general-purpose use. Thus full-duplex operation is most often seen in

- switch-to-switch connections,
- server and router connections, and
- long-distance connections.

Each of these situations is discussed in the following sections.

4.6.1   Switch-to-Switch Connections

It makes sense to use full-duplex mode where possible on connections between switches in a switched infrastructure. Switch-to-switch connections have the following characteristics.

- They often require link lengths in excess of that allowed by the use of CSMA/CD, especially at 100 Mb/s and 1000 Mb/s. This is often the driv-ing force for the use of full-duplex mode in this application.
- They can take advantage of the increased capacity because of the gener-ally symmetrical traffic distribution in a backbone environment.
- They meet the "two-station LAN" requirement of full-duplex mode oper-ation.

Hence, switch-to-switch connections are an obvious and popular appli-cation for deploying full-duplex mode. Figure 4–8 depicts full-duplex Ether-net used in a switch-to-switch environment.

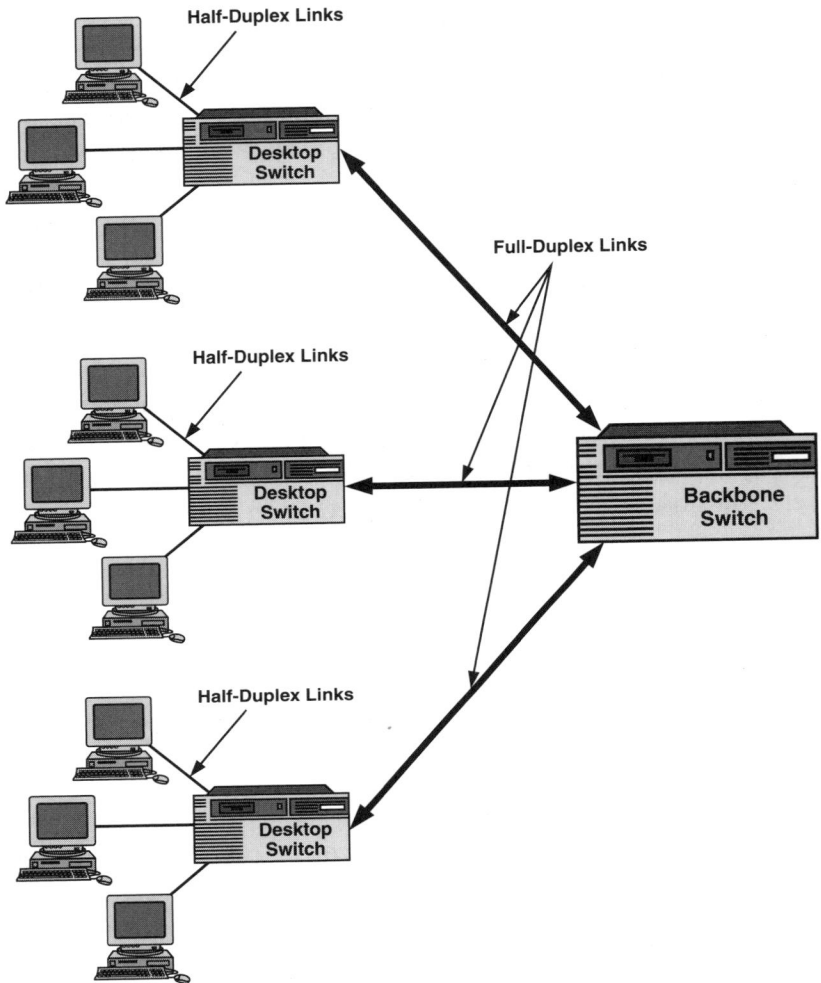

Figure 4–8 Switch-to-switch connections.

4.6.2   Server and Router Connections

Full-duplex connections are also popular for connecting network servers to a LAN, particularly when connecting to a high-speed or backbone switch port. Network server connections have the following characteristics.

■ They can take advantage of the increased capacity because of their multitasking nature.

■ They are relatively few in number and can therefore be justified (on a cost basis) in using dedicated switch ports, even at very high speeds.

As traffic patterns tend to be from many clients to one server, server connections are often made to a high-speed full-duplex port on a switch, with clients connected to lower-speed ports. This prevents the server port speed from becoming a point of network congestion. This was depicted in Figure 4–6.

A router is simply a station connected to more than one network whose purpose is to forward traffic among those networks. From a duplex mode perspective, there is no real difference between a switch and a router.[11] Similarly, a router can be thought of as an *internetwork server*. As such, it becomes an ideal candidate for deployment of full-duplex interfaces, for the same reasons presented previously.

4.6.3   Long-Distance Connections

In some environments, there may be a small number of end stations that need to be connected to a particular workgroup but that are physically separated beyond the limits of half-duplex operation at the speed in use. To allow the connection of such remote devices, a full-duplex connection to a workgroup switch can be used, since full-duplex eliminates the distance limitations of CSMA/CD. Optical fiber is the most common medium for this application, since it can support distances far in excess of that offered by twisted-pair. Figure 4–9 depicts this application environment.

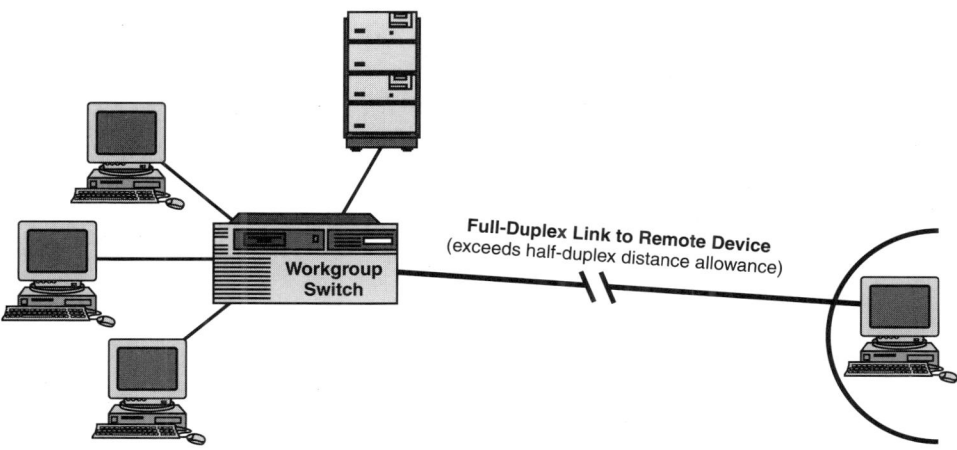

Figure 4–9 Long distance connection.

---

11. Of course, from an *internetworking* perspective, there are huge differences, but these are unrelated to whether it is appropriate to use full-duplex mode interfaces.

The use of a dedicated switch port in this application can be justified by the need for connectivity, not by the need for any improvement in throughput or performance.

4.7   Application of Full-Duplex Mode to Gigabit Ethernet

Gigabit Ethernet can take advantage of full-duplex operation in the bulk of its target applications:

- Using CSMA/CD at gigabit speeds leads to impractical distance restrictions and unnecessarily reduced performance. (See Chapter 10 for a detailed explanation.)
- The capacity offered by Gigabit Ethernet is far beyond what desktop workstations require, at least for the near-term. Also, the cost of gigabit connections will not soon be justified for the volume desktop marketplace. This means that Gigabit Ethernet will be deployed primarily in backbones and for server and router connections. All of these applications can leverage full-duplex mode, as discussed previously.

The vast majority (probably 100%) of Gigabit Ethernet connections will therefore operate in full-duplex mode. Many manufacturers build (and are building) interfaces that support *only* full-duplex operation. This is because such a restriction is not really a serious limitation on the usefulness of the product and the complexity of the half-duplex MAC algorithm can be eliminated. This would not be practical for a 10 Mb/s product; there are simply too many legacy CSMA/CD networks.

Chapter 6 looks at how full-duplex operation eliminates the natural congestion control afforded by the CSMA/CD MAC. An explicit flow control algorithm was developed to overcome this problem.

5 Frame Formats

This chapter examines the various formats of Ethernet frames. There have been some minor (but incredibly annoying!) changes that have occurred from the original DIX Ethernet frame format design to the present usage. The recent work of IEEE 802.3x has finally resulted in the convergence of the various frame formats into one combined format, with industry-wide approval.

Although not relevant to the discussions in this chapter, all of the frame formats examined are further encapsulated by the underlying Physical Layer, including Start-of-Stream and End-of-Stream Delimiters, idle signals, and so on, as appropriate for the particular physical implementation.

5.1 But First, a Word on Notation and Bit/Byte Ordering

Throughout this book, I discuss data units that are longer than 1 bit. While the underlying physical channel may be carrying data in serial fashion, most of the interesting fields and frame contents are much longer than a single bit. Since it is rather inconvenient (not to mention wasteful of paper and ink!) to express multibyte data values as long strings of individual bits, we need to agree on a convention for shorthand notation of fields longer than a single bit.

5.1.1 Bit Ordering

Strictly speaking, the Ethernet is totally insensitive to the interpretation of bits within a byte. That is, it is not really necessary to consider the byte as having an 8-bit numerical value. However, some convention is useful to allow easier description of the bit order and to prevent needless incompatibilities. Ethernet (like most data communications systems) transmits bits within a byte from the *least-significant bit* first (the bit corresponding to the 2^0 numerical position), to the *most-significant bit* last (the bit corresponding to the 2^7 numerical position). Also by convention, when writing binary fields, the least-significant bit is shown as the leftmost bit and the most-significant bit as the rightmost. This is known as "Little Endian," or canonical, form.[1] In contrast, Token Ring and FDDI LANs transmit from the most-significant bit to the least-significant bit within each byte in what is called "Big Endian" format.

A byte is written as two hexadecimal digits, with the most-significant digit first (leftmost digit) and the least-significant digit second (rightmost digit). Following are a few examples of Little Endian bit transmissions for various byte values:

Byte Value (hexadecimal)	Bits Transmitted (from left to right) 2^0 2^7
01	1 0 0 0 0 0 0 0
55	1 0 1 0 1 0 1 0
AA	0 1 0 1 0 1 0 1
4E	0 1 1 1 0 0 1 0

Throughout this book, you should assume that all bytes are transmitted in Little Endian bit order unless stated otherwise.

5.1.2 Byte Ordering

If all of the interesting data values were only 1 byte long, we would now be finished with the discussion of bit ordering! Unfortunately, this is not the case, so we must deal with fields that are longer than a single byte. These fields are represented by a string of bytes arranged from left to right and separated by the hyphen character (-). Each byte consists of two hexadecimal digits.

The bytes of a multibyte field are sent from first byte to last (that is, left to right), with each byte sent in Little Endian bit order. For example, the 6-byte field

08–00–60–01-2C-4A

would be transmitted serially as (read from left to right)

0001 0000 - 0000 0000 - 0000 0110 - 1000 0000 - 0011 0100 - 0101 0010

(The spaces and hyphens are shown for visual convenience only.)

---

1. The terms Little Endian and Big Endian for bit ordering were coined by Danny Cohen in his landmark paper, "On Holy Wars and a Plea for Peace," originally published privately in April 1980 and then in the *Communications of the Association for Computing Machinery*. It is widely available on the World Wide Web. The terms come from the eighteenth-century novel, *Gulliver's Travels*, by Jonathan Swift.

This convention is used throughout all of the IEEE 802.3 standards and is also used in this book.

A Philosophical Aside

Note that I have not referred to any byte as being the "most-significant byte" or the "least-significant byte." This is because in almost all Ethernet uses, *there is no significance to the bytes*. The terms "most-significant" and "least-significant" are used when discussing fields with numerical significance, where one number may be compared with another to see which is larger or smaller. With only one exception, there is no numerical significance to the fields of an Ethernet frame. For example, addresses are used to uniquely identify stations, but they are not *numbers* in the sense that it would be meaningful to discuss the importance of one address being "less than" another. So you can say that in Ethernet, you send the "first byte" first, the "second byte" second, and the "last byte" last, but it is not strictly correct to say that Ethernet sends the "most-significant byte" or the "least-significant byte" first.

The one exception is the IEEE 802.3 Length field, which contains 2 bytes that indicate the number of valid bytes in the Data field. In this one case, the first byte is more numerically significant than the second.

5.2   Ethernet Addresses

An address is an identifier denoting a particular station or group of stations. Ethernet addresses are 6 bytes (48 bits) in length. Figure 5–1 depicts the Ethernet address format.

The first bit of the address, when used as a Destination address, indicates whether the frame is being sent to an individual station or to a group of stations. When used as a Source address, the first bit must be zero. (It is meaningless to have a frame sent *from* a group of stations!)

It is critical that station addresses be unique; there must be no ambiguity over the intended source or target(s) of a given frame. Uniqueness can be either:

- **Local to this network.** Addresses are guaranteed unique on this particular LAN but are not guaranteed to be unique between disjoint LANs. A network administrator is required to assign addresses (and to ensure uniqueness) when locally unique addresses are used.
- **Global.** Addresses are guaranteed unique across all LANs, for all time and all technologies. This is a powerful mechanism, as it

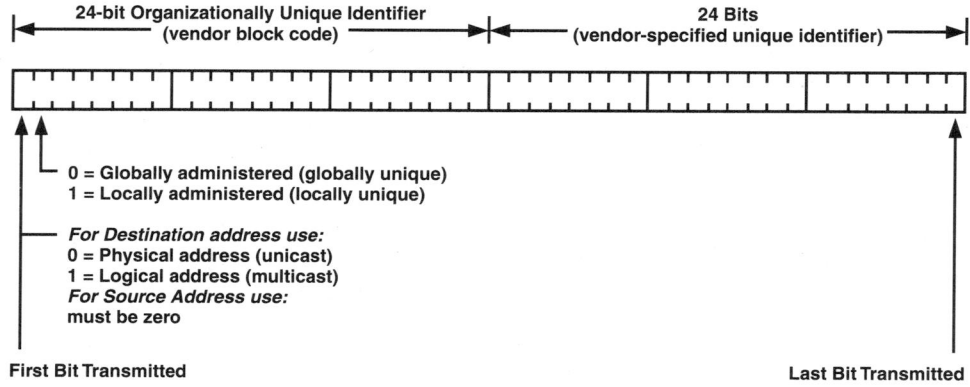

Figure 5–1 Ethernet address format.

- frees the network administrator from having to worry about assigning addresses,
- allows stations to move among LANs without having to reassign addresses, and
- allows practical Data Link bridge/switch implementations.

Globally unique addresses are assigned in blocks, with the blocks administered by the IEEE. An organization (typically a manufacturer) obtains a unique block assignment (called an Organizationally Unique Identifier, or OUI) from the IEEE and can use this to build up to 2^{24} (16,777,216) devices.[2] It is the manufacturer's responsibility to ensure that its portion of the address space (the last 3 bytes) is assigned uniquely.

The second bit of the address indicates whether the address is *globally unique* or *locally unique.* Historically, Ethernets have always used globally unique addresses, with very few exceptions.[3]

---

2. See *http://standards.ieee.org/db/oui/forms/index.html* for an application to obtain an OUI from the IEEE.

3. The original DIX Ethernet specification did not provide for locally unique addresses. The definition of the second bit of the address as indicating global/local uniqueness was introduced in the IEEE 802 specification and is applicable across all IEEE 802 technologies. Token Ring systems have historically used locally administered addresses, particularly to allow assignment of the same address to multiple NICs on a mainframe host. This aids the fault-tolerance of source routing, which is used exclusively in Token Ring systems. The "global/local" bit is sometimes called the "IBM bit" in deference to the company that lobbied for its inclusion in the standard and that is the primary user of this option.

5.3   The DIX Ethernet Frame

Figure 5–2 depicts the original DIX Ethernet frame.

The frame consists of six fields:

1. **A *preamble* containing 8 octets.**[4] The first 7 octets contain the value 0x55, and the last octet contains the value 0xD5. The effect is to send a serial stream of alternating ones and zeros (1 0 1 0 1 0 1 0 . . .) for

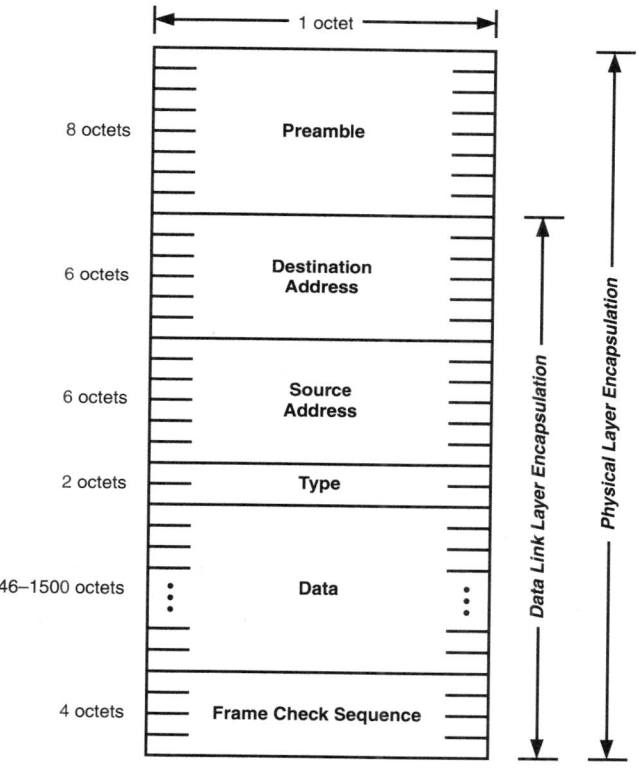

Figure 5–2 DIX Ethernet frame.

---

4. Network protocol specifications generally use the term "octet" to indicate an 8-bit data unit, rather than the more common term, "byte." Strictly speaking, a byte is a group of bits comprising the "natural quantum" of data for a particular computer. While virtually all computers today use 8-bit bytes, there have been machines that used other memory organizations. In the 1970s, 6-bit bytes were not uncommon. Network protocol specifications refer to octets rather than bytes so as to avoid confusion and to allow the specifications to be independent of the computers on which they are implemented. This book uses the terms interchangeably.

62 bits, followed by 2 ones in a row, signifying the start of the Data Link frame. In DIX Ethernet, the preamble is considered part of the Physical layer encapsulation, rather than the Data Link layer.

2. A *Destination address (DA)* **containing 6 octets.** The DA identifies the target destination station(s) for the frame. A DA may carry a unicast address (individual destination) or a multicast address (group destination).

3. A *Source address (SA)* **containing 6 octets.** The SA indicates the station sending the frame. An SA is always a unicast address (that is, its first bit is always a zero).

4. A *Type field* **containing 2 octets.** A Type field indicates the nature of the client protocol running above the Ethernet. Using type fields, a single Ethernet can upwards multiplex among various higher-layer protocols (IP, IPX, AppleTalk, and so on). Ethernet controllers do not typically interpret this field but use it to determine the destination process within the attached computer. Originally, Type field assignments were made by Xerox Corporation. However, in 1997 this responsibility was transferred to the IEEE.

5. A *data field* **containing from 46 to 1500 octets.** The data field encapsulates the higher-layer protocol information being transferred across the Ethernet. Ethernet frames must be of a certain minimum length due to the restrictions of the CSMA/CD algorithm. It is the responsibility of higher-layer protocols to ensure that there are always at least 46 octets in this field. If fewer actual data octets are required, the higher-layer protocols must implement some (unspecified) padding mechanism. The upper bound of the data field length is arbitrary but has been set at 1500 octets.[5]

6. A *Frame Check Sequence* **(FCS) containing 4 octets.** The FCS is a checksum computed on the contents of the frame from the DA through the end of the data field, inclusive. The checksum algorithm is a 32-bit Cyclic Redundancy Check (CRC). The generator polynomial is[6]

---

5. There are many pros and cons of allowing longer maximum Ethernet frames, including the effect on access latency and frame error rates. However, the real reason for the 1500-octet maximum was the cost of memory in 1979 (when the 10 Mb/s Ethernet was being designed) and the buffering requirements of low-cost LAN controllers. For a more detailed discussion, see [SEIF91].

6. A complete discussion of CRCs is beyond the scope of this book. The reader is referred to [PETER72] for a general discussion and to [HAMM75] for the detailed behavior of the particular algorithm used in Ethernet.

$$G(x) = x^{32} + x^{26} + x^{23} + x^{22} + x^{16} + x^{12} + x^{11} + x1^0 + x^8 + x^7 + x^5 + x^4 + x^2 + x + 1.$$

The FCS field is transmitted such that the first bit is the coefficient of the x^{31} term and the last bit is the coefficient of the x^0 term. Thus the bits of the CRC are transmitted: $x^{31}, x^{30}, \ldots, x^1, x^0$.

5.4   The IEEE 802.3 Frame Format (1983–1996)

Between the publication of the original Ethernet specification in 1980 and the first IEEE 802.3 standard in 1983, some minor changes were introduced into the frame format. The IEEE 802.3 frame format (as the standard existed from 1983 through 1996) is shown in Figure 5–3. The frame format is almost identical to the DIX Ethernet frame. There are some differences, however:

■ The 8-octet preamble from the DIX frame has been replaced with a 7-octet preamble and a 1-octet *Start-of-Frame Delimiter (SFD)*. This is a

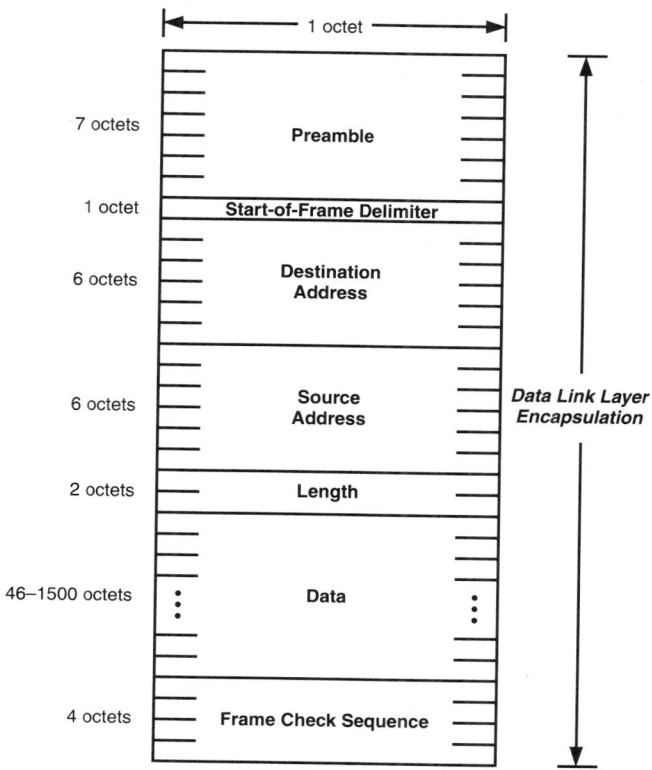

Figure 5–3 IEEE 802.3 frame format, 1983–1996.

nomenclature change only, since the IEEE 802.3 preamble field is defined to be 55-55-55-55-55-55-55 and the SFD is 55-D5.[7] That is, the catenation of the IEEE 802.3 preamble and SFD constitute the exact same bit pattern as the DIX Ethernet preamble.

- The preamble/SFD are considered part of the Data Link Layer encapsulation, rather than the preamble's being considered part of the Physical Layer, as in DIX Ethernet. This appears to be a nomenclature change also, since it does not affect the actual frame format. However, the fact that IEEE 802.3 considers the preamble/SFD part of the Data Link Layer is why these fields have been retained even when Physical Layer implementations that don't require them are used, such as 100BASE-X and 1000BASE-X. It would be possible to eliminate these fields (and thereby improve channel efficiency) if not for this minor change in architectural positioning.

- The Type field has been replaced with a Length field. This 2-octet field is used in IEEE 802.3 to indicate the number of valid data octets contained within the data field. This eliminates the need for higher-layer protocols to provide their own padding mechanism, since the Data Link Layer will provide the pad and indicate the length of the unpadded data in the Length field.

  However, with the Type field eliminated, there is no way to indicate the higher-layer protocol client (upwards multiplexing point) within the sending or receiving station. Frames using the IEEE 802.3 format are assumed to encapsulate Logical Link Control (LLC) data. LLC is specified by IEEE 802.2 and provides both a set of service specifications and a method for upward multiplexing of higher-layer protocols. [IEEE94, IEEE90]

With these three exceptions, all fields are the same in the IEEE 802.3 frame format as in the DIX Ethernet format. Historically, network architects and users have (rightly) focused on the difference between the use of a Type field and the Length field as the main difference between the two. DIX Ethernet used a Type field for upward multiplexing and did not use LLC. IEEE 802.3 required LLC for upward multiplexing because it replaced the Type field with a Length field.

In practice, the two schemes can coexist. The 2-octet field can carry a numerical value between 0 and $2^{16}-1$ (65,535). The maximum numerical

---

7. The standard [IEEE96] actually specifies this field as a string of binary digits. The hexadecimal strings shown here are equivalent, if sent in canonical order (see Section 5.1).

value for a Length field is 1500, as this is the longest valid length of the Data field. Thus the values from 1501 through 65,535 can be used for Type field identifiers without interfering with the use of the same field for a Length indication. We have simply made sure that all of the Type field value assignments were made from this non-interfering space. In practice, all values of this field from 1536 through 65,535 (0x0600 through 0xFFFF inclusive) are reserved for Type field assignment and all values from 0 to 1500 are reserved for Length field assignment.[8]

In this manner, Ethernet clients using the IEEE 802.3 format (with LLC) can communicate among themselves, while clients using the DIX Ethernet format (with Type fields) can communicate among themselves, on the same LAN. Of course, the two types of clients cannot intercommunicate, unless a device driver or higher-layer protocol understands both formats. Most higher-layer protocols use the DIX Ethernet frame format even today. This format is the most common format employed by TCP/IP, IPX (NetWare), DECnet Phase 4, and LAT (DEC's Local Area Transport). IEEE 802.3/LLC format is most commonly used with AppleTalk Phase 2, NetBIOS, and some IPX (NetWare) implementations.

5.5   The IEEE 802.3 Frame Format (1997)

During 1995–96, the IEEE 802.3x Task Force developed a supplement to the existing IEEE 802.3 standard to support full-duplex operation. As part of that effort, a mechanism for flow control was developed. This flow control mechanism (generalized into a MAC Control protocol) is described fully in Chapter 6. The important change from a frame format perspective was that the MAC Control protocol used a DIX Ethernet-style Type field to uniquely differentiate MAC Control frames from other protocols. This was the first time that any IEEE 802 committee had used such a frame format.[9] As long as the Task Force had to "legitimize" the use of Type fields for the MAC Control protocol, they went the rest of the way and legitimized the use of Type fields for any IEEE 802.3 frame. IEEE 802.3x became an approved IEEE standard in 1997. [IEEE97]

---

8. The range of 1501–1535 was intentionally left undefined.

9. The driving force behind using a Type field was to avoid the need for the complexity and overhead of parsing and decoding LLC fields in a protocol that generally must be implemented in hardware.

This made the old distinction of "Ethernet uses Type fields and IEEE 802.3 uses Length fields" disappear. IEEE 802.3, as supplemented by the IEEE 802.3x standard, supports the use of both Type and Length interpretations of the field. Both are "IEEE 802.3 format," as shown in Figure 5–4.

The distinction between Length and Type field interpretations is done as described previously in this chapter. As part of the standardization of Type field usage, the IEEE assumed the responsibility for assigning unique Type fields (Xerox had been assigning them since 1980). Gigabit Ethernet uses this combined frame format.

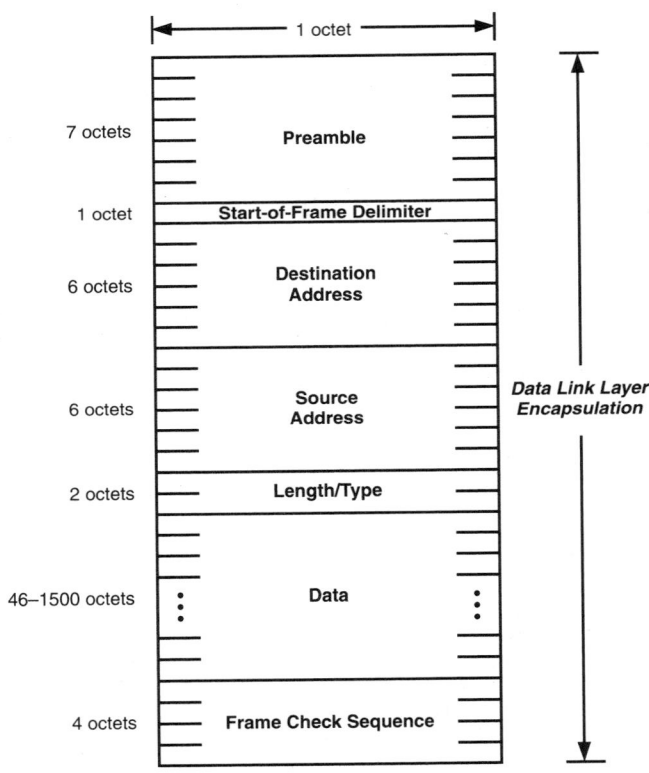

Figure 5–4 IEEE 802.3 frame format (1997).

6 Ethernet Flow Control

6.1 The Need for Flow Control in Ethernet

Ethernets (and virtually all other LAN technologies) are connectionless in nature. As such, there is no concept of a virtual circuit and no guarantee made regarding the delivery of a given frame. Frames are transferred without error to a high degree of probability, but there is no absolute assurance of success. In the event of a bit error, receiver buffer unavailability, or any other abnormal occurrence, an Ethernet receiver will simply discard the frame without providing any notification of that action. This allows Ethernet interfaces to be built at very low cost. A connectionless system is much simpler to implement than a system that includes mechanisms for error recovery and flow control within the Data Link Layer.

The probability of bit errors on LANs is extremely low. Ethernet specifies a bit error rate (BER) of 10^{-8} worst-case.[1] [IEEE96, Clause 14] A typical Ethernet in a benign (office automation) environment has a BER on the order of 10^{-11} or better. This translates into a frame loss rate (FLR) on the order of 10^{-7}, or 1 in 10 million.[2] This is low enough to be ignored at the Data Link Layer and dealt with in higher-layer protocols or applications requiring reliable data delivery.

However, the loss of a frame due to buffer unavailability has the same effect as a frame lost due to a bit error. In both cases, the frame is not deliv-

---

1. This is for copper media at 10 Mb/s. At 100 Mb/s and 1000 Mb/s and with fiber media, the BER is specified to be orders of magnitude better.

2. Frame Loss Rate can be calculated from Bit Error Rate by:

$$FLR = 1 - (1 - BER)^n,$$

where n is the number of bits in a frame, assuming a uniform distribution of errors across bits in the frame. The figure given in the text assumes the worst-case Ethernet frame length of 12,144 bits.

ered to the receiver and there is no indication at the Data Link Layer of the event. The probability of frame loss due to buffer congestion can be much greater than for bit errors, especially at high data rates and within internetworking devices (for example, switches).

The original Ethernet design did not provide any means for flow control, that is, ensuring that senders did not transmit faster than receivers were able to receive. When the network consists of communicating end stations, such mechanisms can (and usually are) provided by higher-layer protocols. With the advent of transparent bridges (switches), the immediate receiver of a frame may be unknown to the sender. That is, a switch is receiving and forwarding frames on behalf of attached stations without those stations' knowledge or participation. Without a protocol to provide flow control, excessive frame loss can occur due to switch buffer congestion.

6.1.1 Switch Behavior

A switch receives frames on its input ports and forwards them onto the appropriate output port(s) based on information (typically the DA) in the received frame. Depending on the traffic patterns, switch performance limitations, and the available buffer memory, frames may possibly arrive faster than the switch can receive, process, and forward them. When faced with such an overload condition (hopefully temporary), the switch has little choice but to discard incoming frames until the congestion condition clears. Thus the default behavior of a switch (or any device in a connectionless internetwork) is to discard frames when faced with a congestion condition.

6.1.2 The Effect of Frame Loss

Any higher-layer protocol or application that requires reliable delivery must implement some form of error control. A variety of such mechanisms has been implemented. [TANEN88] Most reliable transport layer protocols (for example, TCP, SPX, NFS, and so on[3]) use some form of *Positive Acknowledgment and Retransmission* (PAR) algorithm. In this scheme, data being transferred in one direction between stations is acknowledged in the other direction. The originating station does not assume that the data has been successfully delivered until an acknowledgment has been received. If the

---

3. Transmission Control Protocol, used in the TCP/IP suite; Sequenced Packet eXchange, used in the NetWare suite; and Network File System, used in the Sun/NFS suite. While NFS is not strictly a Transport protocol, it is responsible for reliable message block delivery across a connectionless network.

acknowledgment is not received in some predetermined period of time, the originator assumes that the data has been lost en route (or the acknowledgment has been lost *etuor ne*[4]). It then initiates a retransmission of the original data. In this way, acknowledged, reliable, end-to-end data communication can occur despite the possibility of frame loss in the underlying networks. The same mechanism is used to recover from frame loss regardless of the reason for the loss. Remember that the predominant source of frame loss may be buffer congestion rather than bit errors.

A PAR protocol will operate correctly in the face of lost frames, but it will incur a performance penalty in doing so. A lost frame will (in general) require that the higher-layer protocol acknowledgment timer expire before initiating retransmission. These timers must (at a minimum) be set to allow for the end-to-end propagation delay of the entire network, plus an allowance for processing time and delay variance. Typical protocols will use times on the order of seconds to operate across a large internetwork. Thus a single lost frame can incur the penalty of idling a data transfer for seconds.

This can have a devastating effect on throughput. Consider the case of NFS [RFC1094] faced with a persistent underlying frame loss, as depicted in Figure 6–1. Because the loss of a single frame can cause NFS to halt (waiting for an acknowledgment) for seconds, the overall throughput degrades rapidly with the frame loss rate (FLR). For an NFS acknowledgment timer of 5 seconds, a 1% FLR results in a performance degradation of almost 98%.[5]

The message is clear. While higher-layer protocols can and do recover from frame loss, this should be considered a boundary or exception case and not something that should be allowed to occur regularly. It would be better (in the previous example) to flow control the underlying links so that only 10% of their capacity was available to the application, rather than letting them run at full speed and incur a 1% FLR (due to buffer overflow).

Frame loss is not catastrophic, but reducing its probability is desirable. Frame loss due to bit errors may be unavoidable, but mechanisms can be

---

4. That is, en route in the other direction (loud groan appreciated here).
5. For a given FLR, frame length (length) in bytes, data rate (rate) in bits/second, and acknowledgment timer (acktime), the performance degradation due to frame loss will be

$$degradation = 1 - \left[\frac{(1 - FLR) \times frametime}{(FLR \times acktime) + frametime} \right],$$

where
$$frametime = \frac{length \times 8}{rate}.$$

The graph is derived from this equation.

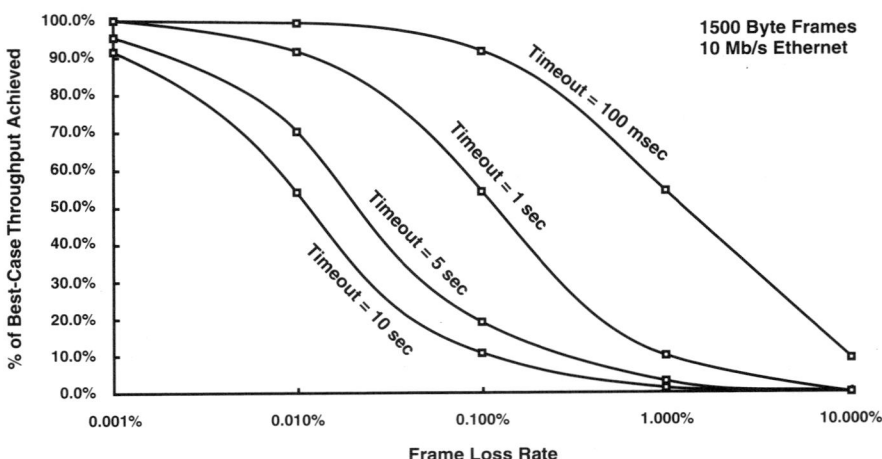

Figure 6–1 NFS throughput as a function of acknowledgment time and frame loss rate.

designed to avoid unnecessarily discarding frames due to buffer congestion in switches and end stations.

6.1.3 End-to-End Flow Control

Reliable transport protocols often provide a means for end-to-end flow control. That is, they ensure that the originator of a data stream does not transmit when there are insufficient resources (for example, buffers) at the receiver to process the data.[6] However, this ensures only that resources are available at the ultimate receiver of the data. A protocol operating between end stations cannot ensure that there are adequate resources available at every intervening switch or router to receive and process the data stream.[7] Thus end-to-end flow control does not guarantee that frames will not be discarded (due to insufficient buffer memory) by those intervening internetworking devices. The problem of link buffer overflow must be addressed at the link layer; end-to-end flow control does not solve it.

---

6. In some protocols, this mechanism used for flow control may be the same as that used for error control. That is, an acknowledgment of data receipt indicates to the sender that it may continue sending. In other protocols (for example, ISO TP-4 [ISO84]), the error and flow control mechanisms are decoupled.

7. An analogy can be made using highway traffic. Just because there are adequate parking spaces (buffers) available for all patrons at the ballpark does not mean that the road to the ballpark can handle all of the traffic going there.

6.1.4   Cost/Performance Trade-offs

If we design and implement a link flow control mechanism, we will incur additional complexity and therefore increase the cost. This cost may not be justifiable in networks on which high performance is not a major concern, for example, 10 Mb/s desktop LANs. In this environment, not only is the impact of a performance degradation less significant, but also the probability of frame loss is lower, since it is not difficult to design switches that can process frame arrivals from multiple 10 Mb/s Ethernet ports at wire-speed. However, as the data rate increases and the focus shifts from the desktop to backbone networks, the decision goes the other way. Especially at gigabit data rates, there is a much greater probability that a device can be overloaded by frame arrivals, especially on a device with a large number of ports. In addition, we are already paying a premium for the higher-speed LAN. If we do not address the frame loss problem, then we may not really be getting value from the increased expenditure.

The flow control mechanism discussed in Section 6.3 was developed as a result of the difficulties in switch design at 100 Mb/s. With Gigabit Ethernet, flow control becomes absolutely necessary in order to provide good application performance at reasonable cost.[8]

6.1.5   Backpressure in Half-Duplex Networks

In the case of a switch port connected to a shared LAN (half-duplex network), it is possible to forestall incoming traffic by manipulating the behavior of the MAC algorithm itself to prevent potential transmitters from actually sending their traffic. This is called *backpressure*. On a CSMA/CD LAN, two methods are available to prevent switch input buffer overflow[9]:

1. **Force collisions with incoming frames.** On the surface, this appears to be a reasonable tactic. The collision will cause the sending station to reschedule the transmission of the frame. This does prevent the buffer overflow, as intended. Unfortunately, there are some undesirable side effects:

---

8. While the flow control mechanism discussed in Section 6.3 is usable at any data rate, 10 Mb/s full-duplex switches had been shipping for years—without flow control and without significant problems—before the protocol was designed.

9. The explanations in this section assume some familiarity with the Ethernet MAC algorithm. Readers unfamiliar with the terminology and behavior discussed here should see Chapter 10 for a thorough discussion of the Ethernet half-duplex MAC.

- The sending station(s) may be throttled *too* much, so the throughput of the system will actually be lower than the available capacity (that is, there will be unnecessary idle time on the channel). This is because the collision will cause the end station to calculate an exponentially increasing backoff. The station will select a time that is initially in the range of 0 to 1 *slot times*[10] but that increases from 0 to 1023 slot times for later collisions. It is possible (likely) that switch input buffers will become available during this very long time, as the switch will be emptying this queue onto the output ports in the meantime. Even though the queue is emptied, the channel will remain idle until the backoff timer expires. It seems a shame to waste bandwidth solely due to an inefficient backpressure algorithm.
- In the event of sustained input buffer congestion, a station can experience 16 successive collisions on the frame at the head of its queue. Following the MAC algorithm, the station will discard such a frame and report it as an error to station management. To the higher-layer protocols, this appears the same as if the switch had discarded the frame. This has the same long-timeout and performance problems discussed previously, although only under sustained congestion conditions.
- Management counters and statistics will indicate very high numbers of collisions, as well as higher numbers of "excessive collision errors." While the statistics will be correct (strictly speaking), the interpretation by a human network administrator will likely be that there is some serious problem with the network. "Normal" Ethernets do not experience extremely high collision rates or large numbers of excessive collision errors. The latter events especially are indicative of systematic network problems that require reconfiguration or repair.

2. **Make it appear as if the channel is busy.** This method uses the "deferral" mechanism rather than the collision backoff mechanism of the Ethernet MAC. As long as the station sees that the channel is busy (that is, Carrier Sense is asserted) it will defer transmission. However, it imposes no additional backoff delay, and the frame remains at the head of the queue and is not discarded regardless of the duration of the deferral. This is a superior approach to the forced collision method.

---

10. A *slot time* is the fundamental time unit of a half-duplex Ethernet MAC. It is derived from the round-trip propagation delay and represents the minimum length of a frame as well as the quantum of retransmission for backoff purposes. See Chapter 10 for more detail on slot times and the operation of the half-duplex Ethernet MAC.

It is relatively simple to cause Carrier Sense to be asserted in the stations attached to a shared LAN; it requires only that validly formed bits be present on the Ethernet connecting the switch to the station(s). The simplest approach is to generate preamble onto the desired input port whenever the switch wants to throttle offered load in the face of congestion.[11] The end of the stream should never be a Start-of-Frame delimiter. This ensures that receiving station(s) will not interpret the stream as a real frame.

Preamble can be sent in this manner for as long as necessary. It eliminates the forced collisions completely and has no serious side-effects (believe it or not). The only problem is that standard 10 Mb/s transceivers may assert *jabber control* (disabling their transmitter) if preamble is sent for longer than 20 ms. On 100 Mb/s and 1000 Mb/s systems, this is not an issue at all.[12]

The use of false Carrier Sense is especially elegant when there is only one end station connected to each switch port (microsegmentation). In this case, the only reason for input buffer congestion is the ability of the end station to offer more load than the switch can forward to its outputs. The false Carrier Sense algorithm will throttle this station perfectly. When the false carrier is dropped, the station will simply begin sending the frame at the head of its queue. There will be no collisions or backoff, even in the congested case.

There is a slight difference if there is more than one station connected to the switch port (shared LAN). When congestion occurs, Carrier Sense is asserted and all stations will withhold transmissions. When the congestion clears, Carrier Sense is dropped. At this time, more than one station has likely queued a frame for transmission. This guarantees a collision among those stations, at least for the first attempt. However, this is exactly what is expected in Ethernet. The stations will resolve their *Ethernet* congestion using the proper collision-detect and backoff method. (*Buffer* congestion has been resolved through the backpressure mechanism.) Thus, while collisions may be generated as an indirect result of the false Carrier Sense algorithm, they are normal and resolve properly.

A complete treatment of CSMA/CD backpressure algorithms and implementation issues can be found in [SEIF96].

Similar backpressure mechanisms can be used on shared LANs using MAC algorithms other than CSMA/CD. In a token-passing network, for

---

11. Of course, the interface must obey the normal MAC algorithm in this regard. The switch simply sends preamble when appropriate, thereby making it appear as if a frame is being transmitted.

12. In addition, stations that implement the *excessiveDeferral* management object of IEEE 802.3 should expect to see an increase in this statistic counter.

example, a switch can "hold the token" for an extended period to forestall incoming frames (subject to timing limitations of the token-passing protocol itself).

6.1.6 Explicit Flow Control in Full-Duplex Networks

The backpressure methods discussed in Section 6.1.5 provide a form of *implicit flow control* on half-duplex LANs. Stations are being prevented from sending frames and overflowing switch buffers, but they do not realize that it is the switch that is manipulating the MAC algorithm to this end. As far as any station can tell, it is simply obeying the normal access rules for the network. The reduction in load on the switch is achieved without any explicit mechanism in the station being throttled.

On a full-duplex Ethernet, neither the false Carrier Sense nor the forced collision algorithm will work. A full-duplex Ethernet interface does not detect collisions and ignores Carrier Sense for the purpose of deferring its transmissions. A full-duplex network therefore requires an explicit flow control mechanism to allow a switch to throttle a congesting end station. To achieve this, a standard mechanism (IEEE 802.3x) was developed for flow control of full-duplex Ethernet [IEEE97].

6.2 MAC Control

Rather than define just a protocol for explicit flow control of full-duplex Ethernet (that would have been too easy!), the IEEE 802.3x Task Force chose to specify a more generic architectural framework for control of the Ethernet MAC (*MAC Control*), within which full-duplex flow control was the first (and currently, the only) operation defined. This allowed for the future:

- Expansion of explicit flow control to half-duplex networks
- Specification of alternative full-duplex flow control mechanisms (besides the simple PAUSE function, discussed shortly)
- Definition and specification of other functions (besides flow control)

While no such standard extensions of the MAC Control protocol have been developed, the architecture makes this a relatively easy task.

MAC Control is an optional capability in Ethernet. Making it optional avoided the need to declare preexisting Ethernet-compliant devices to be non-compliant with a later revision of the specifications. Clearly, the use of flow control provides significant advantages in high-speed, full-duplex switched networks, but an implementor (and user) is allowed to choose performance versus price. The cost of implementing the MAC Control protocol (specifically, the PAUSE function used for full-duplex flow control) is extremely low (it can typically be implemented in hardware, in the Ethernet controller silicon itself). Hence most vendors of full-duplex Ethernet products likely will implement this capability, especially at gigabit data rates.

6.2.1   MAC Control Architecture[13]

Figure 6–2 depicts the MAC Control architectural layering.

MAC Control constitutes a *sublayer* of the Data Link Layer. It is an optional function inserted between the traditional Ethernet MAC and the client of that MAC. That client may be a Network Layer protocol (for example, IP) or the relay function implemented by bridges (switches) within the Data Link Layer itself.

If the client of the MAC does not know about, or care to use, the functions provided by MAC Control, then the sublayer "disappears"; normal transmit and receive data streams pass from the MAC to and from its control-unaware client(s) as if the MAC Control sublayer were not there. MAC Control-aware clients (such as a switch desiring to prevent buffer overflow) can use the added capabilities of this sublayer to control the operation of the underlying Ethernet MAC. In particular, it can request that the MAC at the other end of a full-duplex link cease further data transmissions, thereby preventing the impending overflow.

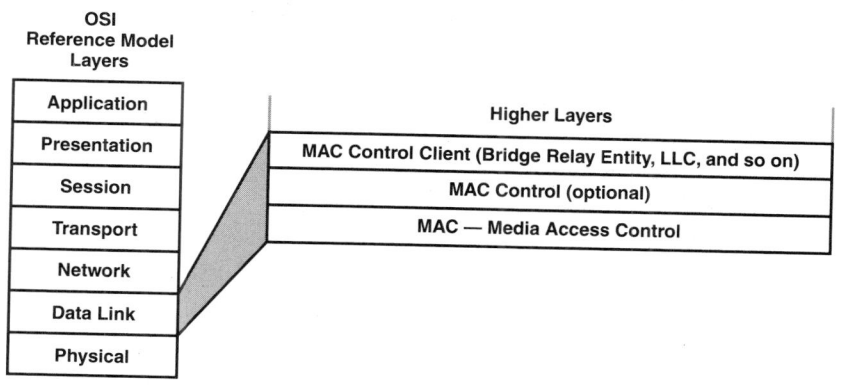

Figure 6–2 MAC Control architectural positioning.

---

13. Readers interested in reality, as opposed to architecture, may skip this section and go directly to the discussion of PAUSE operation in Section 6.3, with no loss of continuity.

Upon request from a MAC Control-aware client, MAC Control can generate *control frames,* which are sent on the Ethernet using the standard underlying MAC. Similarly, an Ethernet MAC will receive MAC Control frames (generated by a MAC Control sublayer in another station) and pass them to the appropriate function within the MAC Control sublayer. This is depicted in Figure 6–3. On the Ethernet, MAC Client (that is, normal) data frames are thereby interspersed with MAC Control frames.

Before the invention of MAC Control, every frame transmitted on an Ethernet was a result of a request to transmit data by a higher-layer protocol or application and each carried data relevant to that protocol or application. MAC Control introduced the concept of frames being generated and received (that is, *sourced* and *sunk*) within the Data Link Layer itself. This concept exists in many other MAC protocols (for example, IEEE 802.5 Token Ring and FDDI), but it was new to Ethernet.

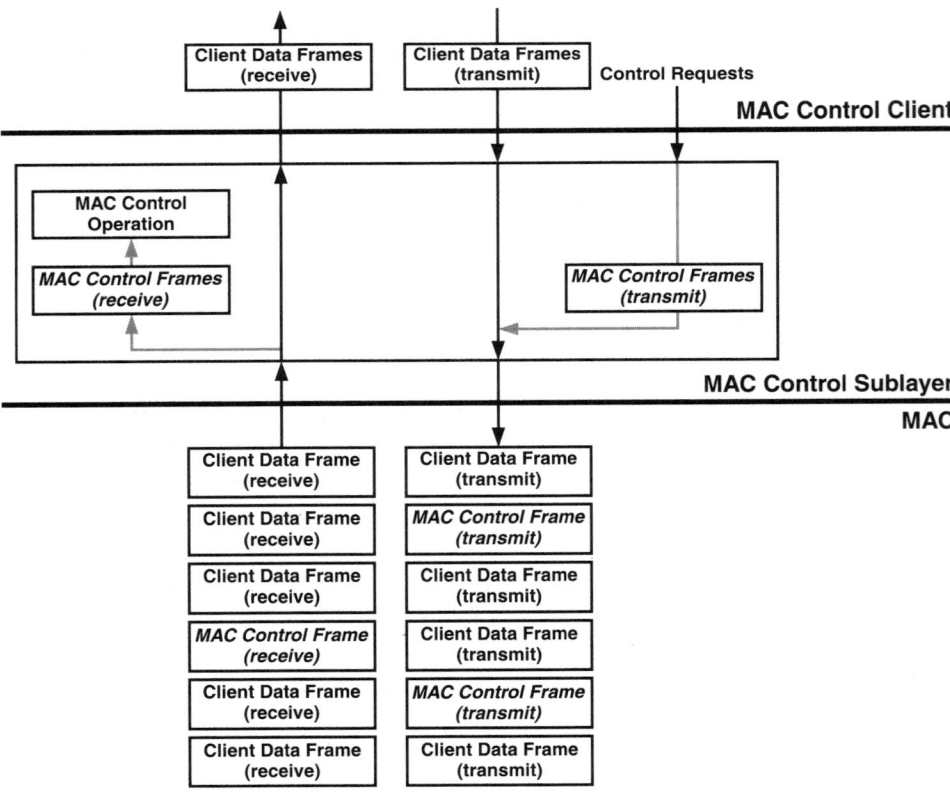

Figure 6–3 Client and control frames.

6.2.2   MAC Control Frame Format

MAC Control frames are normal, valid Ethernet frames. They carry all of the fields discussed in Chapter 5 and are sent using the standard Ethernet MAC algorithms. Other than the unique Type field identifier (discussed in 6.3.2.3), MAC Control frames are unexceptional when transmitted or received on the network. All MAC Control frames are exactly 64 bytes in length—minimum-length Ethernet frames—not including the preamble and Start-of-Frame delimiter. Figure 6–4 depicts the MAC Control frame format.

MAC Control frames are identified by a unique Type field identifier (0x8808) in the frame. This Type field has been reserved for Ethernet MAC Control.

Within the Data field of the frame, the first two octets identify the MAC Control opcode, that is, the control function that is being requested by the

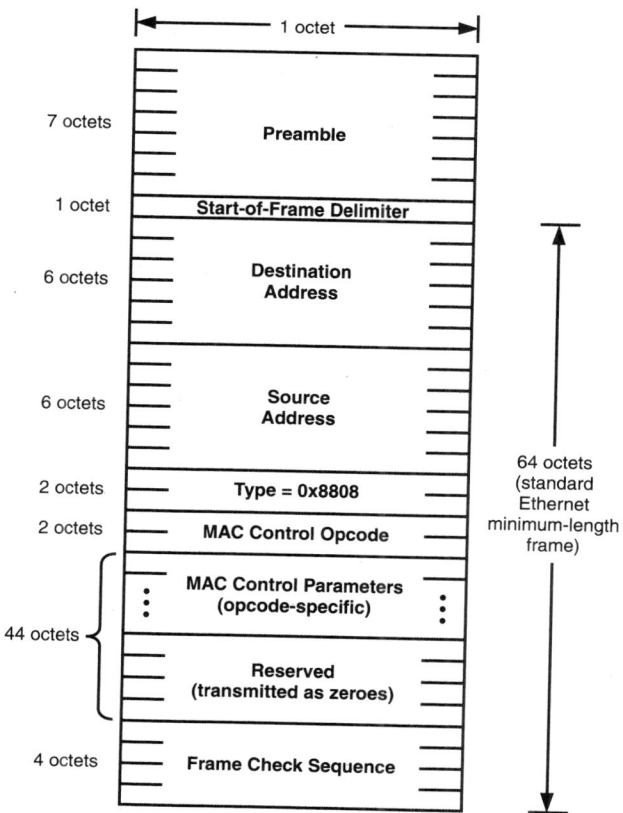

Figure 6–4 MAC Control frame format.

frame. Currently, only one such opcode is defined (the full-duplex PAUSE operation, discussed shortly). It is assigned opcode 0x0001.

Following the opcode field, the frame carries parameters specific to the requested opcode (if any are needed). If the parameters do not use all available 44 bytes, the remainder of the frame is padded with zeroes.

6.3   PAUSE Function

The PAUSE function is used to implement flow control on full-duplex Ethernet links. PAUSE operation is implemented using the MAC Control architecture and frame format described in Section 6.2. The operation is currently defined only for use across a single, full-duplex link. That is, it cannot be used on a shared (half-duplex) LAN. Nor does it operate across or through intervening switches. It may be used to control data frame flow between

- a pair of end stations (a simple, two-station network),
- a switch and an end station, or
- a switch-to-switch link.

The PAUSE function is designed to prevent switches (or end stations) from unnecessarily discarding frames due to buffer overflow under short-term transient overload conditions. Consider a device designed to handle the expected steady-state traffic of the network, plus an allowance for a certain amount of time-variance of that load. The PAUSE function allows such a device to avoid discarding frames even when the short-term load increases above the level anticipated by the design. The device can prevent internal buffer overflow by sending PAUSE frames to its partner on the full-duplex link; the reception of the PAUSE frame by the partner will cause it to stop sending data frames. This gives the first device time to reduce its buffer congestion, either by processing frames in the queue that are destined for the device (end station operation) or by forwarding them to other ports (switch operation).

The PAUSE function does not:

- **Solve the problem of steady-state network congestion.** The protocol is designed to alleviate temporary overload conditions by reducing inbound traffic in the face of buffer overflow. If the sustained (that is, steady-state) traffic level exceeds that for which the device is designed, this must be considered a *configuration problem*, not a flow control problem. The PAUSE function cannot cure a sustained overload.

- **Provide end-to-end flow control.** The PAUSE operation is defined across a single full-duplex link only. There is no mechanism provided for either end-to-end flow control or the coordination of PAUSE operations across multiple links.[14]

- **Provide any complexity beyond a simple "stop-start" mechanism.** In particular, it does not directly provide for credit-based schemes, rate-based flow control, and so on, although these could be provided in future enhancements to the protocol.

6.3.1   Overview of PAUSE Operation

The PAUSE operation implements a very simple "stop-start" form of flow control. A device (end station or switch) wishing to temporarily inhibit incoming data sends a PAUSE frame that contains a parameter indicating the length of time that the full-duplex partner should wait before sending more data frames. When a station receives a PAUSE frame, it stops sending data frames for the period specified. When this timer expires, the station resumes sending data frames where it left off.[15] PAUSE frames inhibit the transmission of data frames, but they have no effect on the transmission of MAC Control frames (for example, PAUSE frames from the other direction).

A station issuing a PAUSE may cancel the remainder of the pause period by issuing another PAUSE frame that contains a parameter of zero time. That is, newly received PAUSE frames override any PAUSE operation currently in progress. Similarly, the issuing station can extend the PAUSE period by issuing another PAUSE frame that contains a nonzero time parameter before the first PAUSE period has expired.

Since the PAUSE operation uses the standard underlying Ethernet MAC, there is no guarantee of frame delivery to the receiver. PAUSE frames could be corrupted by errors, and the receiver would not know that such frames were ever sent. The design of a PAUSE transmission policy (discussed in Section 6.4.2) must take this into account. For the formal, detailed specification of the PAUSE operation, refer to [IEEE97].

---

14. Of course, it is possible to design a higher-layer application or mechanism that does this coordination by using the primitive PAUSE function as a tool for more complex flow controls, but the PAUSE function itself provides no such feature.

15. The use of a timer-based mechanism prevents the (unintentional) permanent disabling of another station from sending data frames.

6.3.2 PAUSE Frame Semantics

A PAUSE frame contains all of the fields indicated in Figure 6–4. Preamble, Start-of-Frame delimiter, and FCS are the same as for all Ethernet frames, discussed in Chapter 5. The remaining fields take the values explained in the following sections.

6.3.2.1 Destination Address

The Destination address is the intended destination of the PAUSE frame. It always contains a unique multicast address reserved for PAUSE operation and is equal to 01-80-C2-00-00-01.

Why does a Destination address need to be specified at all? Since the PAUSE function is defined only for full-duplex links, clearly the target of the PAUSE is the station at the other end of the link! Even stranger, why is the destination specified to be a multicast address, since there can be only one other device on the link? The reasons are subtle, but important.

- In the event that a PAUSE frame is inadvertently sent on a shared LAN (through a configuration error), the use of a specific multicast address ensures that the only stations that receive and interpret such frames will be those that actually understand the PAUSE protocol (that is, the address is reserved for this purpose exclusively).
- The use of a multicast address relieves the sender of PAUSE frames from having to know the unicast address of its link partner. While this address is likely known by higher-layer protocols, there is no need for the Data Link Layer to be aware of it.
- The specific multicast address selected is a member of a special, reserved group of addresses that are blocked (sunk) by all standard bridges and switches. Frames sent to addresses in this group are never forwarded onto other ports of a switch.[16] This keeps PAUSE frames local to the single full-duplex link on which they are relevant. For more information about this reserved group of multicast addresses, see [IEEE93a].

6.3.2.2 Source Address

The Source address field contains the unicast address of the station sending the PAUSE frame. While it seems unnecessary to specify a Source address

---

16. The default behavior of a switch with respect to multicast destinations is to forward them onto all ports except for the port on which the frame arrived. That rule is suspended for this reserved block of multicast addresses. That is, frames with destination addresses in this block are never forwarded from one port of a switch to any other port. The reserved block includes all addresses in the range 01-80-C2-00-00-00 through 01-80-C2-00-00-10, inclusive.

because the frame could have been emitted only by one device, including a Source address provides the following benefits.

- Consistency with all other Ethernet frame types (that is, the Source address in all Ethernet frames contains the unicast address of the station sending the frame)
- Proper updating of management counters in monitoring devices (for example, RMON [RFC1757]) that may be keeping track of frames generated on a per-station basis
- Ease in determining the sender if PAUSE frames are inadvertently emitted onto a shared LAN due to a misconfiguration

6.3.2.3 Type Field

The Type field contains the reserved value used for all MAC Control frames, equal to 0x8808.

6.3.2.4 MAC Control Opcode and Parameters

The MAC Control opcode for a PAUSE frame is 0x0001.

The PAUSE frame takes a single parameter called the *pause_time*. This parameter is a 2-byte unsigned integer value that indicates the length of time for which the sender is requesting that data frames not be sent by the receiver. The time is measured in 512 bit-time increments; that is, the receiver should pause for a period equal to the pause_time multiplied by 512 bit-times at the data rate currently in use. The range of values for the pause_time is shown in Table 6–1.

The use of a data-rate-dependent parameter was chosen for two reasons.

1. When the PAUSE operation is specified in this manner, it can be thought of as stopping the partner from sending a specified number of *bits,* regardless of data rate, rather than for a specified period of time. Since the original purpose of the PAUSE function was to allow memory-constrained switch implementations, an interface can be designed such that it emits PAUSE frames with a constant pause_time parameter

TABLE 6–1 PAUSE TIMER RANGES

10 Mb/s	0–3.36 sec (in 51.2 μs increments)
100 Mb/s	0–336 ms (in 5.12 μs increments)
1000 Mb/s	0–33.6 ms (in 512 ns increments)

when there is a constant number of bits of buffer remaining, regardless of the data rate. This can simplify some designs.

2. In a half-duplex Ethernet, the collision backoff counter measures time in increments of the slotTime, which is 512 bit-times for all data rates except 1000 Mb/s. Since the PAUSE function is used only on full-duplex links, this counter (if implemented) is not needed for backoff timing and can be used for PAUSE timing without change.[17]

6.3.3   Configuration of Flow Control Capabilities

It is important that the two partners on a full-duplex link agree on whether they will be sending and/or are capable of responding to PAUSE frames. If a switch implementation is betting on the fact that it can prevent buffer overflow by sending PAUSE frames, then it is important that the device at the other end of the link be capable of pausing properly. Since the implementation of MAC Control and the PAUSE function are optional, this cannot be assured without some form of configuration control. This configuration can generally be accomplished in two ways: manual or automatic.

1. Manual configuration implies that a human network administrator must properly configure the two ends of the link as desired. This would typically be done using some software tool (utility program) that can enable or disable various features and capabilities of the device. Such tools are typically vendor- or device-specific, but use of a generic tool may also be possible (for example, a standard Network Management station). While manual configuration is tedious and prone to error (those darn humans!), it may be the only configuration method possible for many devices.

2. Some Ethernet physical media provide an industry-standard mechanism that allows for automatic negotiation of link parameters. When such a mechanism is available, it is clearly the preferred means of configuring the flow control capabilities of the full-duplex link partners. On copper media using RJ-45 connectors, the Auto-Negotiation protocol described in Chapter 8 can be used to automatically configure the flow control capabilities of the link. On 1000BASE-X media, the equivalent protocol described in Chapter 12 is used. Table 6–2 indicates, for all full-duplex capable media, which configuration methods are possible.

---

17. When the PAUSE function was being designed, Gigabit Ethernet had not yet defined a slot-Time that was not 512 bits, thus this benefit accrued across all data rates. The later change to a 4096-bit slotTime by the IEEE 802.3z Task Force eliminated some of this benefit.

Of course, the ability to automatically determine the capabilities of the attached devices and configure the link cannot make a device do something that it cannot. If a switch requires the ability to flow control the attached devices and that capability isn't there, then the switch must choose between working without flow control (and incurring the possibility of higher frame loss) or disabling the link entirely.

6.4   Flow Control Implementation Issues

This section discusses a number of issues related to the implementation of Ethernet systems that support and use the PAUSE mechanism described previously. Readers not interested in the low-level design of hardware and software for Ethernet interfaces can safely skip this section.

6.4.1   Design Implications of the PAUSE Function

Flow control (specifically, the transmission and reception of PAUSE frames) imposes some new twists that previously did not exist for the design of Ethernet devices. Prior to flow control, all Ethernet frames transmitted by a given interface were provided by a higher-layer protocol or application. Similarly, all received frames were checked for validity and then passed up to the higher-layer entity without the contents being inspected, interpreted, and acted upon by the Ethernet interface. This all changed with the implementation of flow control. Now, the link interface can generate PAUSE frames,

---

TABLE 6–2 FLOW CONTROL CONFIGURATION OPTIONS

Media Type	Manual	Automatic
10BASE-T	✔	✔
10BASE-FL	✔	
100BASE-TX	✔	✔
100BASE-FX	✔	
100BASE-T2	✔	✔
1000BASE-CX	✔	✔[1]
1000BASE-LX	✔	✔[1]
1000BASE-SX	✔	✔[1]
1000BASE-T	✔	✔

1. Auto-Negotiation of flow control is mandatory for all 1000BASE-X media.

must inspect incoming frames to determine if it is a PAUSE request from its link partner, and then act on those requests. This raises some important issues in the design of Ethernet interfaces supporting the PAUSE function.

6.4.1.1 Inserting PAUSE Frames in the Transmit Queue

Without the PAUSE function, an Ethernet interface simply transmits frames in the order they are presented by the device driver. Since Ethernet has no concept of priority access (or user priority), a single-queue model can be used for the transmitter. However, the effective use of flow control requires that PAUSE frames be emitted in a timely manner.

A higher-layer application (for example, the bridge relay function) will typically signal its need to assert flow control on the link due to an impending buffer overflow condition. If the PAUSE frame generated by this signal is simply inserted on the transmit queue like any other frame, its transmission may be delayed while it waits for all other frames in the queue to be transmitted. Depending on the size of the interface's transmit queue, flow control may not be asserted in time to prevent the buffer overflow and so the effort would be wasted.

Clearly, PAUSE frames must be given priority in transmission. In general, there is no need to have an actual transmit queue for PAUSE frames, since there can be only one outstanding flow control action in effect at any given time. In addition, the contents of the PAUSE frame are relatively fixed; the only field that may need to vary over time is the value of the pause_time parameter. An implementation can simply keep a well-formed PAUSE frame in a static buffer (or even hard-coded in logic) available for transmission on request.

The transmission of a PAUSE frame cannot preempt a data transmission in progress. So the interface should (upon getting a signal to send a PAUSE frame) complete the transmission of any frame in progress, wait an inter-frame spacing, and then send the requested PAUSE frame. After the end of the PAUSE frame, the interface can continue transmitting frames from the transmit queue in the normal manner. This is depicted in Figure 6–5.

6.4.1.2 Parsing Received PAUSE Frames

An interface capable of being flow controlled must be able to inspect and parse the fields in all incoming frames to determine when a valid PAUSE has been received in order to act upon it. The following fields must be checked:

- **Destination Address.** This field must be checked for a match against *either* the well-known multicast address reserved for the PAUSE function

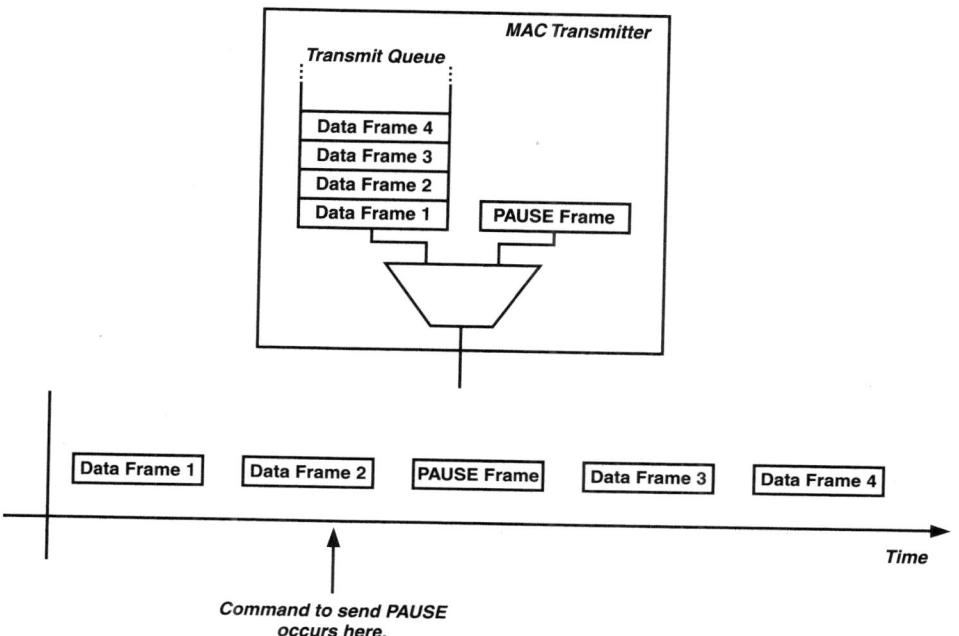

Figure 6–5 PAUSE frame insertion.

(01-80-C2-00-00-01) or the unicast address of the port on which the frame is received. While (current) transmitters of PAUSE frames should never send to this unicast address, this provision in the receiver allows for future extension of the PAUSE function to half-duplex MACs.

- **Type Field.** This field must be checked against the reserved value for MAC Control frames (0x8808).
- **MAC Control Opcode.** This field must be equal to the value for the PAUSE function (0x0001).
- **Frame Check Sequence.** This field must contain the valid CRC for the received frame. Since the earlier fields may be parsed and checked before the reception of the FCS, some provision must be provided for ignoring a PAUSE frame that has already been received and decoded in the event of a subsequent FCS error.

After the parsing and decoding, the receiver must extract the pause_time parameter from the frame and supply it to the logic that is performing the PAUSE function within the interface. PAUSE frames are not passed up to the device driver but are absorbed within the interface.

6.4.1.3 PAUSE Timing

Because the PAUSE function is used for real-time flow control across the link, it is important that the implementation decode and act on received PAUSE frames in a timely manner. Following the reception of the PAUSE frame itself (that is, starting from the end of the last bit of the received FCS), the interface has a maximum of 512 bit-times (1024 bit-times for Gigabit Ethernet) to validate, decode, and act on the PAUSE frame. If, during this time, the transmitter begins transmission of a frame, then that frame is completed. (Note that the transmitter is completely independent of the receiver, since this is a full-duplex interface.) However, it is not permissible to begin the transmission of a data frame more than 512 bit-times (1024 bit-times for Gigabit Ethernet) after the receipt of a valid PAUSE frame that contains a nonzero value for the pause_time. This is depicted in Figure 6–6.

Without this upper bound on the response time of a PAUSE receiver, it is impossible for a sender of a PAUSE frame to know how much additional data may be received before the flow stops. There would be no way to use the mechanism to effectively prevent buffer overflow.

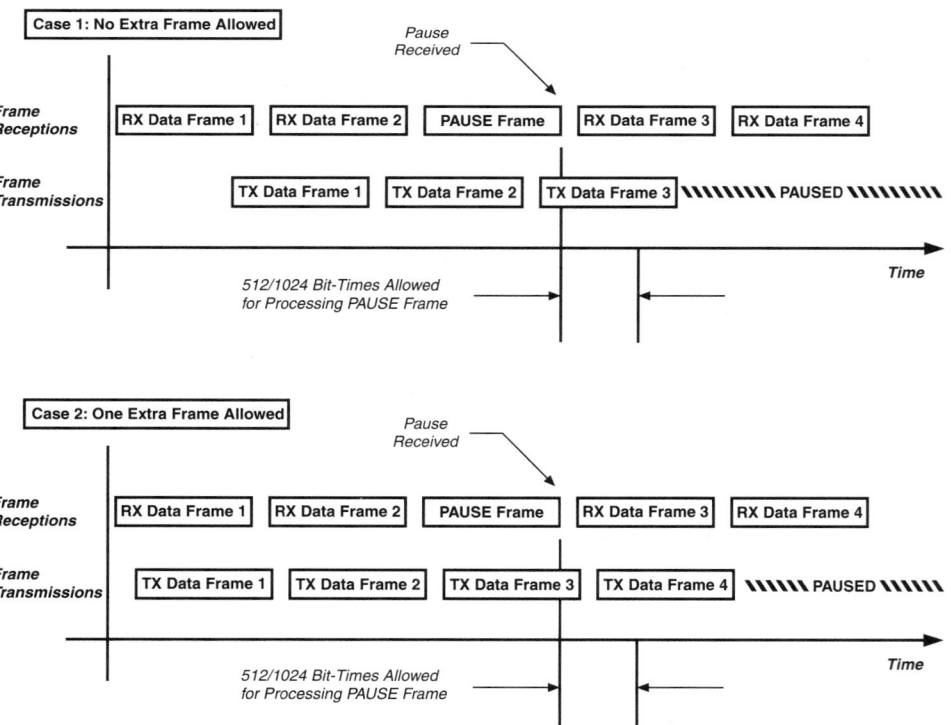

Figure 6–6 PAUSE timing.

6.4.1.4 Buffering Requirements

Since flow control operates on a full-duplex link and there is both a propagation delay and a response time delay between the link partners, the sending of a PAUSE frame cannot immediately stop the flow of data in the other direction (into the sender's receiver). Thus the sender must allow for this additional data to be received and send the PAUSE frame well before buffer overflow occurs. The maximum amount of data that could possibly be received after a request to the MAC Control entity to assert flow control (that is, the amount of buffering required above the threshold for sending the PAUSE) is the sum of the following:

TABLE 6–3 LINK ALLOWANCES

One maximum-length frame on transmit	12,336 bits[1]
(This is a frame from the sender's transmit queue that could have just been started when the flow control signal was asserted and that cannot be preempted.)	(1542 bytes)
One PAUSE frame time	512 bits
(This is the PAUSE frame itself.)	(64 bytes)
The PAUSE frame decode time allowance	512 or 1024 bits (64 or 128 bytes)
One maximum-length frame on receive	12,176 bits[2]
(This is a frame from the receiver's transmit queue that could have just been started when the PAUSE was decoded and that cannot be preempted.)	(1522 bytes)
The round-trip propagation delay of the link	See Table 6–4

1. This amount includes an allowance for a data payload of 1504 bytes, which is a maximum-length Ethernet data field appended by a Virtual LAN (VLAN) tag of 4 bytes, plus preamble, Start-of-Frame delimiter, addresses, Length/Type field, CRC, and interframe gap.
2. This amount includes an allowance for a data payload of 1504 bytes, plus header fields as before, but it does not include preamble, Start-of-Frame delimiter, or the interframe gap, as these do not typically impact receive buffering.

The required buffering "headroom" is therefore ~3.2 Kbytes plus an allowance for the propagation delay of the link. This link allowance can be significant, as shown in Table 6–4.

Thus, in the worst-case (a 3 km Gigabit Ethernet link), there can be a total of ~7 Kbytes of data "in the pipeline" that must still be received and buffered after the assertion of a flow control signal. After this time, the

TABLE 6–4 LINK PROPAGATION DELAYS

Type of Link	Maximum Propagation Delay in Bit (Byte) Times[1]		
	10 Mb/s	100 Mb/s	1000 Mb/s
100-m UTP[2]	12 bits	114 bits	1140 bits
	(2 bytes)	(15 bytes)	(143 bytes)
2 km multimode fiber[3]	200 bits	2000 bits	20,000 bits
	(25 bytes)	(250 bytes)	(2500 bytes)
3 km single-mode fiber[4]	300 bits	3000 bits	30,000 bits
	(38 bytes)	(375 bytes)	(3750 bytes)

1. Rounded up to the nearest bit or byte.
2. Supported by 10BASE-T, 100BASE-TX, 100BASE-T2 and 1000BASE-T.
3. Supported by 10BASE-FL and 100BASE-FX.
4. Supported by 1000BASE-LX.

PAUSE frame should stop the flow from the link partner. The design of buffers and flow control threshold selection must take this delay into account to effectively use flow control to prevent frame loss. The use of nonstandard, even longer single-mode fiber links further increases the buffering requirements for effective flow control.

6.4.2 Flow Control Policies and Use

The PAUSE mechanism that is provided for flow control of full-duplex links is only a tool. The specification of the protocol defines what actions occur upon the sending or receiving of PAUSE frames, but it says nothing about when a device should assert flow control and when it should resume the flow. This section considers some of these *flow control policy* issues for practical implementations.

In a typical implementation, flow control is used to prevent buffer overflow in a switch.[18] This allows a switch to be built that can accommodate *average* traffic levels without slowing throughput, while also preventing undesirable frame loss under short-term overload conditions—all without incurring the cost of huge buffer memories to accommodate the overload

---

18. It may also be used to prevent buffer overflow in an end station. However, an end station can use end-to-end flow control mechanisms (for example, TCP window advertisements), which are not available to a switch.

case. The result is a less-expensive switch that performs perfectly well (from the user's perspective) under a wide range of traffic conditions.

6.4.2.1 Buffer Thresholds

A typical switch will have some amount of input buffering available for each port (input queue). The queue holds frames until either the output port or the switching fabric itself is available to accept the frame, as depicted in Figure 6–7.[19]

Depending on the traffic patterns and the total load offered to the switch, frames will experience a delay in this queue while waiting to be unloaded. During this time, additional frames are being received on the same port, thus

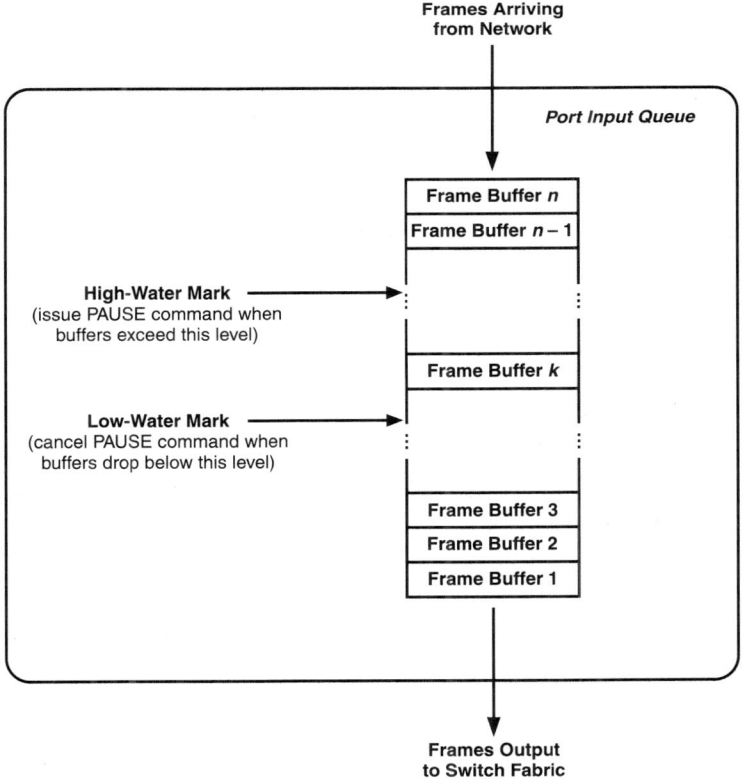

Figure 6–7 Input buffering.

---

19. Many different architectures are possible. A comprehensive treatment of the internal design of switches is beyond the scope of this book.

causing the queue to fill. A reasonable flow control policy would be to send a PAUSE frame (with a non-zero value for the pause_time) when the buffer fills up to a predetermined *high-water mark* so that the switch can prevent frames from being dropped at the input due to buffer unavailability. While the link partner is throttled in this manner, the switch will be unloading frames from this queue and forwarding them out other ports of the switch. When the buffer empties below a predetermined *low-water mark,* the flow control can be canceled (by sending a PAUSE frame with a value of 0 for the pause_time), and then normal operation resumes. In this manner, the switch can be used at maximum capacity without discarding any frames.

The high-water mark should be set such that there is still sufficient buffering available above the mark to accommodate the additional traffic that can still be in the pipeline. This is a function of the data rate, media type, and length of the link. Similarly, to ensure that buffer starvation does not occur, there should be sufficient room below the low-water mark such that incoming frames can arrive before the queue is completely emptied.[20] The room required below the low-water mark is less than the room required above the high-water mark, since the only factors are the PAUSE frame transmission time (512 bits), the decode time (512 or 1024 bits), and the round-trip link delay (see Table 6–4). There is no issue of maximum frame times as for the overflow case, since by definition there will be no frames transmitted by the link partner while paused.

6.4.2.2 Selection of PAUSE Times

The implementor has a choice of what pause_time to specify in the PAUSE frame. This can vary depending on the flow control policy being used. In the previous example, the value is relatively unimportant. In fact, a perfectly acceptable policy could be to use the value 0xFFFF when the queue depth crosses the high-water mark and a value of 0x0000 when it crosses the low-water mark. No heuristic is necessary to select "optimum" values for the pause_time. A different flow control policy (perhaps dictated by a different switch implementation) might optimize behavior by careful selection of pause times.

It is important that a link not be flow-controlled indefinitely. Higher-layer protocols may be depending on at least *some* frames being delivered across

---

20. This is less of a problem than buffer overflow, since starvation will cause only a minor performance degradation (that is, the switch could be temporarily idle, waiting for frames to arrive) rather than an end-to-end time-out, as would be needed in the event of a frame discard on overflow.

the network. In the event of an extended period of flow control, they could time-out connections, break virtual circuits, and so on. In particular, timers in the Spanning Tree Protocol state machine (used to maintain a loop-free topology in a bridged/switched network) may time-out, thereby causing a recalculation of the spanning tree and a consequent topology change [IEEE93a].

6.4.2.3 Dealing with Unreliable Delivery

There is no guarantee that PAUSE frames will be delivered to the link partner. They are subject to the same error characteristics of the link as any other frame (although in a proper implementation, they should *not* be subject to loss due to buffer unavailability). The sender of PAUSE frames can deal with this explicitly (for example, by implementing a policy of sending PAUSE frames multiple times). Alternatively it can ignore the problem and accept that at some very low level (that is, the inherent frame loss rate of the link), the flow control mechanism may not always work.

In any case, the worst that would happen if a PAUSE frame was not delivered is that flow control would not be asserted and frames would be discarded. This is no worse than if flow control was not available on the link at all. Higher-layer protocols and applications must already deal with the possibility of frame loss across a LAN. While performance may degrade significantly, correctness should still be maintained and applications should behave (relatively) normally. Assuming that the PAUSE frame was lost due to a transient error, the system should quickly revert to proper operation (including flow control) on subsequent error-free transmissions.

6.5   Flow Control Symmetry

Flow control can be either symmetric or asymmetric. In certain network configurations, it may be desirable to allow either device at the ends of a full-duplex link to throttle the transmissions of the other. In others, it may be desirable to allow flow control in one direction only.

6.5.1 Symmetric Flow Control

Symmetric flow control makes sense under the following circumstances:

- Both devices must deal with a high statistical variance of frame arrivals (that is, short-term transient overloads around some lower average traffic level).

- Both devices have similar buffer memory constraints (that is, neither one is inherently capable of absorbing the transients better than the other).
- The traffic pattern is relatively uniform (that is, the traffic flows are not weighted heavily in either direction).
- Neither device is the source or sink of much of the traffic.

One common scenario meeting all of these conditions is a switch-to-switch full-duplex link, depicted in Figure 6–8.[21]

6.5.2 Asymmetric Flow Control

In some circumstances, it may be better to allow one link partner to throttle the other but not vice versa. The most common scenario for this is an end station that is connected to an internetworking device (for example, switch or router) through a dedicated full-duplex link, as depicted in Figure 6–8.

There are two possible directions to the asymmetric flow control, and both have their uses.

1. **The switch can throttle the station but not vice versa.** This is the most common application of asymmetric flow control. This allows a switch to push back directly on end stations when network congestion causes internal buffer overflow (or near-overflow). Since end stations ultimately are the source of all frames in the network, pushing back on the end stations reduces the congestion at the source.

   Within the end station, internal interlayer flow controls (for example, memory allocation mechanisms in the device drivers and operating system programming interfaces for higher-layer protocols) will propagate the flow control right back to the application program, where it belongs. Thus a switch asserting flow control in this manner not only prevents its own internal buffers from overflowing, it also actually reduces the total offered load to the network, thereby effectively reducing or eliminating the true cause of the congestion.

   The use of asymmetric flow control in this manner also allows the implementation of extremely throughput-constrained switches, referred to as *Buffered Distributors,* discussed in detail in Chapter 11.

2. **The station can throttle the switch but not vice versa.** If the link capacity (data rate) is much greater than the ability of the attached station to process data, frames might be dropped in the end station's interface

---

21. A router-to-router link would also meet all of these criteria and would also be a good candidate for symmetric flow control. The choice of a switch in this context is purely exemplary.

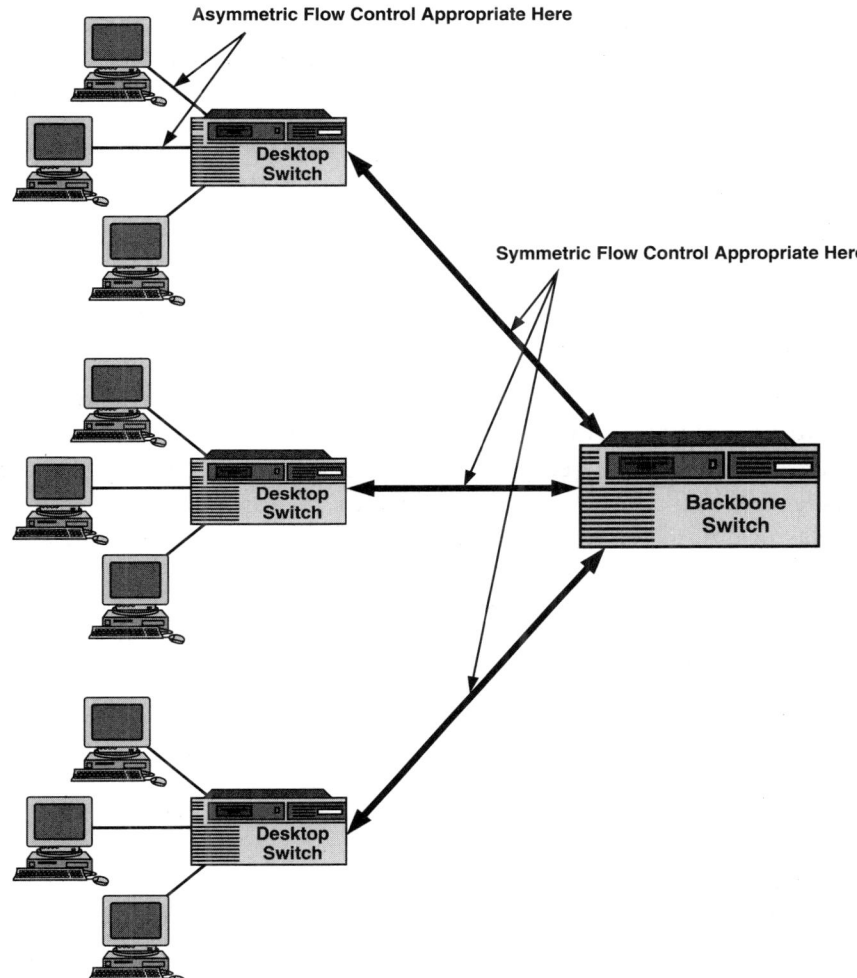

Figure 6–8 Symmetric and asymmetric flow control.

controller due to link buffer overflow. This situation is unlikely in a
10 Mb/s Ethernet, but it is a real concern at gigabit rates. Data may be
coming in from multiple sources (especially in the case of a server) at a
rate greater than the station can process the data and free up link
buffers.[22] Asymmetric flow control can allow the station to throttle the

---

22. End-to-end flow control mechanisms, such as window advertisements in TCP, can prevent
buffer overflow for a single data stream, but they cannot necessarily prevent end-station link
overflow for multiple, uncoordinated data streams.

switch to prevent frame loss in this situation. In this way, the end station "borrows" buffer capacity in the switch for its own use.

If the station can process data at wire-speed, asymmetric flow control in this direction is never needed.

A given link can be configured to use any of the following:

- No flow control
- Symmetric flow control
- Asymmetric flow control (in either direction)

The original specification for the Auto-Negotiation of flow control (used on UTP media only, at 10 Mb/s and 100 Mb/s [IEEE97]) permitted automatic configuration only for symmetric flow control (or no flow control at all). Asymmetric flow control required manual configuration in all cases. The Auto-Negotiation protocol used in 1000BASE-X (discussed in Chapter 12) allows the automatic configuration of symmetric or asymmetric flow control for Gigabit Ethernet networks using 1000BASE-X technology. 1000BASE-T will extend the UTP-media Auto-Negotiation protocol to support automatic configuration of asymmetric flow control on UTP links (for all data rates), but at the time of this writing, this is not an official standard.

7 — Ethernet Medium Independence

When an Ethernet is deployed, some physical medium must be provided for exchanging information among the stations. Ethernets are often characterized by the medium used, for example, coaxial cable Ethernet, optical fiber Ethernet, or twisted-pair Ethernet.[1] Thus the "Ethernet connector" can be a coaxial cable connector (for example, BNC), an optical fiber connector (for example, duplex SC), or an RJ-45 connector for unshielded twisted-pair. The Ethernet architecture also incorporates a second attachment point to allow partitioning of the subsystems within an Ethernet station. This chapter looks at how this second attachment point allows manufacturers to build devices that perform their intended function independent of the physical medium used to interconnect the stations in the Ethernet.

7.1 Ethernet Is Multimedia!

Originally, 10 Mb/s Ethernet was designed to operate over thick coaxial cable. Period. There was no intent to provide for, or allow the use of, multiple media types. In fact, allowing different cable types would have fostered non-interoperability, as you would not be able to connect two such different devices to the same network. Over time, the 10 Mb/s Ethernet media options increased from the original thick wire cable (10BASE5) to include the following media types, which are more popular today:

- Thin-wire coaxial Ethernet (10BASE2), which was developed as a means to reduce the cost and installation complexity of 10BASE5. Relinquished

---

1. Ē-ther-net mē-di-um, *n.*
    1. The physical cable used to communicate among stations on an Ethernet LAN.
    2. A psychic who can determine which network products will ship next year. (ref: *marketing.*)

in exchange for these benefits was network extent, maximum number of attachments, and network reliability.

■ Optical-fiber Ethernet (10BASE-F), which was developed primarily to allow operation between buildings (electrical isolation) and in harsh electromagnetic environments. In exchange, fiber Ethernets are more costly and difficult to install than copper-based systems.

■ Twisted-pair Ethernet (10BASE-T), which was developed to ease the problem of moves/adds/changes in large networks. Although 10BASE-T is more costly than coaxial cable-based systems, the benefits in network administration, management, and fault isolation outweigh the cost penalty.[2]

Similarly, 100 Mb/s Ethernet supports operation over twisted-pair (both shielded and unshielded) and optical fiber.

Unless the system architecture provides a means for medium independence, the designer of an Ethernet device or interface must either

■ build separate versions of the product for each possible medium that the end customer may wish to use (not desirable from a product proliferation perspective), or

■ support only one medium type in the product (not desirable from a market penetration perspective).

Fortunately, each generation of Ethernet has provided a medium-independent interface. This interface allows designers to build network controllers and stations that can connect with relative ease to any available physical medium.

7.2   10 Mb/s Attachment Unit Interface

In 10 Mb/s Ethernet, the medium-independent interface is called the Attachment Unit Interface (AUI) [IEEE96, Clause 7].[3] An AUI allows medium-

---

2. Many people mistakenly believe that twisted-pair Ethernets (10BASE-T) are less expensive than coaxial cable-based Ethernets (10BASE2). While the cost per-unit-length of twisted-pair cable is less than coaxial cable, the cost of a twisted-pair Ethernet *system* is greater. This is because:

1. Much more cable is needed in a twisted-pair system, since each station requires a dedicated "home run" to the wiring closet.
2. Twisted-pair systems require a hub, which is unnecessary in coaxial cable systems.
3. The transceiver electronics is more expensive for twisted-pair due to the poor transmission characteristics of the medium (which must be compensated for in the transceiver).

3. The original DIX Ethernet specification calls this the *transceiver cable* interface.

independent Ethernet controllers to connect to medium-specific transceivers. The controller is completely isolated from any of the details of the physical medium; its behavior is identical in all cases. In fact, when an AUI is used, the controller is completely unaware of the nature of the physical medium.

7.2.1 Medium Independence Was an Accident

Interestingly, the creation of the AUI had nothing to do with medium independence. The original 10BASE5 design demanded a separation between the controller and the transceiver for altogether different reasons:

- For electrical reasons, the transceiver had to be physically adjacent to the coaxial cable. There could be not more than a few centimeters distance between the coaxial cable and the transceiver electronics.[4] Unless there was a separation between controller and transceiver, the thick cable would have to be routed to each station. This is unwieldy (to say the least) and would use excessive lengths of cable for station attachments.
- It was desirable to keep the transceiver electronics to the absolute minimum necessary, since the transceiver often resided in a dropped ceiling or raised floor. Minimizing the active circuitry in this physically harsh (high and low temperatures and humidity, shock, vibration, and so on) and inaccessible environment increased the overall system reliability and availability.
- The technologies used in the controller and transceiver were fundamentally different. Controllers used primarily digital techniques and could be implemented using high-integration MOS processes. Transceivers were primarily analog, using (at the time) ECL and discrete transistor technology. Thus there was a logical partitioning along technology lines.

The AUI was created to allow this controller-transceiver separation, with no real thought to its ability to support multiple LAN media. (Sometimes you get lucky.)

7.2.2 AUI Architecture

Figure 7–1 depicts the logical separation of functions across an AUI.

All of the functions that are most easily implemented in high-integration digital logic are performed within the controller. This includes the bus interfac-

---

4. This is also true for 10BASE2, but it is accomplished by bringing the coaxial cable itself to the integrated controller/transceiver, rather than providing a physical interface between a separate controller and transceiver.

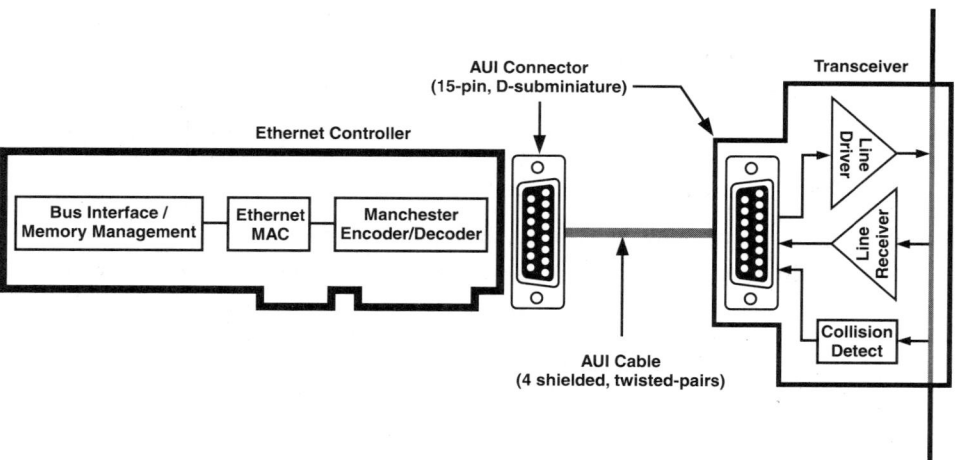

Figure 7–1 AUI architecture.

ing, memory management, Ethernet MAC, and the Manchester encoder/ decoder. The transceiver comprises the minimal set of required circuitry and is generally implemented using analog techniques. The AUI demarcation was chosen to support this logical and physical separation. It was believed that the technologies were sufficiently different that it was likely that manufacturers of controller products would not build transceiver products and vice versa, since the skills required to design a product were completely different at the two ends of the AUI. This was almost invariably true in the early days of Ethernet and is generally true even today. While there are companies that successfully build and market both digital controller and transceiver circuits, most companies' expertise lies clearly in one camp or the other. Even those firms that are successful on both sides of the AUI connector often develop those products in separate internal divisions or technology groups.

As applications demanded the use of alternative LAN media, the AUI was an obvious choice for standardizing the interface between the medium-independent controller and the medium-dependent transceiver. Transceivers with AUI interfaces were designed for thin-wire coaxial cable, optical-fiber, and twisted-pair media that allowed the use of existing controllers without change.

One result of this choice of separation is that the encoder/decoder is on the controller side of the interface. This implies that 10 Mb/s Ethernet must use Manchester encoding regardless of the medium employed. Manchester is a rather inefficient line code. It requires 2 baud for each bit of transmitted data; that is, the bandwidth required is twice that needed if the data were transmitted unencoded (non-return-to-zero, or NRZ).[5] This is not a problem for coaxial cable media, which have considerably more inherent bandwidth than is needed to transmit and receive 10 Mb/s signals. However, when Ethernet moved to UTP, this was no longer true. Had Ethernet been designed from the beginning to operate on UTP, Manchester would not have been the line code chosen.[6] However, because of the legacy installed base of AUI-based Ethernet controllers, 10BASE-T Ethernet also uses Manchester code. This resulted in a transceiver design that is considerably more complex and difficult than would otherwise be necessary.

7.2.3   AUI Design

The AUI consists of four signals:

1. **Transmit Data.** This signal carries Manchester-encoded data from the controller to the transceiver for transmission on the medium.
2. **Receive Data.** This signal carries Manchester-encoded data from the transceiver to the controller.
3. **Collision Presence.** This signal indicates to the controller that the transceiver has detected that there are multiple, simultaneous transmissions on the medium.
4. **Power.** Power (+12—15 VDC, differential) is provided by the controller for operating the transceiver.

All signals (except Power) use differential ECL voltages. Figure 7–2 depicts the AUI connector, signals, and pin assignments.

The AUI uses a 15-pin, D-subminiature connector and a 4-pair, individually shielded cable. The AUI is specified to be able to drive cables of up to 50 m in length.

---

5. Using Manchester coding, a 10 Mb/s (10 million bits-per-second) signal generates 20 Mbaud (20 million transitions-per-second on the medium, worst-case). The additional 10 Mbaud are used to transfer clock information. Other codes can be more efficient by sending the clock information less frequently than every bit time.

6. Manchester code is also sensitive to the absolute value of the voltage; a polarity reversal of the twisted-pair wires results in an inversion of the data. Differential Manchester code (as used on Token Ring) is sensitive only to the transitions (that is, the changes in voltage without regard to their absolute value) and thus transmits data correctly regardless of the polarity of the wires. Token Ring was originally designed for twisted-pair and so used this slightly more complex code to avoid the polarity problem. 10BASE-T transceivers usually employ some means of polarity detection, automatically reversing the wires when the incorrect polarity is sensed.

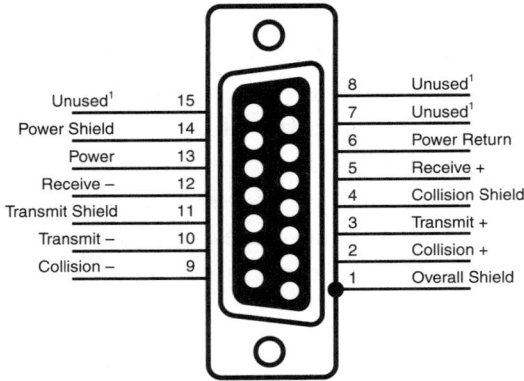

Figure 7–2 AUI signals.

1. The standard specifies an optional "Control Out" pair, which has never been widely implemented. These pins are invariably unused.

Since the AUI supports only 10 Mb/s devices, its use is historical. In particular, not only don't Fast Ethernet and Gigabit Ethernet allow the use of the physical AUI, but also their model of medium-independent interfacing differs somewhat, as discussed in the following sections. The AUI is presented here solely to show the progression from a single-medium system (thick coaxial cable) to a medium-independent Ethernet.

7.3   100 Mb/s Medium-Independent Interface

As part of the development of the 100 Mb/s Fast Ethernet system, a completely new medium-independent interface (with the appropriate abbreviation, MII) for interconnecting controllers and transceivers was designed. This interface provided both a new physical connection mechanism (cable and connectors), as well as a different partitioning of the functions in the controller and transceiver. [IEEE95, Clause 22]

7.3.1   MII Architecture

While medium independence came about almost by accident in the case of the AUI, the MII was specifically designed to provide for this function. Fast Ethernet was seen as being used for desktop applications (using twisted-pair) and backbone applications (using optical fiber). For this reason alone, interface manufacturers wanted to provide medium independence from the start.

Consideration (brief!) was given to "upgrading" the AUI from 10 Mb/s to 100 Mb/s. The problems with this approach were overwhelming because

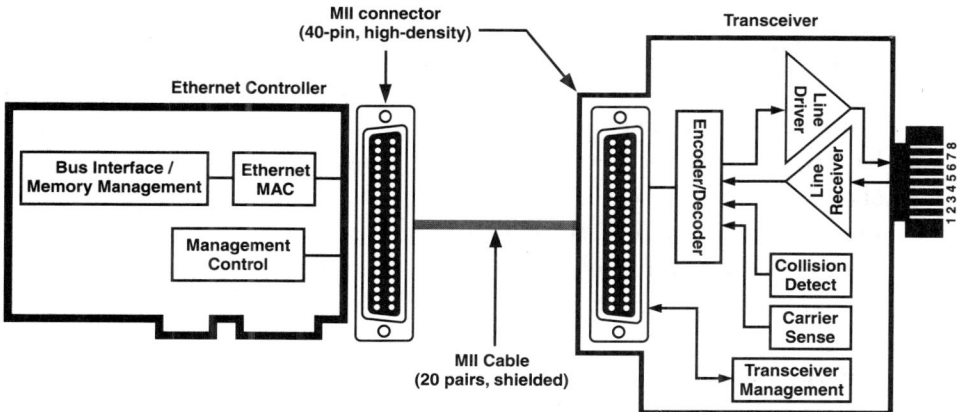

Figure 7–3 MII architecture.

the architectural requirements for a Fast Ethernet MII differ fundamentally from the needs of the original 10 Mb/s system.

■ The MII needed to support 10 Mb/s as well as 100 Mb/s transceivers. Therefore a certain amount of speed independence was necessary.

■ The different Physical Layer implementations of Fast Ethernet (for example, 100BASE-TX, 100BASE-T4, and 100BASE-T2) each use a different encoding scheme. So it makes more sense to move the encoder to the transceiver side of the interface.

■ It was an unnecessary complication to drive serial 100 Mb/s signals across the controller-transceiver interface, especially with the encoder on the transceiver side of the boundary. Thus the MII uses a parallel (nibble wide) data path.

■ Because a transceiver could have multiple capabilities and functions (for example, 10/100 Mb/s operation), a mechanism was needed for management communications with the transceiver to configure and control these functions.

Figure 7–3 depicts the overall MII architecture and system partitioning.

7.3.2   MII Design

The MII signals include five groups:

  1. Transmit signals. These include the nibble-wide Transmit Data, plus associated Transmit Clock, Transmit Enable, and Transmit Error signals. The data is synchronous with the clock, and the clock rate is one-fourth of the data rate (that is, 25 MHz for a 100 Mb/s Ethernet and 2.5 MHz for a 10 Mb/s Ethernet). The transmit signals are used to move data from the controller to the transceiver for encoding and transmission on the LAN.

2. **Receive signals.** These include the nibble-wide Receive Data, plus associated Receive Clock, Receive Data Valid (equivalent to a Receive Enable signal), and Receive Error signals. The data is synchronous with the clock, and the clock rate is one-fourth of the data rate. The receive signals are used to move decoded data from the transceiver to the controller.

3. **Ethernet Control signals.** These are the Carrier Sense and Collision Detect signals generated by the transceiver and used by the controller for medium access control. Note that they are used only in half-duplex mode; they are ignored in full-duplex mode.[7]

4. **Management signals.** These include a serial management I/O signal and an associated clock. Management information is exchanged (bidirectionally) between the controller and the transceiver for configuration and control.

5. **Power.** Power (+5 VDC) is provided by the controller for operating the transceiver. Of course, a return path is provided for both the power and the logic signals.

Figure 7–4 depicts the MII connector, signals, and pin assignments.

The MII uses a 40-pin, high-density D-connector and a 20-pair, shielded cable. While the AUI can drive cables of up to 50 m in length, the MII was designed for very short interconnections (0.5 m, maximum). The intent is to allow "pig-tail" transceiver cables or motherboard-daughterboard interconnections.[8]

---

7. In the AUI, the transceiver detects collisions, but the controller is expected to *infer* Carrier Sense from a combination of the Collision and Receive Data signals. In retrospect, this is a significant flaw in the design of the AUI; it causes a number of subtle timing problems for controllers and repeaters.

8. The AUI was designed for much longer cables because the original thick-wire coaxial Ethernet design envisioned ceiling-installed trunk cables and transceivers with relatively long drop cables to the station. With the use of twisted-pair cabling to the station, there is no need for a large separation between controller and transceiver.

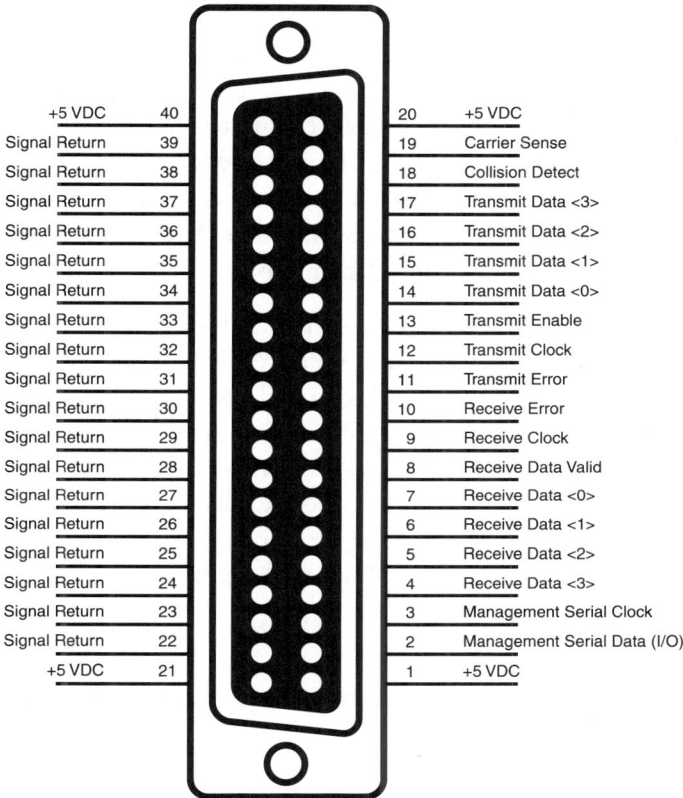

+5 VDC	40	20	+5 VDC
Signal Return	39	19	Carrier Sense
Signal Return	38	18	Collision Detect
Signal Return	37	17	Transmit Data <3>
Signal Return	36	16	Transmit Data <2>
Signal Return	35	15	Transmit Data <1>
Signal Return	34	14	Transmit Data <0>
Signal Return	33	13	Transmit Enable
Signal Return	32	12	Transmit Clock
Signal Return	31	11	Transmit Error
Signal Return	30	10	Receive Error
Signal Return	29	9	Receive Clock
Signal Return	28	8	Receive Data Valid
Signal Return	27	7	Receive Data <0>
Signal Return	26	6	Receive Data <1>
Signal Return	25	5	Receive Data <2>
Signal Return	24	4	Receive Data <3>
Signal Return	23	3	Management Serial Clock
Signal Return	22	2	Management Serial Data (I/O)
+5 VDC	21	1	+5 VDC

Figure 7–4 MII signals.

7.4   Medium Independence and Gigabit Ethernet

Gigabit Ethernet takes medium-independent interfacing from the physical to the ethereal (pun intended). The Gigabit MII (GMII) is intended primarily as a *logical interface,* rather than a physical one. That is, while you can define a system using the GMII as the model for communications between a transceiver and a controller, the GMII itself might exist only inside an IC and not be exposed at all. If it is exposed, it is used exclusively as an IC-to-IC interface; the GMII does not support the use of any connectors or cables.

Logically, the GMII is identical to the MII; the partitioning is exactly that shown in Figure 7–3. The only differences are

1. The GMII data path is byte-wide rather than nibble-wide. This reduces the GMII clock from 250 MHz (if it were nibble-wide) to 125 MHz,

thus making it practical to implement a GMII-compatible IC using CMOS technology. In addition, the clock is sourced from the controller (rather than the transceiver, as is the case with the MII). This is done to eliminate timing errors due to the propagation delays of the ICs and circuit traces used to implement the interface.

2. The GMII signal voltages (if exposed, as an IC-to-IC interface) are compatible with 3.3-V IC processes, rather than the older 5-V technology.[9]

3. The GMII has no connector or cable.

The GMII is discussed in detail in Chapter 12. You should be aware that while the AUI and MII were (and still are) widely implemented in real products, the GMII is more of an architectural construct than a physical interface. In many products, it will often make more sense to physically partition the system such that there is no exposed GMII at all. In particular, the technology and clock speeds used for the encoder/decoder are better matched to the controller than to the transceiver technology. A higher level of integration (and lower cost) can be achieved by integrating the encoder/decoder with the MAC controller logic.[10]

7.5. Summary of Medium-Independent Interfaces

A summary comparison of the characteristics of the AUI, MII, and GMII is provided in Table 7–1.

---

9. As clock rates increase, it becomes important to reduce the signal swing so that power, signal crosstalk, and EMI are reduced. It is acceptable to use 5-V signals with the 25 MHz clock of Fast Ethernet/MII, but the signal swing must be reduced with Gigabit Ethernet's 125 MHz GMII clock.

10. This is precisely the same logic that caused the designers of the AUI (including myself) to put the Manchester encoder/decoder on the controller side of the interface. Plus ça change, plus c'est la même chose. (The more things change, the more they stay the same.)

TABLE 7–1 MEDIUM-INDEPENDENT INTERFACES SUMMARY

Characteristic	AUI	MII	GMII
Cable Employed	4-pair, individual shield	20-pair, overall shield	N/A[1]
Maximum Length	50 m	0.5 m	N/A[1]
Connector	15-pin, D-subminiature (IEC 807-2)	40-pin, high-density D-style (IEC 1076-3-101)	N/A[1]
Data Signaling	Serial, Manchester-encoded	4-bit-wide, NRZ	8-bit-wide, NRZ
Data Rates Supported	10 Mb/s	10/100 Mb/s	1000 Mb/s
Clock Signaling	N/A[2]	2.5/25 MHz	125 MHz
Management Interface	N/A	Serial	Serial
Signal Levels	Differential ECL	CMOS/TTL, 5/3.3-V compatible	CMOS/TTL, 3.3-V compatible
Power Supply	12–15 V, differential	+5 V	N/A
Specification	IEEE 802.3, Clause 7 (Ethernet base document)	IEEE 802.3u, Clause 22 (Fast Ethernet)	IEEE 802.3z, Clause 35 (Gigabit Ethernet)

1. The GMII does not support the use of either a cable or a connector.
2. No separate clock is required. It is encoded into the Manchester data stream.

8 Automatic Configuration

This chapter looks at the mechanisms used to automatically configure stations and hubs in 10 Mb/s and 100 Mb/s twisted-pair Ethernets and which laid the groundwork for automatic configuration of Gigabit Ethernet. Gigabit Ethernet applies these same concepts, extending them to support additional features as well as operation across optical-fiber links. This chapter deals primarily with the history and development of 10 Mb/s and 100 Mb/s automatic configuration. The details of operation for Gigabit Ethernet are provided in Chapter 12.

8.1   The Driving Forces behind Automatic Configuration

Life was easy when the only variety of Ethernet was thick coaxial cable operating at a single data rate (except perhaps for the people who had to install and pay for it). The connectors (both the Type N coaxial and the 15-pin AUI) were chosen in part because no other popular computer connection at the time used those particular connectors. Thus there was little probability of plugging a 10 Mb/s Ethernet cable into a system that was expecting a different mode of operation, and no chance that the station's capabilities were incompatible with the hub.[1] Even as 10 Mb/s Ethernet evolved into its various manifestations—thin coaxial cable, optical fiber, unshielded twisted-pair, and so on—there was still no concern that incompatible devices would be present at the ends of the cable. Each variant of Ethernet used a different cable and (more important) a different connector. It simply was not possible to plug a coaxial cable into a twisted-pair hub. Proper configuration was guaranteed through connector differentiation.

The development of Fast Ethernet, using the same cable and RJ-45 connector used by 10BASE-T, created a fundamental problem. It was now possible

---

1. Especially since 10BASE5 networks don't use hubs!

to have standards-compliant Ethernet systems that were incompatible, yet appeared physically identical. A 10BASE-T-only and a 100BASE-TX-only device each has an RJ-45 LAN connector; however, they will not interoperate if interconnected. Worse yet, the use of full-duplex mode operation and the capability to source and sink flow control frames created even more unobservable, incompatible options. As part of the Fast Ethernet standards development, a method was developed for automatic configuration of twisted-pair links using RJ-45 connectors, dubbed "Auto-Negotiation."

Auto-Negotiation was driven by the following concerns.[2]

- Incompatible devices (for example, 10 Mb/s-only versus 100 Mb/s-only or half-duplex-only versus full-duplex-only) can use the same connector and be inadvertently connected to each other. At best, the systems will not function properly. At worst, this might cause network disruption (for example, the disabling of an entire hub) or even physical damage to the devices.[3]

- Devices can have multiple capabilities using the same connector (for example, 10/100 Mb/s operation, half-/full-duplex, and so on). It is desirable for such devices to be able to determine the maximum set of common capabilities supported by both itself and the device to which it is connected and to configure itself appropriately. This makes the best use of available features and allows easy migration and upgrading to new capabilities as devices are replaced.

- There is usually a considerable distance (up to 100 m) between a device and the hub to which it is connected. Even if one has physical access to the hub (not a good idea in general), it is rather inconvenient in most cases to have to go to the wiring closet and find out what the hub's capabilities are before attaching a new device to a star-wired network.

- Human beings make misteaks.[4] Even if the proper target configuration was known, errors would be made in the execution. Considering that the

---

2. While there are clearly "driving" forces behind the development of Auto-Negotiation, it is not related to the "auto negotiation" process often used to determine the purchase price of a vehicle.

3. This was a real problem with early implementations of dual-speed (4 Mb/s and 16 Mb/s) Token Ring LANs using passive Medium Access Units (MAUs). Inserting a single device of the incorrect speed (for example, a 4 Mb/s device into a 16 Mb/s ring) would cause the entire ring to cease operation. Modern implementations using active MAUs can detect this condition and isolate the offending station(s).

4. Such as forgetting to run a spell checker. Actually, "Miss Steak's" would be a great name for a restaurant.

configuration would have to be done on *every device in the network* (possibly thousands), the likelihood that everything would work properly is quite low.

The need for Auto-Negotiation can easily be seen from the computer installer's perspective. You have a device with an RJ-45 connector on the back, labeled "LAN." The device could operate at 10 Mb/s or 100 Mb/s or both, could be capable of half-duplex operation or full-duplex operation or both, and may have other features, all of which are invisible. There is a jack on the wall with an RJ-45 connector, similarly labeled "LAN." It is connected to a hub in a wiring closet that is at the end of the hall, and probably locked. The hub similarly could support some combination of data rates and duplex operation. How does the installer decide which mode(s) of operation should be configured on this computer?

Auto-Negotiation allows the computer and the hub to determine each others' capabilities and set themselves to the "highest common denominator"—the highest set of capabilities that both support.

8.2   Auto-Negotiation on UTP Systems

In theory, the problem of multiple, incompatible configurations on common media and connectors exists for both UTP and optical-fiber systems. Even before Gigabit Ethernet, there were incompatible, standards-compliant Ethernet systems using optical fibers (for example, 10BASE-FL/FP/FB and 100BASE-FX). However, optical-fiber Ethernet was still a relatively small part of the total market, being primarily deployed in controlled, backbone environments. Thus manual configuration was considered acceptable, since the number of systems was within the realm of human management.

The vast majority of Ethernet systems are now deployed using unshielded twisted-pair wiring. The problem of proper configuration in desktop LANs was the primary focus for the designers of Auto-Negotiation.

8.2.1   Auto-Negotiation Development

The Auto-Negotiation mechanism in wide use today was developed during 1993–95 and standardized as part of the Fast Ethernet project in IEEE 802.3 [IEEE95, Clause 28]. It was based on a system developed by National Semiconductor Corp., called *Nway.* Nway was originally developed for use with isoEthernet [IEEE94a], a system pioneered by National Semiconductor that allowed a UTP/RJ-45 connection to carry a standard 10 Mb/s Ethernet signal, plus a 6 MHz isochronous channel (hence, the "iso" part of isoEthernet). This allowed the integration of voice and video services (using the isochronous channel) with conventional LAN data over the same wires. Nway negotiation allowed isoEthernet devices to determine the capabilities of the partner at the other end of the UTP link and to enable the isochronous services only when they could be supported.

isoEthernet was a commercial failure. Even though it achieved IEEE standardization, it never gained much market acceptance. However, the Auto-Negotiation system derived from Nway has found commercial life in most new Ethernet systems.

8.2.2 Auto-Negotiation Scope

By the time Auto-Negotiation was being developed, there was already a wide range of incompatible options within the scope of Ethernet systems using RJ-45 connectors. In particular, Auto-Negotiation had to deal with the following:

- 10 Mb/s-only, 100 Mb/s-only, and dual 10/100 Mb/s-capable devices
- Within the 100BASE-T family (at least in theory), two possible signaling schemes (-TX, -T4)
- A large installed base of 10BASE-T devices that did not have any Auto-Negotiation capability
- A smaller number of prestandard 100 Mb/s Ethernet devices that did not have Auto-Negotiation capability

Later, additional signaling options (100BASE-T2) and flow control support were added to the Auto-Negotiation capabilities.[5]

8.2.3 Auto-Negotiation Principles

Auto-Negotiation incorporates the following concepts.

- **Auto-Negotiation operates over a single, point-to-point link.** Typically, the negotiation occurs between a station and a hub, as depicted in Figure 8–1.[6] The characteristics of the devices at each end of the link are the

---

5. While in theory it is important to allow the negotiation of different signaling methods for a given data rate (for example, 100BASE-TX, -T4, and -T2), in practice the use of anything except 100BASE-TX has been so minimal that it is not really an issue.

6. In the simple case of a two-station LAN, the negotiation would be station-to-station.

only factors affecting the configuration sequence. There is no concept of "network-wide" negotiation.

■ **Negotiation occurs upon link initialization.** The Auto-Negotiation process is executed when the device initializes the link prior to any data exchanges.[7] This would generally occur as part of a power-up sequence or during a link restart due to a failure or management intervention. Thus Auto-Negotiation is a *quasi-static* configuration mechanism; it does not support dynamically changing the characteristics of a link during normal operation.

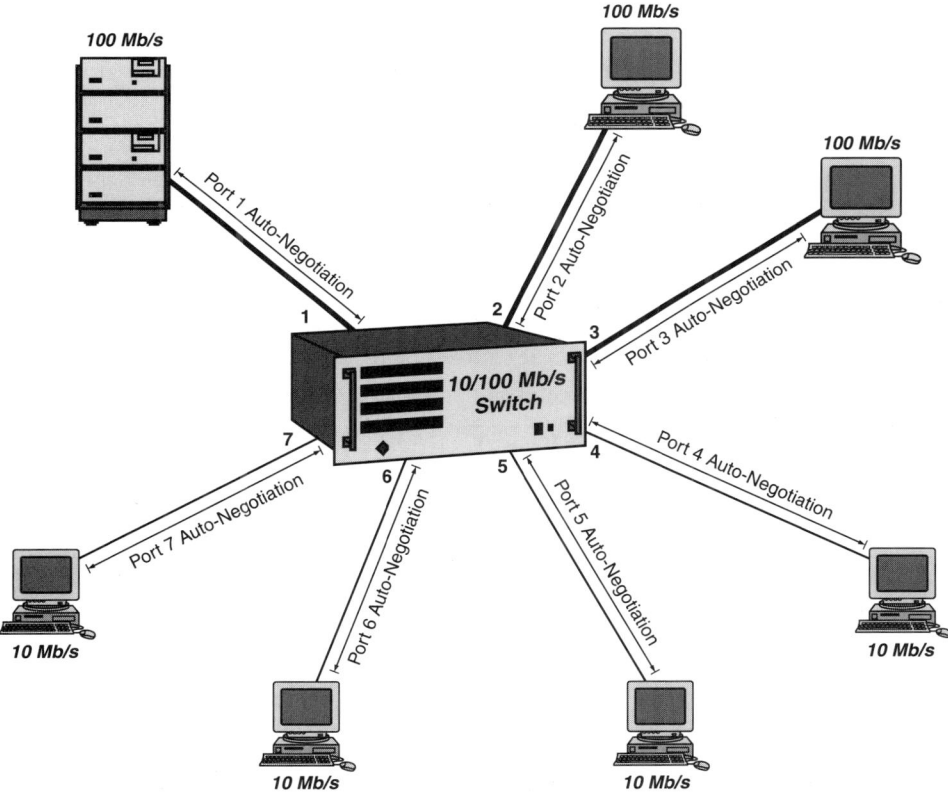

Figure 8–1 Independent Auto-Negotiation.

---

7. This is similar in concept to the way that a dial-up modem negotiates data rates, compression, and so on, upon connection, except that retraining during link operation is not permitted in Auto-Negotiation.

- **Auto-Negotiation signaling is independent of the signaling used for normal data.** On UTP media, one of the items being negotiated is the method of signaling to be used on the link (for example, 4B/5B encoding for 100BASE-TX versus Manchester encoding for 10BASE-T). The Auto-Negotiation mechanism cannot depend on the presence of any particular encoder in its link partner. A very simple signaling scheme is used (described shortly) that is separate from that used for normal data.
- **Each device "advertises" its capability to the other and selects the appropriate configuration based on the set of common capabilities.** Each device on the link transmits to the other a 16-bit "page" of capability information. A standard set of syntax and semantics are applied (that is, the use and meaning of each bit in the page is determined by prior agreement; discussed shortly). One bit is used as an *acknowledgment* mechanism to inform the partner that the device has correctly received the corresponding page of information in the other direction.

  The algorithm defines a hierarchy of functions, so that the highest common denominator can be unambiguously selected. For example, if both devices are capable of full-duplex operation, this will take priority over any half-duplex capability; 100 Mb/s operation takes priority over 10 Mb/s operation, and so on.
- **The mechanism is extensible.** One bit in the page is used as an "escape mechanism" that indicates that there will be additional pages. Each page is completed and acknowledged before proceeding to process additional pages. Additional page semantics can be defined by standard or used in a proprietary manner.
- **Auto-Negotiation cannot determine the type of wiring installed between the stations.** Some types of systems (for example, 100BASE-TX) require Category 5 wire for reliable operation. The signaling mechanism used by Auto-Negotiation operates perfectly well over Category 3 wire.[8] There is no mechanism within Auto-Negotiation to determine the quality of the intervening wire. Thus it is possible to negotiate the use of a system requiring Category 5 wire over a link incapable of supporting it. Quite simply, the complexity required to make such a "wire quality" determi-

---

8. This is necessary because the result of the negotiation could be to use 10BASE-T, which requires only Category 3 wire. In reality, the wire does not even need to meet Category 3 requirements in order to support Auto-Negotiation signaling.

nation was far beyond the level appropriate for Auto-Negotiation and would have increased the cost of implementation to prohibitive levels. It is considered the network administrator's problem to make sure that the wiring system can support the desired mode of operation.

■ **Auto-Negotiation does not support non-Ethernet systems.** There are many other communications systems that use RJ-45 connectors, for example, ISDN telephones and Token Ring LANs. Auto-Negotiation cannot explicitly detect such systems. Fortunately, such systems are unlikely to "masquerade" as anything compatible with Ethernet. That is, a system employing Auto-Negotiation plugged into a non-Ethernet system would not successfully complete its negotiation sequence and therefore would not enable the link.[9]

8.2.4   Auto-Negotiation Operation

The following sections provide detailed information on the syntax and semantics of Auto-Negotiation exchanges.

8.2.4.1   Auto-Negotiation Messages

Upon link initialization, the Auto-Negotiation protocol transmits 16-bit messages to its link partner and receives similar messages from that partner. A message may take as many 16-bit "pages" as needed, but most common negotiations require only the minimum "base page" depicted in Figure 8–2.

There is a capability bit for each type of signaling and duplex mode of operation available, plus 1 bit for indicating whether the device has implemented the flow control protocol described in Chapter 6.[10] Note that there is a full-duplex bit for each signaling method that supports full-duplex operation; it is possible to indicate support for full duplex operation at some speeds and not at others.

---

9. One exception that occasionally must be dealt with is FDDI-over-copper. This system uses the identical signaling method as 100BASE-TX and is "parallel-detected" by a Fast Ethernet device at the other end of the link. FDDI incorporates extensive Connection Management (CMT) protocols at low levels in the system to check the link integrity before enabling the channel for data communications. A 100BASE-TX device connected to an FDDI-over-copper hub (or vice versa) might appear to be using the correct signaling, but it would fail CMT. While the link (and the single device) would not function, there would be no network-wide disruption.

10. The bits used for Auto-Negotiation of some 100BASE-T2 parameters are located on later pages. [IEEE97a]

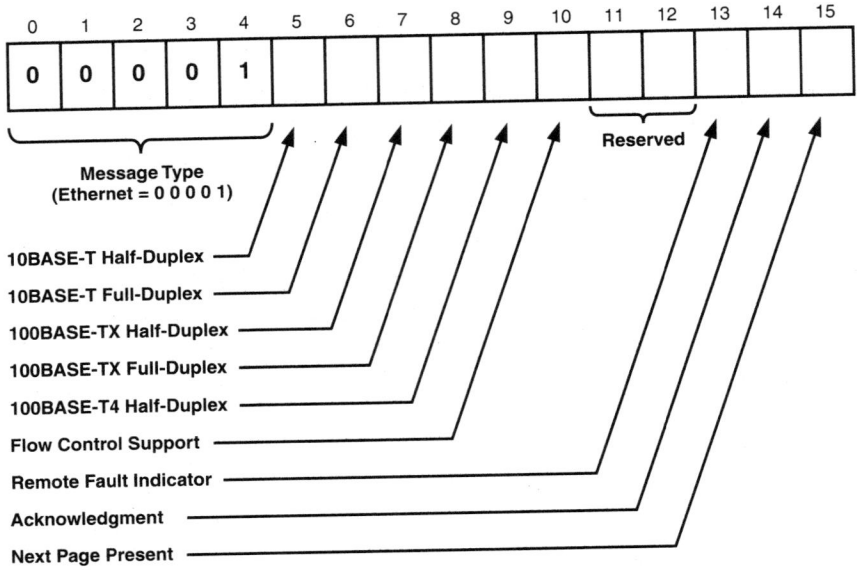

Figure 8–2 Auto-Negotiation base page message.

Figure 8–2 also depicts the mechanism for indicating that more messages are present (Next Page) and whether the corresponding page is being acknowledged. Negotiation messages are sent repeatedly until acknowledged. An acknowledgment is generated after three consecutive messages are received that contain identical information. This improves robustness in the face of bit errors during negotiation. The complexity of implementing a checksum (for example, CRC) on the negotiation exchange was considered excessive.

8.2.4.2 Auto-Negotiation Signals

Auto-Negotiation messages are transmitted as a series of clock and data pulses. Each pulse is nominally 100-ns wide and has the same appearance and characteristics as a 10BASE-T link pulse; clock and data pulses are identical. These pulses are each *roughly* equivalent to a single, 100-ns-wide positive pulse, although the waveshape is quite carefully controlled. [IEEE96, Clause 14] Each bit of the 16-bit message is sent as a pulse (for a logic 1) or a lack of a pulse (for a logic 0), with a clock pulse inserted before the beginning of the message and in between each bit of the message, as depicted in Figure 8–3.

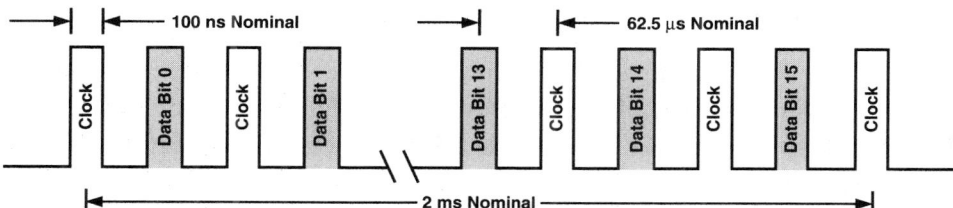

Figure 8–3 Auto-Negotiation signaling.

The entire message is repeated, nominally at 16-ms intervals, until the negotiation is complete.

8.2.4.3 Automatic Configuration without Auto-Negotiation

A device can easily detect whether the signals it is receiving were generated using 10BASE-T, 100BASE-TX, or 100BASE-T4. In the case of 10BASE-T, every device emits characteristic "link pulses" every 16 ms when the link is idle; this constitutes an unmistakable signature.[11] In the case of 100BASE-TX and 100BASE-T4, the signal levels, timing, and encoding used are sufficiently different that determination of the link's nature can be made without the use of Auto-Negotiation. This is often called "parallel detection."

Thus it is possible to automatically configure to any of these three signaling methods without implementing the negotiation protocol. Doing this is fairly common, and it slightly lowers the cost of a product.

However, a great deal of flexibility is lost by not using Auto-Negotiation:

- It is not possible to implement automatic dual-speed capability (for example, 10 Mb/s and 100 Mb/s).
- It is not possible to determine duplex mode.
- It is not possible to determine flow control capability.

The default assumption if Auto-Negotiation is not employed is that the link is operating in half-duplex mode, without explicit flow control. Thus devices not implementing Auto-Negotiation are generally those with only a single mode of operation, for example, a 100BASE-TX (only) repeater hub or a 10BASE-T (half-duplex-only) controller, where there is nothing to be gained by implementing Auto-Negotiation.

---

11. Also called "link beat," these pulses are used to ensure that the link is physically connected. It is the detection of this pulse that usually enables a "Link LED" on a 10BASE-T controller or hub port.

8.3   Auto-Negotiation on Optical Fiber

The problems of incompatible systems using common cables and connectors is not limited to RJ-45 connectors and UTP wiring. When the Auto-Negotiation protocol was being designed, there were also multiple variants of Ethernet systems using optical fibers (for example, 10BASE-FL/FP/FB). The introduction of Fast Ethernet added 100BASE-FX to this list, thereby creating the possibility of even more incompatibilities. There was clearly a need for automatic configuration (and isolation, in the event of incompatible systems) even when optical fiber was the medium employed.

Unfortunately, the problems of signal compatibility with legacy systems were insurmountable. The various optical-fiber-based Ethernet systems had so little in common with each other that even exchanging Auto-Negotiation messages was impossible.[12]

Considerable work went into trying to find some means to support automatic configuration, to no avail. The result is that for optical-fiber Ethernets, the ends of the links must be manually configured to the proper mode of operation (data rate, duplex mode, and flow control capability).

8.4   Automatic Configuration for Gigabit Ethernet

Gigabit Ethernet (at least in its first incarnations) does not operate over UTP wire. Nor does it use RJ-45 connectors. Thus the general problem of desktop device incompatibility that exists for 10 Mb/s and 100 Mb/s systems does not exist at the gigabit data rate. Nonetheless, it is especially important that Gigabit Ethernets not be improperly configured (at least with regard to duplex mode and flow control). This is because they are often deployed in backbone applications, where network-wide disruptions can be catastrophic.

The concepts of Auto-Negotiation have found their way into the gigabit technology in two ways:

■ **1000BASE-X Auto-Negotiation.** When 1000BASE-X signaling is used (discussed in Chapter 12), Gigabit Ethernet employs Auto-Negotiation to determine duplex operation, flow control, and similar capabilities. This mechanism operates over optical fiber as well as over the specialized

---

12. For example, a 10BASE-FL receiver may not even detect the *presence* of a 100BASE-FX driver output, much less decode a negotiation message.

copy media employed by 1000BASE-X systems (although it is still incompatible with existing 10 Mb/s and 100 Mb/s optical-fiber systems).The link configuration protocol (that is, state machine and message format) is identical to the Auto-Negotiation protocol described in this chapter. The only difference between the two is the physical method used to signal the negotiation messages. 1000BASE-X Auto-Negotiation is gigabit-specific; that is, it is not possible to negotiate data rates.

■ **1000BASE-T Auto-Negotiation.** 1000BASE-T, currently under development, will provide a method for gigabit operation over Category 5 UTP using RJ-45 connectors. This standard will extend the existing Auto-Negotiation protocol to support the new capability, most likely through the assignment of currently reserved bits to gigabit functions, or bit assignments on message pages beyond the base page discussed previously. This will allow fully negotiable 10/100/1000 Mb/s operation over UTP wiring.

PART

II

Gigabit Ethernet Technology

9 Architecture and Overview of Gigabit Ethernet

G igabit operation represents an *evolution,* rather than a revolution, in Ethernet technology. Incremental changes have been made almost continuously since the original 10 Mb/s, thick-coaxial-cable-only design, through 10BASE-T, to Fast Ethernet, and now Gigabit Ethernet. While the chapters that follow provide detailed information about all of the features and options under the Gigabit Ethernet umbrella, this chapter looks at the landscape from a fairly high altitude. It identifies the key elements of Gigabit Ethernet and, perhaps more important, the differences with respect to existing Ethernet systems. This is the place to be for readers familiar with Ethernet in general who want a quick update on what's new and what's different for gigabit operation.

9.1 Gigabit Ethernet Architecture

Figure 9–1 depicts a high-level system architecture for a hypothetical Gigabit Ethernet station.[1] This figure differs somewhat from the "standard" OSI layered model—it tries to show the *real* internal modules that would be present in this typical system, rather than using the abstract layering of the OSI model. (The architecturally pure-of-heart should read Chapter 13, which deals with the IEEE standard model for Gigabit Ethernet and has more layers than a Bermuda onion.) The mapping to the standard OSI layers is shown to the right. The shaded blocks indicate system modules that are affected by Gigabit Ethernet. The figure gives somewhat greater granularity for the Gigabit Ethernet-specific modules (that's why we're here, right?). Each of the shaded electronic modules could actually be implemented as a single IC.

---

1. The figure provides a reasonable model of a typical NIC, but it is not intended to imply that all NICs must follow this model. It is used for explanatory purposes only.

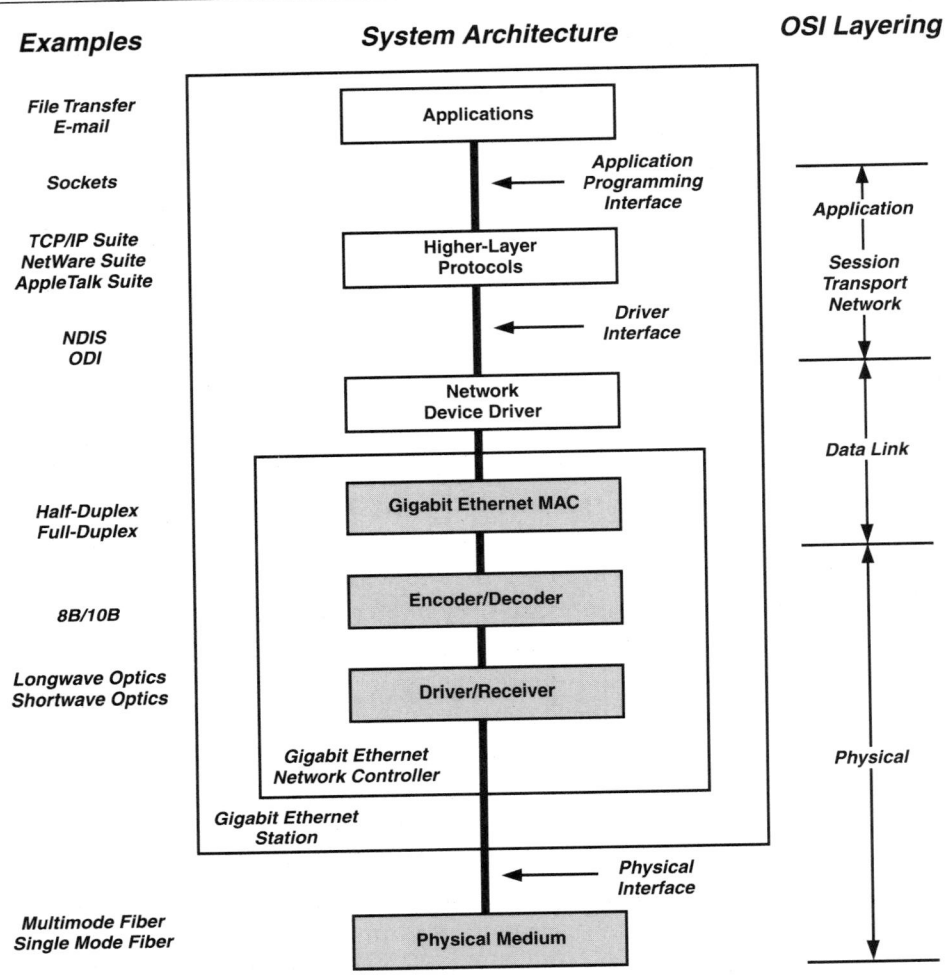

Figure 9–1 High-level system architecture.

Gigabit Ethernet is a Data Link and Physical Layer technology only. As such it requires no changes to higher-layer protocols or applications (although it may be appropriate to "tune" the behavior of higher-layer protocols and applications to properly take advantage of the higher bandwidth available). Existing applications should be able to run identically over an Ethernet, whether at 10 Mb/s, 100 Mb/s, or 1000 Mb/s (although Gigabit Ethernet offers the capability of running a lot faster). A device driver written to a standard driver interface specification (for example, the Network Driver Interface

Standard, NDIS) isolates the higher-layer protocols and applications from the specifics of the underlying LAN.

The Ethernet NIC shown comprises:

- A MAC entity, commonly referred to (and implemented) as an *Ethernet controller*
- An Encoder/Decoder (ENDEC) that converts data to/from the format needed for transmission on the physical medium[2]
- A set of drivers and receivers, as needed, for the particular physical medium in use. These may be electronic circuits (for copper media) or lasers/photodetectors for use with optical media.
- The physical medium used for communications

9.2   Overview of Gigabit Ethernet Technology

The following sections discuss each of these elements and how they are affected by Gigabit Ethernet. This chapter provides an overview. Later chapters contain much more detailed information about the technologies involved. Appropriate chapter references are provided.

9.2.1   Higher-Layer Software and Interfaces

Gigabit Ethernet, like all Ethernets, provides an unacknowledged, connectionless (datagram) delivery service. Frames may be sent to unicast addresses (single destination) or multicast addresses (multiple destination). A single frame can contain from 46 to 1500 bytes of data.

If the system is properly designed, there should be no changes required for higher-layer protocols or applications to use Gigabit Ethernet. You can consider this either fortunate (if you are a user of networks) or a fundamental requirement of the design (if you are a manufacturer of network products). No technology would get very far if it depended on the development of new applications and protocols to take advantage of its capabilities.

For a Gigabit Ethernet end station, the interface can mesh seamlessly with existing protocol stacks (for example, TCP/IP or NetWare) through the use

---

2. In Gigabit Ethernet, the ENDEC block generally includes a device called a Serializer/Deserializer (SERDES), since this allows the high-speed (1000 MHz or greater) clock domain to be restricted to a smaller, specialized device. See Chapter 12 for details.

of a standard device driver interface (for example, NDIS). Of course, having Gigabit Ethernet available will not necessarily make the applications run faster unless the host computer is capable of processing the data at the higher rate offered. Putting racing tires on the family sedan won't make it go any faster; you also need a more powerful engine and transmission, as well as other components, in order to truly increase performance. Only end stations that contain high-performance processing capabilities, buffer memory, and so on, will benefit significantly from Gigabit Ethernet connections. However, the resident protocols, applications, and operating systems do not need to be rewritten (or even recompiled) to use the higher-speed interface. See Chapter 15 for an extensive discussion of performance issues.

Similarly, there is no logical difference between the operation of an inter-networking device (bridge or router) using Ethernet at 1000 Mb/s versus 10 Mb/s or 100 Mb/s. Of course, devices designed for Gigabit Ethernet will need to consider the performance and memory implications in order to achieve real user benefits from the speed.

9.2.2 MAC Operation

The Gigabit Ethernet MAC is a proper superset of the 10/100 Mb/s Ethernet MAC. That is, it contains all of the capabilities that currently exist and adds some additional functions and features specific for gigabit operation.

The Gigabit Ethernet MAC can operate in either full-duplex or half-duplex mode (see Chapter 4). Full-duplex operation is unchanged from other data rates. Half duplex operation at gigabit rates is problematic. The use of CSMA/CD as an access control mechanism implies an intimate relationship between the minimum length of a frame transmission and the maximum round-trip propagation delay of the network. The minimum transmission time must be longer than the maximum round-trip propagation time of the LAN so that a station will still be transmitting a frame when it is informed of a collision. Since the length of time required to transmit a frame scales inversely with the data rate, increasing the speed by an order of magnitude (from Fast Ethernet's 100 Mb/s) reduces the frame transmission time by that same factor of 10. To accommodate this scaling, you need to reduce the size (extent) of the network, to increase the minimum frame, or to change the MAC algorithm.

If there were no other modifications, the network extent would have to have been reduced to the order of 10–20 m to support half-duplex Gigabit Ethernet operation. This is clearly inadequate for most practical uses. So the approach taken was to work with the minimum frame transmission time and the MAC algorithm itself.

Half-duplex Gigabit Ethernet introduces the concept of *carrier extension.* Carrier extension is used to increase the effective length of a frame transmission without actually increasing the minimum length of the frame itself as seen by the device driver and higher-layer software. Because carrier extension imposes a performance penalty for senders of short frames, the concept of *frame bursting* is also introduced. Frame bursting allows stations to send multiple short frames with a single arbitration for the channel. For half-duplex Gigabit Ethernet, carrier extension is a required function (without it, the CSMA/CD algorithm would not work). In contrast, frame bursting is optional (this is a performance issue only and does not affect correctness). Carrier extension and frame bursting are explained in detail in Chapter 10.

In full-duplex mode, neither carrier extension nor frame bursting is necessary. With no need to detect collisions, there is no need to extend the transmission time to ensure that the sender is still transmitting when a collision occurs. In addition, full-duplex Ethernets "naturally" burst; there is no need to provide an explicit mechanism for this. Since most (and probably all) Gigabit Ethernets will operate in full-duplex mode, the complexities of carrier extension and frame bursting are primarily of academic interest and do not affect most networks or users.

Gigabit Ethernet systems, like their slower-speed counterparts, can also use flow control. Indeed, it is expected that most systems (both end stations and internetworking devices) will incorporate this mechanism, since it can prevent unwanted frame loss in the face of transient buffer congestion. With frames arriving at gigabit speeds, the possibility of buffer overflow is much greater, so flow control is a welcome tool. In the time that a 10 Mb/s Ethernet fills 16 KB of buffer memory, a Gigabit Ethernet can fill 1.6 MB!

9.2.3   Signal Encoding

In high-speed networks, it is almost always necessary to *encode* data being transmitted into a self-synchronizable stream. To properly interpret the data at the receiver, you need to know the precise frequency and phase of the clock used to generate the signal. It is generally impractical to send this clock separately from the data. Even if you did, the problems of differential timing skew between the data and the clock transmissions greatly reduce the usefulness of the phase information received. Worse still, it would require two communications channels: one for the data and another for the clock. Therefore, some form of data encoding is employed that combines the clock and data information into a single signal, which is separated at the receiver (decoder).

The original 10 Mb/s Ethernet used Manchester encoding for all media types. Manchester encoding had two important characteristics that made it suitable for Ethernet use.

1. It is perfectly balanced for DC. That is, the amount of time in the logic "high" state is the same as the time in the logic "low" state, regardless of the data being transmitted. This allows the signal to pass through transformers with minimal distortion.
2. It is relatively easy to decode—and even easier to generate.

On the down side, Manchester is a bandwidth-inefficient code, requiring 2 baud/bit (that is, a 10 Mb/s Ethernet signal generates 20 Mbaud when Manchester encoded). This was not considered a serious flaw, however, as the original Ethernet used coaxial cables that had available signal capacity far in excess of the 10 Mb/s data rate. This excess capacity may have been used "wastefully" by the Manchester encoding, but it reduced the overall system cost by requiring less-expensive encoder/decoders.

For Fast Ethernet, Manchester code was impractical. On UTP wire, bandwidth is dear and the cable characteristics are such that 200 Mbaud signaling is simply not achievable. So a "richer" code was needed, one that encoded more data into the same bandwidth. The three versions of Fast Ethernet use different codes, since they operate over different numbers and types of cabling, as shown in Table 9–1.

Coding systems are often referred to with a shorthand notation, such as "4B/5B." This denotes a scheme that encodes 4 bits into 5 baud (equivalently,

---

TABLE 9–1 FAST ETHERNET ENCODING

	Type of Wire	No. of Pairs/Fibers	Coding System	Coding Efficiency
100BASE-X	Multimode fiber, STP, Catalog 5 UTP	2	4B/5B	1.25 baud/bit
100BASE-T4	Catalog 3/4/5 UTP	4	8B/6T	0.75 baud/bit
100BASE-T2	Catalog 3/4/5 UTP	2	PAM 5x5	0.50 baud/bit

"4 data bits into 5 code bits").[3] When more bits are encoded into fewer baud, the code is more bandwidth-efficient and is said to be *richer*. On the other hand, richer codes tend to require more complex encoders and decoders and greater expense.

Operating an Ethernet at gigabit rates does not reduce the encoding burden, to say the least. Even when it's operated over optical fibers and specialized, short copper cables, the data rates and economic factors combine to make rich encoding necessary. Gigabit Ethernet uses a coding system—called 8B/10B—developed for Fibre Channel [ANSI94] and patented by IBM Corporation.[4] [FRAN84] As you might expect, this system encodes 1 byte (8B) of data into 10 baud, or code bits. The Gigabit Ethernet entry in Table 9–1 now looks like that in Table 9–2.

The nickname for this encoding system is 1000BASE-X (similar to the 100BASE-X

> **Seifert's Law of Networking #27**
>
> You can transmit and receive data at a gigabit-per-second through a barbed wire, with acceptable error rates. It's only a matter of how much you are willing to pay for the encoder and decoder.

nickname used for the 4B/5B encoding used in Fast Ethernet). The 1000 Mb/s data rate translates into a 1250 Mbaud signal rate on the actual physical medium (1.25 baud/bit). 1000BASE-X signaling is supported on optical fiber and special shielded twisted-pair cables, as discussed later in the chapter.

At the time of this writing, the coding system for Gigabit Ethernet operation on UTP wire (1000BASE-T) has not yet been standardized. Clearly, it

---

TABLE 9–2 GIGABIT ETHERNET ENCODING

	Type of Wire	No. of Pairs/Fibers	Coding System	Coding Efficiency
1000BASE-X	Single-mode and multimode fiber, STP	2	8B/10B	1.25 baud/bit

---

3. The 8B/6T scheme encodes 8 bits into six ternary (three-level) signals, hence the "6T." PAM 5x5 encodes 4 bits into a two-dimensional 25 code-point (5x5) constellation space.

4. Per IEEE rules, IBM has agreed to allow the use of their patented technology as part of an IEEE standard by providing patent licenses on a nondiscriminatory basis and at a reasonable cost.

will be a richer code than that used on optical fibers because the available bandwidth of UTP is considerably lower. This lower bandwidth implies that the encoder also will be more complex.

The details of the 8B/10B coding system are described in Chapter 12.

9.2.4 Physical Media and Signaling

Gigabit Ethernet is currently supported on optical fiber (both multimode and single-mode) and special 2-pair STP cables (also called *short copper jumpers*) by using 1000BASE-X (8B/10B) encoding. Like the 1000BASE-X encoding system itself, the physical media specifications leverage the work done for Fibre Channel. In the future, Gigabit Ethernet will support the use of 4 pairs of Category 5 UTP (1000BASE-T).

> *The nice thing about standards is that there are so many to choose from.*
> —*Andrew Tanenbaum*
> *[TANEN88]*

9.2.4.1 Optical Fiber

1000BASE-X supports three types of optical fibers:

50-µm multimode

62.5-µm multimode

10-µm single-mode

and two optical wavelengths for the laser drivers:

Short wavelength (850 nm nominal, called 1000BASE-SX)

Long wavelength (1300 nm nominal, called 1000BASE-LX)

Each connection requires two fibers, one each for transmit and receive. The range of fiber lengths supportable with the different wavelengths and fiber types is shown in Table 9–3.

TABLE 9–3 1000BASE-X OPTICAL FIBER MAXIMUM LENGTH

	50 µm Multimode	62.5 µm Multimode	10 µm Single-Mode
1000BASE-SX	525 m	260 m	Not supported
1000BASE-LX	550 m	550 m	3000 m

The lengths shown are the limits based on the physical signaling characteristics (optical attenuation, dispersion, and so on). When the MAC is operating in full-duplex mode, these are the only length limitations that apply. If half-duplex mode is used (that is, a shared LAN), then there may be further restrictions due to the round-trip propagation delay supportable by the MAC. This is discussed in Chapter 12.

As Table 9–3 shows, long-wavelength lasers allow longer distances to be achieved, both with 62.5 µm multimode and 10 µm single-mode fibers. Distances of up to 3 km can be used, thus making this the medium of choice for campus backbone applications. Short-wavelength lasers can achieve practical distances for applications within a building. As expected, however, the extended distance capability of long-wavelength lasers comes with a cost penalty.

All three fiber types are specified and supported by the building wiring standard, EIA/TIA 568 [EIA91, EIA91a]. The standard connector used for all Gigabit Ethernet fiber media is the duplex SC (further discussion and a picture is provided in Chapter 12). This is the same connector specified for 100BASE-FX (Fast Ethernet over fiber).

9.2.4.2 Short Copper Jumpers

For very short distances, another option is provided. Like its Fibre Channel cousin, Gigabit Ethernet supports the use of a 2-pair, 150 Ω shielded, twisted-pair cable for short interconnections. This cable is similar, *but not identical,* to the shielded twisted-pair commonly used in Token Ring systems.[5] This medium uses 1000BASE-X signaling over copper wire and is therefore called 1000BASE-CX (C for copper).

1000BASE-CX is intended for interconnections among equipment within a wiring closet or in a single room (for example, an equipment rack or server cluster). The maximum distance supported is 25 m.

Two connector alternatives are available for this cable.

- The preferred connector is the Fibre Channel High-Speed Serial Data Connector (HSSDC) [ANSI94, FC-PH-3 (3rd revision)].
- Also permitted is the DB-9 (9-pin D-subminiature) connector typically used in Token Ring and 100BASE-TX (STP) systems.

These connectors are discussed in more detail (with pictures) in Chapter 12. The HSSDC is smaller and has considerably better electrical characteristics

---

5. The main difference is a tighter specification for differential timing skew between the pairs.

than the DB-9 (this is important for Gigabit Ethernet) and is the connector of choice for 1000BASE-CX systems.

9.2.4.3 Unshielded Twisted-Pair

At the time of this writing, there is no standard nor any products available for Gigabit Ethernet operating on UTP. Work is ongoing, however, to develop this technology.

1000BASE-T is the designation for Gigabit Ethernet operating over Category 5 UTP. The system under development will support operation using 4 pairs over a distance of 100 m. This is compatible with the EIA/TIA 568 wiring specification and, when available, will allow the upgrade of existing 10 Mb/s and 100 Mb/s systems using Category 5 cabling.

1000BASE-T will not use the 8B/10B encoding system used in 1000BASE-X. A richer code will be required to squeeze gigabit rates out of UTP cable.

9.2.5   Topology

Gigabit Ethernet supports both shared and switched LAN configurations. Because of the modern tendency to use star-wired, hub-centric wiring systems and the extremely tight timing constraints of Gigabit Ethernet, the range of possible shared LAN topologies has been reduced greatly, compared with Ethernet operation at slower speeds. A rich set of topologies is still available for switched Gigabit Ethernet networks.

9.2.5.1 Shared Gigabit Ethernet LANs

The original 10 Mb/s Ethernet supports a wide range of physical topologies for a shared LAN, including

- multidrop coaxial buses (with medium-dependent lengths),
- star-wired topologies in multiple tiers (both in twisted-pair and optical fiber),
- point-to-point links, and
- combinations of these.

In fact, the permissible topologies are so varied that entire books (and entire clauses of LAN standards) are devoted to determining the set of valid configurations. [SPUR96]

Fast Ethernet restricted the legal topologies considerably for 100 Mb/s operation. Only three topologies are permitted for a shared Fast Ethernet LAN:

1. A point-to-point link with exactly two stations
2. A single repeater with either copper or optical-fiber connections, using any combination of encoding methods

3. Two interconnected repeaters with either twisted-pair or optical-fiber connections, using a single encoding method

This restriction (relative to the design freedom afforded 10 Mb/s topological design) is due to the tight timing constraints of propagation delay at the higher, 100 Mb/s data rate. Gigabit Ethernet restricts the available topology options even further, to

■ a point-to-point link with exactly two stations, and
■ a single repeater with either copper or optical-fiber connections using a single encoding method.

These topologies are depicted in Figure 9–2.

This makes the physical design of shared Gigabit Ethernet LANs rather trivial. (It's about time!) The only design task is ensuring that the link lengths are within the maximum specified for the given medium. Repeaters cannot be interconnected within a single collision domain due to the timing restrictions imposed by the data rate.[6] By definition, stations connected to a shared LAN use the half-duplex MAC.

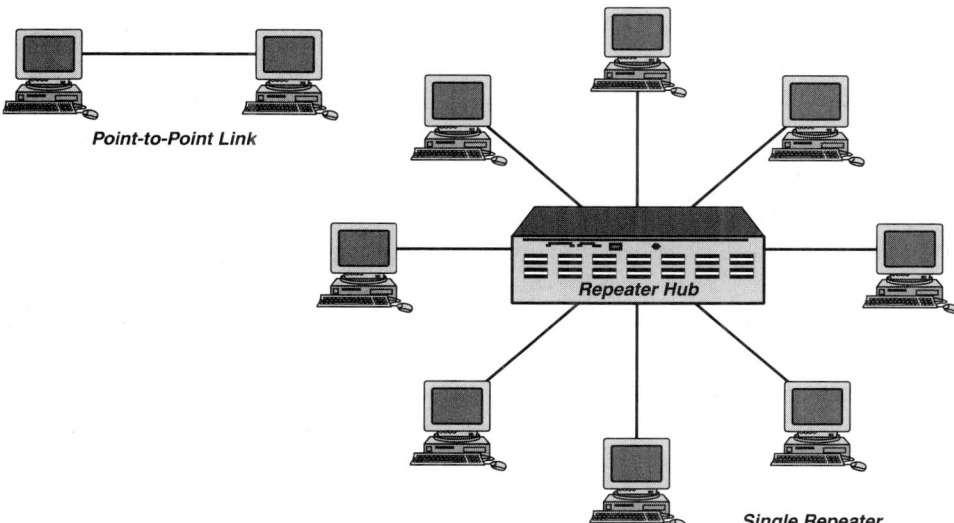

Figure 9–2 Gigabit Ethernet shared LAN topologies.

---

6. A vendor could conceivably implement a proprietary means of interconnecting repeaters (that is, a *stackable repeater*) that makes multiple devices appear to behave as a single repeater. While this is common practice for 10 Mb/s and 100 Mb/s repeaters, the timing constraints of gigabit operation make even this approach difficult.

9.2.5.2 Switched Gigabit Ethernet LANs

Of course, more extensive topologies can be created using bridges (switches) to isolate collision domains. Gigabit Ethernet does not reduce the realm of permitted switched LAN topologies. The only restrictions for switched Gigabit Ethernet design are the maximum lengths supported by the physical media—and the depth of one's bank account. The use of full-duplex operation allows the largest possible network extents, since there are no MAC-imposed distance restrictions.

9.2.6 Medium-Independent Interfacing

Ethernet has a variety of medium options at every data rate. To support coaxial cable, twisted-pair, and/or optical-fiber, each Ethernet system has incorporated (at least logically) a standardized interface between controller equipment (for example, Network Interface Controllers or NICs[7]) and Physical Layer attachment devices (for example, transceivers). This allows manufacturers of controllers and transceivers to build these devices independently, yet retain flexibility for the end user's choice of preferred media. This interface point is the medium-independent interface, discussed in Chapter 7. One has been defined for each of the three common Ethernet data rates, as discussed in that chapter.

Gigabit Ethernet introduced a new Gigabit Medium Independent Interface (GMII). This is a logical extension of the MII designed for Fast Ethernet, with the major design differences being the width of the interface (byte versus nibble-wide) and the clock rate (125 MHz versus 25 MHz).

While the Fast Ethernet MII was designed to allow an exposed physical implementation (that is, a cable and connector for external transceiver connections), the GMII does not permit this, primarily due to the difficulties in maintaining signal integrity with high-speed clocks and very fast signal transitions. Thus the GMII, when it exists within a device, serves as an internal interface used between ICs within a product.

Table 9–4 summarizes the various medium-independent interfaces. Details of the GMII are in Chapter 12.

9.2.7 Auto-Negotiation

As discussed in Chapter 8, Fast Ethernet implemented a mechanism for automatic link configuration called Auto-Negotiation. This was needed because, for the first time, multiple, widely deployed, incompatible Ethernet systems were

---

7. NIC stands for both Network Interface Controllers and network interface cards.

TABLE 9–4 MEDIUM-INDEPENDENT INTERFACES

	10 Mb/s Attachment Unit Interface (AUI)	10/100 Mb/s Medium-Independent Interface (MII)	1000 Mb/s Gigabit Medium-Independent Interface (GMII)
Cable Employed	4-pair, individual shield	20-pair, overall shield	None
Maximum Length	50 m	0.5 m	N/A
Connector	15-pin, D-subminiature (IEC 807-2)	40-pin, high-density D-style (IEC 1076-3-101)	None
Data Signaling	Serial, Manchester-encoded	4-bit-wide, NRZ	8-bit-wide, NRZ
Data Rates Supported	10 Mb/s	10/100 Mb/s	1000 Mb/s
Clock Rate	N/A[1]	2.5/25 MHz	125 MHz

1. No separate clock is required; it is encoded into the Manchester data stream.

available that used the same connector (RJ-45). Gigabit Ethernet continues this policy of making sure that devices self-configure to the maximum extent possible. This policy has been extended to include partial configuration of optical fiber links in addition to copper.

Two separate forms of Auto-Negotiation are provided in Gigabit Ethernet: one for 1000BASE-X systems and another for 1000BASE-T. Gigabit Ethernets using 1000BASE-X signaling can automatically configure themselves for

- half- versus full-duplex operation, and
- flow control, including both symmetrical and asymmetrical operation and the direction of asymmetry.

However, 1000BASE-X Auto-Negotiation is restricted to gigabit operation—it cannot negotiate data rates between link partners. It is still the responsibility of the network installer to ensure that the devices at the ends of the link are both gigabit-capable. Also, the installer must ensure that both ends of each link use the same type of drivers/receivers (for example, long-wavelength versus short-wavelength lasers), since the different driver/receiver systems are all mutually incompatible. Because much of the configuration

TABLE 9–5 SUMMARY OF ETHERNET TECHNOLOGY MIGRATION

Characteristic		10 Mb/s	100 Mb/s	1000 Mb/s
High-Level Software Interface		Unacknowledged, Connectionless Service; Unicast/Multicast/Broadcast Addressing; 46–1500 Bytes Data Payload/Frame		
Topologies	**Half-Duplex (shared LAN)**	Multidrop bus; Point-to-point links; Single and multiple repeaters; Star-wired repeater hubs (multiple tiers)	Point-to-point links; Star-wired hub (single repeater); Star-wired hub (two repeaters)	Point-to-point links; Star-wired hub (single repeater)
	Full-Duplex (switched LAN)		Point-to-point links; Switched hubs	
MAC Characteristics	Min Frame		64 bytes (plus preamble/SFD; 46 bytes data payload)	
	Max Frame		1518 bytes (plus preamble/SFD; 1500 bytes data payload)	
	Slot Time	51.2 µs (512 bit-times)	5.12 µs (512 bit-times)	4.096 µs (4096 bit-times)
	Interframe gap	9.6 µs (96 bit-times)	960 ns (96 bit-times)	96 ns (96 bit-times)
	Carrier Extension	No	No	Yes
	Frame Bursting	No	No	Yes (optional)
Media	**Half-Duplex (100/1000 Mb/s fiber lengths are based on equidistant radii from the repeater)**	Thick coaxial cable, 500 m; Thin coaxial cable, 185 m; Broadband coaxial cable, 1.8 km; Category 3 UTP, ~100 m (10BASE-T); Category 5 UTP, ~150 m (10BASE-T); 62.5-µm MM fiber, 500 m (10BASE-FP)	Category 3/4/5 UTP, 100 m (100BASE-T4, -T2); Category 5 UTP, 100 m (100BASE-TX); 62.5-µm MM fiber, 160 m (100BASE-FX)	Category 5 UTP, 100 m (1000BASE-T; under development); 62.5-µm MM fiber, 111 m (1000BASE-SX/LX); 50-µm MM fiber, 111 m (1000BASE-SX/LX); 10-µm SM fiber, 111 m (1000BASE-LX); 150 Ω STP cable,

TABLE 9–5 SUMMARY OF ETHERNET TECHNOLOGY MIGRATION (Continued)

Characteristic		10 Mb/s	100 Mb/s	1000 Mb/s
Media	Half-Duplex (cont.)	62.5-μm MM fiber, 1000 m (FOIRL) 62.5-μm MM fiber 2000 m (10BASE-FL)		25 m (1000BASE-CX)
	Full-Duplex	Category 3 UTP, ~100 m (10BASE-T) Category 5 UTP, ~150 m (10BASE-T) 62.5-μm MM fiber 2000 m (10BASE-FL)	Category 3/4/5 UTP, 100 m (100BASE-T2) Category 5 UTP, 100 m (100BASE-TX) 62.5-μm MM fiber, 2000 m (100BASE-FX)	Category 5 UTP, 100 m (1000BASE-T; under development) 62.5-μm MM fiber, 260/550 m (1000BASE-SX/LX) 50-μm MM fiber, 525/550 m (1000BASE-SX/LX) 150 Ω STP cable, 25 m (1000BASE-CX)
Signal Encoding		Manchester (all media)	4B/5B (100BASE-X) 8B/6T (100BASE-T4) PAM 5x5 (100BASE-T2)	8B/10B (1000BASE-X) {t.b.d} (1000BASE-T, under development)
Medium-Independent Interface		AUI (15-pin connector, 50 m) Bit-wide interface	MII (40-pin connector, 0.5 m) Nibble-wide interface	GMII (no connector or cable) Byte-wide interface
Automatic Configuration		Auto-Negotiation on 10BASE-T (UTP)	Auto-Negotiation on 100BASE-TX/T4/T2 (UTP)	Auto-Negotiation on 1000BASE-X and 1000BASE-T

must still be performed manually, 1000BASE-X Auto-Negotiation is not quite as useful as its UTP counterpart; it resolves only the problems of duplex operation and flow control configuration. On the other hand, if both ends are connected to compatible 1000BASE-X devices, you can be sure that these devices can communicate using the normal, 1000BASE-X signaling method. As such, the Auto-Negotiation signaling can (and does) use the same 8B/10B encoding and line drivers/receivers used for normal data exchanges, rather than the special-purpose link pulse signaling used on UTP cables.

1000BASE-X Auto-Negotiation uses the same protocol and message format as Auto-Negotiation on UTP cable. It changes only the electro-optical signaling used on the physical medium, and the semantics of some of the bits in the messages themselves. Like its Fast Ethernet equivalent, the Auto-Negotiation mechanism is extensible to support any additional features that may be added in the future.

When Gigabit Ethernet over UTP cable (1000BASE-T) is used, the existing UTP Auto-Negotiation protocol and signaling is used unchanged from Fast Ethernet. The semantics of the negotiated data are extended (love those extensible protocols!) to include the negotiation of the gigabit data rate itself, as well as any other characteristics needed by the physical signaling method employed.

9.2.8 Summary of 10/100/1000 Mb/s Ethernet Technology Migration

Table 9–5 summarizes the key differences among Ethernets operating at 10, 100, and 1000 Mb/s.

10 Gigabit Ethernet Media Access Control

This chapter discusses the Media Access Control (MAC) protocol for Gigabit Ethernet. It provides descriptions of the important changes made to the traditional Ethernet MAC for gigabit operation, as well as the operational parameters for IEEE 802.3z standard operation. While the presentation is thorough enough for all practical uses (and contains everything a network user or planner/administrator should ever need to know about Gigabit Ethernet MACs, and more), designers and implementors of Gigabit Ethernet MACs should use the standard itself for the formal specification of the protocol and interoperability requirements. [IEEE98]

Gigabit Ethernet (like its 10 Mb/s and 100 Mb/s cousins) can operate in either half-duplex or full-duplex mode. The use of a half-duplex MAC at gigabit speed poses some difficult problems that can result in restrictions on the allowable topologies and/or changes to the Ethernet MAC algorithm itself. The specification for the half-duplex Gigabit Ethernet MAC suffers both of these fates.

Full-duplex operation is actually simpler to implement (from a product standpoint) than a half-duplex MAC, but it comes with its own set of concerns. Notable of these are the nature of the devices that can connect, the Physical Layer technologies available, and the higher cost of hub equipment.

This chapter first examines the design of the half-duplex Gigabit Ethernet MAC, including:

- The limitations imposed by half-duplex operation,
- The basic algorithmic procedures of a half-duplex Ethernet MAC and the changes made for gigabit operation
- The specific parameters for operation according to the standard

Second, it considers the equivalent issues for full-duplex mode Gigabit Ethernet MACs. Fortunately, no changes are required to the algorithms for full-duplex Gigabit Ethernet relative to 10 Mb/s and 100 Mb/s operation; that is, none of the complexities encountered in half-duplex operation are applicable to full-duplex Gigabit Ethernet. Last, this chapter looks at the rationale and target applications for half- versus full-duplex Gigabit Ethernet.

10.1 Half-Duplex MAC

Traditionally, Ethernets have always used a half-duplex MAC. Efficient bidirectional communications with a half-duplex system is effected by rapidly changing the direction of communication on the half-duplex channel. In an Ethernet environment, in which stations can quickly arbitrate for the ability to send their frames (that is, align the half-duplex LAN to each station's advantage), this is not a problem. However, the extension of the Ethernet MAC algorithm to gigabit data rates does strain the ability to efficiently operate in this mode. When the arbitration time (equal to the round-trip delay, in the worst-case) approaches or exceeds the time to transmit a typical frame, the efficiency of the algorithm suffers.

10.1.1 Half-Duplex Ethernet MAC Operation[1]

The purpose of any MAC algorithm is to allow stations to decide when it is permissible for them to transmit on a shared physical channel. Ethernet uses a distributed algorithm called Carrier Sense, Multiple Access with Collision Detect (CSMA/CD). The IEEE 802.3 standard contains a precise, formalized specification of the CSMA/CD algorithm in Pascal code. [IEEE96] Readers interested in an exact, detailed description of the operation of CSMA/CD should refer to the standard itself. The description provided here is qualitative in nature and does not take into account some of the low-level details required in an actual implementation. A simplified flow chart of the algorithm is provided in Figure 10–1.

10.1.1.1 Frame Transmission in Half-Duplex Mode

When a station has a frame queued for transmission, it checks the physical channel to determine if it is currently in use (by another station). This process

---

1. If you have read this explanation in another book, you won't be hurting my feelings by jumping right to the new stuff! I am simply fulfilling the requirement that this explanation be present in every book that has the word "Ethernet" in the title. It's a union thing.

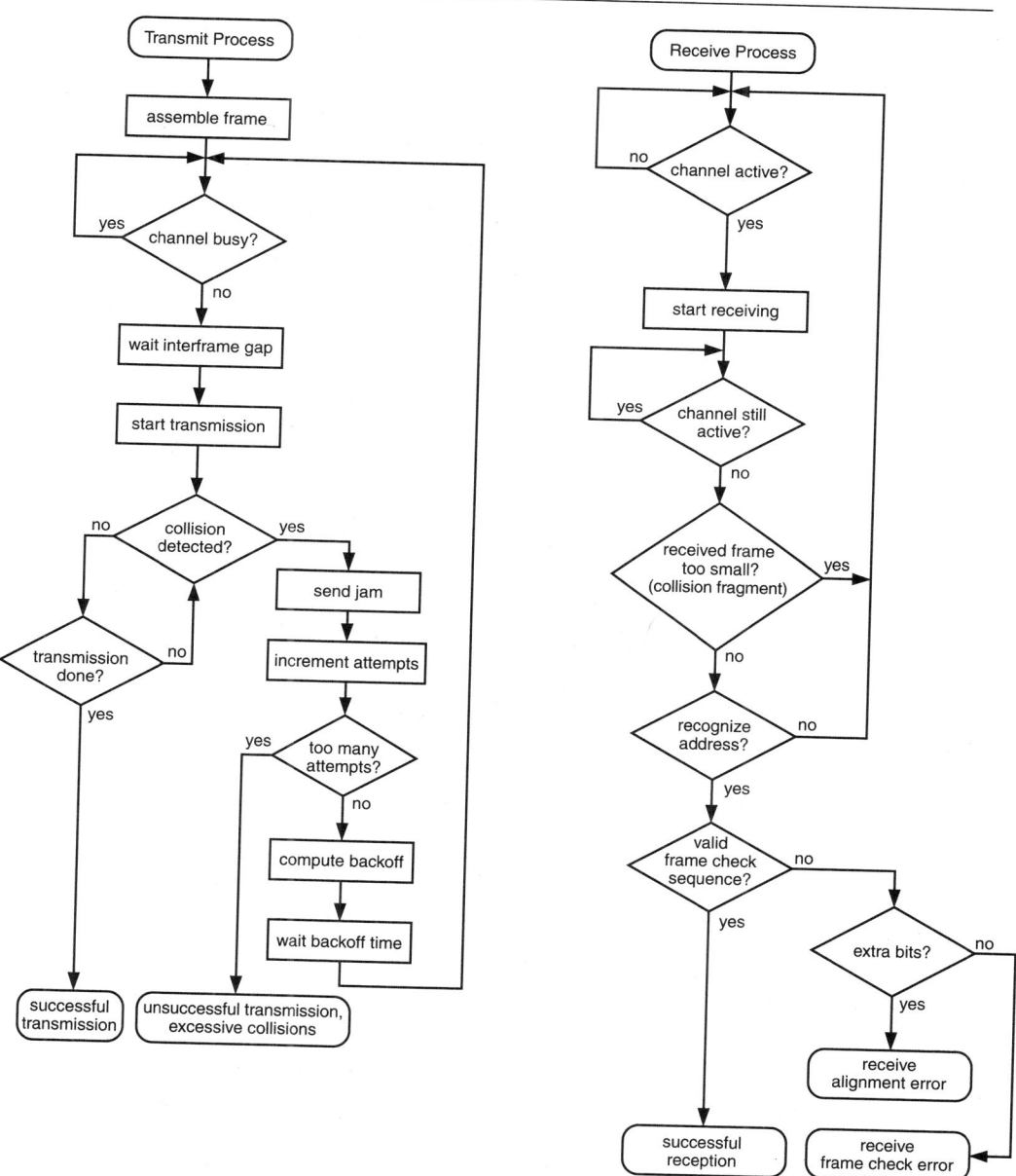

Figure 10–1 Ethernet MAC flow (conventional half-duplex operation).

is called *sensing carrier*. If the channel is busy, the station *defers* to the ongoing traffic to avoid corrupting a transmission in progress.[2]

After the end of the transmission in progress (that is, when carrier is no longer sensed), the station waits for a period of time—an *interframe gap*—to allow the physical channel time to stabilize and also to allow time for receivers to perform necessary "housekeeping" functions, such as adjusting buffer pointers, updating management counters, and interrupting a host CPU. After the expiration of the interframe gap time, the station begins its transmission.

If this is the only station on the network with a frame queued for transmission at this time, the station should be able to send its frame after the expiration of the interframe gap time with no interference from other stations. No other action is required, and the frame is considered delivered by the sending station after the end of the frame transmission. The station can then go on to process the next frame in the transmit queue (if any) using the same access control method.

On the other hand, if there are multiple stations with frames queued at the same time, each will attempt to transmit after the interframe gap expires after the deassertion of carrier sense. The resulting interference is called a *collision*. A collision will always occur if two or more stations have frames in their respective transmit queues and have been deferring to passing traffic. The collision resolution procedure is the means by which the Ethernet arbitrates among the stations to determine which one will be granted access to the shared channel.[3]

---

2. The use of the term "carrier" is historical. The ALOHA network [ABRA85] laid the architectural foundation for distributed MACs such as the one used in Ethernet. ALOHA used radio transmissions, and the presence of a transmission could be sensed by detecting the radio carrier that the station modulated with its data signal. Thus "carrier sense" came to mean "detecting the presence of a transmission on the shared channel." Ethernets do not use modulated carriers to transmit data (except for the relatively obscure 10BROAD36 CATV system [IEEE96, Clause 11]). It is interesting that many of the newer systems being developed for encoding high-speed signals onto transmission media *do* perform amplitude and/or phase modulation, even within a baseband system. This is likely to be the case with 1000BASE-T.

3. The use of the term "collision" is unfortunate. In most of life's activities, collisions (between automobiles, people, and so on) are to be avoided if possible. In Ethernet, a collision is simply a result of the normal arbitration for the use of the shared channel. It is not a "bad" thing, something to be avoided, but rather the way that Ethernet resolves contention. If it were termed an "arbitration cycle" rather than a collision, there would be a lot less concern over measuring collision rates and the world market for yellow LEDs would shrink dramatically.

Even if only one station was actually deferring its transmission to passing traffic, a collision can still occur because there is a non-zero time for signals to propagate across the physical channel. After the expiration of the interframe gap timer, there is a "window" (equal to the signal propagation delay of the physical channel) during which a station can be transmitting and other stations are not yet aware of the transmission. A station that queues a frame for transmission during this window will encounter a collision, even though it did not defer that transmission to passing traffic. Thus just deferring to carrier is insufficient to prevent simultaneous transmissions by multiple stations.

In the event of a collision, all involved stations continue to transmit for a short period to ensure that the collision is obvious to all parties. This process is called *jamming*.[4] After jamming, the stations abort the remainder of their intended frames and wait for a random period of time.[5] This is called *backing off*. After backing off, a station goes back to the beginning of the process and attempts to resend the frame. If a frame encounters 16 transmission attempts, all resulting in collisions, the frame is discarded by the MAC, the backoff range is reset, the event is reported to management (or simply counted), and the station proceeds with the next frame in the transmit queue, if any.

The backoff time for any retransmission attempt is a random variable with an exponentially increasing range for repeated transmission attempts. The range of the random variable r selected on the nth transmission attempt of a given frame is

$$0 \leq r < 2^k,$$

where $$k = \text{MIN}\,(n, 10).$$

Thus the station starts with the range $0 - 1$ on the first collision encountered by a given frame and increases the range to $0 - 3, 0 - 7, 0 - 15$, and so on, up to the maximum range of $0 - 1023$ with repeated collisions encountered by the same frame. The backoff time is measured in units of the round-trip

---

4. The station's behavior while jamming is no different from that during normal data transmission. It simply continues to send for a period of time to ensure that all parties to the collision are aware of it (that is, the collision event lasts for an appreciable time). There is no special "jam" signal.

5. It is the aborting of the remainder of the frame upon the detection of a collision that gives Ethernet its high performance relative to ALOHA-type protocols [KLEIN75]. The detection and resolution of collisions occurs very quickly, and channel time is not wasted sending the rest of a frame that has already been corrupted.

propagation delay of the channel, called the *slotTime*.[6] The range of the backoff variable is reset upon successful transmission of the frame—there is no history maintained between frames.

10.1.1.2 Frame Reception in Half-Duplex Mode

On the receive side, a station monitors the channel for an indication that a frame is being received. When the channel becomes nonidle in this manner, the station begins receiving bits from the channel, looking for the preamble and Start-of-Frame delimiter that indicate the beginning of the MAC frame. The station continues receiving until the end of the frame, as indicated by the underlying channel.[7]

A receiving MAC discards any frames received that are less than one slot-Time in length. This is because, by definition, these frame fragments must be the result of a collision, since valid frames will always be longer than the slotTime (which is equal to the round-trip channel propagation delay). Note that a receiver can therefore detect and discard collision fragments without requiring an explicit collision detection indication from the physical channel (as is required by transmitters) and without depending on checksum (CRC) invalidity.

If the received frame meets the minimum length requirement, the CRC is checked for validity. If the CRC does not match the proper value for the received frame, the frame is discarded. Assuming there is a valid CRC on a valid-length frame, the receiver will check the Destination address to see if it matches either:

1. the physical address of the station (unicast) or
2. a multicast address that this station has been instructed to recognize by software.

If either of these indicate that the frame is indeed destined for this station, the MAC passes the frame to its client (typically through device driver software) and goes back to the beginning, looking for newly received frames.

10.1.2 Limitations of Half-Duplex Operation

The use of CSMA/CD as an access control mechanism implies an intimate relationship between the minimum length of a frame and the maximum

---

6. The use of the term "slot time" is also historical and does not imply that Ethernet uses a slotted access method, such as that used in TDMA systems.

7. Depending on the specific physical channel implementation in use, the end of the frame may be indicated explicitly by an End-of-Stream delimiter (for example, in 100BASE-X and 1000BASE-X) or implicitly by the loss of carrier (for example, 10BASE-T).

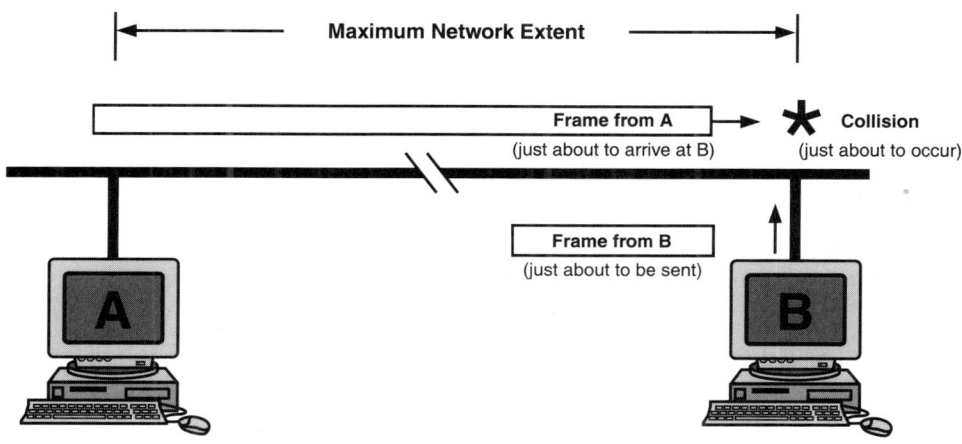

Figure 10–2 Worst-case collision timing.

round-trip propagation delay of the network. Consider the case of two devices separated by a maximum-length network, as shown in Figure 10–2.

If the network is quiescent, station A senses this through its carrier-sense mechanism and begins transmitting. Station B does not yet know of A's transmission, since it takes a non-zero period of time for A's frame to propagate down the medium toward B. If B has a need to transmit (that is, the driver has inserted a frame in the transmit queue before A's frame arrives at B), B will sense that the channel is still available (carrier sense is false until A's frame arrives) and begin its transmission.[8] Almost immediately after starting its transmission, B will sense the collision between its frame and that of A, perform its jam, abort the frame, and reschedule the transmission through the backoff mechanism. But A does not yet know of the collision, since it takes time for this information to propagate back to A. After one round-trip propagation time (from the time that A began sending its frame), A will also know of the collision event and perform its own jam, abort, and rescheduling.

But what if A's frame was so short that it could be completed before the collision information propagated back to A (in the worst-case)? From A's perspective, it would have sensed an idle channel, began a transmission, and completed sending the frame with no collision evident. After this sequence, A could reasonably notify its driver of the successful transmission, free up its frame buffer, and get on with the next frame in the queue. But *we* know

8. While this may seem to be a contrived situation, it is not rare. If station A is sending back-to-back frames and station B has been dutifully deferring to A's first frame, this worst-case collision scenario will always occur on A's second frame.

(being omniscient) that A's frame has irreparably collided with B. A will erroneously think that its frame was sent successfully when, in fact, it should be rescheduled.

This is like the man who complains to his doctor that, "It hurts when I hit my head against the wall." The doctor's response is, "Well, don't do that!" We need to make sure that if a collision occurs on a transmission, all stations know of the collision so that they can take proper action. This implies that the minimum length of a frame must be longer than the maximum round-trip propagation time of the network, plus an allowance for the jam time, synchronization delays, and so on.

We are presented with a tradeoff:

1. If we want to allow very long networks, we can make the minimum frame very long. This means that if a station wishes to send less data than implied by this minimum frame, it must pad the data to fit the minimum. Padding incurs processing overhead and reduces the transmission efficiency of the network for short data exchanges.

2. If we want to avoid the overhead of padding, we must reduce the extent of the network so that collisions can be detected in all cases.

For the original 10 Mb/s Ethernet, a compromise was struck. The minimum frame was set at 512 bits (64 bytes), not including the preamble and Physical Layer overhead. (See Figure 10–3.) The resulting minimum data field of 46 bytes rarely imposes a significant padding overhead. For example, the minimum length of the protocol headers for IP and TCP combined is 40 bytes. This leaves only 6 bytes to be accounted for by higher-layer data.

At 10 Mb/s, 512 bit-times is 51.2 µs. Depending on the type of cable used (for example, coaxial, twisted-pair, or optical fiber) and the configuration of the repeaters, the extent of a 10 Mb/s Ethernet can be on the order of from 2 to 3 km.[9] It is important to note that the minimum-length frame is measured

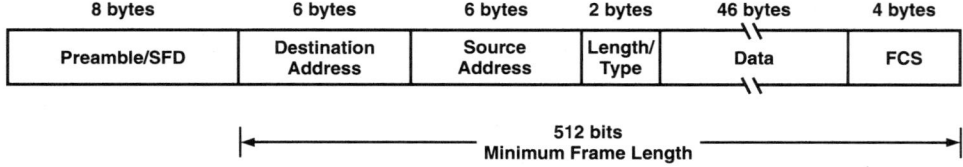

Figure 10–3 Minimum Ethernet frame.

---

9. Using 10BROAD36 (CATV) technology, a 3.6-km extent can be achieved. However, 10BROAD36 networks are rarely seen in practice today.

in *bit-times,* not absolute time. This means that, for a given minimum-length frame, the extent of the network scales inversely with data rate. This is shown in Figure 10–4.

When the 100 Mb/s Fast Ethernet system was being designed, a conscious choice had to be made to do one or more of the following.

- Increase the minimum frame length so that large networks (with multiple repeaters) could be supported.
- Leave the minimum frame as is, and decrease the extent of the network accordingly.
- Change the CSMA/CD algorithm to avoid the conflict.

The decision was heavily influenced by three factors.

1. By the mid-1990s, LANs were predominantly hub-centric, using twisted-pair wiring in a star configuration to a hub in a wiring closet. (See Chapter 2.) Thus the only truly important distance was from the user to the wiring closet. The building wiring standard [EIA91] ensures that this distance does not exceed 100-m radius to the closet (200-m diameter).

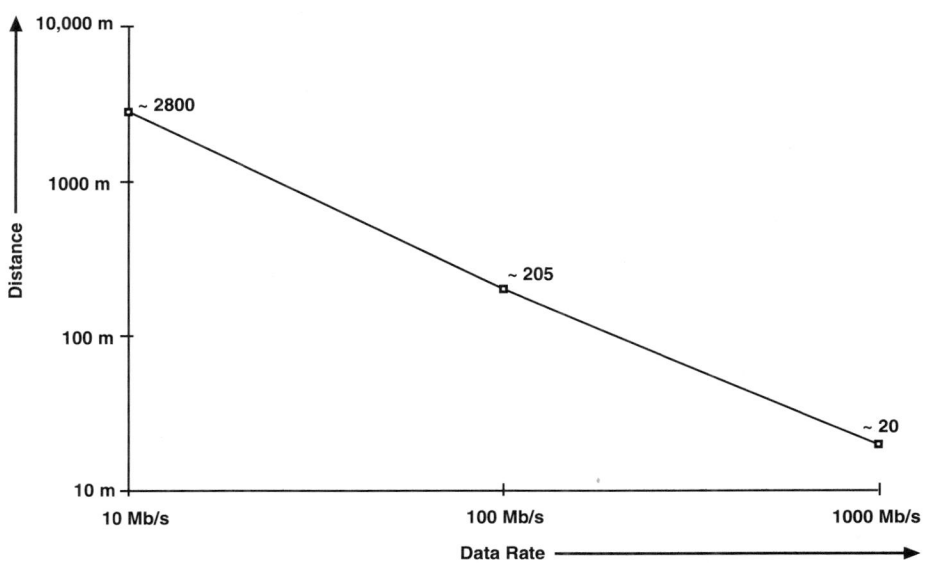

Figure 10–4 Distance scaling with data rate.

2. A change to the minimum frame length would have required changes to higher-layer software, including device drivers and protocol suite implementations. Also, it would be difficult to seamlessly bridge between 10 Mb/s and 100 Mb/s networks if the minimum frame length between the two differed. This would have significantly hampered the rapid deployment of Fast Ethernet.

3. A change to the CSMA/CD algorithm would have significantly delayed the release of the Fast Ethernet standard, which in turn would have delayed product schedules and allowed alternative technologies to obtain market share.

As a result, Fast Ethernet uses the same 512-bit minimum frame—with a concomitant decrease in the maximum network extent to the order of 200 m, using twisted-pair cabling—with no change to the CSMA/CD algorithm.[10]

If the same approach used with Fast Ethernet was used with Gigabit Ethernet (that is, to keep the 512-bit minimum frame and make no other algorithmic changes), the resulting network extent would be on the order of from 10 to 20 m! This is barely adequate for interconnection of devices within a single wiring closet; it is clearly inadequate for traditional LANs that have user and/or server attachments.

The solution adopted for Gigabit Ethernet has three elements:

1. Keep the 512-bit minimum frame, as seen at the software (device driver) interface. This eliminates the need to modify driver designs or existing protocol stacks in order to allow them to migrate to gigabit speed. It also allows seamless bridging (switching) among Ethernets at 10 Mb/s, 100 Mb/s, and 1000 Mb/s, since the frame characteristics are unchanged.

2. Modify the MAC algorithm (using a procedure called *carrier extension*) to artificially extend the frame as seen on the physical channel so that a short frame appears longer. This allows Gigabit Ethernet to continue to support the same wiring closet topology (100-m radius from the closet) without increasing the minimum length of the data portion of the frame.

3. Provide an optional performance enhancement for senders of short frames (called *frame bursting*). This is so that the inefficiency associated

---

10. The use of fiber links in particular configurations can increase the maximum extent to as much as 412 m.

with carrier extension does not significantly degrade the performance of either individual stations or the network as a whole when large numbers of short frames are sent.

The operational details of these techniques are described in the next sections.

10.1.3 Carrier Extension

In the 10 Mb/s and 100 Mb/s Ethernet systems, the minimum frame length is set equal to the maximum round-trip propagation delay of the network (less an allowance for jamming, synchronization, and so on). Thus the minimum frame length and the slotTime are the same value: 512 bits. Similarly, receivers discard frames that are shorter than 512 bits, since, being shorter than a slotTime, they must be collision fragments.

As discussed earlier in the chapter, because of the need to support practical network extents and the desire to maintain backward compatibility of the minimum frame length, something had to give. The solution was to modify the CSMA/CD algorithm to increase the minimum length of a transmission without increasing the minimum length of a frame as submitted or seen by the client of the MAC. This process is called *carrier extension*. A carrier-extended and a non–carrier-extended frame are depicted in Figure 10–5.

The key change is that the slotTime and the minimum frame are no longer the same. The minimum frame is maintained at 512 bits (64 bytes, as

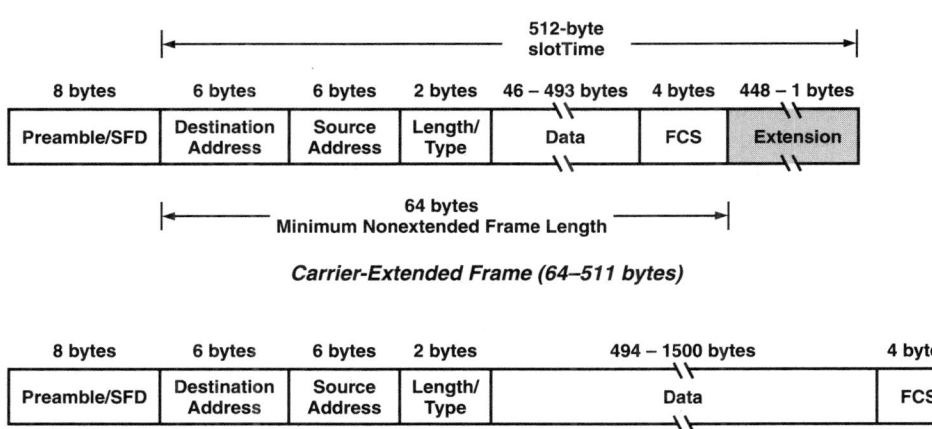

Figure 10–5   Carrier-extended and non–carrier-extended frames.

in 10 Mb/s and 100 Mb/s Ethernets), but the slotTime reflects the longer round-trip delay of the network at gigabit rates and has been set at 4096 bit-times (512 bytes).

As can be seen from the figure, frames that are shorter than the slotTime are artificially extended by appending a carrier-extension field so that they are exactly one slotTime long. This extends the duration of the time that the station transmits on the channel (that is, keeping Carrier Sense asserted in all of the other stations on the network) without extending the data field of the frame or altering the checksum (CRC). The contents of the extension field are sent by the Physical Layer as nondata symbols; that is, they are not interpreted as data at the receiver and are discarded.[11] The extension field is always an integral number of bytes and extends the transmission to the slot-Time (4096 bit-times). Frames that are already one slotTime in length (or longer) are not extended.

The collision window is still one slotTime; a station may expect to see collisions within one slotTime of beginning the transmission of a frame. However, unlike 10 Mb/s and 100 Mb/s Ethernet systems, the station may have completed the transmission of the data portion of the frame (and the CRC) before the occurrence of the collision. The Gigabit Ethernet MAC algorithm has been modified to recognize this possibility.

The MAC transmits the frame, including the extension field, while looking for a collision indication. If a collision occurs during any time from the beginning of the frame to the end of the extension field (as opposed to the end of the CRC only), the MAC will jam, abort, and backoff, as in all Ethernets. The only difference is the addition of the extension field by the MAC, transparent to its client.

A receiver on a 10 Mb/s or 100 Mb/s Ethernet will normally discard a frame that is shorter than the minimum valid data frame length, since the frame also will be shorter than a slotTime and therefore constitutes a fragment resulting from a collision. In Gigabit Ethernet, the slotTime is no longer the same as the minimum data frame length, so receivers need to do something slightly different. A receiver must discard received frames whose length, *including the extension field,* is shorter than a slotTime. This is true regardless of whether the station received the entire "significant portion" (that is,

---

11. Carrier extension can be used only on physical channels that provide an encoding means for nondata symbols. The 8B/10B system used for 1000BASE-X does this, as do most block-coding schemes. Manchester encoding, used in 10 Mb/s Ethernets, does not provide this capability, but this is not a problem, since carrier extension is not used on 10 Mb/s or 100 Mb/s Ethernets.

headers, data, and CRC) of the frame successfully. Since collisions can now occur outside of the boundary of the original MAC frame, the receiver must recognize that collision fragments can be longer than the data portion of the frame and discard them accordingly.

It seems wasteful for a receiver to discard a frame that has been received completely, without error, just because it may have been corrupted at some other point in the network. While a collision did occur, it occurred at a time when the transmitter was sending "filler" data (as seen at the receiver), to artificially extend the carrier. Unfortunately, even though the data portion of the frame may have been seen correctly at a receiver, the sender of the frame will recognize that there was a collision and perform its backoff and retry algorithm. The sender will resend the frame until it is sent without a collision indication. If receivers don't discard all collision fragments, even those carrying valid data frames, they will receive multiple copies of the same frame. This violates an invariant of Ethernet—that is, it delivers a maximum of one frame to a receiver for each one transmitted. Many applications and protocols are not designed to deal with the possibility of receiving multiple copies of the same frame and may produce unexpected results.[12]

10.1.4 Frame Bursting

The use of carrier extension for short frames imposes a significant performance degradation. The time used on the physical channel will always be a minimum of one slotTime (that is, 4096 bit-times), even if the actual frame is shorter than this. In the worst-case, the channel efficiency for a stream of minimum length frames of 512 bits with a 64-bit preamble/SFD and a 96-bit interframe gap is

$$\frac{512}{4096 + 64 + 96}, \text{or } 12\%.[13]$$

While typical Ethernet usage is not dominated by very short frames (sometimes called "tinygrams"), it is still significant. It was considered "bad form" to let the channel efficiency degrade so much under such conditions.

---

12. This is a nice way of saying they may crash.

13. On a 10 Mb/s or 100 Mb/s network, the efficiency for a continuous stream of minimum-length frames is

$$\frac{512}{512 + 64 + 96} = 76\%,$$

where the only inefficiencies are due to preamble/SFD (64 bits) and the interframe gap (96 bits).

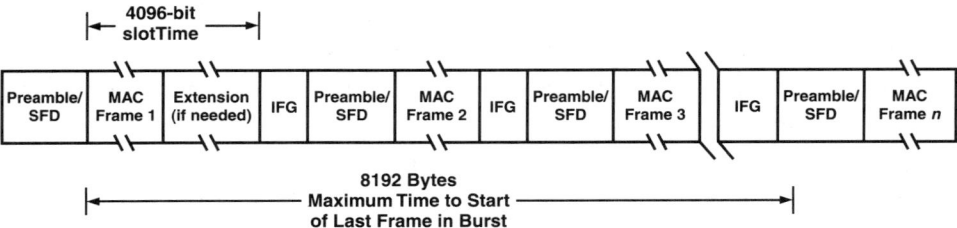

Figure 10–6 Frame bursting.

The solution is to allow a station to send multiple frames, while extending only the first one with carrier extension. This is called *frame bursting* and is depicted in Figure 10–6.

A station may choose to burst frames if there is a frame in its transmit queue when it has finished sending its first frame (plus extension, if necessary). As can be seen from Figure 10–6, the station sends its first frame in the normal manner, extending the carrier if necessary to the slotTime. If the station encounters a collision, it jams, aborts, and backs off as usual. No additional frames are sent if a collision occurs before the slotTime expires.

After that time, the station can begin sending additional frames *without contending again for the use of the channel*. This is because once the station has transmitted for one slotTime without encountering a collision, it is assured that all other stations are deferring to its carrier; thus there will be no collisions after this time. (The exception is called a *late collision* and is discussed shortly.) The station can send multiple frames in this manner. Each is separated from the previous one in the burst by an interframe gap time. The interframe gap is filled with nondata symbols in the physical channel (identical to the carrier extension symbols) so that the receiver obtains the benefit of the interframe gap without the transmitter's dropping its carrier signal on the channel (this would terminate the burst).[14] The bursting station may continue to start new frames for up to one burstLength, which limits the maximum time that a station is allowed to dominate the channel in this manner.

Transmitters are not required to implement frame bursting. This is a trade-off between the added complexity of the bursting algorithm and the performance improvement gained on short frame transmissions. Of course, a receiver must be prepared to receive bursted frames, since transmitters may

---

14. This is called an *active idle* signal.

implement this feature. This is no more difficult than receiving unbursted frames, since the frames are still separated by an interframe gap.

While the frame bursting mechanism was designed specifically to over-come the performance degradation imposed by carrier extension, there is no reason why it cannot be used even if carrier extension is not needed. That is, even if the first frame in a burst is longer than a slotTime, a station may continue to burst frames up to the burstLength time.

What happens if a collision occurs after the first slotTime during a burst of frames? Clearly, this should never happen, since the CSMA/CD algorithm ensures that after this time, all potential transmitters will be deferring to the carrier.

There are two possibilities that can cause such a *late collision:*

1. The round-trip propagation delay of the network exceeds the maximum allowed delay. This may be a configuration error (for example, cascading multiple repeaters in a Gigabit Ethernet) or an inadvertent use of cables that were longer than the installer may have thought them to be.

2. Some device has failed such that either it is unable to properly detect the transmission on the channel (carrier sense failure) or it is disobeying the proper CSMA/CD rules of behavior.

Late collisions are a problem in all Ethernets, not just Gigabit Ethernet. Unlike a normal collision, a late collision indicates a serious problem with the network—either an improper configuration or a faulty device. While the presence of millions of normal collisions may not indicate a problem, the presence of a single late collision should be reported to a network manager.

In a 10 Mb/s or 100 Mb/s Ethernet, a station can treat a late collision identically as a normal collision (for the purposes of backoff and retry). While the event is significant and should be reported, the proper behavior to take with regard to the instant frame encountering the late collision is the same as for a normal collision: jam, abort, backoff, and retry. There is no better course of action to take.

In a Gigabit Ethernet, though, a late collision can occur during a frame burst. The interface controller will have sent the entire first frame (and possibly more) before a late collision is detected. The frame buffers of the completely sent frames may already have been released to the device driver. In this case, it is no longer possible to go back and retry the transmission due to the collision. Worse, the algorithm gets complicated by the fact that a single collision may require the retransmission of multiple frames. The retransmission of those frames could cause frame duplication at the receiver, thus violating an Ethernet invariant. Therefore, upon encountering a late collision, a Gigabit Ethernet MAC simply jams and aborts the frame in progress without invoking any backoff or retry. Any affected frames are simply discarded by the MAC. Fortunately, late collisions are an extremely rare event, so this problem does not significantly affect application performance.[15]

Why not avoid the carrier extension altogether if we are going to burst frames? Why not just start bursting after the first frame and not waste the extension time? Remember that a normal collision can occur at any time up to the slotTime. If we allow multiple frame transmissions within the first slot-Time, then a normal collision could occur after the first frame in the burst but still within the slotTime. This imposes the identical complexity that we wanted to avoid with retransmission of frames in a burst affected by a late collision! The transmitter would have to keep all of the frame buffers outstanding (until the end of the slotTime) and take on the task of rescheduling multiple frames rather than just one.

Even worse, consider the plight of the receiver. It would be possible to burst up to six minimum-length frames within the first slotTime. A receiver could be validly receiving these frames but could not deliver them to the device driver. A normal collision could still occur right up to the end of that sixth frame, thus necessitating that the receiver discard all of the received frames to prevent delivering duplicates to the driver. (The transmitter will be resending all of these frames as a result of the collision.) In the interest of controller simplicity, the first frame is therefore carrier-extended (if necessary) and frames are bursted after that time, when there is no possibility of a normal collision.

10.1.5 Gigabit Ethernet Half-Duplex Operational Parameters

Like its 10 Mb/s and 100 Mb/s counterparts, the Gigabit Ethernet half-duplex MAC has several parameters that control its specific behavior. Of

---

15. A similar problem can occur in 10 Mb/s or 100 Mb/s systems, depending on the architecture of the memory buffers and the DMA engine in the interface controller. One commonly used implementation uses a "scatter-gather" DMA engine with link-listed buffers of 64 bytes or more. If a collision is encountered in the first slotTime (a normal collision), the controller is still operating on the first buffer in the linked list (that is, the first 64 bytes are within the slotTime) and the controller can restart the transmission using the same buffer. If the collision occurs after the first 64 bytes (a late collision), the controller may have already relinquished ownership of the first buffer to the device driver, so it can no longer go back to retry the transmission from the beginning. It must simply abort the frame transmission. With such a controller, the behavior due to a late collision for a single frame that has been scattered over multiple buffers is very much like that of multiple frames being sent as a burst in Gigabit Ethernet.

A Philosophical Aside

The normal Ethernet CSMA/CD algorithm is "fair" in the sense that over time, all stations have an equal probability of obtaining the use of the channel. This fairness is on a "frame basis"; once a station acquires the channel it may send a single frame. If some stations regularly need to send short frames and some regularly send long frames, they will each get an equal opportunity to send their frames. The station sending long frames, however, will use a greater portion of the available channel bandwidth.

Frame bursting is also fair, but on a "bandwidth basis"; that is, once stations acquire the channel, they may send data for up to a burstLength time (plus one frame), regardless of whether the frames are short or long. A station using the frame bursting algorithm is not penalized as much (in terms of available bandwidth) for sending short frames as it is in the traditional CSMA/CD algorithm.

Neither approach is inherently better than the other. Depending on the application requirements and the traffic model, one or the other may be more appropriate. If all stations use a mix of frame lengths, there will be no significant difference (other than the fact that frame bursting is more channel-efficient). If the available channel bandwidth is much greater than the total offered load, then it doesn't make much difference either way.

---

those parameters that apply to all data rates, very few were changed for Gigabit Ethernet. The most notable exception is the slotTime parameter (discussed in greater detail later in the section). This change resulted from the use of carrier extension to increase the effective duration of a minimum frame.

Each of the important parameters of half-duplex Gigabit Ethernet operation are explained in this section. The parameter names come from the IEEE 802.3/802.3z standard [IEEE96, IEEE98], which formally specifies how these parameters control the behavior of the half-duplex MAC (see specifically, the Pascal code in Clause 4).

minFrameSize	512 bits (64 bytes)

This parameter is the minimum length of a valid frame, including Destination address and Source address, Length/Type, Data, and the FCS fields, but not including any preamble and Start- or End-of-Frame delimiter. The Ethernet MAC pads frames containing fewer than this minimum by appending arbitrary data into the Data field. The FCS is computed on the frame after any such padding. The value of minFrameSize is constant across all data rates. This provides consistency for device drivers, higher-layer protocols, and bridges that want to treat all Ethernets identically, regardless of data rate.

maxFrameSize	12,144 bits (1518 bytes)

This parameter is the maximum length of a valid frame, including Destination address and Source address, Length/Type, Data, and the FCS fields, but not including any preamble and Start- or End-of-Frame delimiter. The value of maxFrameSize is constant across all data rates.[16]

In 10 Mb/s and 100 Mb/s systems, a station may transmit only one frame per channel access; that is, frame bursting is not defined for systems other than Gigabit Ethernet. Thus the maximum transmission time for a station operating at 10 Mb/s or 100 Mb/s is the maxFrameSize plus any preamble and Start- or End-of-Frame delimiter. In Gigabit Ethernet, the duration of a single transmission can be more than six times maxFrameSize due to frame bursting.

slotTime	4096 bit-times (4.096 µs)

This parameter simultaneously defines:

- The minimum duration of a *carrier event* (the length of time that the channel is busy) for a valid frame
- The maximum time from the beginning of a transmission during which a normal collision can occur (the *collision window*)
- The maximum round-trip propagation delay of the underlying physical channel (the network extent)
- The quantum of retransmission for backoff calculations

In 10 Mb/s and 100 Mb/s Ethernets, the slotTime and the minFrameSize are identical. In Gigabit Ethernet, the slotTime has been increased to accommodate practical network extents, as discussed earlier in the chapter. Carrier extension is used to keep the channel busy if the first transmitted frame of a burst is shorter than the specified slotTime.

In addition, when a station needs to back off after a collision, the chosen random number is multiplied by the slotTime to produce the actual time

---

16. At the time of this writing, there is work in progress in the IEEE 802.1Q Virtual LAN (VLAN) Task Force that will require Ethernet systems to increase this maximum by 4 bytes in order to accommodate a "VLAN tag" field. [IEEE97c] A project is ongoing within IEEE 802.3 (IEEE 803.3ac, of which I am the editor) to formally extend the maximum frame size to accommodate VLAN tags. Formal approval of these new standards is expected during 1998. [IEEE97d]

value for the backoff interval. This is necessary to ensure that stations choosing different random numbers will not collide again.[17]

extendSize	3584 bits (448 bytes)

This parameter is the maximum length of a carrier extension; it is equal to the slotTime minus the minFrameSize. A minimum-length frame will be carrier-extended by extendSize bits so that its duration is sufficient to ensure proper collision detection by all stations in the network.

10 Mb/s and 100 Mb/s Ethernets did not have carrier extension as part of their MAC, therefore this parameter applies only to Gigabit Ethernet. (In 10 Mb/s and 100 Mb/s systems [slotTime – minFrameSize] = 0, since both are defined as 512 bits.)

burstLength	65,536 bits (8192 bytes)

This parameter is the maximum time from the start of a transmission to the start of the last frame of a burst. That is, a station may continue to send frames (of any valid length) until one burstLength has been sent. If a frame is in progress when this threshold is crossed, that frame is completed normally. Thus the maximum duration of a frame burst is equal to burstLength + maxFrameSize. This maximum will occur if a station begins a maximum-length frame at precisely the time that the burstLength threshold is crossed.

As with carrier extension, 10 Mb/s and 100 Mb/s Ethernets do not have frame bursting as part of their MACs, so this parameter applies only to Gigabit Ethernet.

interFrameSpacing	96 bits

This parameter is the enforced minimum spacing between transmitted frames. Its purpose is primarily to allow receivers some time to recover between frames and to prepare to receive the next frame. It also provides time to allow the physical channel to settle to a quiescent state, if necessary.[18] The interFrameSpacing scales with the data rate. The actual time of the spacing is

---

17. The slotTime is the fundamental time quantum of a CSMA/CD MAC. Lower values for the slotTime will result in improved performance because less time is spent arbitrating the use of the channel and backing off. Unfortunately, lower slotTimes also reduce the permissible extent of the network, so a compromise must be reached.

18. This time is needed in coaxial systems and to a lesser extent in 10BASE-T. It is not needed when a continuous-signaling physical channel is used, such as 100BASE-X or 1000BASE-X.

9.6 µs, 960 ns, and 96 ns, respectively, for 10 Mb/s, 100 Mb/s, and 1000 Mb/s operation.

attemptLimit	16

This parameter is the maximum number of attempts that a MAC will make to transmit a frame in the face of repeated collisions. If all 16 attempts result in a collision, the MAC will discard the frame, report the error, and proceed with the next frame in the transmit queue (if any). This prevents transient network overload from creating a deadlock situation and consequently preventing progress for all stations. The value of attemptLimit is the same for all Ethernet data rates.

backoffLimit	10

This parameter is the maximum number of times that a station will double the upper bound of the range used for selection of random backoff intervals. The first ten attempts resulting in a collision will cause a concomitant exponential increase in the upper bound of the random number range, as indicated in Table 10–1.

TABLE 10–1 BACKOFF RANGES

Attempt	Random Number Range	
1	0–1	(2^1-1)
2	0–3	(2^2-1)
3	0–7	(2^3-1)
4	0–15	(2^4-1)
5	0–31	(2^5-1)
6	0–63	(2^6-1)
7	0–127	(2^7-1)
8	0–255	(2^8-1)
9	0–511	(2^9-1)
10	0–1023	$(2^{10}-1)$ [†]
11	0–1023	$(2^{10}-1)$
12	0–1023	$(2^{10}-1)$
13	0–1023	$(2^{10}-1)$
14	0–1023	$(2^{10}-1)$
15	0–1023	$(2^{10}-1)$
16	discard [‡]	

[†] backoffLimit
[‡] attemptLimit

Limiting the exponential increase in the backoff range reduces the maximum delay in transmitting (or discarding) a frame. If the backoff range doubled 16 times, the resulting backoff times could be excessive. The backoffLimit also places an absolute upper bound (at 1024) on the number of active stations within a single collision domain. The value of backoffLimit is the same for all Ethernet data rates.

jamSize	32 bits

This parameter is the length of the collision enforcement (jam) period. A station continues to transmit jamSize bits after detecting a collision to ensure that all transmitting stations properly see the collision event. The value of jamSize is the same for all Ethernet data rates.

10.2   Full-Duplex MAC

Now, forget everything you just read. (Yeah, right!) When an Ethernet operates in full-duplex mode, all of the complexity of carrier sense, collision detection, carrier extension, frame bursting, backoff ranges, and so on, has no bearing. All of this is needed only when multiple stations are contending for the use of a shared communications channel. Since full-duplex operation implies a dedicated channel (see Chapter 4), it avoids all of the complications of half-duplex operation. The full-duplex MAC is not really a MAC at all. This is because there is no need for a set of rules to determine when a station may transmit in full-duplex mode. With a dedicated channel, a station may transmit at will.

10.2.1   Limitations of Full-Duplex Operation

For full-duplex mode to be used, all of the following must be true.

- The underlying physical channel must be capable of supporting simultaneous, bidirectional communications without interference. This is true for both the 1000BASE-X and 1000BASE-T families of Physical Layer implementations (see Chapter 12).
- There must be exactly two devices on the LAN segment. These may be two end stations or, more commonly, an end station and a switch, or two switches.
- The interfaces in both devices must be capable of and configured to use full-duplex mode.

If all of these conditions are met, then full-duplex mode not only *can* be used, it *should* be used; there is no disadvantage to doing so.[19]

10.2.2 Operation of Full-Duplex MAC

Full-duplex MAC operation is trivial. A station may send a frame (subject to interframe spacing requirements, discussed shortly) any time there is a frame in its transmit queue and it is not currently sending a frame. Stations should similarly receive (and expect to receive) frames from the physical channel at any time, subject to interframe spacing.

Full-duplex MACs do not defer transmissions to received traffic. Nor do they detect collisions, jam, abort, backoff, or reschedule transmissions. The simultaneous transmission and reception of a frame is not considered a collision in full-duplex mode.

Unlike half-duplex operation, there is no need for carrier extension in full-duplex Gigabit Ethernet. Carrier extension was necessary only to ensure that short frame transmissions lasted long enough for the CSMA/CD algorithm to properly arbitrate the channel. Similarly, there is no explicit need for frame bursting in full-duplex. Full-duplex MACs can "burst" at any time (not just after an extended carrier) and for any length of time (not just for a burstLength period). There is no need to be concerned with monopolizing the channel, since the channel is dedicated to the full-duplex device.

10.2.3 Gigabit Ethernet Full-Duplex Operational Parameters

Very few parameters are necessary to control the behavior of a full-duplex Ethernet MAC. Many of the half-duplex parameters discussed in Section 10.2.1 are necessary only to ensure that the CSMA/CD algorithm behaves correctly in all stations attached to a shared medium and that the available capacity is shared fairly. With a dedicated channel, none of this is necessary. Thus, in full-duplex mode, there is no need to specify:

- slotTime
- extendSize
- burstLength
- attemptLimit
- backoffLimit
- jamSize

---

19. An exception is if the full-duplex link did not support flow control (see Chapter 6). Under certain traffic conditions, a half-duplex link using backpressure could result in better application performance.

The remaining parameters of full-duplex Gigabit Ethernet operation are described here. The values are all identical to those for half-duplex operation.

minFrameSize	512 bits (64 bytes)

Strictly speaking, there is no need to specify a minFrameSize for full-duplex operation. The only reason for having a minimum in the first place was to ensure that frames persisted long enough to still be in the transmission process following a round-trip propagation delay of the underlying channel.[20] This allows the collision detection procedures to work properly. Since full-duplex Ethernet does not perform any collision detection, there is no need to have any minimum frame (other than the Address, Length/Type, and FCS fields). Nonetheless, for device driver compatibility between half- and full-duplex MACs and backward compatibility with 10 Mb/s and 100 Mb/s Ethernet (seamless bridging), the minFrameSize constraint is retained in full-duplex Gigabit Ethernet. Since most higher-layer protocols use all (or nearly all) of the specified minimum anyway, this is not a real burden on either the driver software or overall network performance.

maxFrameSize	12,144 bits (1518 bytes)

There is no change in the maximum length of a frame for full-duplex operation.

interFrameSpacing	96 bits

There is no change in the interframe spacing for full-duplex operation.

10.3   Rationale and Target Applications for Half- versus Full-Duplex Gigabit Ethernet

Is a half-duplex (traditional) Ethernet MAC at gigabit rates needed? This is a reasonable question, especially since it is clear that some significant changes had to be made to the Ethernet design in order to support half-duplex operation at this speed.

There is only one advantage of half-duplex over full-duplex operation: Half-duplex (shared) LANs can use a repeater hub rather than a switching hub, thereby potentially saving some system cost.[21] A switching hub will always cost more than a repeater hub (on a per-port basis). However, over

---

20. In half-duplex Gigabit Ethernet, the minFrameSize does not meet this requirement; hence, carrier extension is used.

21. In theory, a half-duplex-only transceiver could be less expensive than a full-duplex-capable transceiver, particularly for 1000BASE-T. However, such transceivers do not currently exist.

time the difference shrinks considerably with competition and the availability of high-integration silicon switching components. The cost of the station attachment (NIC) is identical whether using shared or switched hubs.

So, to the extent that the hub constitutes a cost factor for the system as a whole, the system cost will be greater when using full-duplex rather than half-duplex operation, since full-duplex LANs require switching hubs. However, the ratio of *total system cost* is not the same as the ratio of hub costs. Total system cost includes the costs of station attachments, wiring components, management tools, and so on, all costs of which are the same for both full- and half-duplex networks. There is a premium paid to use full-duplex mode, but it is not very large and it decreases over time. In return for this price premium, you can avoid:

- Having to change the Ethernet MAC algorithms
- The performance degradation of carrier extension (for short frames)
- The performance limitations of CSMA/CD in general
- Any need to reduce network extent (distance)

In fact, you can operate a full-duplex Gigabit Ethernet over longer distances than you can even 10 Mb/s (shared) Ethernets. Further, the use of switching provides greater aggregate bandwidth.

Consider the three potential application areas for Gigabit Ethernet (discussed in detail in Chapter 14):

1. Desktop connectivity
2. Server connectivity
3. Backbone networks (building and campus environment)

The only application areas that can possibly benefit from a lower-cost half-duplex network are the first two. Backbone networks invariably require longer distances than can be supported by half-duplex Gigabit Ethernet, even with carrier extension. However, backbone networks are the primary application area for Gigabit Ethernet, especially during the period of its initial deployment. These networks often experience high traffic loads, which Gigabit Ethernet can well accommodate. Also, the higher cost of Gigabit Ethernet can be justified in the backbone, where it is amortized over a large number of users (for example, an entire campus).

At least initially, desktop devices (workstations) cannot really benefit from Gigabit Ethernet, because:

- Very few desktop computers today can take advantage of a 1 Gb/s communications channel because this speed is faster than the ability of most processors to move data. It makes no sense to upgrade a desktop

NIC to Gigabit Ethernet if the station cannot benefit from the increased speed.

■ The wiring systems in place to desktops (unshielded twisted-pair over distances of up to 100 m) are not initially supported by Gigabit Ethernet.

Server clusters could conceivably benefit from half-duplex Gigabit Ethernet. However, the cost benefit obtained is relatively small. This is because the per-port savings is only for server connections, not for desktop connections, and there are many fewer servers than desktop devices.

Also, the use of Buffered Distributors has the potential to reduce to insignificant the cost difference between half- and full-duplex networks. (A Buffered Distributor is a low-cost, full-duplex switching hub with reduced performance relative to a traditional switch, and is discussed in Chapter 11.) If low-cost Gigabit Ethernet is needed for server and future desktop applications, this need can be served by Buffered Distributor–based systems, without invoking half-duplex operation.

If the primary application area (at least initially) for Gigabit Ethernet is backbone networks (requiring full-duplex operation for distance reasons) and the cost savings for half-duplex operation are small and hard to realize in practice, why did the industry bother to develop a half-duplex Gigabit Ethernet standard?

The answer is more political than technical. Gigabit Ethernet was developed under the auspices of the IEEE 802.3 Working Group. By definition, 802.3 networks must include the capability of CSMA/CD operation. If Gigabit Ethernet offered a full-duplex-only solution, it would have been difficult to justify its development within the IEEE 802.3 Working Group. This would have resulted in some important political difficulties, including the following:

1. A new Working Group would have to have been formed within IEEE 802. Doing this takes considerably more time than a new project within an existing Working Group and would have delayed the development of the standard.

2. The resulting standard would have had difficulty calling itself "Ethernet," since it would not use CSMA/CD (even as an option) and it would not have been developed as part of IEEE 802.3, the recognized "owner" of the Ethernet name.[22]

---

22. This is one reason for the market failure of the 100VG-AnyLAN technology developed by Hewlett-Packard and the IEEE 802.12 Working Group [IEEE95a]. While there was nothing wrong with the technology (indeed, it has some potential advantages over traditional Ethernet), the alternative, Fast Ethernet, was "Ethernet," thus making it much less intimidating to customers as an upgrade option.

So, rather than fight the system, the IEEE 802.3z Task Force chose to work on both half-duplex and full-duplex Gigabit Ethernet, making modifications to the CSMA/CD algorithm to support reasonable distances in half-duplex mode. The real rationales for the specification of half-duplex Gigabit Ethernet are standards-committee machinations and market positioning. Few industry observers believe that there will be much (if any) half-duplex Gigabit Ethernet deployment.

11 Gigabit Ethernet Hubs

Hub is the generic name for a device that is physically located at the center of a star-wired network. With the exception of the degenerate case of a two-station network connected with a point-to-point link, all Gigabit Ethernets require a hub.[1] Originally (in 10BASE-T, the first hub-centric Ethernet system), hubs implemented repeater functionality only. As switching became technologically and economically feasible for large numbers of ports, switching hubs emerged as a practical, higher-performance alternative. It is also possible to deploy a Network Layer router in a wiring hub or to provide combinations of repeater, switch, and routing functionality in a practical product. This chapter explores the available options for Gigabit Ethernet hubs, including

- Repeaters,
- Switches, and
- Routers.[2]

It also considers a special case of a switching hub—the *Buffered Distributor.*

A commercial hub *product* may combine the capabilities of two or more of these approaches (for example, an integrated switch/router, or *swouter*). However, for the purposes of the discussion in this chapter, hubs are considered

---

1. This is also true for 10BASE-T, 10BASE-F, and 100BASE-T networks.

2. Pronunciation guide: **router** (ro͞ot´ər) noun
    A device that forwards traffic between networks.
    router (rou´t ər) noun
    A machine tool that mills out the surface of metal or wood.

from the *functional* perspective only; that is, repeaters, switches, and routers are treated as discrete, separable entities.

11.1 Repeaters

A repeater is the "classic" Ethernet hub. A Gigabit Ethernet repeater, shown in Figure 11–1, does the following.

- Provides a physical port for every attached station.
- Creates a single, shared LAN (single collision domain, see Chapter 3) for all attached stations.

Since none of the physical media supported by Gigabit Ethernet provides for multidrop operation (that is, there are no shared media), a repeater is *required* for all shared Gigabit Ethernets that have more than two stations. The purpose and overall behavior of the repeater is unchanged from that at 10 Mb/s or 100 Mb/s. The total channel capacity (1 Gb/s, in this case) is shared by the attached stations and is allocated by the CSMA/CD MAC algorithm. This algorithm is implemented by the MAC entities in the attached stations (that is, not by the repeater, which does not have a MAC at all). Thus a repeater can be used only by stations operating in half-duplex mode (those implementing the CSMA/CD algorithm).

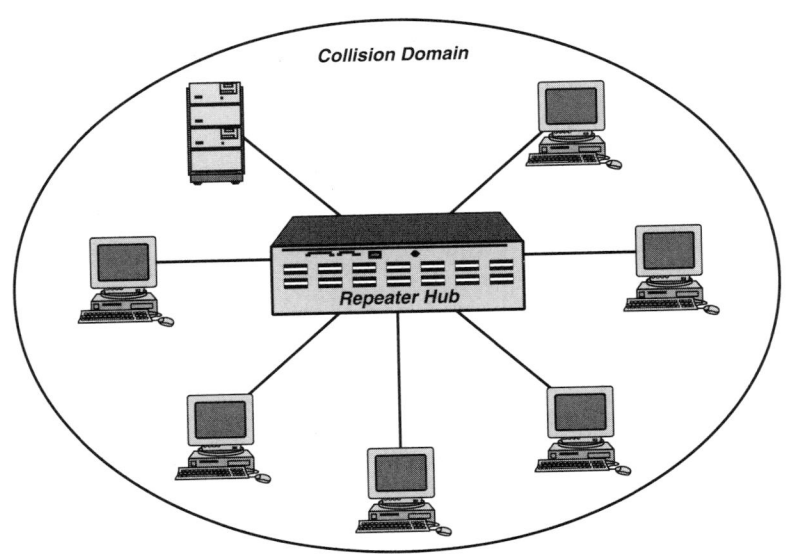

Figure 11–1 Repeater hub configuration.

The number of station connections that can be provided on a given repeater is implementation-dependent, although traditionally, single repeaters have provided between 8 and 24 ports.[3]

11.1.1 Repeater Operation

Figure 11–2 depicts a block diagram of a repeater. (This is a high-level functional depiction and is not intended to be either complete in the details or representative of any particular implementation.) A repeater operates at the Physical Layer of the OSI model [ISO94]. A physical interface is provided for every port, as well as a set of logic (typically implemented as a finite-state machine) that propagates signals as necessary among ports so that the attached stations see the group as *logically* sharing a single physical channel.

A repeater provides the following basic functions.

- **Restores signal amplitudes and timing.** The repeater transmits signals onto each port with the full amplitude, correct waveshape, and proper clock characteristics specified for the medium and encoding scheme in use, regardless of the characteristics present in the received signal being repeated. The signal emanating from a repeater port meets the same requirements as the signal emanating from a transmitting end station. The signal-to-noise ratio and waveshape characteristics are restored, and timing distortion (jitter) is removed by the repeater. Thus communications signal budgets (amplitude, noise, and timing) apply to each link individually; signal degradation is not cumulative among links.

- **Receives and propagates data transmissions.** Under noncollision (and nonidle) conditions, the repeater receives data from a transmitting end station and retransmits it to all repeater ports except the one from which it arrived. The repeater is not a frame store-and-forward device. The only delays through the repeater are those required for receiver, decoder, state machine, clock synchronization, and transmitter operation.[4]

---

3. In the early days of 10BASE-T, there was some demand for repeater hubs with high port densities—on the order of 100 or more. As the bandwidth requirements of the attached stations has grown, the ability of a shared LAN to support such large numbers of devices has disappeared; switching hubs are used instead. It is unlikely that there will be a need for Gigabit Ethernet repeaters that have very high port density.

4. A repeater should introduce as little delay as possible while still performing its required functions. The IEEE 802.3z standard specifies a default round-trip propagation delay of 976 bit-times for a Gigabit Ethernet repeater, but the actual value is implementation-dependent.

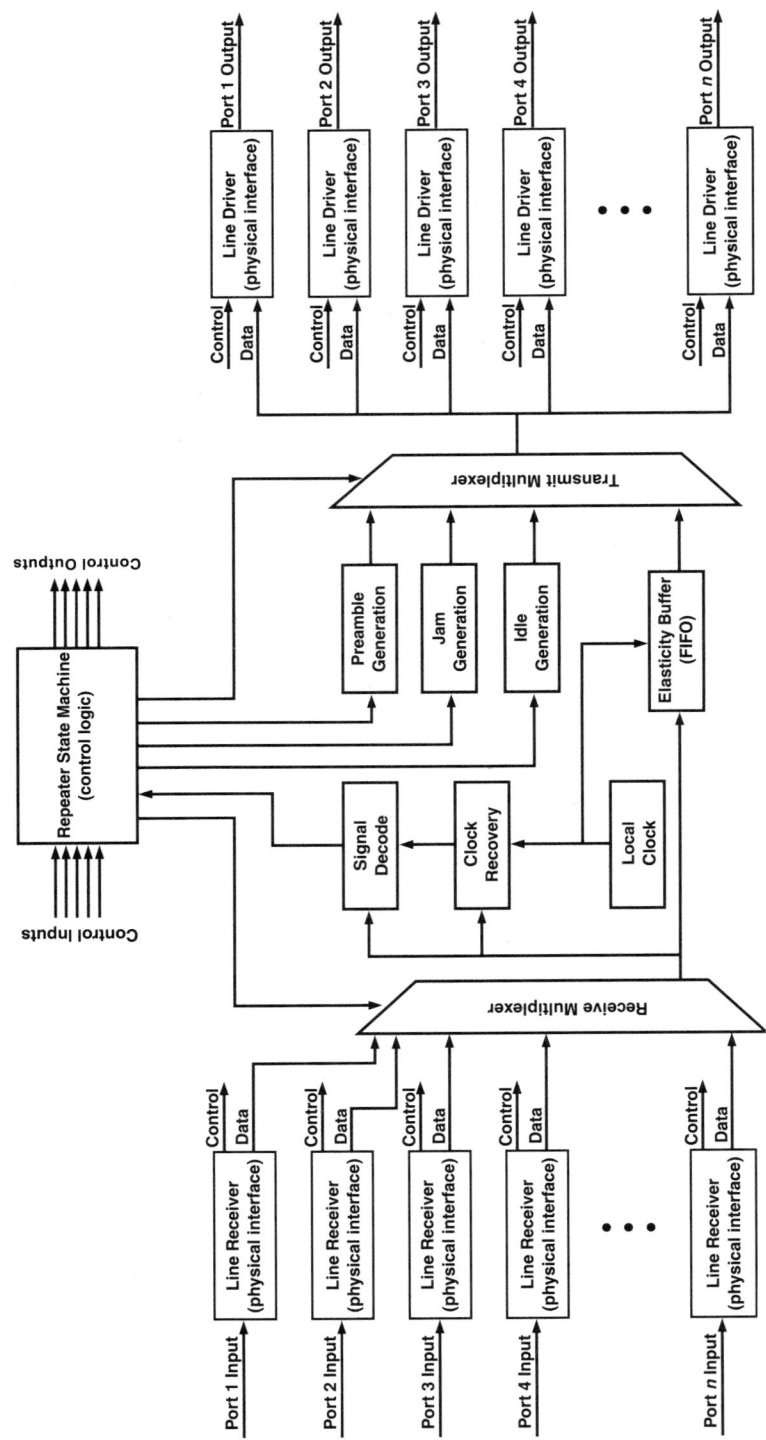

Figure 11–2 Repeater block diagram.

A repeater regenerates preamble (if necessary[5]) to ensure that there is always a guaranteed minimum preamble that precedes actual frame data. Once the repeater begins repeating what it believes is a valid frame, all signals are repeated, including possible errors. The repeater does not perform data error checking on the transmitted data. Instead, transmission errors will be rejected by either the decoder (due to block code validity checking) or the FCS (CRC) calculation performed in the end station's receiver.

- **Detects and propagates carrier sense.** Each repeater port looks for the presence of activity (that is, carrier sense) and, when such activity is detected, triggers the repeater state machine so that all attached stations are made aware of the activity. This is required for proper operation of the MAC entities in the end stations.

- **Detects and propagates collision detect.** Similarly, the repeater looks for simultaneous activity on multiple ports, defining this as a collision. The repeater state machine propagates this collision information to all of the involved parties so that proper collision resolution can occur (jam, backoff, and rescheduling). Note that when there is no true shared medium, the repeater is the *only* device capable of detecting simultaneous transmissions from multiple stations. Unless this collision information is propagated by the repeater, the CSMA/CD MAC algorithm in the end stations would not work properly.

In addition, a Gigabit Ethernet repeater:

- **Detects and isolates faulty links.** A single faulty link could conceivably present signals to the repeater that would propagate to all other segments. This could cause a local fault to become network-wide and catastrophic. While a repeater cannot detect and isolate every possible link fault, many potential problems are eliminated by having the repeater use some discretion before "qualifying" the link for inclusion in the repeated set. In particular, the repeater looks for signals that do not meet the criteria for valid transmissions (called *false carrier*) and will prevent their propagation. Continued false carriers will cause the repeater to isolate that link until the condition is corrected.

---

5. When frame-asynchronous (stop-start) signaling methods are used, such as with Manchester-encoded 10 Mb/s Ethernets, preamble bits may be "consumed" by receiver circuitry. Preamble regeneration is necessary here to ensure that a minimum number of preamble bits is always present (that is, the consumption is not cumulative). With continuous-signaling schemes, as implemented with the 8B/10B block coding used in Gigabit Ethernet (and the 4B/5B block coding used in Fast Ethernet), there is less likelihood of preamble shrinkage.

A Gigabit Ethernet repeater may also detect that the attached device is attempting to operate at a data rate other than 1000 Mb/s and isolate that link. Of course, all stations on a shared LAN must operate at the same data rate.

■ **Detects and isolates "jabbering" stations.** One particularly insidious failure mode for a CSMA/CD network is a station that continuously transmits. This is called *jabbering*. A jabbering station causes carrier sense to be continuously asserted and effectively blocks all use of a shared LAN. A repeater looks for this condition and isolates the offending station.[6]

11.1.2 Repeater Management

For the purpose of creating the shared CSMA/CD LAN, a repeater operates exclusively within the Physical Layer of the OSI model. However, a practical repeater may need to provide certain network management features so as to allow fault isolation, performance monitoring, and so on. These functions require that the repeater incorporate higher-layer capabilities. Figure 11–3 depicts a simplified block diagram of a *managed repeater*. A managed repeater incorporates all of the repeater functions and, in addition, provides what is effectively an entire end-station protocol stack implementation just for management.

It is important to recognize that this higher-layer functionality (including any MAC, CPU, memory, and management protocol implementation) is unrelated to the operation of the device as a repeater. The management subsystem is not involved in any of the repeater functions discussed earlier in the chapter. The repeater state machine is not involved in any of the management protocol interaction. The only commonality is that the repeater subsystem provides a set of managed objects (counters, control variables, and so on) that can be read and/or manipulated by the management subsystem.

The standards, both IEEE 802.3 and the relevant IETF RFCs, specify a set of universal managed objects (a Management Information Base, or MIB) for repeaters. [RFC1516, RFC2108] The standards bodies have extended (or are in the process of extending—MIB extensions are a never-ending task) the Repeater MIB to include Gigabit Ethernet repeaters. Vendors often provide proprietary extensions to the standard repeater MIBs to allow the management of implementation-specific features.

---

6. Research is underway to determine if this mechanism can be extended for use on politicians and university lecturers.

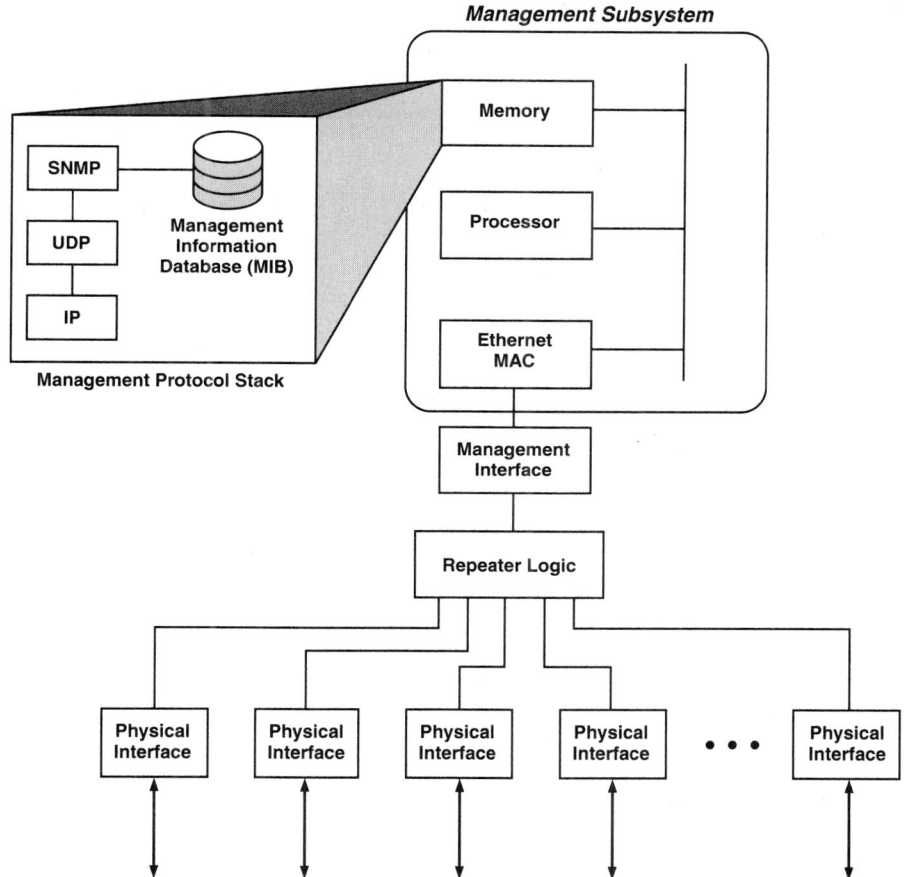

Figure 11–3 Managed repeater.

11.1.3 Allowable Repeater Configurations for Gigabit Ethernet

The height of shared Ethernet configuration complexity occurred in 1993 with the publication of IEEE 802.3j (10BASE-F, [IEEE93]) and its concomitant enhancements to the System Guidelines [IEEE96, Annex B]. This latter document provided a means for calculating (using multiple methodologies, yet!) whether a given configuration mix of coaxial cables, 10BASE-T segments, optical-fiber repeaters, and point-to-point links met the system budget requirements with respect to propagation delay and interframe gap shrinkage.[7]

---

7. This document has also been called the Network Consultant's Full Employment Act of 1993.

TABLE 11–1 LINK LENGTH LIMITS FOR SHARED GIGABIT ETHERNET

Media Type	Maximum Link Length
1000BASE-T (UTP cable)	100 m
1000BASE-CX (STP cable)	25 m[1]
1000BASE-LX/SX (optical fiber)	111 m

1. 1000BASE-CX is limited by the capabilities of the physical medium itself and not the timing constraints of the collision domain.

Since then, the complexity of repeated Ethernet configurations has become progressively simpler, primarily due to the strict timing constraints imposed by higher-speed operation. For Gigabit Ethernet, the rule is trivial. There can be only one repeater for a shared Gigabit Ethernet LAN, period. The minimal configuration shown in Figure 11–1 is also the maximal configuration.

The maximum length of the attached links is a function of the media type used, as shown in Table 11–1.

The lengths listed assume that all links are of the same type—there is no mix of dissimilar media. The diameter of the network (that is, a single collision domain) is twice the length of any individual link shown in the table. Chapter 12 contains a complete discussion of possible configurations, including the (slight) variations possible by mixing media types.

11.1.4 Performance of Shared Gigabit Ethernet LANs

Numerous papers have been written about both the theoretical and measured performance of shared Ethernet LANs under a variety of offered load assumptions. [BOGG88] Most of this work is based on 10 Mb/s Ethernets, but it is generally applicable to Fast Ethernet as well, since there were no changes to the CSMA/CD algorithm for 100 Mb/s operation.

However, the performance of a shared Gigabit Ethernet LAN will be worse than would be predicted from a simple scaling of the numbers from 10 to 100 to 1000, for a few important reasons:

■ The efficiency of traditional Ethernet is due in great part to the fact that very little time is wasted in collision resolution, relative to the time required to transmit typical data frames. That is, the round-trip propagation delay (the slot time) is normally only a small fraction of the frame length.[8] Collisions are detected and resolved within the first slotTime. On a 10 Mb/s or 100 Mb/s Ethernet, a slotTime (512 bit-times) constitutes 4.2% of a maximum-length frame (1518 bytes) and 12% of a work-group-average frame length of 534 bytes [AMD96]. That is, a collision on a 10 Mb/s or 100 Mb/s Ethernet wastes a maximum of 12% of the time required to send an average frame and only 4.2% of the time required to send a long frame. Even less time would be wasted if the stations were physically positioned on the LAN such that they detected the collision in less than one slotTime. The one-slotTime waste is the worst-case for maximally spaced interfering stations.

In Gigabit Ethernet, the slotTime increases from 512 bit-times to 4096 bit-times. This increases the worst-case collision overhead to 96% of the work group-average frame length and 34% of a maximum-length frame. Clearly, frame bursting improves this considerably, as there is no wasted time for subsequent frames in a burst. However, under certain conditions of offered load (for example, heavy load from a large distribution of stations each attempting to send individual frames without bursting), the utilization of the LAN will be less than predicted by the earlier research. Also the end-station performance will not be simply scaled by a factor of 10 or 100 from lower-speed Ethernets.

If there ever exists a significant installed base of shared Gigabit Ethernet LANs, more data will be available to quantify the real reduction in performance seen, in comparison with this theoretical degradation.

■ On a 10 Mb/s network, stations will normally be physically located much closer to each other than the worst-case; that is, there is rarely a slotTime of round-trip delay between potential colliders. Indeed, on a network consisting of a single 10BASE-T repeater (a common configuration), the delay is so low that all collisions occur during the preamble! This shorter *real delay* (compared to the worst-case delay) makes the real performance of 10 Mb/s Ethernet much better than the worst-case predictions.

However, in Gigabit Ethernet, many (if not all) stations will be located at or near the worst-case spacing possible, because:

• Practical distances from a wiring closet are of the same order of magnitude as the maximum allowable distance (tens to hundreds of meters).

---

8. This ratio of round-trip delay to frame length (called *a* in [TANEN88]) is a critical parameter in determining the arbitration efficiency of all CSMA-based networks.

- A significant portion of the overall delay budget is consumed by the repeater itself, which is there even if the stations are physically adjacent to the repeater and each other.

  Therefore, unlike 10 Mb/s Ethernet, the typical performance of 1000 Mb/s CSMA/CD will approximate the worst-case performance.

■ Even when collisions are not considered, the use of carrier extension imposes additional channel overhead. A station will experience a performance degradation relative to earlier incarnations of Ethernet to the extent that a station or application uses frames shorter than a slotTime (512 bytes) and cannot leverage frame bursting (either because the optional feature was not implemented in the device or the frame arrival distribution is such that there are never multiple frames in the transmit queue to burst).

11.1.5 Advantages and Disadvantages of Repeaters

Why should someone use a repeater? There are three driving forces:

1. Cost,
2. Cost, and
3. Cost.

In addition, repeaters can save money. A repeater hub is the lowest-price, lowest-performance hub possible for a Gigabit Ethernet. It represents one extreme of the price/performance trade-off.

The available capacity of a shared Gigabit Ethernet is always less than or equal to 1000 Mb/s. The actual throughput and utilization will be a function of the statistical distribution of the offered load among stations, as well as over time and frame length. Even so, attached devices get gigabit-style throughput and delay characteristics for bulk file transfers under light load. That is, a repeater-based Gigabit Ethernet may make sense if the intent is not to achieve high utilization or to maintain high *sustained* throughput, but to provide very low delay under light, bursty load conditions. This is precisely the model of the original 10 Mb/s Ethernet (at least when it was first conceived). It is only now, when there are devices that can saturate 10 Mb/s, and even 100 Mb/s networks, that shared LANs are considered to be "low performance" and switched hubs with higher aggregate capacity are used regularly.

11.1.6 Applications for Shared Gigabit Ethernet LANs

Cost tends to become more significant to users when the product volumes are high. For a campus backbone, cost is relatively insignificant; no one buys a lot of such products. For desktop connections, cost becomes extremely important because product costs are multiplied by as much as thousands to accommodate all users in a large organization. Hence, Gigabit Ethernet repeaters may become important when the technology moves from the backbone to the desktop.

The use of Gigabit Ethernet at the desk is constrained by several factors:

■ Current building wiring practice provides only UTP to most desktops. Unless and until Gigabit Ethernet provides a transmission solution that works reliably over the installed base of UTP cabling, it will be very difficult to deploy in significant quantities for desktop applications. There is currently no standard technology available for Gigabit Ethernet over UTP.

■ Very few desktop devices can take advantage of Gigabit Ethernet, even if it was available. Network throughput is limited less by network capacity

---

One Man's Opinion

While Gigabit Ethernet repeaters (and shared CSMA/CD gigabit LANs) are discussed here in a technically correct manner, I do not believe that they make much sense as commercial products or that they will be widely deployed.

Currently, the application driving the "need for gigabit speed" is the campus backbone. This application cannot use half-duplex mode (shared LAN) due to the round-trip delay restrictions. All backbone connections will need to use full-duplex mode, with switching or routing hubs. In addition, this is a performance-intensive environment. Why would anyone pay the price for Gigabit Ethernet without getting the capacity that a switched hub provides?

Since the only real advantage of repeaters is their lower cost, they become important only when the technology moves to the desktop, with its increased volumes. This will not happen for a few years at the soonest due to the unavailability of a low-cost UTP delivery mechanism and the lack of real need for this level of performance. By the time Gigabit Ethernet is needed at the desktop, switch costs may be reduced to the point where the savings offered by a repeater is not worth the loss of performance. This is the current situation with 10 Mb/s Ethernet and is rapidly occurring with Fast Ethernet as well. In addition, Buffered Distributors (discussed later in this chapter) offer a solution for Gigabit Ethernet that is cost-competitive with shared repeaters, while providing the longer distances of full-duplex operation and a higher level of performance than a CSMA/CD LAN.

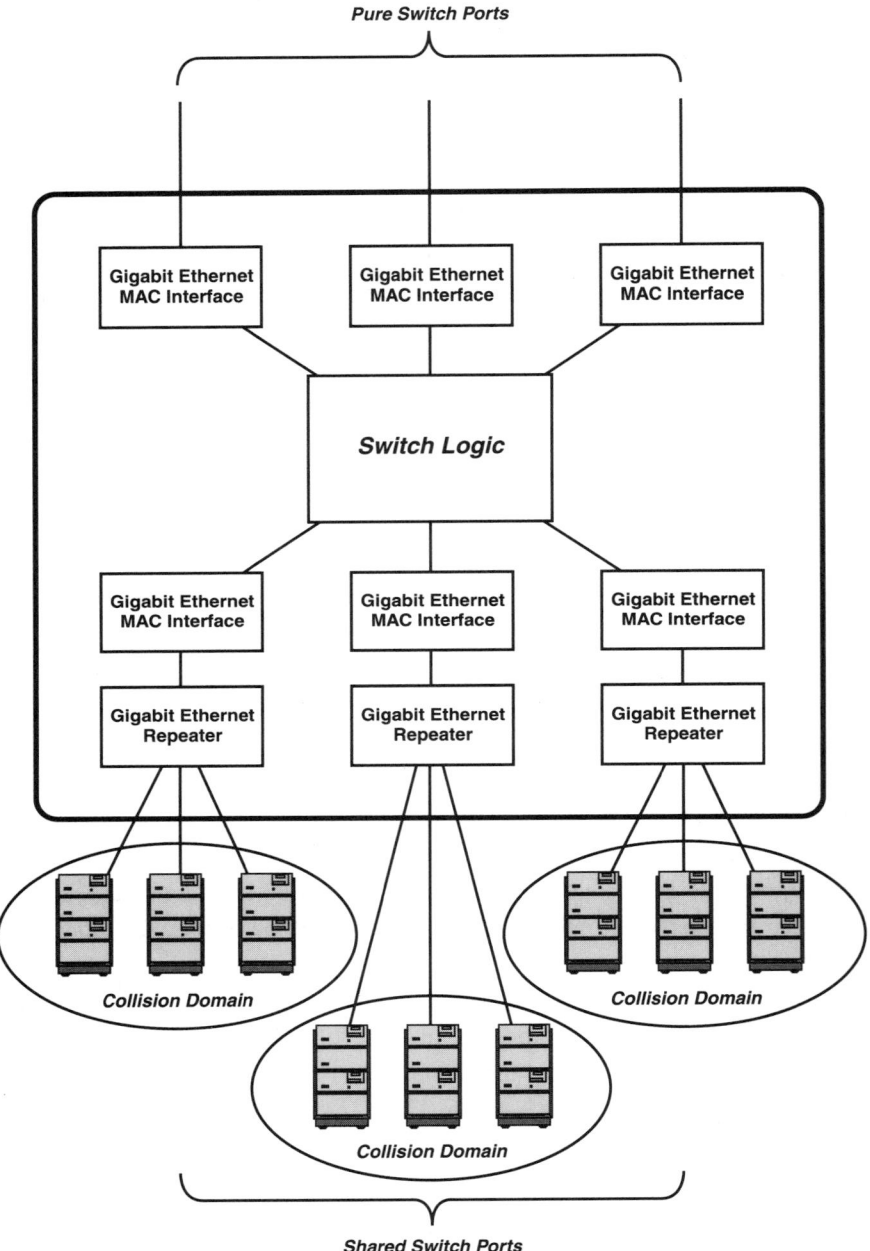

Figure 11–4 Hybrid switch/repeater.

than by disk transfer rates, CPU protocol and application processing overhead, internal bus bandwidth, and so on. (See Chapter 15.)

- The alternative approach of using switched Fast Ethernet (instead of shared Gigabit Ethernet) may be superior. It runs over standard UTP today and is already lower cost (per port) than a shared gigabit connection would be. The only disadvantage is the lower burst throughput (100 Mb/s versus 1000 Mb/s). This is not much of a disadvantage if the attached computer can't sustain gigabit transfer rates anyway.

A second application for shared Gigabit Ethernet today is in server clusters. While a single server may not need a dedicated Gigabit Ethernet connection, a repeater allows a cluster of servers to share a (relatively expensive) Gigabit Ethernet switch port. Some switches targeted at the server cluster market may integrate small repeaters into the switch ports, as depicted in Figure 11–4.

The repeaters function as switch port multiplexers, or *fan-out* devices. The result is a switch with more station/server attachments than ports. The cost-per-port would be between that of a repeater and a switch, as would the performance.

11.2 Switching Hubs

A switching hub is simply another name for a switch (bridge) deployed at the center of a star-wired system. Basic switch operation was discussed extensively in Chapter 3 and is not repeated here (pun intended).

It is expected that the bulk of Gigabit Ethernet hubs will employ switching or routing technology (or a combination of both), rather than the classic repeater hub used for 10BASE-T. This is because:

- Gigabit Ethernet's primary application is in backbone networks. Backbone networks (even for intrabuilding use) require distances longer than possible with shared repeater hubs. Longer distance can be achieved only with full-duplex operation; this implies a switching (or routing) device at the hub.
- Backbone applications are characterized by the need for high bandwidth, as well as for isolation of traffic among workgroups and departments within the organization. Switching (and routing) technology is much better-suited for this application than are repeaters.
- Gigabit Ethernet carries a high initial cost-of-entry (relative to 10 Mb/s and 100 Mb/s systems). It doesn't make much sense to pay that higher

base price and not "go the rest of the way" with the increased performance provided by a switching hub.

11.2.1 Workgroup versus Campus Switches

There are two classes of switch products that will typically include Gigabit Ethernet ports, as shown in Figure 11–5. Chapter 14 discusses the market segmentation and product features of switches in greater depth.

1. **Workgroup switch.** A workgroup switch describes a device used to aggregate traffic within a workgroup or department. It is characterized by having a relatively low number of Gigabit Ethernet ports (typically one or two) used as uplinks to a campus switch and/or a workgroup server.
2. **Campus switch.** A campus switch would typically be used as a *collapsed backbone* for a site consisting of multiple buildings. A campus switch incorporates more high-speed ports (Gigabit Ethernet) than does a workgroup switch.

The distinction between the two switches is important when the architecture and feature sets of the devices are considered. A workgroup switch uses Gigabit Ethernet primarily as a link out of the workgroup, whereas a campus-level device is actually switching among multiple gigabit ports. Therefore a workgroup switch has only one or two Gigabit Ethernet ports, while a cam-

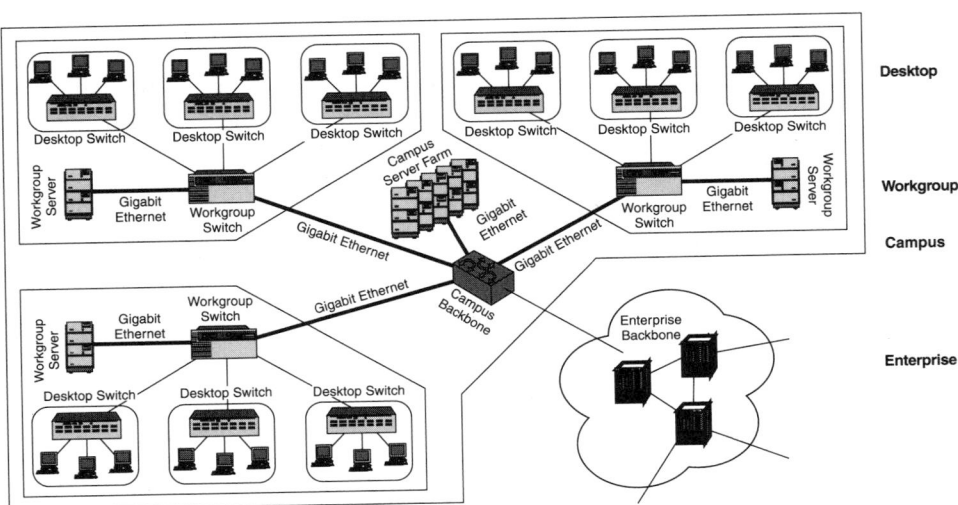

Figure 11–5 Gigabit Ethernet deployment in switches.

pus switch will typically support many more ports. The feature set (and the fundamental architecture) for these devices will be quite different, as will be the acceptable cost.

11.2.2 Gigabit Ethernet Switch Characteristics

This section discusses the following key characteristics of switching hubs that relate to Gigabit Ethernet operation.

- Performance
- Blocking versus nonblocking operation
- Number of stations supported
- Full-duplex operation and flow control

11.2.2.1 Performance

Switch performance may be specified by the following [IEEE93a]:

- **Port filter rate.** This is the rate at which the switch can receive, do any necessary table lookup/update, and make the forward-or-discard decision for the frame. It is usually expressed in frames/second/port and is measured using minimum-length frames (the worst-case).
- **Relay rate (often called Forwarding Rate).** This is the rate at which the switch can actually forward frames onto its output ports, assuming that the output port is available (that is, no output congestion). This is also measured in frames/second/port and is always less than or equal to the filter rate.

While these are commonly used metrics, they don't measure switch behavior under typical or practical network conditions. [RFC1242, RFC1944] They imply a benchmark that streams continuous, back-to-back-to-back minimum-length frames at all ports of a switch. While a switch that can filter and forward at wire-speed (that is, pass this test without missing any frames) will never be the limiting factor in an internetwork, the converse is not true. A switch that cannot pass this test may be perfectly acceptable under normal (or even extreme) cases of network load.

In the early days of bridge design, Gigabit Ethernet did not exist and wire-speed bridges, even at 10 Mb/s, were rare. Achieving wire-speed performance was a major concern of switch manufacturers, particularly for the "battle of the data sheets." Today, however, wire-speed operation is fairly common, at least at 10 Mb/s and 100 Mb/s. Indeed, a 10/100 Mb/s switch that cannot operate at wire-speed is generally considered a low-end product, useful only for low-performance applications. Gigabit data rates make the question of wire-speed operation interesting again. In Gigabit Ethernet, the ability to operate at wire-speed implies a filter/forward rate on the order of 1.5 million frames/second/port—this is no small feat. Making a frame forwarding decision in under 700 ns implies some high-performance and potentially expensive hardware. A complete treatment of benchmarks and performance metrics for switches is beyond the scope of this book. The point here is that as the data rate of the links increases, wire-speed operation becomes increasingly more difficult and expensive to achieve.

Whether a switch really needs to provide wire-speed performance differs with the application environment. A workgroup switch uses its Gigabit Ethernet port in a somewhat different manner from a campus switch. In a workgroup environment, the Gigabit Ethernet port is an *uplink*. It provides connectivity to a high-speed backbone or workgroup server, but the switch is not concentrating traffic among multiple gigabit-rate ports. A workgroup switch is therefore less likely to ever see sustained wire-speed traffic on its Gigabit Ethernet ports. This reduces the performance requirements of the device. In addition, in the event of short-term transient overload, the use of flow control can prevent undesirable frame discard in the workgroup switch. The workgroup switch can effectively "borrow buffers" from the campus switch, which can be assumed to have more resources available.

A campus switch generally must be designed for sustained, high-performance operation. Unlike the workgroup device, the campus switch aggregates traffic from a potentially large number of very high-speed (gigabit) ports. As the switch is often the (collapsed) backbone for an entire organization, overall network throughput can be adversely affected by an under-powered campus switch. Thus high performance (including wire-speed operation at gigabit rates) is a more critical issue for a campus switch.

11.2.2.2 Blocking versus Nonblocking Operation

In connection-oriented networks, when the offered load exceeds the designed-in capacity of the switch, the switch *blocks* the overload. For example, in a telephone switch, when the number of simultaneous callers exceeds the number of circuits available, the switch prevents overload by not issuing a dial tone to new potential callers. If this situation can never occur, the switch is said to be *nonblocking*. In the telephone example, this would be the case if there were sufficient outside circuits to accommodate all callers. Note that nonblocking operation does not ensure that all callers will necessarily be able to communicate as they desire; the line being called may be busy. It is just that the switch will not be the limiting factor for communications; traffic patterns will.

Connectionless networks do not perform circuit-switching; they move frames among their ports. In a connectionless (Ethernet) switch, the term "non-blocking" refers to a switch whose internal switching (data moving) capacity is greater than or equal to the sum of the capacities of all attached links. This is conceptually similar (but not identical) to the idea of nonblocking operation in connection-oriented switches. A nonblocking LAN switch architecture provides the mechanism for wire-speed frame forwarding. On the other hand, an inherently blocking architecture is not necessarily bad; it means simply that the switch cannot support traffic patterns in which all links are carrying sustained traffic at full speed without either discarding frames or invoking flow control. The (potentially) higher cost of a non-blocking switch may not be justified if the traffic load is such that the switch is never operated at its full capacity or if occasional reduced throughput due to flow control is acceptable.

In practice, if the switch is to behave in a nonblocking manner, the internal switching bandwidth must be *greater* than simply the sum of the capacities of the attached ports. This avoids excessive queuing delays (or queue overflow) due to the statistical distribution of traffic arrival. Consider a 24-hour supermarket that has a business level of 2400 customers per day and whose checkout clerks can serve 10 customers per hour on average. To ensure adequate checkout capacity, the store appears to need only 10 clerks:

$$\text{clerks} = \frac{2400 \text{ customers/day}}{24 \text{ hours/day} \times 10 \text{ customers/hour/clerk}} = 10$$

This result would be valid if the 2400 customers arrive at uniformly distributed times throughout the day. If they all show up at 6:00 P.M. on their way home from work, however, the store may have adequate service *capacity*, but the service delay will be 12 hours (average) and 24 hours for the unlucky last customer who walked in at 6:01![9] Depending on the arrival statistics, the switch needs to have excess internal capacity to prevent excessive delays. This is called *undersubscribing* the bandwidth. Common practice in nonblocking switch design is to use an undersubscription ratio on the order of 1.5:1 to 2:1. By definition, an *oversubscribed* fabric cannot be nonblocking.

---

9. Any resemblance between this analogy and actual facts is intentional. However, do not attempt to engage the store manager in a discussion of queuing theory while in a "quick checkout" line that stretches into the produce department.

Note that just because the switching fabric may be nonblocking does not mean there cannot be congestion due to output port blocking. (This is the equivalent of a nonblocking telephone switch trying to make a call to a busy line, as discussed earlier in the section.) The switch may have adequate capacity to move data from each port to every other port. However, if there is more traffic destined for a given output port than that port can handle, there is little the switch can do about it, other than buffering the traffic (and possibly using flow control to prevent buffer overload). A nonblocking switch can support maximal flows only if the traffic patterns are uniform across its ports.

11.2.2.3 Number of Stations Supported

A switch performs an address lookup to determine the appropriate output port(s) for a given received frame. The performance of the switch (and the basic design architecture) is affected by the maximum number of stations that the switch can know about. If the actual number of stations exceeds this design maximum, traffic destined for stations that are not presently in the address table must be flooded onto all output ports. This reduces the capacity of the overall system.

In general, organizations do not build huge, "flat" switched networks.[10] Beyond some number of users, it becomes desirable to provide the administrative separation, security/firewall capabilities, and multicast traffic isolation provided by routers. While there are internetworks (for example, the Internet) that support literally millions of computers by using routers, rarely does a single switched LAN comprise more than a few thousand active stations. A station capability of 64K addresses is considered adequate for even the largest switched catenet.

In this regard, a workgroup switch has a slightly easier job than a campus switch. From the perspective of traffic arriving from other ports, the Gigabit Ethernet uplink port can be viewed as a *default port*. That is, the workgroup switch can take the policy of directing traffic among its lower speed (nonuplink) ports in the normal fashion, forwarding traffic to a port when the destination address lookup indicates that the target receiver is reachable through that port. In the event of a lookup failure (that is, the destination is unknown to the workgroup switch), the switch can choose to forward

---

10. A switched LAN is called "flat" because there is no hierarchy to the address space. Network layer protocols (as used in a routed internetwork) always provide some structure in their address space, for example, using network or subnetwork identifiers to make routing decisions independent of the individual station identifiers.

this traffic onto the uplink port, rather than flooding this traffic onto all ports. This is done on the assumption that the intended receiver is connected to some switch reachable through the campus backbone.

This policy enables the address capability of the workgroup switch to be greatly reduced. It needs to support only the maximum number of stations that are connected to its *local ports;* it does not need to keep track of all stations in the catenet (as is normally required by a bridge). Thus a practical workgroup switch needs to support only a few thousand stations, rather than tens of thousands. This can reduce the cost and complexity of the product. The campus switch is the only device that needs to maintain address tables for the entire catenet.

11.2.2.4 Full-Duplex Operation and Flow Control

A switch incorporating Gigabit Ethernet ports will typically need to operate over distances greater than that allowed by CSMA/CD (half-duplex) operation. Connections to campus switches require distances on the order of hundreds or thousands of meters; this necessitates both full-duplex operation and optical-fiber media. In practice, virtually all Gigabit Ethernet connections are (and will be) full-duplex.

Full-duplex connections can take advantage of explicit flow control as provided by IEEE 802.3x [IEEE97], discussed in Chapter 6. This is a universally desirable feature in a Gigabit Ethernet switch at any layer in the hierarchy. Flow control prevents undesirable frame loss under transient overload conditions. It also reduces the cost of a switch because the designer does not need to provide huge buffer capacity just to handle the most extreme cases of offered load. Relative to the previous discussion, flow control allows a blocking switch architecture to behave acceptably in the network by throttling incoming traffic when the switch fabric becomes temporarily oversubscribed. In this sense, flow control acts as a "safety net" for the switch design.

In the case of a switch port connecting directly to an end station (for example, a server or high-performance workstation), flow control can be implemented in an asymmetrical manner. This allows the switch to throttle the end station without allowing the end station to throttle the switch. The difference is that an end station is the true source of the traffic. Preventing the station from transmitting actually reduces the overall internetwork load, rather than just shifting it from one device to another (as occurs with switch-to-switch flow control). The penalty is a loss of performance; the station is prevented from sending traffic, and application delay is increased. However, this is usually preferable to allowing the application to send its traffic, and then forcing that traffic to wait in intermediate switch buffers. The delay is the same, but flow control prevents the station from imposing a burden on intervening switch resources.

11.2.3 Gigabit Switch Architectural Issues

The design of the internal switching fabric is critical to the performance of a switch. A complete treatment of this subject would fill its own book. However, the following is an overview of three popular switching architectures that have been used in products to date, with an eye toward the needs of Gigabit Ethernet-capable switches:

- Shared memory
- Shared bus
- Crosspoint matrix

11.2.3.1 Shared-Memory Switches

A shared-memory architecture (depicted in Figure 11–6) uses a single common memory as the exchange mechanism for frames between ports. The main advantage of this approach is that memory is relatively cheap and one single, large memory can be used for all of the ports, rather than separate per-port

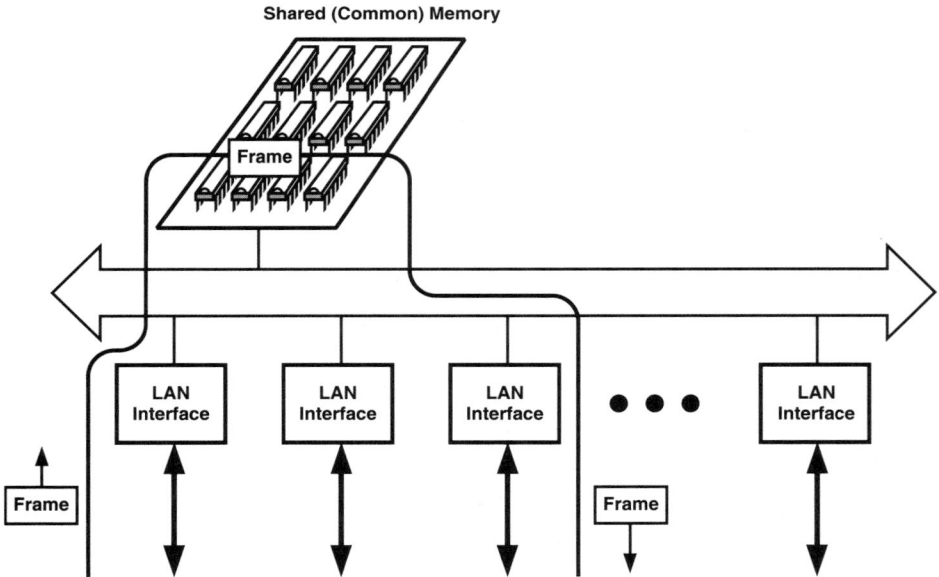

Figure 11–6 Shared-memory architecture.

memories being required. Also, the techniques for designing systems based on shared memory are well-known in the industry. A shared-memory switch can be built using "off-the-shelf" technology. The downside is that the limiting factor for performance is usually the bandwidth of the memory.

For example, consider a 32-bit-wide memory bus that uses low-cost 60-ns Dynamic Random Access Memory (DRAM). Even with the performance improvement offered by streaming data (that is, the first access may take one or more 60-ns memory cycles, but subsequent sequential accesses take less time), the switch capacity is limited to about 500 Mb/s.[11] This figure accounts for the fact that every frame must be both written to, and read from, the memory, thereby effectively halving the memory bandwidth available for switching. Unbounded queuing delays can be prevented by undersubscribing the available switching capacity. This results in a usable capacity on the order of from 300 to 350 Mb/s.

This capacity is adequate for 10 Mb/s switches with port counts of from 12 to 16 or more, or even an 8–12 port 10 Mb/s switch with one or two 100 Mb/s uplinks. Full-duplex operation is assumed here; with ports operating in half-duplex mode, the design can either support more ports or offer more design margin. Static RAM (SRAM), being much faster than DRAM, can allow an increase either to the total number of ports or the number of higher-speed ports, in either case with a concomitant penalty in price. (For performance reasons, most shared-memory switches are built using SRAM.)

A simple shared-memory architecture is impractical for a switch comprising Gigabit Ethernet ports. A single such port would overwhelm the capacity of the entire memory. The architecture could be stretched, perhaps by using a combination of SRAM, a wider memory bus, and/or faster clocks. However, even a 64-bit-wide, SRAM-based switch using 66 MHz clocks can support only one or two Gigabit Ethernet ports. The architecture is simply not appropriate for the application.

11.2.3.2 Shared-Bus Architecture

A shared-bus architecture (depicted in Figure 11–7) uses a common bus as the exchange mechanism for frames between ports. Each port (or small group of ports) has its own memory, both for input and output queues, depending

---

11. 32 bits $\times$ 16 MHz $\times$ 2 (streaming factor) $\div$ 2 (write and read each frame) = 512 Mb/s.

The actual performance improvement due to memory streaming is a function of the design of the messaging system used to move frame data into and out of the memory. The factor of 2 used here is just one possible value and is used for exemplary purposes.

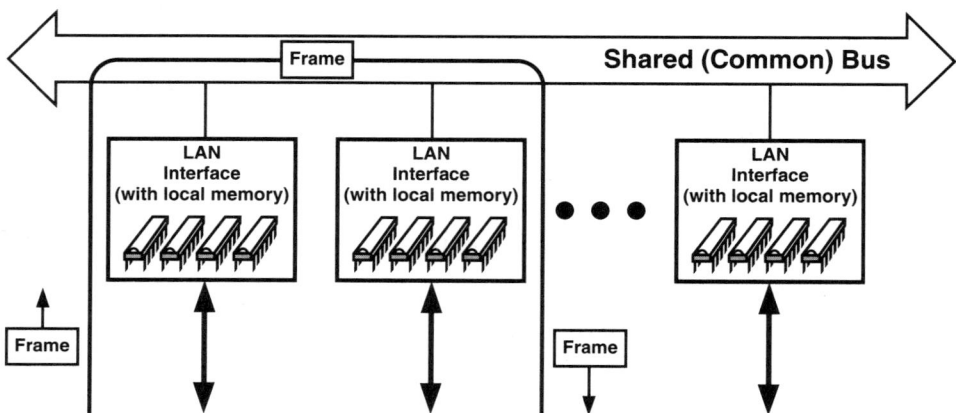

Figure 11–7 Shared-bus architecture.

on the design. The advantage of this approach is that a shared bus can have higher bandwidth than a memory can. For example, a 32-bit, 33 MHz PCI has a theoretical maximum capacity of slightly over 1 Gb/s. Proprietary busses can be used to achieve even higher capacities, by using either wider bus widths or faster clocks. A 1 Gb/s shared-bus architecture can support a moderate number of 100 Mb/s ports (typically eight) and/or a very large number of 10 Mb/s ports. In addition, the bus is needed only *once* per transaction (rather than once in and once out, as in the shared-memory case), so the effective capacity is doubled relative to the shared-memory approach. The downside of this architecture is that a separate memory is needed for each port (or group of ports). This increases the cost.

Conceivably, a shared bus could be used for a workgroup switch that incorporates a single Gigabit Ethernet uplink. If the bus capacity was on the order of 2 Gb/s or more (for example, by using a 64-bit-wide bus, a faster clock, or both), a reasonable number of 100 Mb/s ports can be accommodated in addition to a single uplink. This architecture does not scale well, however. It also will not support the large number of Gigabit Ethernet links that are needed in a campus switch.

11.2.3.3 Crosspoint Matrix Switch

A crosspoint matrix, shown in Figure 11–8, essentially creates a very transient "circuit" between ports for the duration of a frame (or subset of a frame) exchange. There is an electronic switch located at each crosspoint in the matrix between every input and every output. The switch controller connects an input to the appropriate output(s) on a frame-by-frame basis in a matter of nanoseconds and then disconnects the ports in preparation for the next

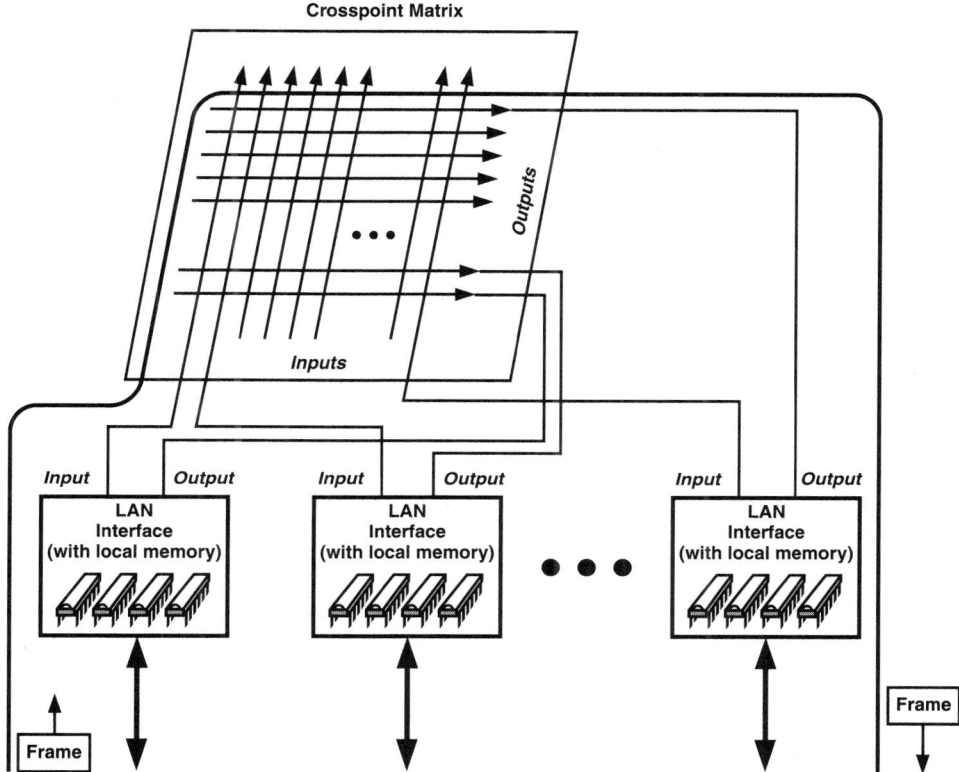

Figure 11–8 Crosspoint matrix architecture.

frame exchange. While the inputs and outputs in the figure are shown as single lines, they can, in reality, be parallel paths (for example, two, eight, or more signals per port) to increase both the total and the per-port available bandwidth.

Depending on the clock speed and the width of the interface to the matrix, a huge switching capacity can be created. For example, an eight-port, 16-bit-wide (16 signals per port) matrix with a 50 MHz clock has an effective bandwidth of 6.4 Gb/s. This is clearly suitable for huge numbers of 100 Mb/s ports and/or quite a few Gigabit Ethernet ports. This architecture requires memory at each port (like the shared bus), plus a complex crosspoint matrix device, which is typically implemented as either a custom integrated circuit or an ASIC(s).[12]

---

12. With *lots* of pins! The matrix described would need 256 pins for the data paths alone, plus pins for clocks, control, and so on.

Each approach (shared-memory, shared-bus, and crosspoint matrix) provides an improvement in performance over its predecessor at an increase in price. Shared-memory switches provide a practical, low-cost solution for desktop 10 Mb/s switches with 100 Mb/s uplinks. A shared-bus can be an effective approach for a workgroup concentrator that has moderate numbers of 100 Mb/s ports. A crosspoint matrix is virtually a necessity at gigabit speeds.

The architecture used is intimately related to the application environment. The price and performance of a given switch is controlled by the underlying design approach. Therefore, while it is possible to use a campus backbone switch with all-gigabit port capability in a workgroup environment, it is generally not cost-effective to do so. Similarly, there could be a performance bottleneck if a switch designed for a workgroup environment is used in a backbone application.

11.2.4 Buffered Distributors

Consider a special case of a switch with:

- One station attachment per port (microsegmentation)
- End-station attachments only (that is, no cascaded or switch-to-switch links)[13]
- No address table (that is, the switch does not keep track of the addresses of the attached stations)
- All stations operating at 1000 Mb/s
- All stations operating in full-duplex mode
- All stations capable of receiving and acting on PAUSE (flow control) messages

Such a device is called a *Buffered Distributor*[14] and is depicted in Figure 11–9. From a switch-behavior perspective, every frame received from each attached station must be forwarded (flooded) onto every output port except that on

---

13. One exception is the inclusion of an uplink port to a workgroup or backbone switch to connect this device to the rest of the network. However, the uplink port would likely use more conventional bridge technology, including an address table for traffic isolation.

14. This device is sometimes called a *Full-Duplex Repeater* and, occasionally, a *Gigabuffer.* The name Buffered Distributor (abbreviated BD) was coined by Bernard Daines (also abbreviated BD), of Packet Engines, Inc., its leading proponent. A similar device, known as a *Buffered Repeater,* was built and sold by Ungermann-Bass, Inc., during the 1980s and 1990s. This device, while also essentially a bridge without any address table, had only two ports, operated at 10 Mb/s, and did not use full-duplex mode or flow control.

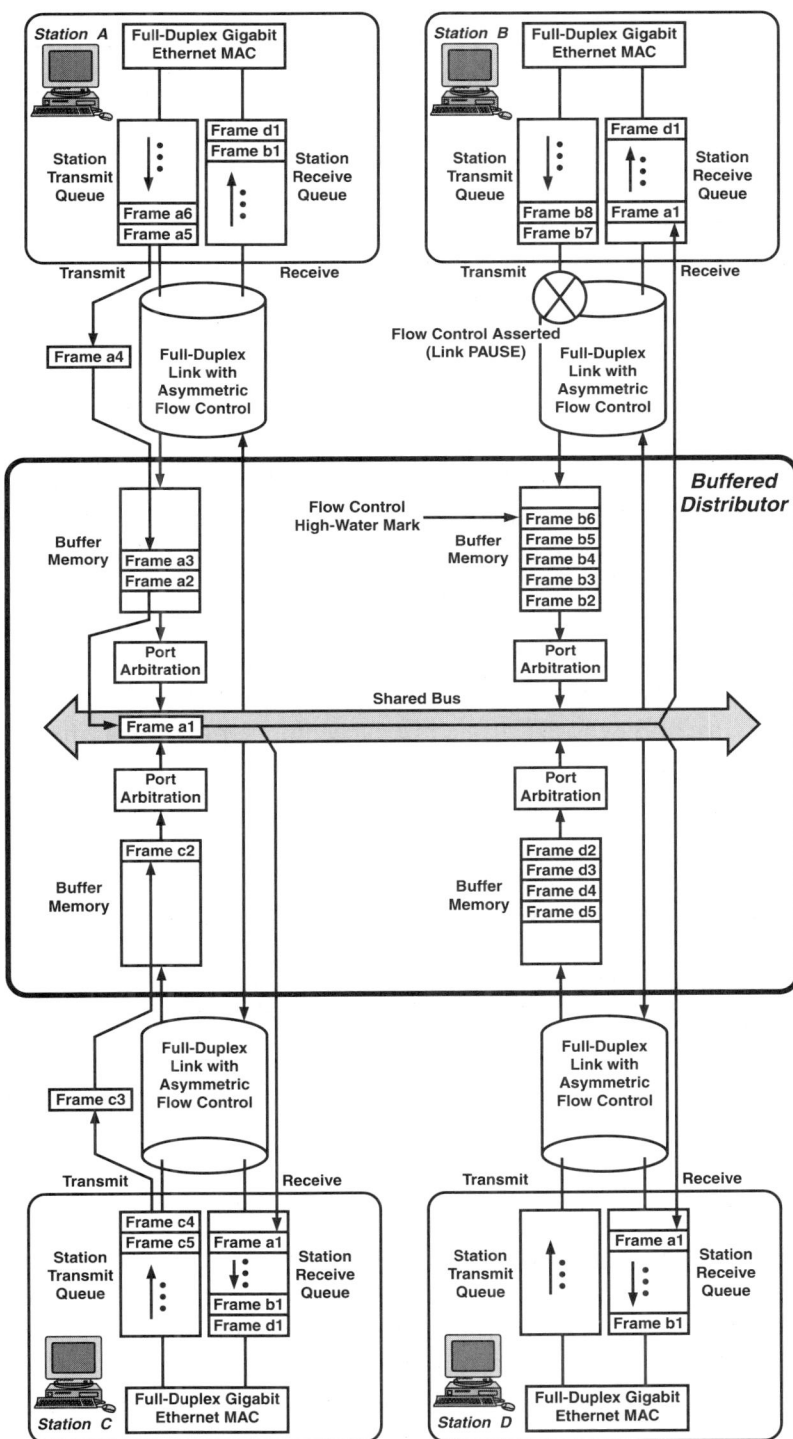

Figure 11–9 Buffered Distributor.

which the frame arrived. This is because there is no address table to keep track of relative station locations, so the switch must revert to the default behavior for a frame sent to an "unknown" destination address (since *all* addresses are "unknown"!).[15]

The maximum throughput of a Buffered Distributor is equal to the maximum throughput of any *one* of its links. This is unlike a traditional switch, which can have an aggregate capacity equal to the sum of the capacities of its links. The reduction in capacity is because every frame must be transmitted on every link, and therefore uses bandwidth on every link, since there is no address table or filtering algorithm to provide traffic isolation. Clearly, there is a potential for switch overload, for many stations may wish to send traffic at the same time, yet the switch must flood all traffic to all ports. Said another way, the offered load can be many times 1 Gb/s (depending on the number of ports), but the total switch capacity is only 1 Gb/s. Something has to give.

This is where the use of flow control comes in handy. If the total load offered to the switch (the input traffic) exceeds the forwarding capability of the switch (the output traffic), then input buffers will fill. The Buffered Distributor can use the PAUSE mechanism (see Chapter 6) to throttle transmissions from any port whose buffers are exceeding some maximum threshold (called "high-water mark"). This will reduce the offered load and prevent switch overflow. Flow control is effective here because the attached device is an end station rather than a switch. The flow control is asserted to the true source of the offered load, rather than the congestion problem simply being moved to a different internetworking device. It is also important that the flow control be asymmetric—the Buffered Distributor can stop end stations from sending additional frames, but end stations cannot throttle the Buffered Distributor (they better not!). If a station was allowed to flow control the Buffered Distributor, it would halt all traffic through the hub. If a Buffered Distributor cannot send traffic out on all ports, it cannot send traffic out on *any* port!

This may seem a strange way to design a switch, but it has some interesting advantages (and some equally important disadvantages). On the plus side:

+ This device can be built more cheaply than a switch designed for higher capacity. Not only can you avoid the need for address tables and lookup hardware, but, in addition, the internal bandwidth of the switch does not

---

15. Perlman [PERL92] calls such a device a "No-Frills Bridge."

need to be more than 1 Gb/s. This allows the use of a less-expensive shared-bus switching architecture, rather than the crosspoint matrix traditionally required for multigigabit switches.

+ The availability of asymmetric flow control allows the designer to reduce the per-port buffer memory. Only that amount of memory necessary to deal with the round-trip latency required for proper flow control operation is needed. And unlike a traditional switch, additional port buffer memory will not improve performance.

+ The throughput of a Buffered Distributor can be a full 1000 Mb/s, regardless of the statistical distribution of load among stations and frame lengths. This differs from a repeater, whose throughput is limited by the CSMA/CD algorithm (the performance of which *is* a function of the statistics of the load distribution).[16]

+ Since it connects only to end stations, the likelihood of a bridge loop through a Buffered Distributor is low. This lets you avoid the need to implement the Spanning Tree Protocol [PERL92, IEEE93a].[17]

On the other hand:

− The cost savings may not be worth the performance loss relative to a true switch. There is a certain base cost associated with a Gigabit Ethernet port, regardless of whether it is in a Buffered Distributor or a traditional switch. There are Physical Layer devices, MAC devices, memory, and CPU, plus connectors, power supply, PC board, and so on. The savings in the Buffered Distributor are primarily in memory, address logic, and, to a certain extent, the switching fabric.

− A Buffered Distributor cannot be used in a mixed data rate environment. All ports must operate at 1000 Mb/s. If a Buffered Distributor allowed a

---

16. CSMA/CD becomes an inefficient arbitration algorithm when the round-trip delay of the network is long relative to the frame transmission time. A Buffered Distributor essentially moves a portion of each station's transmit queue from the station to the hub and arbitrates within the hub for access to the internal shared bus. Since this arbitration is occurring over extremely short distances (typically a single circuit board), a "perfect scheduling" algorithm can be implemented. The arbitrator "knows" the complete state of the network at all times (that is, which stations have frames to transmit) and can schedule access to the shared bus without wasting any time waiting for information to propagate across the network.

17. While this is true in theory, in practice there will need to be a processor and memory within the Buffered Distributor anyway for housekeeping and network management purposes. The additional burden of implementing the Spanning Tree Protocol on this processor is insignificant, both in terms of memory and performance. Little is gained by eliminating the Spanning Tree.

mix of speeds, the total throughput would be equal to the *lowest* data rate attachment due to the flooding algorithm. It would not make any sense to have Gigabit Ethernet devices limited to 100 Mb/s or less.[18]

‒ A Buffered Distributor is useful only in an end-station environment. It is not applicable for backbone connections because it has limited throughput and depends on asymmetric flow control for proper operation.

Probably the best application today for a Buffered Distributor is for server cluster connections. In this regard, it competes more with a repeater than with a classical switch. One can envision a range of products, from the lowest price and performance (repeater) to the highest (classical switch/router), with the Buffered Distributor falling between. Whether there is a large enough "market niche" for this idea depends on whether the cost is sufficiently less than that of a classical switch in order to justify its lower performance.

Buffered Distributors, while available as a product (under various names), are not mentioned or specified in the IEEE 802.3z Gigabit Ethernet standard.[19] In reality, it is a degenerate case of a standard IEEE 802.1D bridge, with an address table depth of zero entries.

11.3 Routing Hubs

Historically, LAN hubs have used either repeater or bridge (switching) technology. Routers are not normally considered in the same context as repeaters or switches, which are treated more as wiring concentrators than internetworking devices. While a switch might have incorporated some routing functionality (especially with regard to a high-speed uplink port), routing was rarely the primary function of a hub product. Reasons for this include:

■ Routers are more complex than repeaters or switches. Since network protocols provide functionality well beyond that provided by Physical Layer repeaters or Link Layer bridges, the device implementing that protocol (that is, a router) is necessarily more complex and therefore more expensive. For a given level of performance, a router traditionally costs more

---

18. In theory, there is no reason why someone couldn't build a 100 Mb/s or 10 Mb/s Buffered Distributor. However, the cost of "real" switches at these data rates is already so low that the savings from using the Buffered Distributor approach is generally unwarranted.

19. This was a matter of intense debate in the committee during the development of the standard.

than a switch. (Or looked at the other way, for a given cost, a router will have a lower level of performance than a switch.)

■ Until recently, numerous network protocols were in widespread use in typical networks, so a router would have to implement multiple network protocols in order to support the installed base. IP, DECnet, IPX, and AppleTalk (as well as some other, more obscure protocols) might be needed in a marketable product. In addition to the network protocol, each suite also incorporates a number of supporting functions, such as routing protocols, error reporting, network management, and so on, thus further increasing the complexity and cost.

■ Routers have traditionally been implemented purely in software. This is because until recently, the complexity of the state machine(s) needed for even the simpler network protocols made implementation in silicon impractical.[20] In addition, network protocols (especially the more complex ones, such as the Internet Protocol [RFC791]), were still considered "fluid." That is, changes were being made to the design at the subtlest levels of detail that made hardware implementations of network protocols risky from the perspective of implementing changes as the protocol matured. In contrast, a switch or repeater has a bounded, well-defined set of behaviors that is amenable to hardware deployment.

■ Because of the software implementation, the performance of a router was limited by the performance of the processor executing the protocol code. To achieve wire-speed routing, one had to use very high-performance processors together with large memories. This translated into higher cost.

---

20. There were two fairly well-known early attempts to build "hardware routers." During the late 1980s and early 1990s, a company called Protocol Engines unsuccessfully attempted to build a hardware-based Transport and Network Layer protocol chipset. [CHES91]. They failed, primarily because their approach involved developing a new protocol suite (the eXpress Transport Protocol, XTP) that was simpler than TCP/IP and more amenable to silicon implementation. They required that applications use this new protocol in lieu of TCP/IP to achieve the higher performance level. This was met with significant resistance from the industry, especially once high-speed software-based IP routers became widely available, quashing the notion that hardware was necessary for speed. They also failed because, even with the reduced protocol requirements, the complexity was at the limit of (some say beyond) the capability of then-available silicon technology.

cisco Systems has for many years successfully deployed a *Silicon Switching Engine* (SSE) in their high-performance router product line. While this doesn't implement the entire IP protocol as a state machine, it performs certain time-critical tasks (for example, routing table/ARP cache lookups, and so on) as "hardware subroutines," thus significantly accelerating the company's standard IP routing software.

■ Routers create (or assume) a separate network at each port; that is, a router interconnects *networks* as opposed to stations. Repeaters and switches can be used to interconnect stations, since they operate below the Network Layer of the architectural model. At the desktop level of a wiring hierarchy, routers make no sense; they would create a large number of networks, with one station in each network.

Thus, while software-based wire-speed routing was possible with 10 Mb/s connections, or with a relatively smaller number of 100 Mb/s ports, the cost and architectural implications forced routers to play one of two primary roles:

1. As an "edge" or boundary device, connecting a workgroup to a campus or enterprise backbone
2. As the campus or enterprise backbone itself, deployed in either a distributed or collapsed manner

However, these roles are precisely the key initial application areas for Gigabit Ethernet. As depicted in Figure 11–5, workgroup devices concentrate 10 Mb/s and 100 Mb/s links into 1000 Mb/s connections to a campus concentrator; the campus concentrators (collapsed backbones) themselves will be the primary vehicles for Gigabit Ethernet ports. These devices are also the locations in the network that traditionally have used Network Layer (routing) capability to provide administrative isolation, security/firewall protection, traffic isolation, and so on. Unlike its lower-speed cousins, a Gigabit Ethernet hub designer may find it hard to avoid having to implement routing capability if the product being designed is to be successful.

11.3.1 Routing Gigabit Ethernet

Here is where we get hit with the "double-whammy":

■ Gigabit Ethernet products are likely to be deployed in applications that need routing capability.
■ Routing is already expensive (or performance-limiting); 1000 Mb/s operation only exacerbates this problem.

Fortunately, other changes in technology (both networking and silicon) have changed the landscape for implementing high-speed routers. These include the following.

■ The number of protocols that are important in products today is much less than 10 years ago. While there is still a significant installed base of

DECnet, AppleTalk, IPX, and even some XNS-based systems, the vast majority of new internetworks are based on IP. Most corporations, universities, and other institutions are building (and migrating) their enterprise networks to IP-only operation. In addition, most of the "legacy" protocols can be encapsulated into IP, thereby making an IP-only routing solution acceptable for high-speed backbone networks.

■ IP has matured as a protocol. The operation and behavior of the IP routing "core" is well-defined and unlikely to change significantly. Indeed, it would be quite difficult to gain widespread acceptance for any change that caused an incompatibility with the millions of installed IP devices.[21]

■ Silicon capability has improved to the point where highly complex systems can be built on a single IC. The use of 0.35 µm and smaller silicon geometries enables ASIC implementations of five million gate-equivalents or more. Embedded memory (S/SRAM, S/DRAM) and microprocessors are available in addition to high-density logic. This makes it possible to build single-chip, low-cost routing solutions that incorporate both hardware and software as needed for best overall performance.

In addition, experience has shown that while an IP router must, in general, perform a myriad of functions, in practice the vast majority of packets need only a few simple operations performed in real-time. Thus we can implement the performance-critical functions in hardware and the remaining (necessary, but less time-critical), functions in software. This creates an optimized routing solution that can route Gigabit Ethernet at reasonable cost.

A router with even a few ports operating at Gigabit Ethernet speeds must be prepared to handle millions of packets per second. IP contains many features and functions that are either rarely used (for example, routing options) or that can be performed in the background of high-speed data forwarding

> **Seifert's Law of Networking #92**
>
> Optimize for the *typical* case, not the *boundary* case.

(for example, routing protocol operation and network management). A practical product does not need to be able to perform wire-speed routing when

---

21. While there is considerable activity in the area of new routing protocols, multicast operation, resource reservation (RSVP), and so on, the *core* functionality of an IP router is quite stable. The operations required to perform packet parsing, routing table lookup, lifetime control, fragmentation, and other functions are unlikely to change and can be committed to silicon with little risk.

infrequently used options are present in the packet. Since packets having such options comprise a small fraction of the total traffic, they can be handled as exception conditions. Similarly, there is no need to add (and pay for) performance for housekeeping and support functions such as ICMP and SNMP. The router architecture should be optimized for those functions that must be performed in real-time, on a packet-by-packet basis, for the majority of packets. This is called the *fast path* of the flow.[22] Most routers supporting moderate-to-large numbers of Gigabit Ethernet ports implement this fast path in hardware, and high performance is usually guaranteed only for these fast-path functions.

11.3.2 Fast-Path Routing Functions

What *are* those functions of the network protocol that are in the fast path? They will vary somewhat from protocol-to-protocol, but this section takes a closer look at IP, because:

- It is today's most widely used protocol suite for enterprise networks.
- It a superset of the functionality of popular connectionless network protocols; that is, most other protocols incorporate a subset of the capabilities of IP. The IP fast path is the most complex that needs to be investigated.

The following discussion is intended as an overview, not a comprehensive treatment of routing.[23] The fast path of IP routing requires:

- **Validation.** The router must check that the received packet is properly formed for the protocol before it proceeds with protocol processing. In the case of IP, this means
  - checking the version number,
  - checking the header length field (also needed to determine whether any options are present in the packet),

---

22. The term "fast path" comes from the way protocol processing software is typically designed. The code thread that is traversed most often is scrutinized and optimized most by the programmer, as it has the greatest effect on system performance. Packets that do not deviate from the typical (that is, they generate no exception conditions) receive the highest performance because they require fewer instructions to process (this code path is executed faster).

23. Many books have been written on the subject of IP and IP routing. [COME95, STEV94] The interested reader should also consult the relevant RFCs. IPX routing is discussed in the Novell NetWare product documentation and in [MALA90].

- calculating the header checksum, and
- validating the source address (for example, rejecting multicast sources).

■ **Destination address parsing and table lookup.** The router performs a table lookup to determine the output port onto which to direct the packet and the next hop to which to send the packet along this route. This is based on the Destination address in the received packet and the subnet mask(s) of the associated table entries. The result of this lookup could imply:

- A local delivery (that is, the Destination address is one of the router's local addresses and the packet is locally sunk)
- A unicast delivery to a single output port, either to a next-hop router or to the ultimate destination station (in the case of a direct connection to the destination network)
- A multicast delivery to a set of output ports that depends on the router's knowledge of multicast group membership

The router must also determine the mapping of the destination network address to the data link address for the output port (address resolution, or ARP). This can be done either as a separate step or integrated as part of the routing lookup.

■ **Lifetime control.** The router adjusts the *Time to Live* (TTL) field in the packet used to prevent packets from circulating endlessly throughout the internetwork. A packet being delivered to a local address within the router is acceptable if it has any positive value of TTL. A packet being routed to output ports has its TTL value decremented as appropriate and then is rechecked to determine if it has any life before it is actually forwarded. A packet whose lifetime is exceeded is discarded by the router (and may cause an error message to be generated to the original sender).

■ **Checksum calculation.** Finally, the header checksum must be recalculated due to the change in the TTL field. Fortunately, the checksum algorithm employed (a 16-bit one's complement addition of the header fields) is both commutative and associative, thereby allowing simple, differential recomputation.[24]

That's it. The vast majority of packets flowing through an IP router needs to have only these operations performed on them. While they are not trivial,

---

24. If the only change to the IP header is a decrement of the TTL field, the new checksum can be generated by taking the old checksum value and performing a "subtract-with-borrow" of the same value decremented from the TTL field. This is simple to perform in hardware.

it is possible to implement this complete set of operations in hardware, thereby providing performance suitable for Gigabit Ethernet.

The fast-path for IPX requires even less work, as follows.

- Since IPX uses a fixed-length network identifier (that is, there is no subnet mask), there is no issue of extracting a network identifier from the address field.
- IPX does not incorporate the concept of generalized network layer multicast. This reduces the number and complexity of the possible routing decisions.
- IPX Lifetime Control is implemented as an increment of 1 to a *Hop Count* field, rather than as a potentially variable decrement, as in IP.
- IPX implementations almost invariably disable checksumming; thus no update to the checksum field is usually required.

Therefore, hardware capable of performing IP fast-path routing can be adapted to perform IPX routing as well. There is little extra cost associated with supporting both protocols in the same product (if it is designed with this in mind from the outset).

11.3.3 Not-So-Fast Path Routing Functions

There are many functions that must be implemented in a router other than those in the fast path. Some are performed on a packet-by-packet basis (that is, optional or exception conditions) and some as background tasks. All of these can be implemented in software, as they are not time critical. For IP, these functions include those shown in Table 11–2.

It is worth looking more closely at the issue of fragmentation and reassembly, since it appears that user throughput may be adversely affected if this is not considered to be in the fast path.

TABLE 11–2 NON-FAST-PATH ROUTER FUNCTIONS

Packet-by-Packet Operation	Background Tasks
Fragmentation and reassembly	Routing protocols (RIP, OSPF, BGP, and so on)
Source routing option	Network management (SNMP)
Route recording option	Configuration (BOOTP, DHCP, and so on)
Timestamp option	
ICMP message generation	

In theory, an IP packet can be fragmented by a router. That is, a single packet can arrive, thereby resulting in multiple, smaller packets being transmitted onto the output ports. This capability allows a router to forward packets between ports where the output port is incapable of carrying a packet of the desired length; that is, the *Maximum Transmission Unit* (MTU) of the output port is less than that of the input port. Fragmentation is good in the sense that it allows communication between stations connected through links with dissimilar MTUs. It is bad in that it imposes a significant burden on the router, which must perform more work to generate the resulting multiple output datagrams from the single input datagram.

Fortunately, this is not a problem for a "pure" Ethernet router (including Gigabit Ethernet)—all Ethernets have the same MTU. There is never a need to fragment a packet being routed between Ethernets, whether they operate at 10, 100, or 1000 Mb/s. If a Gigabit Ethernet router supports some other link technology that has a different MTU (for example, FDDI [ISO89]), then the possibility of fragmentation must be considered. A hardware-based router is unlikely to implement fragmentation in the fast path. Thus the router may be able to fragment but not at the same forwarding rate as for packets that do not need to be fragmented. This is generally acceptable because fragmentation is considered an "exception condition," outside of the fast path. The need for fragmentation can be avoided by configuring the devices (for example, servers) on the large-MTU link (for example, FDDI) to use smaller packets than allowed by the technology. If an FDDI device never emits packets larger than would be allowed on an Ethernet, then a router will not need to fragment these packets when forwarding them to an Ethernet segment.

Reassembly of fragments may be necessary for packets destined for entities within the router itself. These fragments may have been generated either by other routers in the path between the sender and the router in question or by the original sending station itself. Fragment reassembly is a resource-intensive process (both in CPU cycles and memory); however, the number of packets sent to the router is normally quite low relative to the number of packets being routed through. The number of fragmented packets destined for the router is some subset (hopefully, a small percentage) of the total sunk traffic. Thus the performance of the router for packet reassembly is not critical and should not significantly affect the design or cost of the router.

12 — Gigabit Ethernet Physical Layer

This chapter gets "down and dirty," and looks into the Physical Layer design of Gigabit Ethernet. In spite of abstract architecture, high-level software, device drivers, and access control mechanisms, ultimately all communication occurs through physical devices that move individual bits across a copper or optical fiber cable.

This part of the system often can be the most difficult to design, especially at high data rates. Physical Layer complexity necessarily increases with higher speeds, longer cables, cables with poor transmission characteristics, and higher environmental stress (noise). In the case of Gigabit Ethernet (especially using UTP), all of these factors come into play simultaneously. The skills required to properly design and implement physical communications channels are highly specialized and quite different from any other aspect of computer networking. At the Physical Layer, you must deal with all of the states *between* zero and one.[1]

In 1980, achieving reliable communications at 10 Mb/s over quadruply shielded coaxial cable was considered a formidable challenge. Ten years later, similar performance was obtained over Category 3 UTP (10BASE-T)—a much worse communications medium, electrically speaking. This feat was achieved primarily through careful conditioning and control of drive signals and without any changes to the serial Manchester line-coding scheme. By 1995, Ethernet designers had pushed the UTP medium to an order-of-magnitude higher data rate (100 Mb/s) without sacrificing error performance. Simply controlling drive signals was not enough to achieve the desired result, however. 100BASE-TX required changes to the medium itself

---

1. I have always felt that digital logic designers had a much easier job: They can guess and be right half the time!

(Category 5 cable) and a new two-tiered coding scheme (4B/5B block coding, plus MLT-3 line coding. [IEEE95])

Gigabit Ethernet comprises two separate families of Physical Layer communications systems:

1000BASE-X supports operation over multimode fiber, single mode fiber, and 150 Ω balanced shielded, twisted-pair cable.

1000BASE-T supports operation over Category 5 UTP.

Let's take a look at what had to be done to achieve gigabit transmission rates over practical cables and distances.

12.1 Physical Layer Architecture

The Physical Layer takes a data stream from an Ethernet MAC controller and transforms it into electrical or optical signals for transmission across a specified physical medium. Similarly, the receiver takes these signals (now degraded through the wonders of the laws of physics), reconstructs the original data presented by the sender, and passes it to the receiving MAC controller. Figure 12–1 depicts the architecture of the Gigabit Ethernet Physical Layer.

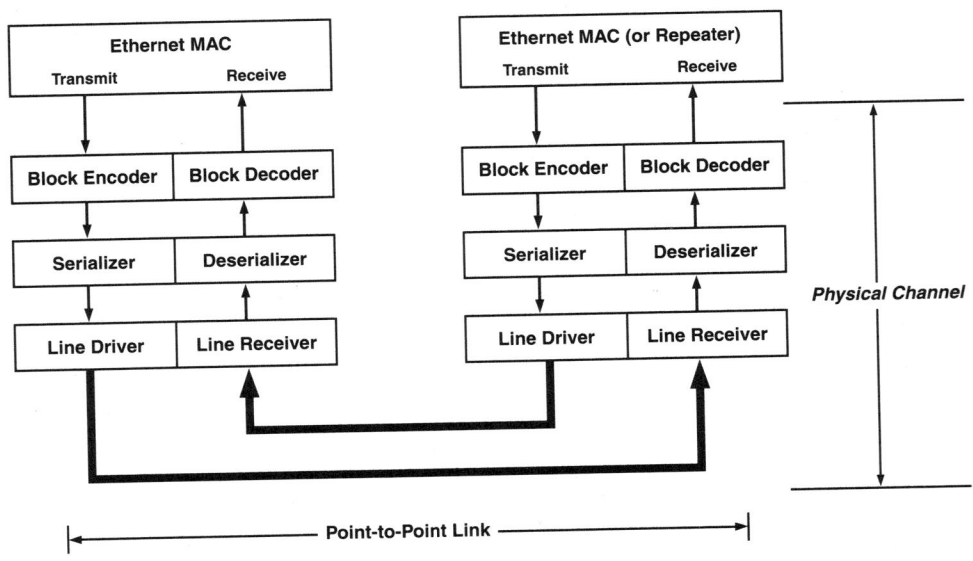

Figure 12–1 Physical layer architecture.

12.1.1 Point-to-Point Links

The physical communications channel for Gigabit Ethernet consists of a pair of point-to-point simplex links (that is, a single point-to-point duplex link) between two Ethernet stations (MACs) or, in the case of a shared LAN, an Ethernet station and a repeater. Similar to the 100 Mb/s system, Gigabit Ethernet does not support any shared-bus medium (such as coaxial cables in 10 Mb/s Ethernet).[2] As a result of this constraint and the timing restrictions imposed by repeaters (discussed in Chapter 11), there are only two permissible single-LAN Gigabit Ethernet physical topologies (see also Figure 12–2):

1. Two stations connected by a single point-to-point link (operating in either half-duplex or full-duplex mode)
2. A group of stations (in half-duplex mode) connected to a single repeater through individual point-to-point links

That's it for single-LAN configurations. There are no complex topological design rules for Gigabit Ethernet analogous to those for 10 Mb/s or

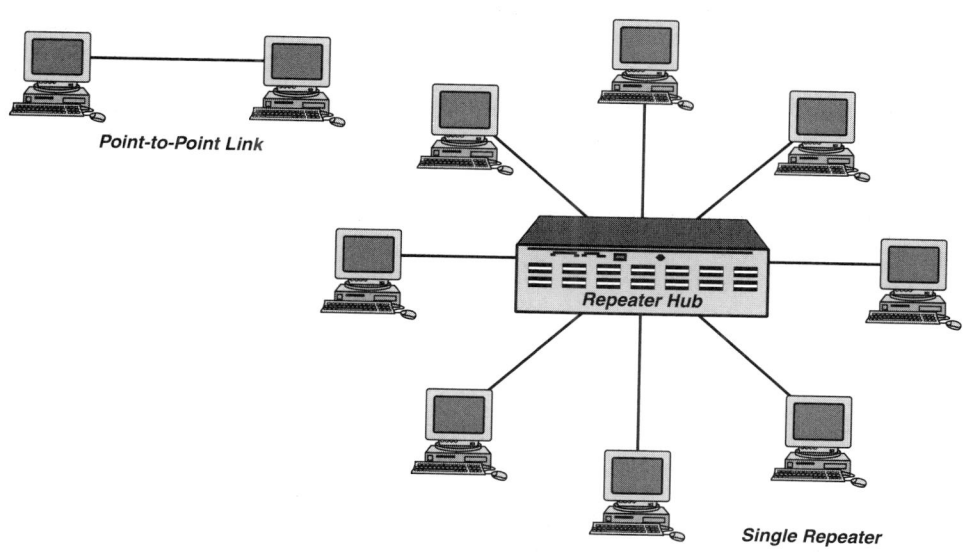

Figure 12–2 Single LAN Gigabit Ethernet topologies.

---

2. Due to electrical issues (for example, tap capacitance and reflections) with tapped transmission lines, shared media become problematic at very high data rates. It is much easier to design a reliable communications system using a point-to-point topology as opposed to a multidrop channel.

100 Mb/s LANs. Of course, complex *logical* structures can be built using bridges/switches and routers. However, regardless of the numbers of devices or the complexity of the arrangement, the physical channel still appears to be one of the two configurations depicted previously.[3]

12.1.2 Block Coding

Gigabit Ethernet (like its 100 Mb/s counterpart) uses a block coding scheme, whereby a group of data bits are encoded into a larger space of code bits. Examples of block codes include:

- 4B/5B as used in 100 Mb/s Ethernet and FDDI. [IEEE95, ISO89a] This code takes 4 bits of data (4B) and expands it into 5 code bits (5B) for transmission on the physical channel.
- 8B/6T as used in 100BASE-T4. [IEEE95] This code takes 8 bits (8B) of data and expands it into 6 ternary (three-level) symbols for transmission.
- 5B/6B as used in 100VG-AnyLAN. [IEEE95a] As should be obvious by now, this code takes 5 bits of data and expands it to 6 code bits for transmission.

There are many other codes that are also used in various communications systems. When dealing with block codes, engineers speak of "data space" (the unencoded bits, that is, 4B, 8B, and 5B from the previous examples) and "code space" (the coded bits, that is, 5B, 6T, and 6B from the previous examples). A grouping of encoded code bits is called a *code-word*. The code space must always be at least as large as the data space; it is usually larger. In the case of 4B/5B, there are 16 possibilities (2^4) for the 4-bit data space and 32 possibilities (2^5) in the 5-bit code space. In the 8B/6T case, there are 256 points (2^8) in the data space, and 729 points (3^6) in the code space. The expanded code space allows us to:

1. **Choose the encoded values of the data such that some important characteristic(s) are ensured.** To properly decode the data at the receiver, you may need to provide some number of signal transitions (one-to-zero or zero-to-one) in the transmitted code-bit stream, regardless of the data being transmitted. You can choose encodings such that this characteristic is guaranteed. Similarly, you can choose your encodings such that over time there are an equal number of ones and zeroes in the

---

3. Remember that the connection between a station and a switch or router is, from the perspective of the physical channel, just a point-to-point link between two Ethernet stations.

coded bits independent of the data, so that an electrical analog of the code-bit stream can pass through a transformer or other AC coupling without undue distortion.

2. **Encode control signals in the transmitted stream.** If the code space is larger than the data space, there can be unused codes that do not correspond to data values. These can be used for control purposes, for example, Start-of-Frame and End-of-Frame delimiting, Idle or Carrier Extension signaling, and error indications.

12.1.3 Serializer and Line Driver

The serializer takes a block of coded bits (a code-word) and converts those bits to a serial (bit-by-bit) stream for actual transmission on the channel. The output of the serializer (and similarly, the input of the deserializer) is a data stream at the actual channel transmission rate; this is usually the highest speed signal in the entire system. It is therefore generally desirable to serialize as late in the process as possible so as to minimize the amount of circuitry that must operate at these extremely high clock rates.

The output of the serializer is converted to the appropriate electrical or optical signals for transmission on the underlying medium. The driver circuit generally incorporates some form of *line coding*. The line coding performs the actual translation of a logic level in code space to a signal on the medium and is totally separate from any block coding that may have been previously applied.[4]

Line coding can be either simple or complex. In general, a complex line code can be used to reduce the frequency spectrum of the transmitted signal. This is useful when transmitting high data rates on a medium that has inherently low bandwidth or poor protection from electromagnetic interference. Some examples of line codes (depicted in Figure 12–3) include:

■ **Non-Return-to-Zero (NRZ).** This simplest of codes transmits a high voltage for a logic one and a low voltage for a logic zero. (Most people don't think of it as a "code" at all.) NRZ is used in systems from RS-232 [EIA69] to Gigabit Ethernet (yes!). For self-synchronous operation, this code

---

4. If binary block coding is used, the logic levels in code space are limited to zero or one. However, if a ternary or higher-power code is used (for example, 8B/6T, or 4B/1Q), the logic levels in code space will have values besides just zero or one. The number of logic levels in code space is equal to the power of the code.

requires that there be some minimum number of logic transitions in the code stream in order to provide clocking information. In the case of Gigabit Ethernet, the block code used guarantees this transition density.

NRZI—Non-Return-to-Zero, Invert on Ones—is a variation of NRZ that leaves the signal unchanged for a logic zero and inverts the signal from its previous state for a logic one. NRZI is used in FDDI and 100BASE-FX; the 4B/5B block code guarantees a sufficient "ones density."

- **Manchester code.** This code, used in all 10 Mb/s Ethernet systems, eliminates the need for any transitions or one's density in the data stream—at the expense of increasing the maximum transmission frequency by a factor of 2.
- **Multilevel Threshold-3 (MLT-3).** This code uses three signal levels. The maximum transmission frequency is reduced by half (relative to NRZ), at the expense of reduced noise margin. The code leaves the signal unchanged for a logic zero and moves the signal to the "next state" for a logic one, where the states are zero voltage, high voltage, zero voltage, low voltage, zero voltage, and so on.

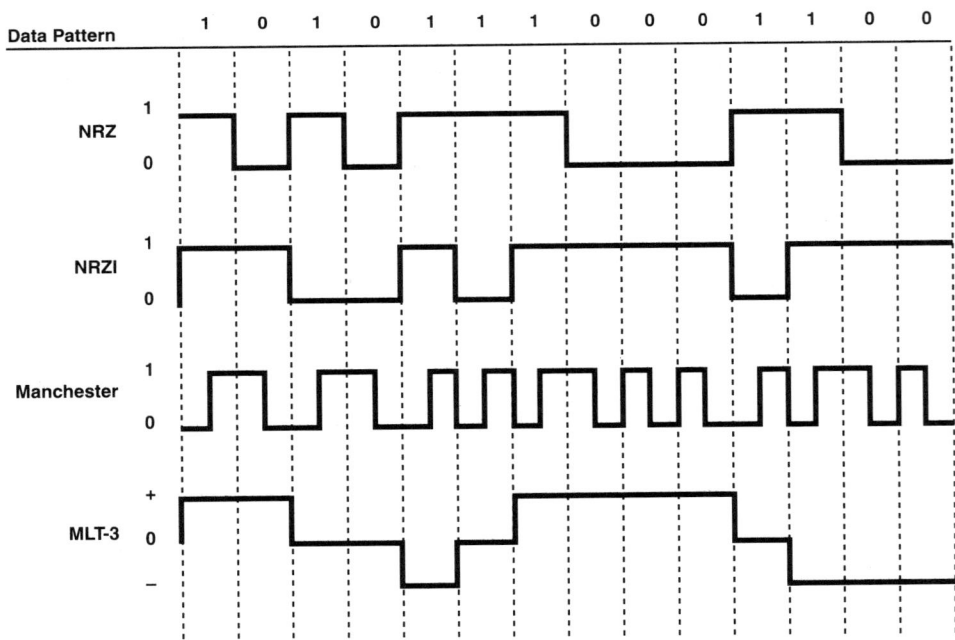

Figure 12–3 Line coding.

The selection of a line code involves a trade-off among:

- Transmission spectrum (minimizing bandwidth requirements and EMI)
- DC balance (keeping the number of ones and zeroes equal)
- Maximum "run length" (the length of time that the code can stay in one state without a transition; this affects short-term DC offset)
- Noise immunity
- Complexity in generation and detection, and so on.

Finally, the block-and-line-coded signal is transmitted onto the medium, either electrically or optically.

12.2 1000BASE-X

The 1000BASE-X family of Physical Layers was the first to be developed under the Gigabit Ethernet umbrella. It was derived directly from the Physical Layer design for Fibre Channel. [ANSI94] In the same way that 100 Mb/s Ethernet adapted the FDDI-over-copper Physical Layer design for use with an Ethernet MAC (see Chapter 16), 1000BASE-X adapted the Fibre Channel Physical Layer design (specifically the FC-0 and FC-1 sublayers) for Ethernet use. The only significant difference is a slight speed increase from Fibre Channel's 1.0625 Gbaud to Gigabit Ethernet's 1.250 Gbaud.

12.2.1 1000BASE-X Block Coding

1000BASE-X uses an 8B/10B block code; 8 bits of data (1 byte) are encoded into 10 code bits. The coding scheme was developed and patented by IBM Corporation and licensed for use in both Fibre Channel and Gigabit Ethernet. [FRAN84] This particular code provides a number of important characteristics:

1. The coding ensures sufficient signal transitions for clock recovery at the receiver.
2. The code space allows control signals to be encoded in the data stream.
3. The specific choices of code mappings significantly increase the likelihood of detecting single- and multiple-bit errors through code violations (without depending on the Ethernet 32-bit CRC).
4. Some of the encodings (used for control signals) contain a unique, easily recognizable code-bit pattern (known as a *comma*) that aids in rapid synchronization and receiver alignment.

12.2.1.1 8B/10B Notation and Terminology

To make it easier to deal with the 256 possible data values and 1024 theoretically possible code-words for every transmitted byte, a shorthand notation was developed for the 8B/10B code. The code space is divided into two groups of codes:

1. The "D" group, used to encode data bytes
2. The "K" group, used to encode special control characters[5]

Figure 12–4 depicts the mapping of data bytes (8B) into code-words (10B).

The 8 bits of the data byte are denoted A, B, C, D, E, F, G, and H (least-significant bit to most-significant bit), as indicated. The encoder translates these 8 bits into a 10-bit code, designated a, b, c, d, e, i, f, g, h, and j. The code-word is treated as two subgroups, one containing 6 code bits (a, b, c, d, e, and i) and one containing 4 code bits (f, g, h, and j). A given code is referred to by the shorthand /D$x.y$/ (for data codes) or /K$x.y$/ (for special codes), where x is the decimal value of EDCBA (E being the most-significant bit of the string) and y is the decimal value of HGF (H being the most-significant bit of the string).

A few examples are given in Table 12–1. The entire 8B/10B code table is provided in Appendix A.

The encoded 10B code-words are transmitted (and received) serially in the order abcdeifghj.

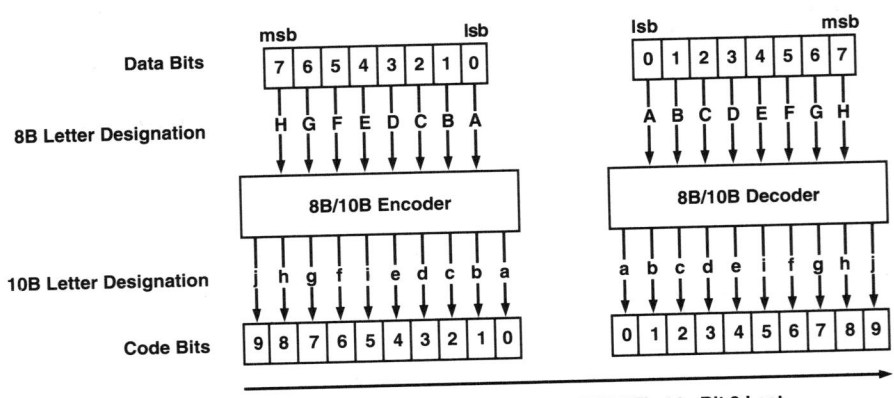

Figure 12–4 8B/10B mapping and notation.

---

5. Yes, the special group is referred to as "K" because of the breakfast cereal of the same name.

TABLE 12–1 EXAMPLE 8B/10B CODING

Name	Byte Value (8B space)	8B Bits HGF EDCBA	10B Code-Word abcdei fghj
/D3.1/	0x23	001 00011	110001 1001
/D25.2/	0x59	010 11001	100110 0101
/D21.5/	0xB5	101 10101	101010 1010
/D28.5/	0xBC	101 11100	001110 1010
/K28.5/	0xBC	101 11100	001111 1010[1]

12.2.1.2 DC Balance and Running Disparity

In order to ensure that the 10B-encoded signal can be AC-coupled onto the medium (for example, pass through a transformer or capacitor) without distortion or the use of a bandwidth-increasing line code, the number of ones and zeroes in the encoded stream must be equal over time for any arbitrary data transmission. Also, the maximum number of consecutive ones or zeroes should be minimized (even if the long-term averages are equal) so as to avoid any short-term DC offset. This is called minimizing the *run length* of the code.

Thus the code-words are carefully chosen out of the 2^{10} possible code groups. The code-words used for data codes never

■ generate more than 4 consecutive ones or zeroes, or
■ have an imbalance of greater than one; that is, the 10 bits in the code always comprise either 5 ones/5 zeroes, 6 ones/4 zeroes, or 4 ones/6 zeroes.

Those codes that have large numbers of consecutive ones or zeroes or that are highly unbalanced are simply not used for data (some are used for special codes). This is one of the advantages of using a large code space: There are 1024 available codes for 256 possible data values, so you can "throw away" those codes that have undesirable properties.

In addition to selecting only the most balanced codes, we define *two* 10B encodings for every 8B group. If the 10B encoding chosen for a given value has the same number of ones and zeroes (five of each), then the two 10B

---

1. Only one of the two possible encodings of /K28.5/ is shown. See Section 12.2.1.2 for a discussion of dual encodings for DC balance.

TABLE 12-2 MULTIPLE BB/10B ENCODINGS

Name	Byte Value (8B space)	8B Bits HGF EDCBA	10B Code-Word abcdei fghj
/D23.2/	0x57	010 10111	111010 0101
			000101 0101

encodings may be the same. This would be a perfectly balanced code point requiring no compensation. The code for /D3.1/ shown in Table 12–1 is an example of a balanced code point.

If the 10B encoding has more ones than zeroes (or more zeroes than ones), then the alternate encoding uses the inverse of the bits within the subgroups [abcdei] or [fghj] (or both) in which the imbalance occurs.[6] Thus /D23.2/ has two different valid encodings, as shown in Table 12–2.

Since the [acbdei] subgroup has more ones than zeroes, the second encoding uses the inverse of this subgroup (which has more zeroes than ones).[7]

The transmitter keeps a running tally, on a code-word by code-word basis, of whether there have been more ones than zeroes transmitted or more zeroes than ones. Since a code-word can comprise (at most) an imbalance of only one additional one or zero, only a single bit of information is required for the running tally. This is called the *running disparity* (RD). RD is a measure of whether the patterns are "leaning" toward too many ones (RD+ or positive disparity) or toward too many zeroes (RD– or negative disparity). The encoder selects one of the two possible codes for each transmitted byte depending on whether the current running disparity is positive or negative. As a result of a given code-word being sent, the running disparity will either invert ("flip") or be left the same. Thus a very tight DC balance is maintained over the entire frame.

In addition, the receiver can detect many errors by checking the disparity of the received code-words. Since a transmitter will never attempt to move the DC balance between code-words by more than 1 bit either way, a code word so received can be assumed to be an error.

---

6. An exception is made in special code groups, in which the second encoding is always the inverse of the first, regardless of balance.

7. To prevent long runs of ones or zeroes, which makes clock synchronization more difficult at the receiver (even in balanced codes), the rules for determining the alternate coding for a given code point also invert patterns of [111000] and [1100] (and their inverses) in the [abcdei] and [fghj] subgroups, respectively.

12.2.1.3 Ordered Sets

Control information (as opposed to data) is communicated through the transmission of *ordered sets*. An ordered set is a string of one or more code-words, always beginning with a code from the Special group. The use of Special codes makes ordered sets easily distinguishable from data. This distinction allows the system to unambiguously pass both data and control information across the same communications channel; that is, ordered sets provide an "out-of-band" signaling method.

Gigabit Ethernet defines and uses eight such ordered sets, given in Table 12–3.

The Configuration sets are used for Auto-Negotiation of link character-istics, which is discussed in Section 12.2.7.

The Idle sets are used between transmissions (frames or bursts). /I1/ is sent first (if necessary) to restore a known (negative) running disparity for the beginning of the next frame. The rest of the idle time is transmitted as /I2/.

The /S/ and /T/ sets are used as delimiters that indicate the beginning and end of each transmitted frame, respectively.[8] In half-duplex systems, during carrier extension (and during the interframe gap of frames in a burst), the /R/

TABLE 12–3   ORDERED SETS

Name	Description	Number of Code-Words in Set	Encoding
/C1/	Configuration 1	4	/K28.5/D21.5/config-message
/C2/	Configuration 2	4	/K28.5/D2.2/config-message
/I1/	Idle 1	2	/K28.5/D5.6/
/I2/	Idle 2	2	/K28.5/D16.2/
/R/	Carrier Extend	1	/K23.7/
/S/	Start of Packet	1	/K27.7/
/T/	End of Packet	1	/K29.7/
/V/	Error Propagation	1	/K30.7/

8. The /S/ and /T/ ordered sets delimit the data bit stream in the Physical Layer encapsulation, denoting the end of idle or interframe gap and the beginning of preamble. This is distinct from the Start-of-Frame Delimiter (SFD) used by the Data Link to indicate the end of preamble and the beginning of the Destination address. The Data Link SFD is signaled "in band," as opposed to the "out-of-band" signaling used by the /S/ ordered set. The standard [IEEE98] uses the term "Start of Packet Delimiter" for the /S/ ordered set rather than "Start of Frame" to indicate this differentiation. However, I prefer to reserve the term "packet" for the Network Layer encapsulation (for example, an IP datagram).

set is transmitted as a "fill" character, rather than one of the Idle sets being used. This provides a spacing between frames without causing the receiving MAC to think that the channel has gone idle, which would cause it to deassert carrier sense.

The /V/ set is used by repeaters to propagate an error detected in the receive stream to all attached stations.

Figure 12–5 depicts the usage of various ordered sets in a data stream. The example shown comprises a frame burst in half-duplex mode, primarily to show how carrier extension and burst interframe gaps are signaled with ordered sets.

12.2.1.4 Commas

The 10B encoding of the special code /K28.5/ contains the bit pattern b'0011111' (or its inverse, b'1100000'), called a *comma*. A comma is unique in that it contains five sequential ones or zeroes. Gigabit Ethernet's use of the 8B/10B coding scheme ensures that unless an error occurs, the comma pattern is unique to /K28.5/. It cannot appear anywhere else in the data stream, even allowing for misalignment of the incoming code bits.[9]

The /K28.5/ code consists of a comma followed by an alternating sequence of zeroes and ones (that is, b'0011111010' or b'1100000101') and was consciously selected for use in the Configuration and Idle ordered sets. This bit pattern provides an easy way to align and synchronize the incoming bit stream at link startup and between frames.

12.2.2 Line Coding

1000BASE-X uses simple NRZ line coding. A logic one in 10B code space is transmitted as either a high voltage (on copper media) or as a high light intensity (on fiber media). A logic zero is transmitted as a low voltage or light intensity. It doesn't get much simpler than that.

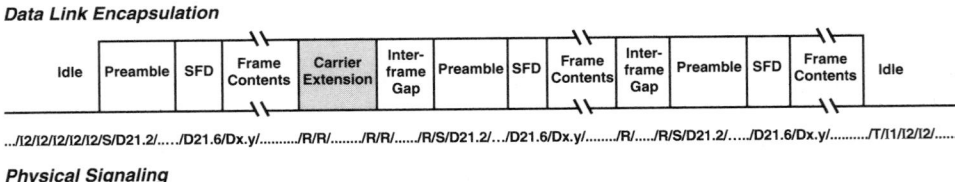

Figure 12–5 Ordered set usage.

---

9. Two other special codes, /K28.1/ and /K28.7/, also contain commas, but these are not used in Gigabit Ethernet.

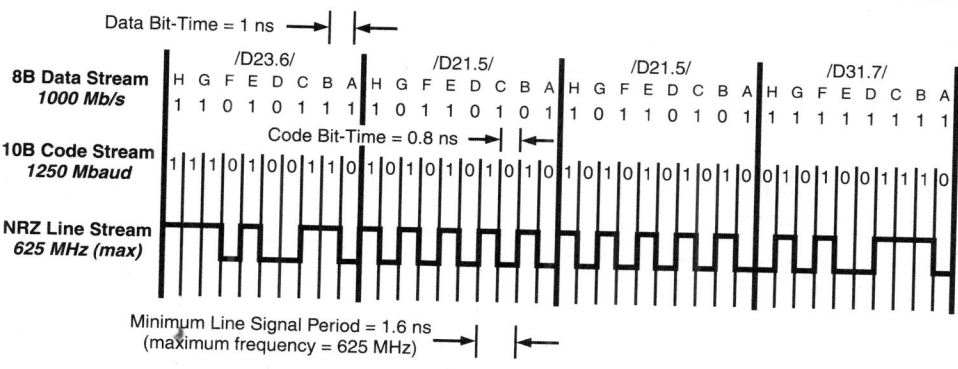

Figure 12–6 Data, code, and line symbol rates.

Using NRZ line coding, the transmitted baud rate is therefore 1.25 Gbaud for a 1 Gb/s data rate (1 Gb/s × 10/8, due to the 8B/10B block coding).[10] The maximum transmitted fundamental frequency is 625 MHz, since NRZ coding requires 2 bits to complete a "cycle" as depicted in Figure 12–6. (The 625 MHz frequency would result from a worst-case code pattern of alternating ones and zeroes, for example, a repeating string of /D21.5/.)

12.2.3 Physical Layer Interfaces

There are two standardized points of interface between a Gigabit Ethernet controller and a device implementing the Physical Layer (a transceiver):

1. **Gigabit Media-Independent Interface (GMII).** Discussed briefly in Chapter 7, this interface is designed to allow a Gigabit Ethernet controller to connect to any transceiver, both 1000BASE-X and 1000BASE-T.
2. **"Ten Bit" Interface (10B or TBI).** Suitable for use only with the 1000BASE-X family, this interface provides a more convenient (and optimized) partitioning of functions along technology and clock domain lines.

In theory, it is also possible to build a completely integrated controller/transceiver, in which the only interface would be to the actual communications medium. This is currently impractical at gigabit data rates with existing technologies. For the foreseeable future, there will need to be some demarcation between logic devices implementing the Ethernet controller (and possibly,

---

10. The line coding rate (1.25 Gbaud) is maintained to ±100 ppm (0.01%).

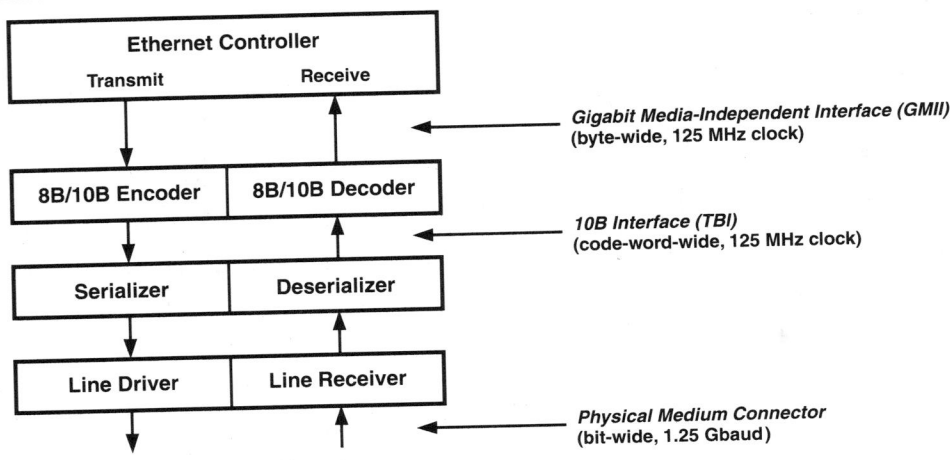

Figure 12–7 Physical layer interfaces.

portions of the Physical Layer logic) and the transceiver used to signal directly on the communications medium.

Figure 12–7 depicts the relationship among these Physical Layer interfaces.

12.2.3.1 Gigabit Media-Independent Interface (GMII)

The GMII is based on the 100 Mb/s MII design (see Chapter 7) and consists of four groups of signals:

1. **Transmit signals.** These include the byte-wide Transmit Data, plus associated Transmit Clock, Transmit Enable, and Transmit Error signals. The data signals are synchronous with the clock, at one-eighth of the data rate, or 125 MHz (1 Gb/s = 125 MB/s). The transmit signals are used to move data from the controller to the transceiver for encoding and transmission on the LAN.

2. **Receive signals.** These include the byte-wide Receive Data, plus associated Receive Clock, Receive Data Valid (equivalent to a Receive Enable signal), and Receive Error signals. Similar to the transmit signals, the receive data is synchronous with the 125 MHz receive clock. The receive signals are used to move decoded data from the transceiver to the controller.

3. **Ethernet Control signals.** These are the Carrier Sense and Collision Detect signals generated by the transceiver and used by the controller

for medium-access control. Note that these signals are used only in half-duplex mode. They are ignored by a controller operating in full-duplex mode.[11]

4. **Management signals.** These include a serial management I/O line and an associated clock. Management information is exchanged (bidirectionally) between the controller and the transceiver for configuration and control.

Table 12–4 summarizes the GMII signaling.

Because of the very high clock rates, the GMII is inappropriate as an externally exposed interface. There is no connector or cable specified for GMII (unlike for the 10/100 Mb/s MII). If it is exposed at all, it is used exclusively for IC-to-IC connections. Even over these short distances, designers must concern themselves with transmission-line effects of printed circuit traces and the behavior of the IC pins and pads themselves.

The GMII is a convenient abstraction for describing how controllers and transceivers interact; the IEEE 802.3z standard specifies most such interactions as an exchange of signals across the GMII. However, the GMII is less useful as a physical interface, unless a designer is really building a component or system that must integrate seamlessly with both 1000BASE-X and 1000BASE-T transceivers.

12.2.3.2 The "10B" Interface

In a product designed to use one family of Gigabit Ethernet Physical Layers exclusively (for example, 1000BASE-X only), it makes more sense to physically partition the system such that there is no exposed GMII, not even as an IC interconnect. The technology and clock speeds used for the encoder/decoder are better matched to the controller than to the transceiver. A higher level of integration (and lower cost) can be achieved by integrating the encoder/decoder with the MAC controller logic. Rather than connecting a controller IC to a separate 8B/10B encoder/decoder, the two functions can be integrated in the same device. The encoder/decoder logic is not particularly large or complex, and the clock speed is exactly that of a controller dealing with a byte-wide data stream. This provides a natural integration scenario.

---

11. If a GMII-compatible device (either controller or transceiver) is designed to operate *only* in full-duplex mode, these signals (as well as the TX_ER signal) may be omitted completely.

TABLE 12–4   GMII SIGNALS

Name	Description	Direction (relative to controller)	Synchronous To
Transmit Signals			
TXD [7:0] Transmit Data	Byte-wide data for transmission on the channel.	Output	GTX_CLK
GTX_CLK Gigabit Transmit Clock	125 MHz (nominal) clock for transmission of data.	Output	
TX_EN Transmit Enable	Indicates when valid data is present on the TXD lines.	Output	GTX_CLK
TX_ER Transmit Error	Used to propagate errors through a repeater. (Used in shared, half-duplex LANs only.)	Output	GTX_CLK
Receive Signals			
RXD [7:0] Receive Data	Byte-wide data received from the channel.	Input	RX_CLK
RX_CLK Receive Clock	Recovered clock (125 MHz, nominal) from received data.	Input	
RX_DV Receive Data Valid	Indicates when valid data is present on the RXD lines.	Input	RX_CLK
RX_ER Receive Error	Indicates that an error was detected while received data was being decoded.	Input	RX_CLK
Ethernet Control Signals			
CRS Carrier Sense	Indicates when the physical channel is active, either with a received or transmitted signal.	Input	Asynchronous
COL Collision Detect	Indicates when one or more stations (other than this station) are concurrently transmitting on the channel.	Input	Asynchronous
Management Signals			
MDIO Management Data Input/Output	Used to transmit and receive management information between the controller and transceiver.	Input/output	MDC
MDC Management Data Clock	2.5 MHz clock (maximum) used for management data exchange.	Output	

The resulting interface for 1000BASE-X is 10 code bits wide, called a "10B" interface (10 [code-] bits).[12] This interface was designed into many commercial Fibre Channel serializer/deserializer (SERDES) components and was naturally carried over to Gigabit Ethernet. The popular 10B interface consists of three groups of signals (Transmit, Receive, and Control) and is summarized in Table 12–5.[13]

Some vendors use a variant of this interface called a "20B" interface. The main difference is that a 20B interface clocks two code-words across the interface for each clock cycle, rather than one at a time. This reduces the clock rate to 62.5 MHz (in both the transmit and receive direction), which makes it more attractive for low-cost CMOS implementations. The need for the split-phase receive clock is also eliminated; a single 62.5 MHz clock is used. The downside is that it requires twice as many IC pins for the transmit and receive data paths.

12.2.4 Optical Fiber Media (1000BASE-SX/LX)

The 1000BASE-X family supports three types of optical fibers:

50-µm multimode

62.5-µm multimode

10-µm single-mode.[14]

It also supports two different wavelengths of laser drivers:

1. Shortwave (nominally 850 nm, designated 1000BASE-SX)
2. Longwave (nominally 1300 nm, designated 1000BASE-LX).

The various combinations of drivers and fibers result in different maximum usable lengths. Further complications result from any distance restrictions imposed by a half-duplex MAC. A complete guide to allowable topologies and lengths is in Section 12.4.

---

12. The standard [IEEE98] refers to this as the *TBI* (Ten-Bit Interface). However most commercial products use the 10B designation.

13. Specific components may use different signal names than those used here and may implement additional signals as well. Table 12–5 is representative of a number of common products, as well as the TBI specified in [IEEE98].

14. Common commercial single-mode fiber core diameters vary over the range of approximately 8–10 µm. They are collectively referred to as 10-µm fiber in the text.

TABLE 12–5 10B SIGNALS

Name	Description	Direction (relative to controller)	Synchronous To
Transmit Group			
TX_CODE_GROUP [9:0] Transmit Data	Code-word-wide data for transmission on the channel.	Output	TX_CLK
TX_CLK Transmit Clock	125 MHz (nominal) clock for the transmission of data.	Output	
Receive Group			
RX_CODE_GROUP [9:0] Receive Data	Code-word-wide data received from the channel.	Input	RX_CLK [1:0]
RX_CLK [0] Receive Clock 0	One-half frequency recovered clock (62.5 MHz, nominal) from received data, used to clock. odd-numbered code groups.[1]	Input	
RX_CLK [1] Receive Clock 1	One-half frequency recovered clock (62.5 MHz, nominal, 180° phase-shift relative to RX_CLK [0]); used to clock even-numbered code groups	Input	
Control Group			
EWRAP Enable Wrap	Used to put the transceiver into a loopback mode.	Output	Asynchronous
COM_DET Comma Detect	Indicates that a comma was received in the incoming stream.	Input	RX_CLK [1]
EN_CDET Enable Comma Detect	Used to enable/disable comma detection and alignment.	Output	Asynchronous
-LCK_REF Lock to Reference	Forces the clock recovery circuitry to lock to the TX_CLK signal rather than the incoming data.	Output	Asynchronous

1. The use of a half-frequency, split-phase receive clock is an artifact of some existing Fibre Channel components and was incorporated into the standard for Gigabit Ethernet use.

12.2.4.1 Multimode Fiber

Gigabit Ethernet is supported over both 50-μm and 62.5-μm fiber at distances up to 550 m. Both fibers use 125-μm cladding and accommodate the same connectors; this is discussed in Section 12.2.4.5.

Because of the distance limitations of multimode fiber, its primary application is for intrabuilding connections (building backbones) and direct end-station connections (servers and high-performance workstations). Campus backbone networks often require distances longer than 550 m and are better suited to single-mode fiber.

The predominant installed base of multimode fiber for intrabuilding use is 62.5 μm. This fiber is already standard for 10BASE-F, 100BASE-FX, and FDDI applications and is supported by the EIA building wiring standard [EIA91]. Unfortunately, this fiber supports Gigabit Ethernet operation up to only 550 m. This is in contrast to the 2 km distance supportable at 10 or 100 Mb/s. Network designers planning to use already-installed 62.5-μm fiber for Gigabit Ethernet (perhaps as an upgrade from 100BASE-FX or FDDI) will have to make sure that the distance limitations are not exceeded.

Systems that use 1000BASE-SX can get a distance advantage by using 50-μm fiber, but at a cost in flexibility. That is, it may be difficult to use this fiber for data communications applications other than Gigabit Ethernet. In any case, the maxima are achievable only when using Gigabit Ethernet in full-duplex mode. Half-duplex (shared) systems will be limited by the timing restrictions of the MAC, rather than the physical limitations of the cable.[15] See Section 12.4 for a complete discussion of the Physical Layer design rules for Gigabit Ethernet.

12.2.4.2 Single-Mode Fiber

1000BASE-X is the first Ethernet system to specify operation over single-mode optical fiber. This was necessary in order to support a key application of Gigabit Ethernet, namely, campus backbone networks. The distances expected in this environment, as well as the data rate employed, mandated a medium beyond the capabilities of multimode fiber. Gigabit Ethernet uses industry-standard, 10-μm, single-mode fiber; the same connector type can be used as for multimode fiber (discussed shortly).

Single-mode fiber requires the use of long-wavelength optical laser drivers and can operate over distances of up to 3 km in full-duplex mode. It makes little sense to use single-mode fiber for half-duplex Gigabit Ethernet, since the length limitations for shared LANs fall well within the capabilities of multimode fiber and shortwave lasers. There is no benefit to be gained by

---

15. Fiber links are limited to 320 m (nominal) for station-to-station connections and 111 m (nominal) for station-to-repeater connections in half-duplex mode.

The Saga of Controlled Launch

During the development of Gigabit Ethernet, an anomaly was discovered with the use of laser optics and multimode fiber. Normally, multimode fiber is used with LED drivers, which launch incoherent light over the entire diameter of the fiber. Thus LEDs will excite all of the mode groups in a multimode fiber; this is exactly how such a fiber is designed to operate.

Gigabit Ethernet is the first standard system to specify the use of laser optical drivers with multimode fiber. Lasers generate coherent light over a very small "spot" (smaller than the diameter of a multimode fiber). This alone should not have caused a problem. However, the manufacturing process of many commercial multimode fibers occasionally introduces a slight defect (a small "glitch" in the index-of-refraction) to appear exactly in the center of the fiber. Coherent light launched onto this defect tends to "split" into two distinct propagation modes, which then travel down different paths in the fiber. Due to the graded index of multimode fiber, they travel at different speeds, and arrive at the receiver out of phase. This timing distortion (called Differential Mode Delay) can degrade the signal to the point where the receiver is no longer able to properly decode it. This results in excessive errors.

This anomaly could reduce the worst-case maximum length that Gigabit Ethernet could support over multimode fiber. The effect is small and causes a problem only in a very small percentage of actual fibers (in most cases, the effect would not be noticeable in a real system). However, good design practice requires specifying the worst-case lengths so that field installers do not have to worry about whether the fibers they are using will exhibit the problem (known as "plug and pray"). The anomaly is most noticeable with longwave lasers; shortwave laser drivers exhibit these symptoms to a much lesser degree. [CUNN97, FRAZ97]

To avoid having to specify unacceptably short distances for Gigabit Ethernet over multimode fiber, a simple "fix" was designed. When longwave laser drivers are used on multimode cable, a short adapter cable is used whose output connector offsets the fiber core slightly. This *controlled launch* sidesteps the problem (literally) by launching the optical power away from the center of the fiber in which the manufacturing defect may occur. Thus a 1000BASE-LX device can be used with single-mode fiber directly (centered launch) or with multimode fiber using the offset cable.

Since 1000BASE-SX devices can be used *only* with multimode fiber, the controlled launch can be built into the laser device itself, thereby avoiding the need for an adapter cable. In practice, adapter cables will rarely be needed. This is because shortwave lasers provide adequate distance coverage for virtually all applications using multimode fiber. Longwave lasers are used primarily with single-mode fiber, which does not require controlled launch.

employing the higher-cost longwave laser drivers required to use single-mode optical fiber.

12.2.4.3 Shortwave Lasers (1000BASE-SX)

Short wavelength lasers (770–860 nm) are used with multimode fiber only. Distances of up to 260 m are supported when using 62.5-µm fiber; 525 m is possible when using 50-µm fiber. The shorter distance (relative to longwave lasers) is offset by a lower cost.

Optical drive levels are in the range of -10 to 0 dbm (light on), with an extinction ratio (on/off) of at least 9 dB. Receive levels (at the end of a maximum length cable) are in the range of -17 to 0 dbm (light on). The system link budget includes allowances for fiber attenuation, modal bandwidth effects, connector attenuation, return loss, and so on. Beyond the optical power levels, the transmit waveshape is very carefully specified (for example, rise/fall times and symmetry). Complete specifications are provided in [IEEE98].

12.2.4.4 Longwave Drivers (1000BASE-LX)

Long wavelength lasers (1270–1355 nm) are used primarily with single-mode fiber. However, they can be used with multimode fiber as well. In this case, they actually allow longer distance coverage than is possible with shortwave lasers. Distances of 550 m are possible when using multimode fiber (62.5 µm or 50 µm) and 3000 m with 10-µm single-mode fiber.

Optical drive levels are in the range of -13.5 to -3 dbm (light on), with an extinction ratio of at least 9 dB. Receive levels (at the end of a maximum length cable) are in the range of -19 to -3 dbm (light on). The system link budget includes allowances for fiber attenuation, modal bandwidth effects, connector attenuation, return loss, and so on. As with shortwave drivers, the transmit waveshape is very carefully specified in [IEEE98].

12.2.4.5 Optical Fiber Connectors

The Gigabit Ethernet standard [IEEE98] specifies only one optical-fiber connector: the (very common) duplex SC, depicted in Figure 12–8. This is the same connector type used for 100BASE-FX, Fibre Channel, and many other systems. The connector is keyed to ensure proper transmitter/receiver matching of the fibers. However, there is no keying to ensure that shortwave drivers are not plugged into longwave receivers or to prevent fiber type mismatches. When using SC connectors, the network installer must make sure that the system is properly configured in this regard.

It is also possible to go outside the standard (gasp!) and use other connectors. There are many different types and styles of fiber connectors available today. Some advantages of using nonstandard connectors include:

- Ability to key for wavelength and/or fiber type
- Smaller size
- Lower cost
- Easier installation

Clearly, if an equipment manufacturer chooses to use a nonstandard connector, then the user of that equipment needs to accommodate that choice in the wiring system. While the duplex SC connector is the "official" standard, it remains to be seen whether any other connectors will gain popularity (due to some particular advantage) and become a de facto standard.[16]

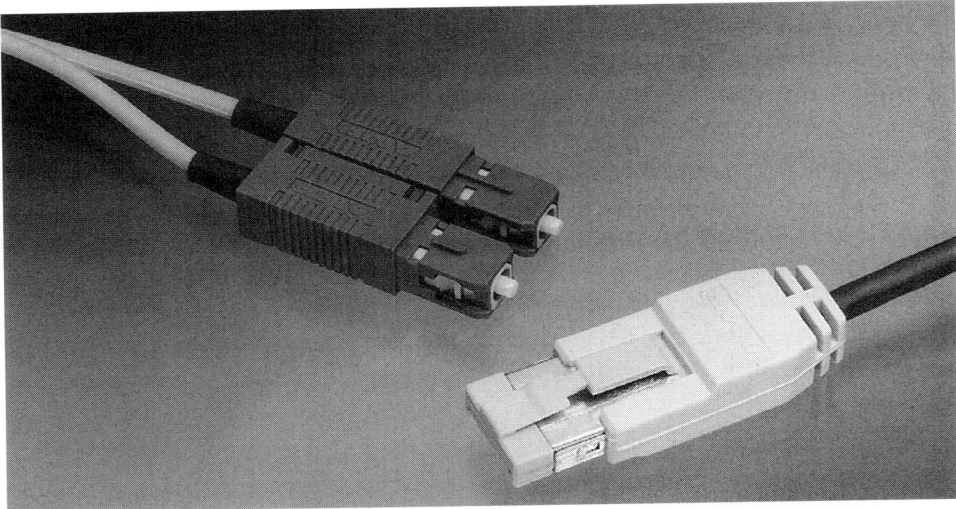

Figure 12–8 Gigabit Ethernet connectors. Left: duplex SC for optical fiber; Right: Fibre Channel Style 2 for 1000BASE-CX. Courtesy AMP Incorporated.

---

16. During the development of the Gigabit Ethernet standard, there was a concerted effort by a number of fiber connector manufacturers to include a second connector within the standard. Of course, every manufacturer wanted *their* particular connector to be the alternative standard connector. Thus began the makings of a "connector war." Teams of engineers and marketers from various connector manufacturers made presentations to the standards committee, all of which could be summed up as, "My (relatively immature, nonstandard) connector is better than their (relatively immature, nonstandard) connector." In the end, the standards committee elected to avoid choosing *any* alternative connector. It decided to allow the market to decide if the duplex SC was adequate—but not before it consumed large quantities of free food and beverages provided night after night, at each connector manufacturers' "Hospitality Reception." The motto of the committee became, "We can't be bribed, but we invite your attempts to try!"

12.2.5 Copper Media (1000BASE-CX)

The 1000BASE-X family also supports operation over dual, 150 Ω shielded twisted-pair cable. The official designation for this signaling system is 1000BASE-CX (C for copper); the cables are commonly called "short copper jumpers." With a maximum useful length of 25 m, its primary application is for equipment interconnection within a wiring closet, that is, for connections between bridges, switches, routers, and so on, within a single rack or closely situated racks of equipment. It also may be useful for connections to servers that are colocated with the wiring room. 1000BASE-CX was designed with the expectation that copper jumpers could provide a lower-cost solution for the wiring room environment than optical-fiber connections could. However, the cost of shortwave lasers is dropping rapidly (due in part to CD-ROM technology). That, plus the simplicity for both manufacturer and user of having fewer options and variations may result in 1000BASE-SX being used in this environment and rendering 1000BASE-CX moot.

12.2.5.1 1000BASE-CX Cables

1000BASE-CX cables consist of two pairs of shielded, 150 Ω cable. The cable is quite similar in appearance to the Type 1 STP wire used in Token Ring networks and 100BASE-TX [IEEE95b, IEEE95], but there are some differences in the detailed electrical specifications (in particular, tighter control of differential skew). In any case, due to the short distance and typical application for 1000BASE-CX, the use of a cable plant with existing wire is irrelevant.

1000BASE-CX cables require "compensation networks" at each end of the cable. These are passive networks (resistors, capacitors, inductors) that provide line equalization and compensation, and they generally must be designed for a particular length and type of cable. The amount of compensation required varies, even over the relatively short range of values between 0 and 25 m. Thus, as a practical matter, all 1000BASE-CX cables are sold and used as manufactured assemblies, with compensation networks and connectors installed at the factory. Also, since the compensation networks are length-dependent, 1000BASE-CX jumper cables cannot be linked together like extension cords. Rather, a single cable must cover the entire distance between the interconnected devices.

12.2.5.2 1000BASE-CX Connectors

Two connectors are specified for short copper jumpers[17]:

- **8-pin High-Speed Serial Data Connector (HSSDC, or Fibre Channel Style 2).** This connector (shown in Figure 12–8) provides both improved electrical characteristics and a smaller form factor than the alternative D-subminiature connector. It is the preferred connector for 1000BASE-CX.
- **9-pin shielded D-subminiature connector.** This connector (shown in Figure 12–9) is available as an alternative to the Style-2 connector. It is the same connector used for Token Ring, 100BASE-TX (STP), and other systems using 150 Ω shielded twisted-pair. While perhaps not the greatest choice for electrical characteristics at 625 MHz, it is low-cost, widely available, and easy to terminate.

Pin assignments are shown in Table 12–6.

12.2.5.3 Electrical Signaling

1000BASE-CX uses differential drivers, with positive ECL (PECL) signaling. Thus for a logic one, the "+" output is driven 1.1–2.0 V more positive than the "−" output. For a logic zero, the "−" output is driven 1.1–2.0 V more positive than the "+" output.[18] Rise/fall times are in the range 85–327 ns,

Figure 12–9 9-pin D-subminiature connector. Courtesy AMP Incorporated.

---

17. The Fibre Channel committee selected the Style-2 connector after going through its own connector war. Gigabit Ethernet simply adopted the Fibre Channel solution with no bloodshed.

18. It is interesting to note that PECL signaling with almost the identical drive levels was used for the original 10 Mb/s AUI (see Chapter 7). The reason for its use is also the same: It provides high-speed signaling with very low differential skew.

TABLE 12–6 1000BASE-CX CONNECTOR PIN ASSIGNMENTS

Signal	Fibre Channel Style-2	9-Pin D-Subminiature
Transmit +	1	1
Transmit −	3	6
Receive +	8	5
Receive −	6	9
Shield	Connector shell	Connector shell

with differential skew (the difference between the rise and fall time) matched to 25 ps. At the receiver, the signal is degraded through the cable and connectors such that the resulting amplitude can be as weak as 400 mV p-p. The receiver is responsible for detecting proper logic levels, even though the signal is significantly degraded in amplitude, distorted in time, and affected by noise.

12.2.5.4 Electrical Isolation

While DC isolation may be provided in the compensation networks used with 1000BASE-CX cables (for example, series capacitance), the shield of the cable is connected to the chassis reference at both ends of the link. Since the chassis of a device is usually connected to the earth reference (green wire) of the power supply, any difference in the power reference will result in current (possibly a huge current) flowing through the shield between the connected devices. The bottom line is that 1000BASE-CX should be used only to interconnect devices that are powered from the same electrical branch circuit. This is generally not a severe restriction within a wiring closet, which is the target application space for this technology. However, if 1000BASE-CX is used to connect devices in separate rooms (or worse, separate floors), the network planner should make sure that the equipments are powered from the same source.[19]

---

19. The word "ground" was carefully and purposefully omitted from the discussion in the previous paragraph. This is because that word means different things to different people; for example:

- The shield of the cable (the communications system designer)
- The reference plane in a circuit board (the logic designer)
- The third wire in the power cord (the power supply designer)
- The chassis of the device (the mechanical designer), and so on.

These different grounds may or may not be connected to each other, depending on requirements for system signal integrity. In any case, they serve very different purposes and should be considered separately.

12.2.6 1000BASE-X Media Summary

Table 12–7 provides a summary of the signaling characteristics of 1000BASE-X media.

12.2.7 Automatic Configuration

1000BASE-X incorporates an automatic mechanism to properly configure certain link characteristics at link initialization time (for example, at power-up or due to a reset command issued by a network management application). This mechanism is modeled after the Auto-Negotiation function originally designed to configure 10/100 Mb/s devices over UTP cables (see Chapter 8), but it does less in the way of allowing systems with multiple capabilities to accede to their highest common denominator. Proper 1000BASE-X operation still depends heavily on a human network installer ensuring that interconnected devices are compatible with each other and with the cables used to connect them.

TABLE 12–7   1000BASE-X PHYSICAL LAYER CHARACTERISTICS SUMMARY

	Maximum Distance Supported				Optical Wave-length	Drive Signal	Drive Rise/Fall Time
	50-μm Fiber (multi-mode)	62.5-μm Fiber (multi-mode)	10-μm Fiber (single-mode)	150 Ω STP			
1000BASE-SX Shortwave Laser Optics	525 m	260 m	—	—	770–860 nm	−10 to 0 dbm[1]	260 ps max.[2]
1000BASE-LX Longwave Laser Optics	550 m	550 m	3000 m	—	1270–1355 nm	−11.5 to −3 dbm	260 ps max.
1000BASE-CX Short Copper Jumpers	—	—	—	25 m	—	±1.1 to 2.0 V p-p, differential	85–327 ps[3]

1. The maximum power may be limited by laser safety regulations to a level lower than 0 dbm.

2. The maximum rise/fall time is reduced to 210 ps if the wavelength used is < 830 nm.

3. A differential skew of not more than 25 ps must be maintained, regardless of the absolute rise/fall time.

12.2.7.1 1000BASE-X versus UTP Auto-Negotiation

The key differences between UTP Auto-Negotiation and 1000BASE-X Auto-Negotiation are:

- **1000BASE-X Auto-Negotiation is used only to configure parameters for the operation of Gigabit Ethernet; it is not used to negotiate data rate.** The network installer is still responsible for ensuring that a cable from a Gigabit Ethernet device is not accidentally plugged into a 10 Mb/s or 100 Mb/s Ethernet device (or some other type of device). This is less of a problem with 1000BASE-X (which does not operate over UTP cables) than in the world of desktop LANs, in which offices are often pre-wired with RJ-45 outlets and many different systems use the same physical connectors. With UTP cabling, it is not at all obvious for what data rate a given jack is configured. 1000BASE-X systems use either optical-fiber cables (for which there never was any mechanism for Auto-Negotiation) or specialized copper jumpers (which are unique to 1000BASE-CX and generally used within a single room[20]).

- **1000BASE-X Auto-Negotiation does not use "fast link pulses" for Auto-Negotiation signaling.** Since it is assumed that the network installer has connected devices that have fundamentally compatible physical signaling (that is, 1000BASE-X), there is no need to use a lower-level "common language," such as the fast link pulses used in UTP Auto-Negotiation. Similarly, there is no need to maintain backward compatibility with 10BASE-T link pulses (as is achieved with fast link pulse signaling), since a 10BASE-T device will never connect to a 1000BASE-X device. Thus 1000BASE-X Auto-Negotiation can use normal 1000BASE-X signaling (the same as used for data transmissions) for determining the proper link configuration.

- **1000BASE-X Auto-Negotiation defines new syntax and semantics for the exchanged messages.** While 1000BASE-X exchanges 16-bit configuration messages (just like UTP Auto-Negotiation), some of the bit definitions are changed.

1000BASE-X Auto-Negotiation cannot resolve an improper configuration of wavelength and/or fiber type. If a 1000BASE-LX device (1300 nm

---

20. The significance of this is that the network installer can usually see, or easily find, the device at the other end of the cable.

laser) is plugged into a 1000BASE-SX device (850-nm laser, using the same duplex SC connector), the link will simply fail to operate. There is little that Auto-Negotiation could do for this misconfiguration anyway because there is a fundamental signal incompatibility. Similarly, if a single-mode fiber is plugged into a device designed for multimode fiber only (for example, 1000BASE-SX), the optical receiver will not respond properly and communication will be impossible. Fundamental matches of signaling (1000BASE-X), wavelength, and fiber mode must be coordinated by the network installer.

So what does 1000BASE-X Auto-Negotiation actually achieve? The only behaviors that can be "negotiated" are

- half- versus full-duplex operation, and
- flow control.

The mechanism is extensible to allow for the addition of other capabilities in the future.

12.2.7.2 1000BASE-X Auto-Negotiation Exchanges

Upon link initialization, the 1000BASE-X Auto-Negotiation protocol transmits 16-bit messages to its link partner and receives similar messages from that partner. A message may take as many 16-bit "pages" as needed, but most common negotiations require only the minimum "base page" depicted in Figure 12–10.

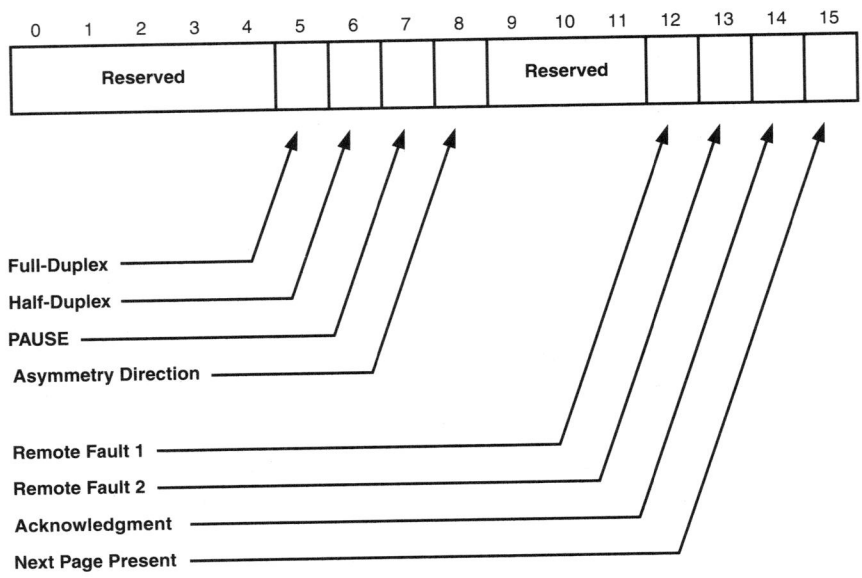

Figure 12–10 Auto-Negotiation base page message format.

Duplex Mode. The "Full-Duplex" bit indicates that the device is capable of operating in full-duplex mode; the "Half-Duplex" bit indicates that the device is capable of operating in half-duplex mode. Full-duplex mode (if available in both negotiating devices) will take precedence over half-duplex mode. If one device is capable of half-duplex only and the other of full-duplex only, then no communication is possible.

Flow Control. The PAUSE and Asymmetry Direction bits are used together to determine if the device is capable of Ethernet flow control (see Chapter 6) and, if so, whether it is capable of symmetric and/or asymmetric operation. The encoding is shown in Table 12–8.

Depending on the capabilities of the two link partners, any of four possible outcomes can result:

1. No use of flow control
2. Asymmetric flow control (toward the partner)
3. Asymmetric flow control (from the partner)
4. Symmetric flow control

Each device performing the negotiation considers its own advertised capability and that of its link partner and makes a decision on the use of flow control, as shown in Table 12–9.

Remote Fault. The Remote Fault bits are used to indicate error conditions to the link partner and are encoded as shown in Table 12–10.

TABLE 12–8 FLOW CONTROL ENCODING

PAUSE	Asymmetry Direction	Advertised Capability
0	0	No Ethernet flow control capability.
0	1	Can send flow control messages but cannot respond to them (asymmetric operation toward the link partner only).
1	0	Can both send and receive flow control messages (symmetric operation only).
1	1	Can both send and receive flow control messages (either symmetric operation or asymmetric operation from the link partner possible).

TABLE 12–9 FLOW CONTROL RESOLUTION

Local Device		Link Partner		Result
PAUSE	Asymmetry Direction	PAUSE	Asymmetry Direction	
0	0	Any	Any	No flow control
0	1	0	Any	No flow control
0	1	1	0	No flow control
0	1	1	1	Asymmetric operation toward link partner
1	0	0	Any	No flow control
1	Any	1	Any	Symmetric flow control
1	1	0	0	No flow control
1	1	0	1	Asymmetric operation from link partner

TABLE 12–10 REMOTE FAULT ENCODING

Remote Fault 1	Remote Fault 2	Indication
0	0	No error
0	1	Device offline (link disabled)
1	0	Link failure
1	1	Auto-Negotiation error

Any indication from a link partner other than "No Error" indicates a fault that can prevent the link from becoming operational for network usage.

Acknowledgment and Next Page. These bits are used in the same manner as for UTP Auto-Negotiation. Negotiation messages are sent repeatedly until acknowledged. The Acknowledgment bit indicates that the device has successfully received three auto-negotiation messages in a row (from its partner) with the same contents; this is assumed to mean that the data received is correct. The Next Page bit is used as an "escape mechanism." It indicates that there will be additional pages sent after this page. This allows the Auto-Negotiation mechanisms to be extended in the future for additional functions.

12.2.7.3 Auto-Negotiation Signals

1000BASE-X provides a convenient means for ensuring that Auto-Negotiation messages are not incorrectly interpreted as Ethernet frame data. Two ordered sets of the 8B/10B code (/C1/ and /C2/, from Table 12–2) are reserved exclusively for transmitting Auto-Negotiation configuration messages. Thus Auto-Negotiation messages are sent as a series of:

/K28.5/D21.5/config-message/
/K28.5/D2.2/config-message/
/K28.5/D21.5/config-message/
/K28.5/D2.2/config-message/

•
•
•

This continues until the Auto-Negotiation process completes, with each link partner learning and acknowledging the others' capabilities and setting the configuration appropriately (or detecting an error condition). Each ordered set is a sequence of 4 bytes: one for the /K28.5/ special code, one for the /D21.5/ or /D2.2/ data code, and two for the 16-bit Auto-Negotiation configuration message.

12.3   1000BASE-T

At the time of this writing, 1000BASE-X is the only Physical Layer fully specified within the IEEE standard and implemented on commercial Gigabit Ethernet products. 1000BASE-X can be used over optical fiber and specialized, short copper jumpers, but it is not usable over the unshielded twisted-pair wiring commonly used for desktop computer connections. Bringing Gigabit Ethernet to the desktop required that a new signaling method be developed, designated 1000BASE-T ("T" for twisted-pair). The technology and standards for 1000BASE-T are under development.

Many companies are actively (nay, fervently!) pursuing 1000BASE-T solutions. The problems are daunting, but it is believed that a workable solution can be achieved. Regardless of the technical details of the ultimate solution (or solutions), 1000BASE-T is expected to:

- Operate over 100 m of Category 5 UTP.
- Require 4 twisted-pairs, dedicated for 1000BASE-T use.
- Support both half- and full-duplex Ethernet operation.
- Support UTP Auto-Negotiation, including negotiating data rates of 10/100/1000 Mb/s (backward compatible with 10BASE-T and 100BASE-T).

While it is no small feat to achieve reliable communications at gigabit data rates over 1000BASE-X media, the challenges for 1000BASE-T are even greater. The transmission characteristics of UTP wire do not lend themselves well to such high-speed signals. In particular, the following difficulties must be overcome.

- The attenuation of UTP is much higher per-unit-length than either the copper jumpers or optical fibers used for 1000BASE-X. A 1000BASE-T receiver must deal with much smaller signals and with a much wider dynamic range (ratio of maximum to minimum amplitude).
- The attenuation of UTP cable degrades rapidly with frequency, in a non-linear manner.
- UTP cables introduce high levels of timing distortion (intersymbol interference) for which compensation is necessary.
- Imperfect line termination and variations in cable characteristic impedance cause reflections (echoes) that require cancellation.
- UTP cables exhibit significant near- and far-end crosstalk. As the signaling rates increase, this crosstalk can potentially cause interference signals that exceed even the levels of the actual transmitted data as seen at the receiver (that is, the data can be weaker than the noise).
- The electromagnetic interference characteristics of UTP cables are much worse than those of shielded cables or optical fiber. This increases the noise seen by the receivers (ingress) and creates difficulties in meeting regulatory requirements (FCC, IEC, and so on) for emissions.
- Category 5 UTP is characterized up to only 100 MHz operation. Signaling with frequencies beyond this limit may require dependence on untested (or unknown) cable characteristics.
- UTP wire installation practices are rarely as carefully controlled as for optical fiber or specialized cables. While there are design rules governing proper system installation, these rules are often overlooked by (or unknown to) the cable installers. The resulting installation may not meet the strict requirements of Category 5 wiring. This may not cause any

noticeable problems when the cable is used for telephony or 10BASE-T, but it may render the cable useless for 1000BASE-T operation.

This is quite a list of technical challenges. A robust 1000BASE-T design must allow for all of these factors, as well as the traditional issues of cost, power consumption, and the feasibility of its use with existing semiconductor technology. Most engineers working on the problem agree that the best approach for 1000BASE-T is to keep the line signaling rate relatively low (that is, comparable to 100BASE-TX) and to achieve higher capacity through very rich, multi-level coding, with digital compensation for crosstalk and line echoes.

Formal IEEE approval of a 1000BASE-T standard is anticipated for 1999. Stay tuned for further developments.

12.4 Physical Layer Design Guidelines

As has been shown, Gigabit Ethernets can be built using a wide variety of media and line drivers. This section looks at the trade-offs involved in using the various media options, as well as the distance limitations for the various supported configurations. The configuration rules given here cover the design guidelines applicable to 1000BASE-X, as well as anticipate 1000BASE-T operation over 100 m of 4-pair Category 5 UTP.

12.4.1 Media Selection

Each media type has some trade-off between cost and distance limitations. Also, some media types are less likely than others to be able to use existing, pre-installed cable; a requirement to install new cable further increases the cost and inconvenience of using those media types. Clearly, if cost and lack of installed cable could be ignored, every Gigabit Ethernet link would use longwave optics with single-mode fiber. In practice, each media type fits well with specific classes of use.

- **Category 5 UTP (1000BASE-T).** This medium offers low system cost and a huge installed base of cable, but it is useful over only short distances (up to 100 m) within a building. The key application is for desktop computer connections. Server attachments (especially when servers are spatially distributed throughout an office environment) can also be accommodated. 1000BASE-T (when it becomes available) provides a logical upgrade for 10BASE-T and 100BASE-TX devices to move to Gigabit Ethernet.

■ **150-Ω STP (1000BASE-CX).** This medium provides a relatively low-cost means of interconnecting Gigabit Ethernet devices over very short distances (up to 25 m). It can be used for equipment interconnections within a rack or a wiring closet and for server attachments to that same equipment within a computer room.

■ **62.5-μm multimode fiber.** This cable has the advantage of a healthy installed base due to its widespread use in 10BASE-F, 100BASE-FX, and FDDI. The network designer can select interfaces that employ moderate-cost shortwave lasers for use up to 260 m or increase the distance achievable (up to 550 m) by using higher-priced longwave laser drivers. Because 1000BASE-T is currently unavailable, 62.5-μm cable with shortwave lasers is the medium of choice for connecting servers, for high-performance workstations, and for intrabuilding backbones within its length restriction.[21] This medium also provides the logical upgrade path for existing, slower-speed systems using optical fiber to migrate to Gigabit Ethernet. Price reductions of 1000BASE-SX components (through product maturity and volume) will probably make 62.5-μm fiber attractive for wiring room interconnections as well, thereby obviating the need for short copper jumpers. It is also possible that the price of 1000BASE-SX components will drop below even that of UTP transceivers, although displacing 1000BASE-T would require that users provide fiber to the desktop.

■ **50-μm multimode fiber.** This cable sees little use today. Its inclusion in the 1000BASE-X family is primarily an artifact of its Fibre Channel roots. If new cable installations are being planned, designers can achieve longer distances with 50-μm fiber than with 62.5-μm fiber (525 versus 260 m), using moderately priced shortwave lasers. However, a sacrifice is made in flexibility; few systems other than Gigabit Ethernet support 50-μm fiber in a standard manner. There is no benefit in using longwave lasers with 50-μm fiber, since it results in a higher cost with no significant increase in distance.

■ **10-μm single-mode fiber.** This is the most expensive alternative due to the requirement for longwave lasers (the cable itself is no more expensive than multimode fiber), but it is the medium of choice for campus (interbuilding)

21. Without 1000BASE-T, 1000BASE-SX using 62.5-μm fiber is the lowest-cost option for lengths in excess of 25 m.

backbone applications. The 3000-m distance allowed exceeds even that of FDDI, the most widely deployed campus backbone technology to date.

Table 12–11 summarizes the trade-offs of the various media and the application environments best suited to each.

TABLE 12–11 SUMMARY OF GIGABIT ETHERNET MEDIA AND APPLICATIONS

Media Type	Likelihood of Existing Cable	Distance Limit	Applications
Category 5 UTP (1000BASE-T)	High	100 m	Desktop computers Server connections
150-Ω STP (1000BASE-CX)	None[1]	25 m	Interconnection of bridges/switches/routers within a rack or wiring closet Server attachments within a computer room
62.5-μm multimode fiber with shortwave lasers (1000BASE-SX)	Moderate[2]	260 m	Server connections High-performance workstation connections Intrabuilding backbones
50-μm multimode fiber with shortwave lasers (1000BASE-SX)	Low	525 m	Server connections High-performance workstation connections Intrabuilding backbones
62.5-μm multimode fiber with longwave lasers (1000BASE-LX)	Moderate[2]	550 m	Intrabuilding backbones
50-μm multimode fiber with longwave lasers (1000BASE-LX)	Low	550 m	[3]
10-μm single-mode fiber with longwave lasers (1000BASE-LX)	Low–Moderate	3000 m	Intrabuilding/interbuilding backbones Campus backbones

1. 1000BASE-CX jumpers are generally available only as manufactured assemblies in specific lengths and do not use preinstalled cable.

2. 62.5-μm multimode fiber is commonly used in existing 10BASE-F, 100BASE-FX, and FDDI systems.

3. There is an additional cost to using longwave optics but no real benefit with respect to distance when using 50-μm multimode fiber. Thus there is no reason to use 1000BASE-LX with this cable.

The standard installation practices and local codes appropriate for each wire type apply to their use for Gigabit Ethernet as well. That is, there are no special constraints on bend radii, connector configurations, and so on, due to Gigabit Ethernet.

12.4.2 Full-Duplex Link Limits

Full-duplex links are limited only by the physical characteristics of the medium and the transceivers themselves; there is no limitation imposed by the Ethernet MAC algorithm. Thus full-duplex operation allows the maximum network extent. Table 12–12 summarizes the link length limits (that's easier to write than to say) for all Gigabit Ethernet media types in full-duplex mode.

12.4.3 Half-Duplex Link Limits

Half-duplex Ethernet link lengths face two potential limiting factors:

   1. The limit imposed by the physical medium itself (this is the same limit as for full-duplex links)

TABLE 12–12 FULL-DUPLEX LINK LENGTH LIMITS

	50-µm Fiber (multi-mode)	62.5-µm Fiber (multi-mode)	10-µm Fiber (single-mode)	150-Ω STP	Category 5 UTP
1000BASE-SX Shortwave Laser Optics	525 m	260 m	—	—	—
1000BASE-LX Longwave Laser Optics	550 m	550 m	3000 m	—	—
1000BASE-CX Short Copper Jumpers	—	—	—	25 m	—
1000BASE-T Category 5 UTP	—	—	—	—	100 m

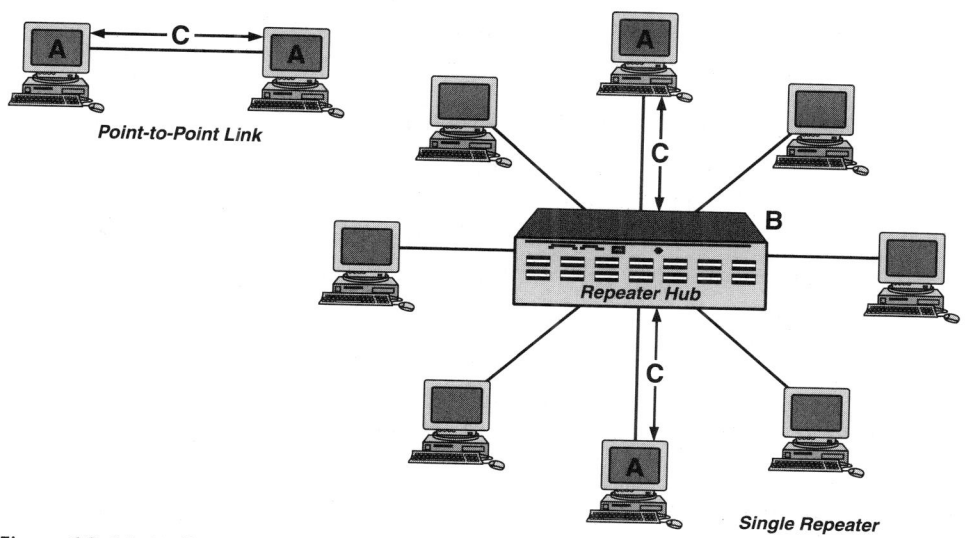

Figure 12–11 Half-duplex configurations.

2. The limit imposed by the Ethernet MAC, whereby the maximum round-trip delay of the network must be less than a slotTime (4096 bit-times; see Chapter 10)

A given configuration must pass both tests. That is, a half-duplex link can never be longer than an equivalent full-duplex link and may need to be shorter due to Ethernet timing requirements.

Fortunately, the range of half-duplex Gigabit Ethernet topologies is rather limited, as shown in Figure 12–11. Unlike 10 Mb/s Ethernet, there are no multidrop coaxial cables and no allowance for multiple repeaters. To determine if a given configuration meets the 4096-bit slotTime limitation, the network designer needs to draw out the proposed topology and perform the following steps:

1. Verify that each individual link (C) meets the physical medium-imposed length limit for that type of link, as shown in Table 12–12.
2. Determine the longest path between any pair of stations in the network. This will be either the single link, for repeaterless, station-to-station connections, or the path including the two longest links in the system, for repeater configurations.
3. Add up the delay contributions (in bit-times) of the three (potential) elements in the path, as follows.

A. Two stations[22]   864   bit-times
B. Repeater (if present)   976   bit-times
C. Cables
   Category 5 UTP cable (if present)
        11.12 × cable length (meters) =   bit-times
   150-Ω STP (if present)
        10.10 × cable length (meters) =   bit-times
   Optical-fiber cable (if present)
        10.10 × cable length (meters) = _____   bit-times
   Total   < 4096   bit-times

The total delay must be less than 4096 bit-times (one slotTime). Ideally, there should be some margin (32 bits is recommended) to allow for variations in cable manufacture and installation, as well as the possibility that cable lengths might need to be extended in the future.

While tedious, this calculation of round-trip delays is necessary to ensure that half-duplex Ethernets operate properly. Networks longer than permitted can exhibit undesirable behaviors. A higher error rate may result, and performance can suffer, especially between devices at the extreme ends of a too-long network. "Late collision" errors can often indicate an improperly configured half-duplex Ethernet.

Fortunately, Gigabit Ethernet is likely to be deployed predominantly in full-duplex configurations. For backbone applications, the distance restrictions of half-duplex operation (not to mention the performance limitations) mandate the use of full-duplex links. Even in desktop applications, the use of Buffered Distributors (discussed in Chapter 11) can allow full-duplex operation with little or no cost penalty, thereby effectively eliminating the need for Gigabit Ethernet repeaters. With any luck, no one will ever need to apply the rules given here.

---

22. The values shown for (A) and (B) are constants that have been calculated to include all internal station delays incurred by a Gigabit Ethernet controller and repeater, respectively.

13 — The Hitchhiker's Guide to the Gigabit Ethernet Standard

Most of this book has emphasized the technology, operation, and applications of Ethernet, and of Gigabit Ethernet in particular. Care has been taken to concentrate on the real behavior and characteristics of Ethernet systems, without getting overly concerned with official standards terminology or the alphabet-soup of arcane architectural abstractions and acronyms (AAAAAs). This chapter veers slightly from that main road and ventures into the Twilight Zone of IEEE LAN standards, where many have dared to tread, but few have lived to tell the tale.

This chapter is not intended as an exhaustive treatise on the nature, operation, or history of LAN standards. Instead, it shows how the technologies described in other chapters are reflected in the official standard. For the reader who may be peripherally familiar with the official standard (or who needs a road map to navigate it), this chapter provides a concise guide to the Gigabit Ethernet supplement. Don't panic, and bring your towel.

> **Cole's Law**[1]
>
> Network standards are like sausages: If you intend to use them, you really don't want to see how they are made.

13.1 What Is IEEE 802.3?

The IEEE 802 Local Area Network/Metropolitan Area Network Standards Committee (LMSC) first met in February 1980 and is now both the de facto and *de jure* organization for the development of international LAN standards. At this time, it comprises eight active (and five dormant) Working Groups

---

1. Attributed to Gerald Cole, University of California (Los Angeles). Not to be confused with coleslaw, attributed to an exceptionally good harvest of cabbage.

and Technical Action Groups (WGs and TAGs), each chartered with the development of standards for particular LAN/MAN technologies.

The IEEE 802.3 Working Group comprises hundreds of individuals from dozens of companies with an interest in defining standards for Ethernet technology. This is not an altruistic effort; most participants represent (and are paid by) companies that manufacture and sell Ethernet products. Their participation in the standards organization helps them to stay at the forefront of technology in a rapidly changing field. With product development cycles taking months or years, a successful vendor cannot simply wait for the standard to be decided and then start building products. By then it is too late—the market is already crowded with competition. The vendor must begin designing products *before* a standard is available. Hence, leading-edge suppliers must track (or try to direct!) the standard in parallel with their product development cycles.

The official standard for Ethernet is IEEE 802.3, which currently comprises a base document [IEEE96] plus approved supplements for 100 Mb/s operation [IEEE95], Full-Duplex/Flow Control [IEEE97], 100BASE-T2 [IEEE97a], and Gigabit Ethernet [IEEE98]. This document, first published in 1985, has grown from the original 10 Mb/s-only, thick-wire coaxial Ethernet reference (consisting of nine chapters, or *clauses*), to its current state of more than 40 clauses and providing specifications for operation at data rates from 1 to 1000 Mb/s over numerous media types. While virtually all Ethernet products conform to some subset of this standard, the standard makes no statement on:

- What products are appropriate in the marketplace
- Which features should be included in a product
- How a product should be implemented

The standard addresses the *behavior* of the various system components and key requirements for interoperability among vendors as an "enabling tool" to allow the marketplace to flourish. The free market decides the proper level of integration, cost/performance trade-offs, features, and so on, as determined by user requirements, cost, and competition.

13.2   What Is IEEE 802.3z?

In November 1995, the IEEE 802 LMSC authorized a High-Speed Study Group (HSSG) to investigate the possibility of extending Ethernet operation from 100 Mb/s to higher speeds. Due to the overwhelming success of products derived from the similar effort three years earlier that resulted in 100 Mb/s

Fast Ethernet, the 1995 HSSG[2] attracted over 200 participants from more than 85 companies. [IEEE96a] Over the next few months, the study group determined that:

- There was a broad market potential for Gigabit Ethernet products (as evidenced by the high level of interest in the study group).
- A Gigabit Ethernet standard could be developed that was compatible with the existing IEEE 802.3 standard (software, frame formats, MAC, and so on).
- A Gigabit Ethernet standard would not duplicate or conflict with other, ongoing standards efforts.
- Gigabit Ethernet was technically feasible (although the details still remained to be worked out).
- Gigabit Ethernet was economically feasible.

Given these conclusions, the IEEE authorized in July 1996 the formation of the 802.3z Gigabit Ethernet Task Force.[3] This Task Force was charged with the development of a standard for Ethernet operation at 1000 Mb/s. Figure 13–1 depicts the organizational relationship of the Task Force with respect to the rest of the IEEE 802 LMSC.

As shown in Figure 13–1, the 802.3z Task Force narrowed its focus slightly from its original goals and developed a standard that supports only optical fiber and short copper jumpers. The work on Gigabit Ethernet over unshielded twisted-pair was moved to a new Task Force, 802.3ab, because this work would have unduly delayed the release of the base standard.

At the time of this writing, the IEEE 802.3z Task Force has completed all technical details of the specifications and passed the IEEE 802.3 Working Group ballot. Final approval by the IEEE Standards Board is anticipated in mid-1998. The rest of this chapter describes the IEEE 802.3z standard.[4]

---

2. The 1992 Fast Ethernet study group was also known as the HSSG. However, what constitutes "high speed" changed by an order of magnitude in three years!

3. Yes, the "z" designation indicates that it was the twenty-sixth such Task Force under IEEE 802.3. Rather than halting new Ethernet development due to a lack of additional letters, 802.3 became the first 802 Working Group to have to use two-letter designations for task forces. There is currently an 802.3aa, an 802.3ab, and an 802.3ac Task Force (and more on the way).

4. While the standard has not achieved final, formal approval at the time of this writing, I am an active member of the Task Force and have made every attempt to present what is expected to be the final content. Of course, it is possible that changes to the standard in the "final hours" could invalidate some of the specifics presented here.

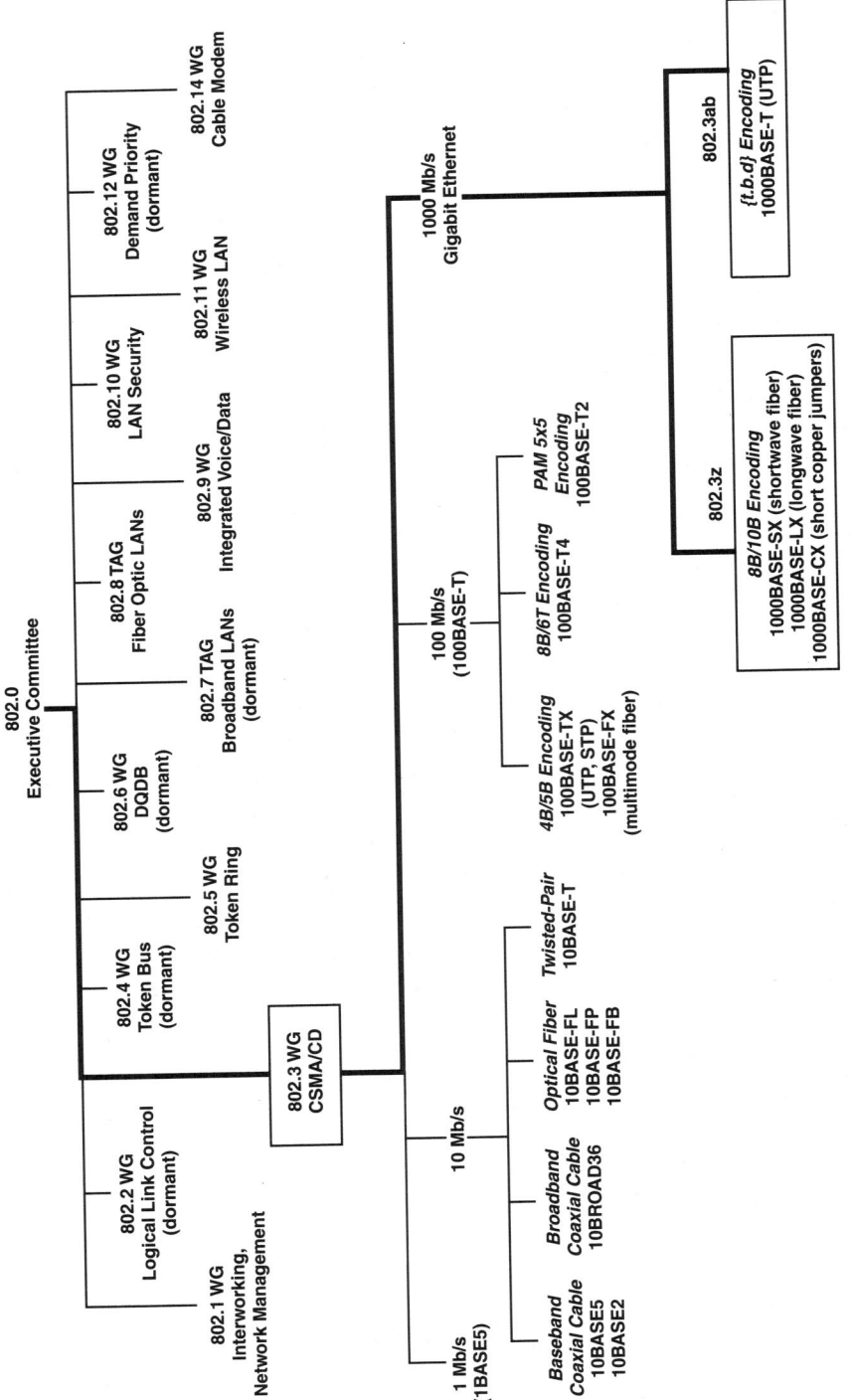

1. WG is an abbreviation for Working Group.
2. TAG is an abbreviation for Technical Action Group.

Figure 13–1   IEEE 802 organization.

13.3   Target Audience and Reader Assumptions

IEEE standards are not "light reading."[5] They are written in a very controlled and formalized style, with many commonly used words taking on very different meanings from those of ordinary use.[6] The purpose of the standard is not to inform or educate the reader (that is left to books like this one!), but to clearly state the precise requirements for the operation and interoperation of network devices. As such, they appeal to a very limited audience. Few *users* of networks would understand or gain much from reading the standards. In fact, many manufacturers have difficulty interpreting the precise meaning and application of standards in specific product implementations. There is considerable work for knowledgeable consultants to help network equipment designers ensure that their products meet the applicable requirements.

IEEE network standards assume the following:

- The reader is a knowledgeable networking professional. There is very little explanatory or tutorial information provided.
- The reader understands "standard-ese," the precise language used to specify behavior of interoperable products. In many cases, the actual conformance requirements are specified as state-machine diagrams or computer code.
- The reader is familiar with all of the other documents referenced by the standard. In some cases, a standard refers (or defers) to another document for important specifications, without which it is impossible to design an interoperable product.[7]

---

5. In fact, they have been known to cure insomnia and increase aspirin sales, as well as be an effective contraceptive if read immediately prior to amorous activities (same effect as for the "insomnia cure").

6. This can make it very difficult to read a standard and understand the real implications of certain statements. A good example is the very careful use of the words "shall" and "shall not." These are the *only* words used in an IEEE standard to denote a conformance requirement. Words such as "must," "will," "has to," and similar have no effect on the conformance requirements of the standard. Thus the statement, "A device *must always* do so-and-so," creates no requirement for it to do so in order to comply with the standard! In this same vein, the term "may" (in an IEEE standard) is exactly synonymous with the term "may not." Really. (Think about it. Send me an e-mail if you don't get the idea.)

7. For example, the parts of the 100 Mb/s Fast Ethernet standard that specify the actual physical drivers and receivers for 100BASE-TX/FX are simply a set of instructions on modifications to be made to the equivalent ANSI FDDI specification.

In addition, standards tend to be full of acronyms—after a while, many of them start to look alike. Other chapters of this book have attempted to avoid all such standards acronyms, except where using one really *helps,* rather than confuses you. However, this chapter succumbs to a certain level of acronym usage, because it deals directly with the standard and the standards terminology can get exceedingly long without the use of short-form acronyms.[8]

For those still interested, copies of IEEE standards (including Gigabit Ethernet) can be ordered directly from the IEEE Operations Center, using the following methods:

Phone: (800) 678-IEEE (United States and Canada)
Phone: (908) 981-0060 (outside the United States and Canada)
Fax: (908) 981-9667
Telex: 833233
Mail:
    IEEE Operations Center
    Sales Office
    445 Hoes Lane
    P.O. Box 1331
    Piscataway, NJ 08855–1331 USA

or see *http://stdsbbs.ieee.org* for more information.

13.4 The IEEE 802.3z Standard

The Gigabit Ethernet standard (IEEE 802.3z and 802.3ab) is a *supplement* to the base 802.3 document. It neither replaces the existing standard nor stands alone as a self-contained document. As described later in this chapter, the supplement provides:

- Updates to existing clauses of 802.3, where a clause contains information that is not gigabit-specific
- Nine new clauses that contain information specific to Gigabit Ethernet

Over the years, the 802.3 standard has grown considerably, both in scope and weight. In several cases, the standards committee has not only added new capabilities, but also changed the *model* (architecture) of the system. This was especially true for Fast Ethernet, but it is also the case, to a lesser degree,

---

8. Why call something a "serializer" when you can call it a "Physical Medium Attachment Sublayer (PMA)"?

with Gigabit Ethernet. For example, all 10 Mb/s systems use Manchester encoding regardless of medium type. Thus, there are no coding-specific sublayers in the architecture for 10 Mb/s Ethernet. Both Fast and Gigabit Ethernet provide for multiple coding schemes, depending on the physical medium in use. So, the respective supplements added new sublayers to the architecture to reflect this separation of function from the original model.

13.4.1 IEEE 802.3z Standard Architecture

IEEE LANs correspond to the Data Link and Physical Layers of the OSI model [ISO94], and Gigabit Ethernet is no exception. It is impractical, both from the perspective of writing a standard, as well as from understanding system behavior, to treat these layers as monolithic blocks. Within the two layers described by the standard are numerous arbitrary subdivisions. While this results in having many more layer entities, the spirit of layered architecture is maintained in that each layer provides a specific function, with a well-defined interface to the sublayers both above and below it.

> *If you know what you are doing, 3 layers are enough. If you don't, even 17 won't help.*
> —*Mike Padlipsky*
> *[PADL85]*

Figure 13–2 depicts the layered architecture model for the entire IEEE 802.3 standard. All flavors of Ethernet have a common model at the Data Link Layer. This layer is sublayered into the Logical Link Control (LLC), MAC Control, and MAC sublayers.

At the Physical Layer four different sublayerings (stacks) are possible, depending on the data rate and media type:

1. A stack providing only an Attachment Unit Interface (AUI) as the physical signal model (far left), usable with 1 Mb/s and 10 Mb/s systems only
2. A stack providing both a Media-Independent Interface (MII) and an AUI as physical signal models (second from left), usable with 10 Mb/s only, but supporting Auto-Negotiation (through the MII) to be compatible with the next model[9]
3. A stack providing an MII as the physical signal model (third from left), for use with 100 Mb/s systems

---

9. This model was added as part of the Fast Ethernet standard for backward compatibility with existing 10 Mb/s systems.

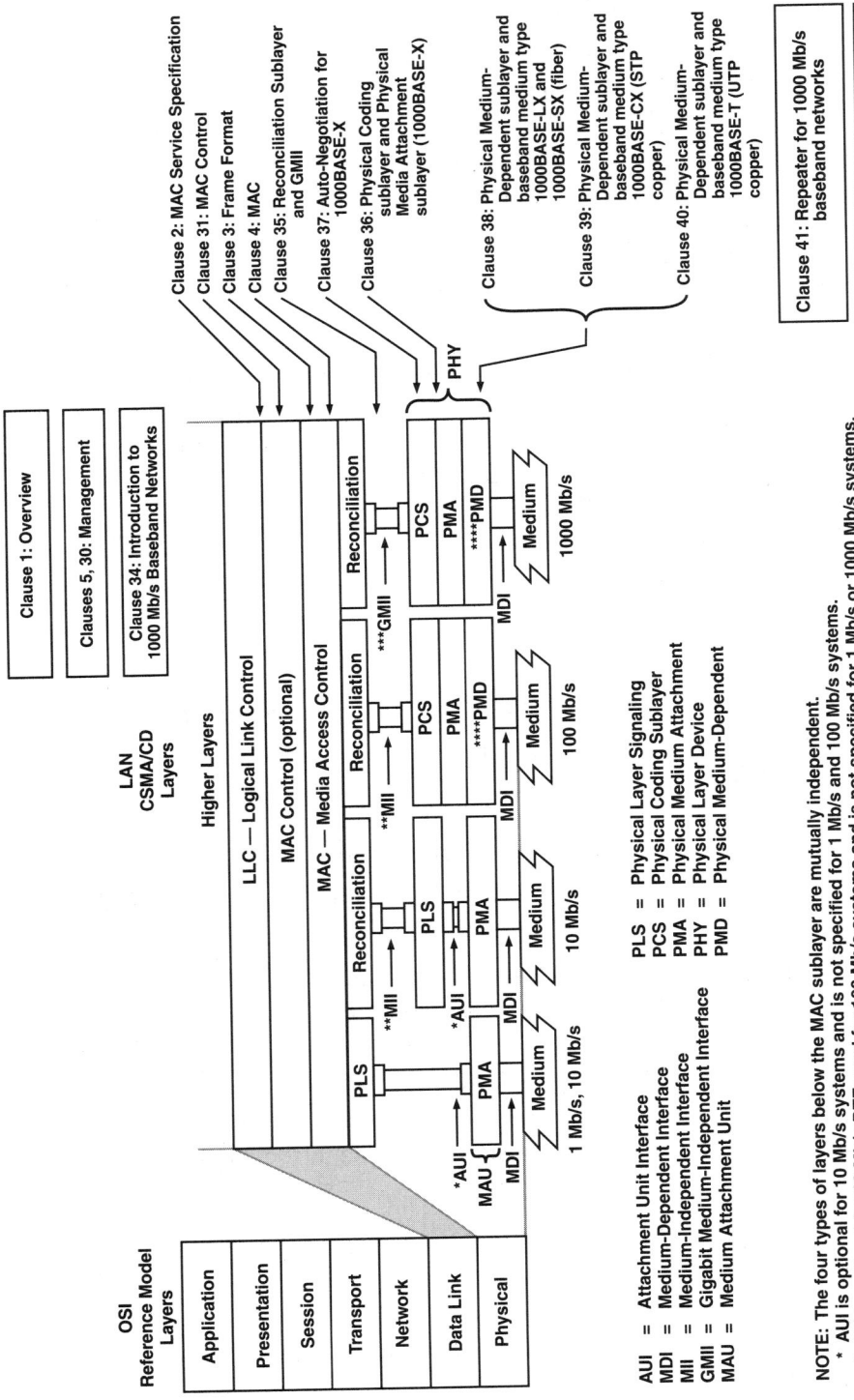

Figure 13–2 IEEE 802.3 Standards architecture and 802.3z clauses.

4. A stack providing a Gigabit MII (GMII) as the physical signal model (far right), for use on Gigabit Ethernet systems

This latter stacking was added to the model by 802.3z. Regardless of the architectural presentation, there is never any requirement to physically *implement* the AUI, MII, or GMII. While the standard uses these interfaces to describe various functions and behaviors, a practical system can conform to the specification without a physical manifestation of any of these interfaces.

Note that some of the layering is "baggage" carried around so that existing standards need not be rewritten when new features and capabilities are added. A good example is the Reconciliation sublayer, which is needed mostly because the architecture of the MII did not map cleanly to the existing MAC-Physical Layer interface.

13.4.2 AUI? MII? SOS!!

Are you maddened by MIIs? Perturbed by PMDs? Addled by acronyms? Unfortunately, the standard is riddled with them. Every sublayer adds new architectural concepts—and new acronyms and abbreviations as well. Table 13–1 explains not only the words, but the meaning of the various sublayers, acronyms, and abbreviations presented in Figure 13–2.

TABLE 13–1 IEEE 802.3 ARCHITECTURAL TERMINOLOGY

Term	802.3 Clause	Term Expansion	Description
PLS	6, 7	Physical Layer Signaling Sublayer	The sublayer that provides Manchester encoding/decoding and maps the logical signals required by the MAC (for example, Transmit Data, Carrier Sense, and Collision Detect) to the physical signals of the AUI cable. Included as part of the original 802.3 (1983) standard.
AUI	7	Attachment Unit Interface	An exposed physical interface for connecting controllers to transceivers at 10 Mb/s. Uses a 15-pin D-subminiature connector and a 4-pair cable. Commonly called a *transceiver cable* or a *drop cable*.
MAU	8, 10, 11, 12, 15–18, 23, 25, 26,	Medium Attachment Unit	The physical means of connecting to the LAN medium. Also called a *transceiver*. Separate clauses define the requirements

TABLE 13–1 IEEE 802.3 ARCHITECTURAL TERMINOLOGY (*cont.*)

Term	802.3 Clause	Term Expansion	Description
MAU (*cont.*)	32, 38–40		for each of the various data rates and media types supported.
PMA	7, 23, 24, 32, 36	Physical Medium Attachment Sublayer	A mechanism for providing serialization (for example, byte-wide to bit-wide conversion) and medium-independence for each encoding mechanism (for example, Manchester, 4B/5B and 8B/10B).
MDI	8, 10, 11, 12, 15–18, 23, 25, 26 32, 38–40	Medium-Dependent Interface	The standards name for the electrical driver/receiver and connector that attaches to the LAN medium (part of the MAU).
RS	22, 35	Reconciliation Sublayer	A mechanism that provides a logical mapping from the Physical Layer interface primitives to the logical signals on an MII or GMII. This is an architectural abstraction only, with no particular (or required) physical implementation. The RS was added to the model for Fast Ethernet and continued with Gigabit Ethernet.
MII	22	Medium-Independent Interface	An (optional) physical interface to connect a MAC controller to a Physical Layer subsystem. Uses a 40-pin connector. The MII was introduced with Fast Ethernet. MIIs can support both 10 Mb/s and 100 Mb/s Physical Layers.
PCS	23, 24, 32, 36, 40	Physical Coding Sublayer	The sublayer that defines the specifics of encoding/decoding for 100 Mb/s and 1000 Mb/s systems (for example, 4B/5B and 8B/10B). For 10 Mb/s systems, this function was performed by the PLS, since all 10 Mb/s systems use Manchester encoding.
PMD	25, 26, 38, 39	Physical Medium-Dependent Sublayer	The sublayer that provides the medium-dependent specifications for encoding systems that support multiple media types.

TABLE 13–1 IEEE 802.3 ARCHITECTURAL TERMINOLOGY (*cont.*)

Term	802.3 Clause	Term Expansion	Description
GMII	35	Gigabit Medium-Independent Interface	A 1000 Mb/s version of the MII. Because of the higher speed, the GMII cannot be used externally (that is, with cables and connectors). If implemented, it is used as a chip-to-chip interface. The GMII is new for Gigabit Ethernet.
PHY		Physical Layer device	A generic term used to describe a transceiver for 100 Mb/s or 1000 Mb/s operation. A PHY would connect between an MII/GMII and an MDI and consist of PCS, PMA, and PMD functionality.

13.4.3 Architecture: Where the Rubber Meets the Sky

It doesn't seem as if the "standards-view" of networking has any correspondence to the "real-world view." In the real world, you can buy transceivers, network interface cards (NICs), and LAN cables; no network equipment supplier sells PCSs, PMAs, or PMDs. Standards define *function*. They are intentionally written in such a way that they are completely independent of the implementation in any particular product. Vendors are free to design products (and subsystems) that use any internal organization they choose, as long as the *external (observable) behavior* conforms to the requirements of the standard. This provides for interoperability without constraining suppliers to specific design practices. A more implementation-specific specification might be easier to understand, but it might stifle creativity by narrowing the range of options available to designers.[10]

The architectural partitioning used in the standard allows for very modular standards writing. It is relatively easy to add new capabilities (for example,

---

10. At one point during the development of the original DIX Ethernet Standard, we consciously chose to pursue an architecturally oriented versus an implementation-oriented approach. The architectural approach defined the Data Link Layer and Physical Layer functions. The implementation approach defined a controller (NIC) and a transceiver. We actually wrote the standard both ways during the early draft stages. Interestingly, the proponents of the implementation approach were the "network architects," while the proponents of the architectural approach were the design engineers (including myself).

new coding methods, data rates, and media types) without having to rewrite the entire standard each time. In practice, the subsystem partitioning used in a particular product (for example, IC functions) will not follow the architectural model. This is because a product performs a specific function in a specific way; it is, by definition, *not* implementation-independent. The proper partitioning of a real network product is normally determined by:

- **Technology capabilities.** It is more cost-effective to combine all functions that can be easily implemented in a given technology (for example, CMOS, Bipolar, or Software) into a single device or subassembly, regardless of how this crosses architectural boundaries.
- **Product modularity.** A product that does not need to support multiple media types (for example, a fiber-only NIC) has no need to incur the cost of any medium-independent interfaces (such as an MII). Product modularity can be much narrower than standards modularity.

Figure 13–3 depicts a representative network product (a Gigabit Ethernet NIC for use on optical fiber) and shows how a practical partitioning of the NIC internals maps to the architectural partitioning of the standard.

In the figure, a single component is used for the MAC Control, MAC, and PCS implementation. A second component is used for the serializer/deserializer (PMA) and an additional pair of devices for the optical driver and receiver.

While not "architecturally pure," this partitioning makes perfect sense, when you realize that:

- The "MAC Controller" can be implemented as a single, high-density CMOS IC, thus lowering the overall cost and increasing reliability.
- The Serializer/Deserializer (SERDES) is the only logic device requiring access to sensitive gigabit-rate clock circuits.
- The SERDES and optical driver/receiver are available off-the-shelf as standard components. This reduces design risk and time-to-market.

Note that not only have the architectural sublayers (MAC, PCS, and so on) been combined into the controller IC, but OSI layer boundaries have even been crossed. The interface between the Data Link Layer and the Physical Layer is not exposed anywhere in the system; it exists only as an architectural abstraction, buried inside the controller. This is not only acceptable, it is also desirable (and typical). Product partitioning is driven by technology, cost, and performance; architectural partitioning is driven by isolation of discrete functions. There is no reason for them to coincide.

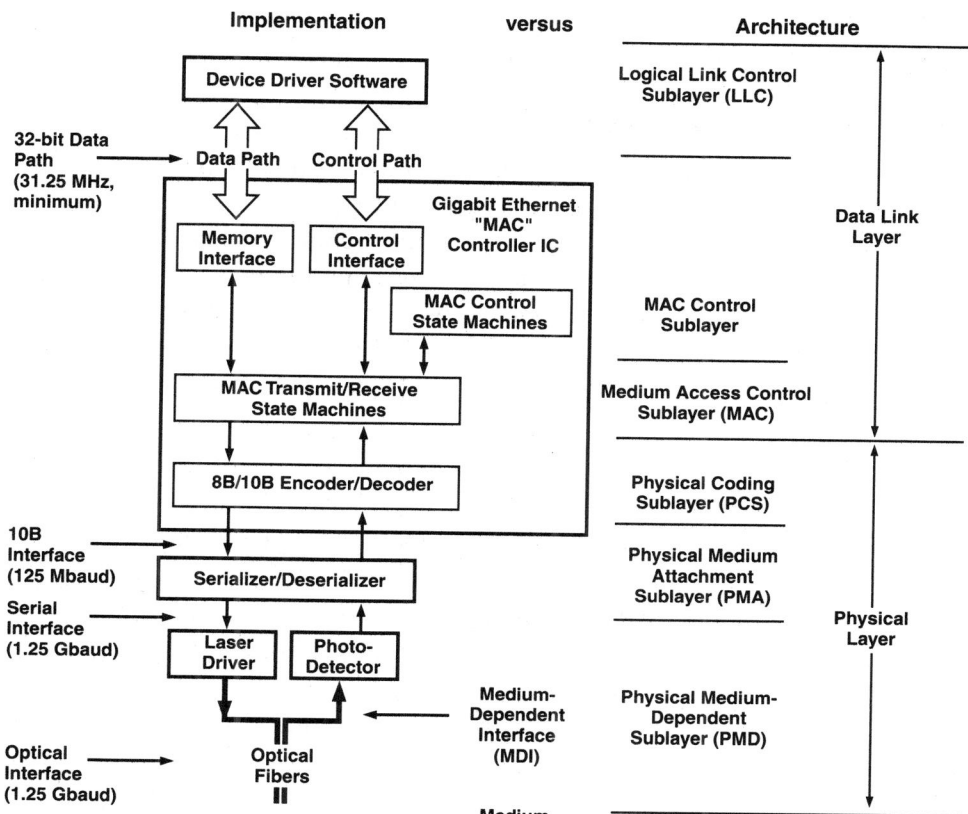

Figure 13–3 Implementation versus architecture.

13.4.4 Chapter, Verse, and Clause

When Gigabit Ethernet was developed, the IEEE 802.3 standard contained 32 separate clauses (chapters), numbered 1–32. Fortunately (!) not all of them were affected by gigabit operation. The following sections briefly describe the changes made to existing clauses and the key elements of the new clauses (34–42) generated by the 802.3z supplement to the standard.[11]

Clause 1: Introduction

This existing clause gives the reader an overview of the entire 802.3 family of standards. Gigabit Ethernet incurred some minor changes to this clause so that the introduction would apply to 1000 Mb/s operation as well as 1, 10,

---

11. A prize will be awarded to the reader who can figure out what happened to Clause 33.

and 100 Mb/s. In addition, some definitions were added that were relevant to Gigabit Ethernet. There is no substantive technical content in this clause.

Clause 2: MAC Service Specifications

This existing clause defines the abstract architectural interface between the MAC and its client (for example, a higher-layer protocol or a bridge relay function). The 802.3z supplement changed the architectural layer drawing to reflect the GMII and Physical Layer options available in Gigabit Ethernet. (Figure 13–2 is an adaptation of that drawing, which is used throughout the 802.3 standard.) No changes were made to the service specification itself. That is, Gigabit Ethernet looks to higher-layer protocols exactly as its lower-speed counterparts do.[12]

Clause 3: MAC Frame Structure

This existing clause defines the format of an Ethernet/IEEE 802.3 frame. It would seem that no changes would be necessary to this clause, since Gigabit Ethernet does not change the minimum length, maximum length, or any of the fields as seen by higher-layer protocols. However, for ease of specification of the half-duplex Gigabit Ethernet MAC, the format was modified to include the carrier extension field as part of the frame structure. A frame is now formally defined as shown in Figure 13–4.

At 1000 Mb/s, the Extension field length varies as necessary to ensure that the minimum transmission lasts for at least one slotTime in half-duplex mode (see Chapter 10). At 100 Mb/s or less, the length of the Extension field is always defined as zero bits, so the frame format is really unchanged except for gigabit operation. This is a specification artifact only and does not change the way applications or protocols perceive or use Ethernet frames. The inclusion of the carrier extension field as part of the MAC frame itself simplifies the formal definition of the MAC operation in Clause 4.

Clause 4: MAC

This existing clause provides the definition of the CSMA/CD algorithm itself. A textual description of CSMA/CD operation is provided, but the formal, conformance-controlling specification is presented as a program in Pascal,

---

12. 802.3x, the supplement that introduced full-duplex operation and flow control, did make significant changes to this clause to support MAC Control functions, which are also available to Gigabit Ethernet implementations.

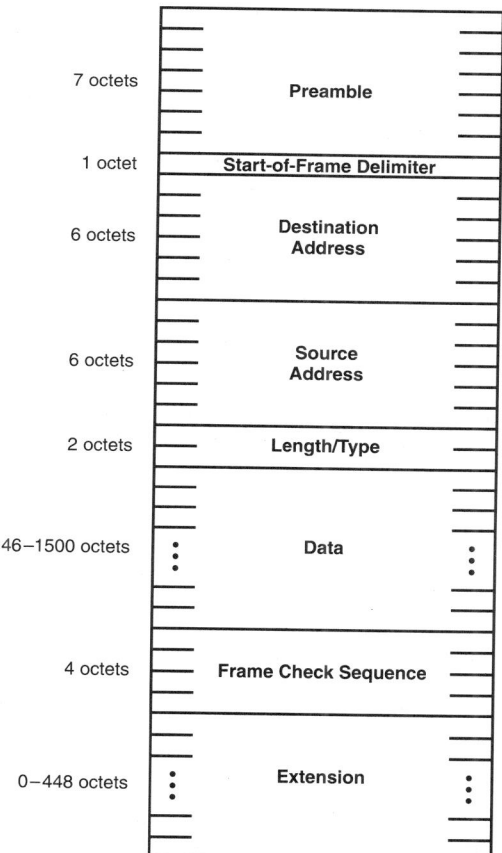

7 octets	Preamble
1 octet	Start-of-Frame Delimiter
6 octets	Destination Address
6 octets	Source Address
2 octets	Length/Type
46–1500 octets	Data
4 octets	Frame Check Sequence
0–448 octets	Extension

Figure 13–4 Gigabit Ethernet frame format.

rather than as text. This was done to eliminate the ambiguity inherent in textual descriptions. The use of Pascal is historical. When the original Ethernet specification was written in 1979–80, Pascal was a popular language and a reasonable choice for a protocol specification.[13]

The changes to this clause mandated by Gigabit Ethernet were primarily to support the use of carrier extension and frame bursting. Changes were made both to the Pascal code and to the text description of CSMA/CD operation. As specified, carrier extension and frame bursting are allowed only when a system

---

13. Also, the writers of that document, including myself, were comfortable with the Pascal language. If the project was started today, Verilog might be a better choice.

is operating at speeds greater than 100 Mb/s (that is, at the gigabit rate). There is no change to the MAC algorithms for any existing systems.

This clause already supported the use of both half-duplex and full-duplex modes by an Ethernet operating at any data rate, so no specific changes were required to support both modes for Gigabit Ethernet.

Clauses 5 and 30: Layer Management

These existing clauses contained the definitions of managed objects for 802.3 devices. These include MAC entities, MAUs (transceivers), and repeaters. IEEE 802.3z adds a number of objects to various categories to support the management of Gigabit Ethernet. Additions were made to the MAC objects (for carrier extension and frame bursting), repeater objects, MAU types, and so on, to support the new capabilities created by gigabit operation. A collection of managed objects relating to a specific entity is called a MIB (Management Information Base).

Management of 802.3 devices is purely optional. While a practical product will typically provide some management capability, this is not required for conformance to the standard.

An annex to Clause 30—30A—provides a formalized description of the managed objects in a language called GDMO (Guidelines for Definition of Managed Objects). This is the language used for managed object definitions in the Common Management Information Protocol (CMIP), the network management protocol of the International Organization for Standardization (ISO) suite. [ISO89b] Standards developed within IEEE 802 generally become ISO standards as they move through various national and international levels of approval. Thus the definitions provided in IEEE 802.3 follow the model of the ISO family of standards.

In practice, very few systems employ the ISO network management protocol (CMIP). For management, the de facto standard is the Simple Network Management Protocol (SNMP), as defined by the Internet Engineering Task Force (IETF). [RFC1157] This is part of the Internet (TCP/IP) suite of protocols. SNMP MIBs are not defined in GDMO but instead use a language comprising a subset of the Abstract Syntax Notation (ASN.1, [ISO87]). SNMP MIBs are defined in Requests for Comment (RFCs), which serve as standards in the Internet community. [ROSE96]

The result is that while Clauses 5 and 30 provide an extensive set of definitions of managed objects for 802.3 networks (including Gigabit Ethernet), in reality the controlling standards are the SNMP MIBs as defined in the Internet RFCs. Virtually no vendor provides a network management system based on the specifications in IEEE 802.3 Clauses 5 and 30. All is not without hope, though, as much of the work done for Clause 30 becomes the basis for the definition of the SNMP MIBs in the IETF. (In fact, it is often the same people doing the work in both standards organizations.) In general, there is a lot of commonality between the two sets of standards. There also are some subtle differences. Most products implement management according to the SNMP definitions. Some products may support both sets of object definitions, but few, if any, implement the 802.3 MIBs exclusively.

Clause 34: Introduction to 1000 Mb/s Baseband Networks

This new clause provides an introduction and overview of Gigabit Ethernet. There is no substantive technical content in this clause.

Clause 35: Reconciliation Sublayer and GMII

This new clause introduces two concepts:

1. A *Gigabit Medium-Independent Interface (GMII)* that allows a MAC controller to perform its functions independent of the coding or signaling methods used by the underlying Physical Layer
2. A *Reconciliation Sublayer (RS)* that provides a mapping between the Physical Layer signaling primitives and the signals on the GMII

The GMII is intended to be a standard means of communication between Physical Layer devices (PHYs) and MAC controllers. It is modeled after the MII of Fast Ethernet. The significant differences between the two are:

- **The GMII uses a byte-wide interface, rather than the nibble-wide interface of Fast Ethernet.** This reduces the clock rate of the GMII from 250 MHz (which it would be if a nibble-wide interface were retained) to 125 MHz. While still high, 125 MHz clocked interfaces can be implemented in current CMOS technology.

- **The GMII eliminates support for external connectors and cables.** A Fast Ethernet MII can be used as an exposed physical interface, with a 40-pin connector and short cables. The timing requirements, the drive levels needed for external cables, and the EMI implications make an exposed GMII with a 125 MHz clock impractical. Thus the GMII is envisioned either as an abstraction only, or as an internal (chip-to-chip) interface.

- **The GMII operates with a different set of electrical and timing specifications.** With the increased clock rate, the elimination of external drive capability, and the desire to support implementations using 3.3V CMOS

TABLE 13-2 RECONCILIATION SUBLAYER MAPPING

Transmit Requests	←→	**GMII Transmit Signals**
		Transmit Data <7:0>
		Transmit Enable
		Transmit Error
		Transmit Clock
Receive Indications	←→	**GMII Receive Signals**
		Receive Data <7:0>
		Receive Error
		Receive Clock
		Receive Data Valid
Control Indications	←→	**GMII Control Signals**
		Carrier Sense
		Collision Detect

processes, the electrical and timing specifications on the GMII are different from the original MII of Fast Ethernet.

It is important to note that there is no requirement to implement the GMII at all. Depending on the partitioning of the components in a real system, there may be no physical interface (even chip-to-chip) that corresponds to the GMII. (This is precisely the case in the diagram of Figure 13–3.) While the GMII may not actually be implemented, the 802.3z specification uses a "logical GMII" as a reference tool. That is, many clauses provide specifications in terms of GMII signals, even though the GMII may not be physically present in a product. This makes the specification internally consistent and does not have any adverse impact on product design.[14]

---

14. From a technology perspective, the most cost-effective chip partitioning may indeed be that of Figure 13–3. This partitioning allows all of the logic operating at 125 MHz and below to be concentrated in a single IC, with a separate IC (serializer/deserializer) handling the conversion to gigabit speeds. Such a partition leverages the best use of CMOS technology (at 125 MHz and below) and bipolar technology (at gigabit speeds). No GMII is present or needed with this partitioning, as the MAC-PHY interface is internal to the CMOS controller IC. Because of this, serious consideration was given during the standards development process to not include *any* electrical or timing specifications for the GMII because they are unnecessary for most practical products. (That is, the committee considered defining the GMII only as a logical interface and allowing vendors who design products that use a physical GMII to provide their own electrical specification.) This idea was abandoned, and the standard does include a set of electrical and timing specifications for a physical GMII.

The Reconciliation Sublayer is a purely architectural abstraction that provides a logical mapping from the Physical Layer interface primitives to the logical signals on the GMII. This is shown in Table 13–2.

It is important to remember that the Reconciliation Sublayer is only an abstraction provided for architectural consistency. There is no specific logic, hardware, or software required in a real product to implement this sublayer. It is simply a way of describing, in an implementation-independent manner, how the GMII signals translate into service primitives used in other clauses of the standard.[15]

Clause 36: PCS and PMA Sublayers, 1000BASE-X

This new clause includes the specifications for the encoding/decoding and serialization of signals for use on the 1000BASE-X family of media. The 1000BASE-X family includes:

- **1000BASE-LX:**   Long-wavelength laser on optical-fiber media
- **1000BASE-SX:**   Short-wavelength laser on optical-fiber media
- **1000BASE-CX:**   150 Ω STP (short copper jumper) media

All three systems use a common encoding scheme, 8B/10B. This clause provides the coding tables, plus the rules for determining carrier sense and collision detect from the received, encoded stream (see Chapter 12.) These functions comprise the Physical Coding Sublayer of 802.3z.

The PMA sublayer specified in this clause defines the mechanism for converting the 10B codes to and from a serial stream, as presented on the actual underlying medium, in a manner independent of the medium itself. A specification for a physical implementation of the 10B interface (Ten-Bit Interface, or TBI) is also provided.

Logically, the PCS and PMA Sublayers combine to take byte-wide GMII data and convert it into an encoded, serial bit stream (and vice versa).

Physical Layer implementations that use a different encoding scheme (for example, 1000BASE-T, for use on UTP cabling) must provide a different PCS/PMA Sublayer specification.

Clause 37: Auto-Negotiation Function, Type 1000BASE-X

This new clause provides the specification for automatic configuration of 1000BASE-X links. The algorithms and state machines provided are logically

---

15. A vendor selling Reconciliation Sublayer ICs will likely also offer bridges in lower Manhattan and prime real estate in central Florida.

equivalent to those used in Auto-Negotiation for UTP copper media, as discussed in Chapter 8 and specified in 802.3, Clause 28. However, Clause 28 is specific to UTP cable and RJ-45 connector systems. Clause 37 provides an equivalent mechanism for 1000BASE-X use on optical fiber and short copper jumpers.

Note that unlike UTP Auto-Negotiation, 1000BASE-X Auto-Negotiation cannot negotiate data rates between attached devices. There are two reasons for this:

1. When 1000BASE-CX is used, the connectors are incompatible with any other Ethernet system. This renders speed negotiation moot.

2. While a number of Ethernet systems use the same fiber and connectors as 1000BASE-SX/LX (for example, 10BASE-F and 100BASE-FX) and it might indeed be desirable to negotiate data rates between devices that support multiple data rates, the optical-fiber signaling systems used in those different systems are all mutually incompatible. There is no practical method to use a single signaling mechanism that is understandable by all of the standard fiber systems, even for the purpose of Auto-Negotiation. (Believe me, we tried.)

As a result, the only capabilities that can be negotiated are these:

- Duplexity (that is, half- or full-duplex operation)
- Flow Control (that is, the ability to support transmission and/or reception of PAUSE MAC Control frames)

Clause 38: PMD Sublayer and Medium, 1000BASE-LX and -SX

This new clause provides the specifications for the optical media, laser drivers, and photodetector receivers for Gigabit Ethernet. This Physical Medium-Dependent (PMD) Sublayer (architecturally) takes the serial bit stream provided by the PMA Sublayer and converts it to/from optical signals across a fiber medium.

Three media types are specified:

62.5-μm multimode fiber

50-μm multimode fiber

10-μm single-mode fiber

and two optical wavelengths:

Short wavelength (770–860 nm), 1000BASE-SX

Long wavelength (1270–1355 nm), 1000BASE-LX

The clause includes complete specifications for the laser drivers (optical power levels, extinction ratio, and so on), the photodetectors (receive sensitivity, return loss, and so on), and the media itself (dispersion, attenuation, and so on). Complete link power budgets are provided. The specified connector is the industry-standard duplex SC.

The optical specifications closely mirror the Fibre Channel specifications from which they were derived. [ANSI94]

Clause 39: PMD Sublayer and Medium, 1000BASE-CX

This new clause provides the specifications for a 2-pair, shielded, 150-Ω copper medium, along with the necessary line drivers, receivers, and system signal budgets. 1000BASE-CX is sometimes called either *short copper jumpers* or *short haul copper* because it provides a short-distance coverage (typically between equipment in the same room) at low cost. It is architecturally identical to Clause 38 and provides an alternative medium to optical fiber.

The clause includes complete specifications for the

- Line drivers (amplitude, jitter, rise/fall times, and so on),
- Line receivers (sensitivity, input impedance, skew, and so on)
- The medium itself (impedance, attenuation, and so on)

Complete link power budgets are provided. Two connectors are specified: a Fibre Channel Style-2 connector (also called a High-Speed Serial Data Connector, or HSSDC) and a 9-pin D-subminiature connector.

The specifications closely mirror the Fibre Channel specifications from which they were derived. [ANSI94]

Clause 40: PMD Sublayer and Medium, 1000BASE-T

This clause is a placeholder for the specification of the PCS, PMA, and PMD Sublayers for Gigabit Ethernet operation over 4 pairs of Category 5 UTP. At the time of this writing, no approved specifications are available. This is the charter of IEEE 802.3ab, a separate Task Force within the 802.3 Working Group.

Clause 41: Repeater for 1000 Mb/s Baseband Networks

This new clause provides the specifications for the repeater necessary for half-duplex Gigabit Ethernet. Similar to Clause 9 (10 Mb/s) and Clause 27 (100 Mb/s), a set of finite state machines are provided, along with a minimal set of environmental specifications.

Gigabit Ethernet requires the use of a repeater (hub) for half-duplex networks of three or more stations. Networks comprising exactly two stations can use a "crossover cable"; full-duplex networks require a switching hub, rather than a repeater.

Clause 42: System Considerations

This new clause provides guidelines for building basic Gigabit Ethernet systems. For full-duplex networks, the maximum lengths supportable for the various PMD/medium options are provided. For half-duplex networks, a set of rules for calculating path delays is provided so that round-trip delays do not exceed that allowed by the CSMA/CD algorithm.

13.5 Work-in-Progress

At the time of this writing, the IEEE has authorized the formation of a new Task Force, IEEE 802.3ab, charged with the development of a PCS/PMA/PMD/medium specification for Gigabit Ethernet operation over 4 pairs of Category 5 UTP. This specification is intended to support migration of Gigabit Ethernet to desktop systems (which are typically wired in this manner). This medium is sometimes called *long haul copper,* in contrast with 1000BASE-CX. The long haul copper work was separated from the rest of the 802.3z activity in 1996 because the design was expected to take longer than the other portions of Gigabit Ethernet and delaying the 802.3z specification was deemed imprudent. Finalization and approval of the IEEE 802.3ab standard is anticipated in 1999.

Applying
Gigabit Ethernet

14 Application Environments

S ometimes, those of us who work with networks on a daily basis (especially those of us who earn our livelihood from networking) forget that the network is not the *end*; it is just a *means* for enabling distributed applications. It is important to remember that the application determines the network. Well, it *should*. It is all too common for end-user network designers to think and work from the "bottom up." That is, they select technologies and products first, then determine which applications can be reasonably supported on the resulting network. Good enterprise network design should always start from the application requirements. The needs of the users of the network should (within the limits of the user's budget) determine the technologies and equipments that are best suited to the task.

> **Seifert's Law of Networking #2**
>
> The Application Determines the Network

The term "application environment" encompasses a wide range of factors, including:

- Numbers and types of users
- Geographical distribution
- Types of equipment
- Application architecture (client-server, peer-to-peer, and so on)
- Application programs in use and their data communications requirements (offered load and traffic patterns)

The range of possible application program environments and the technologies appropriate for each one is far too broad to consider in this book. The remainder of this chapter considers the requirements for a "typical" scenario of a moderate-to-large corporation or similar organization that has a generally wide internal deployment of LAN-attached desktop computers,

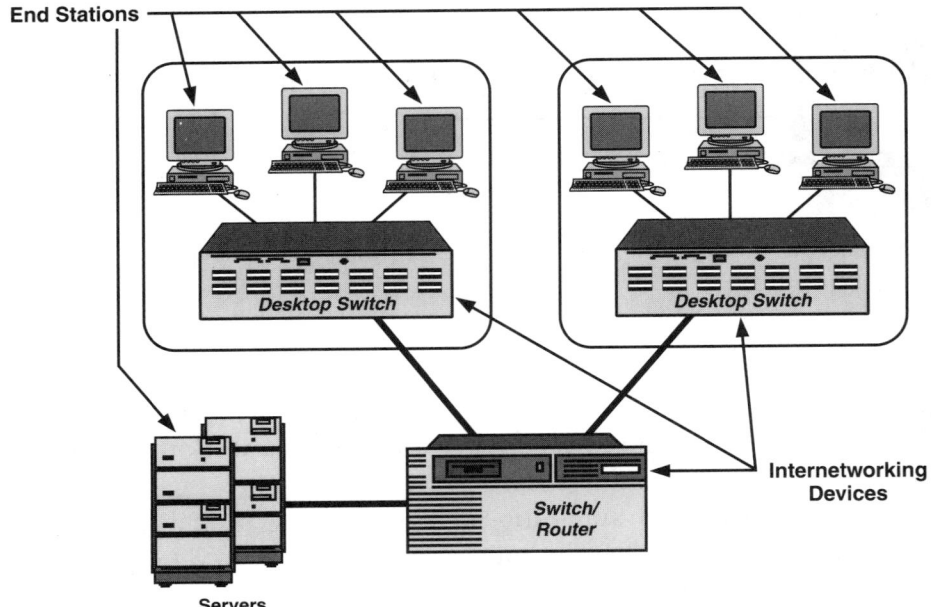

Figure 14–1 End stations and internetworking devices.

LAN-attached workgroup and corporate servers, and backbone networks for LAN interconnection. The focus, of course, is on that subset of environments that can benefit from Gigabit Ethernet. There are two distinct situations in which we need to consider the deployment of gigabit technology: end-station attachments (end users and servers) and LAN interconnection devices (see Figure 14–1).

14.1 End-Station Attachments

End stations are the computers that are actually running applications that make use of the network. The term "end station" applies both to user devices (PCs and workstations) and to servers. They are the source and sink of virtually all traffic on the network.[1]

---

1. A small amount of traffic is generated also by LAN interconnection devices, primarily for the distribution of topology and connectivity information (routing protocols) and for network management. This is usually a small fraction of the total network traffic (although improper configuration and high-granularity management polling activity may increase this significantly). Rarely does a designer making technology decisions need to explicitly consider the modest load offered by these devices.

While most network protocol architectures allow any station to communicate directly with any other station (peer-to-peer communications), many applications use high-performance servers as repositories for large, common data storage (file servers) or for shared resources (print servers, application servers, and so on). The communications requirements of a desktop station (client) are those of a single user. For a server, the requirements are generally much greater, since it is the focal point for data flows to and from multiple clients. Therefore these requirements must be considered independently. Also, clients are separated into two classes for this discussion:

1. The "average" user, who is not using a desktop computer capable of stressing a high-speed network and is not running extremely network-intensive applications

2. The "performance" user, whose applications demand greater network capability and whose desktop computer can take advantage of that capability, if available. Performance users may include computer-aided design (CAD); engineering, animation or intensive graphics manipulation; and other computing and network-intensive applications.

For both desktop and server environments, the primary communications product of interest is a NIC. A NIC, together with appropriate driver software, provides a means to attach the computer to the LAN for application communications. The NIC may be an add-on board that plugs into the I/O bus provided by the station or may be integrated into the design of the station itself ("on the motherboard"). This section considers some of the variables affecting the selection of end-station NICs, both for desktop and server applications. Of course, the issue at hand is determining which environments can best benefit from Gigabit Ethernet and which can obtain equivalent (or at least acceptable) performance with a lower-speed interface, at lower cost.

This discussion should be considered generic. Your needs will vary according to your precise application scenario. In addition, application and product requirements will change over time as new technologies evolve.

Table 14–1 provides a summary of the NIC application space. The discussion in the sections that follow should help you to understand the relevance and interpretation of the data in this table.

14.1.1 Hardware Platform and I/O Bus

A NIC generally must be designed for a specific hardware platform. Different computer families (and in particular, different I/O bus architectures) will require different NIC implementations. Client stations are usually PC-class (Intel Pentium, Pentium II, and so on) or Macintosh platforms. Performance

TABLE 14–1 END-STATION APPLICATION ENVIRONMENT MATRIX

| | Desktop Attachments | | Server Attachments |
	Average User	Performance User	
Hardware Platform	Intel PC (80x86/ Pentium/Pentium II) Apple Macintosh	Intel PC (Single-processor/ multiprocessor Pentium/P–II) SPARCstation MIPS/SGI, Alpha	Intel PC (Single-processor/ multiprocessor Pentium/P–II) SPARCserver MIPS/SGI, Alpha
I/O Bus	ISA/EISA PCI (32-bit/33 MHz)	PCI (32/64-bit, 33 MHz) SBus, SGI	PCI (32/64-bit, 33/66 MHz) SBus, SGI
Operating System	Windows 3.*x*, Windows 9*x* Mac O/S	Windows NT UNIX/SunOS/ Solaris	Windows NT NetWare UNIX/SunOS/Solaris
Data Rate	10 Mb/s, migrating to 100 Mb/s	100 Mb/s, migrating to 1000 Mb/s	100 Mb/s, migrating to 1000 Mb/s[1]
Media Type	UTP (10BASE-T, 100BASE-TX)	UTP (100BASE-TX, 1000BASE-T) multimode fiber (1000BASE-SX)	UTP (100BASE-TX, 1000BASE-T) STP (1000BASE-CX) multimode fiber (1000BASE-SX)

1. For servers in particular, it is also common practice to aggregate multiple 100 Mb/s links to provide incremental bandwidth increases, rather than going directly from 100 Mb/s to 1000 Mb/s. This is called *trunking*. For more information, see the discussion of Fast EtherChannel in Chapter 16.

users generally use either the highest-performance versions of these platforms or engineering workstations built on the Sun Microsystems' SPARC, Silicon Graphics (SGI), DEC Alpha, or similar architectures.

Older PC-class machines commonly used an ISA or Extended ISA (EISA) I/O bus, but this is rarely seen on newer machines due to the inherent low throughput possible with these buses. The most common I/O bus implemented today is the Peripheral Component Interconnect, or PCI [PCI95]. PCI is widely used as a general-purpose I/O interconnect in machines ranging from low-cost PC-class devices through high-end workstations. Most existing PCI implementations use a 32-bit-wide data path, with a 33 MHz system clock, for a peak burst-mode data transfer capacity of 132 MB/s (1.06 Gb/s). In typical use (interleaved, nonburst mode transfers using standard PCI bus components), the effective capacity of this bus is on the order of 500–600 Mb/s.

Issues relating to I/O bus throughput and the resulting performance limitations are discussed extensively in Chapter 15. However, it should be obvious that it will not be possible to support wire-speed operation at gigabit data rates using a 32-bit, 33 MHz PCI (especially in full-duplex mode). Newer, higher-performance systems (both workstation and server) are implementing 64-bit wide PCI, albeit still at 33 MHz. This doubles the I/O bus capability to over 2 Gb/s (peak). In the future, 64-bit wide, 66 MHz PCI bus implementations will provide the capability to support wire-speed gigabit operation. Such implementations will initially be available on servers and performance-class workstations.

14.1.2 Operating System

The first issue relating to the host operating system is the NIC device driver. Obviously, a driver must be available to support the intended target system. Second, it is important to recognize that some operating systems are less likely to be able to take advantage of Gigabit Ethernet technology as follows:

- Single-threaded operating systems (such as Windows 3.*x*/9*x*) cannot take advantage of a full-duplex connection, since there cannot be multiple, simultaneously executing tasks moving data in opposite directions. While a full-duplex NIC can be used on such a system, the system will not be able to use the doubled capacity.

- Driver interfaces (such as the standard NDIS drivers supplied with Windows) that use a single-interrupt-per-frame communications model incur a high overhead for every frame transmitted and received. Throughput may be limited by the frame interrupt processing, rather than the data rate of the underlying network.

- Drivers that assume Data Link-only interaction with a NIC cannot take advantage of any performance enhancements (such as IP checksum calculation, discussed shortly) that may be provided in Gigabit Ethernet interfaces. This will require that higher-layer protocols replicate (in software) functions that may already be implemented on the NIC (in hardware).

An operating system designed for server or performance-user environments (for example, Windows NT and many UNIX-variants) will incur the necessary design complexity to be able to provide the expected level of performance. This includes the implementation of multithreaded code with preemptive multitasking capability and the integration of the network protocol stack into the operating system kernel, thereby allowing more optimized hardware/software trade-offs at the expense of driver complexity. This is discussed further in Chapter 15.

14.1.3 Data Rate Requirements

This is the heart of the matter. It should be obvious that most desktop users today will not benefit greatly (or at all) from a direct Gigabit Ethernet connection to their computer. The typical end user, with a PC-class machine running office automation applications under a Windows 3.x/9x operating system, would gain little or nothing from a 1000 Mb/s connection relative to a 100 Mb/s NIC. In many cases, while the hardware/software platform may be able to sustain data transfers approaching 100 Mb/s under test conditions, most applications would be adequately served by 10 Mb/s LAN attachments. Fast Ethernet and Gigabit Ethernet may create a lot of industry interest and attention, but the vast majority of users are quite well-served by legacy 10 Mb/s Ethernet. Due to the exceptionally low (and ever-decreasing) cost of 100 Mb/s NICs (and the associated hubs and switches), many desktops nonetheless will migrate to 100 Mb/s. This capacity should satisfy the average user for a number of years.

The real application for Gigabit Ethernet end-station attachments is for servers and high-performance workstations. It is only in these applications that both the application(s) and the hardware/software platform can take advantage of speeds greater than 100 Mb/s.

14.1.4 Media Type

Most desktop computers (both for average and performance users) use star-wired, unshielded twisted-pair, with dedicated media between the workplace and the wiring closet. As discussed in Chapter 2, the evolution of structured wiring, building wiring standards [EIA91], and 10BASE-T/100BASE-T networks has resulted in most desktop environments being served by Category 5 UTP connections, with distances of up to 100 m. This huge (and growing) infrastructure of desktop wiring will effectively limit the deployment of Gigabit Ethernet to end stations until the standardization and availability of 1000BASE-T (Gigabit Ethernet over UTP) is complete.

For the performance-user who needs 1000 Mb/s sooner than this, network designers will need to use optical fiber to the desk. This will likely be installed on an as-needed basis because it usually is cost-prohibitive to install fiber-to-the-desk across an entire organization. Short-wavelength optical systems (1000BASE-SX) provide distance coverage in excess of 100 m (see Chapter 12) without incurring the higher cost of the long-wavelength optical systems that will predominate for backbone connections.

Gigabit Ethernet server connections can be provided either with short-wavelength optics (similar to performance users) or in some cases with short-distance copper jumpers (1000BASE-CX). While the distance offered by copper jumpers is only 25 m, the cost is lower than for optics and the distance may be adequate for servers that are co-located with the wiring hub.

14.1.5 Additional Features

In anticipation that operating systems and driver interfaces will have to change to support gigabit speeds, many NIC designs are beginning to incorporate features that can improve the overall performance of a network protocol stack. For example:

- It is quite simple (and virtually cost-free) to calculate higher-layer protocol checksums in hardware in the NIC. IP, TCP, and UDP all incorporate checksum algorithms that are easy to implement in hardware (one's-complement arithmetic). Providing a checksum calculation on receive and automatic checksum generation on transmit can offload the host CPU from performing these calculations in software. In the case of a packet with an invalid received checksum, the packet can be discarded within the NIC; thus the need can be avoided to transfer buffers to host memory or alert the higher-layer protocols at all. Of course, the host operating system and device driver interface must support such features in order to take advantage of the optimized performance.

- Avoiding the need to interrupt the host on a frame-by-frame basis can significantly reduce interrupt overhead and improve overall performance. With careful design, interrupts can be avoided altogether for the normal flow of traffic. However, this requires more complex bus interface logic in the NIC (for example, bus mastering and scatter/gather DMA). The trade-off in cost versus performance can be justified for high-performance workstation and server NIC applications.

- In some system architectures, it may be possible for a NIC to perform virtual-to-physical memory mapping. This allows the NIC to transfer data in and out of virtual memory without requiring host intervention in the event that the desired virtual memory page is not currently resident in physical memory. This is an extremely sophisticated maneuver and requires extra logic in the NIC, interface access to the system page table, and an operating system that supports such operations.

14.2 LAN Interconnection

A primary application for Gigabit Ethernet is LAN interconnection. Typically, this takes the form of a link on a LAN switch or router. This section considers two dimensions comprising the application of Gigabit Ethernet for LAN interconnection:

- The level in the hierarchy at which the interconnection is being deployed
- The features and requirements of a device as a function of its intended position in that hierarchy

14.2.1 Internetworking Hierarchy

LAN interconnection is generally implemented in a hierarchical manner, as depicted in Figure 14–2.

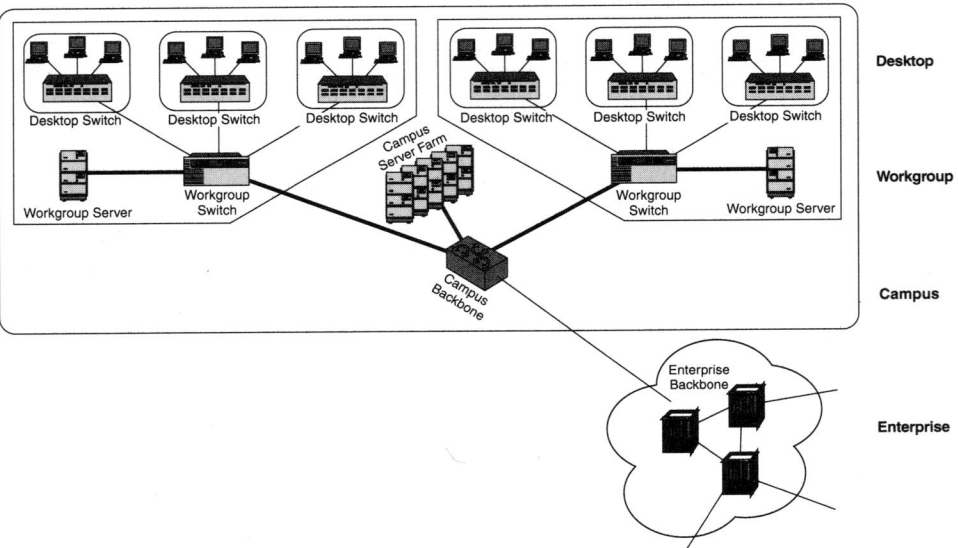

Figure 14–2 LAN interconnection hierarchy.

There are several reasons why such hierarchical structures are often employed.

- The burden imposed on the internetworking device(s) is only that of the level at which it is deployed; for example, desktop switches need only to accommodate the needs of the desktop environment. If a "flat" interconnection strategy were used (that is, a single backbone interconnecting all users with no hierarchy), then every interconnection device would need to deal with the issues and complexities of enterprise-wide internetworking. This would result in the use of many more-expensive devices.
- The burden imposed on the network administrator is similarly restricted to the level at which the given person operates. Local (departmental) administrators need to deal only with the problems associated with the department or workgroup and not the entire enterprise. Similarly, an enterprise administrator does not have to deal directly with the problems of individual users.
- Problems are more naturally isolated; network disruptions typically affect only the users or the interconnection at the level of the fault. For most failure modes, the number of users affected by a network disruption is minimized. A failure of the enterprise backbone disrupts only inter-campus communications and allows most workgroup computing to continue unimpeded. A failure of a desktop switch would affect only the users directly connected.

In a given organization, not all levels of the hierarchy are necessarily required. A small company may operate only within a single building and not require campus or enterprise internetworking. A geographically separate workgroup in a large company may connect from that workgroup directly to the enterprise backbone without imposing a campus level in the hierarchy, even though other sites within the organization may indeed have campus-level interconnection points. Rarely are more than four levels of hierarchy required.

The terminology used here is becoming industry-standard, both for network planners and equipment manufacturers. These four levels are defining the market segmentation for internetworking devices. Most products are specifically designed to meet the needs of one (or at most two) segments of this hierarchy. In fact, some companies' entire product strategy centers on a subset of the hierarchy. It is possible to build a successful business without offering products at all levels (although interoperation with products from other manufacturers becomes critical).[2]

Each level provides a *backbone* for the level below it. A backbone is a network whose primary purpose is the interconnection of other networks. In practice, end users are connected only at the desktop level, not directly to a backbone. The only devices generally attached directly to a backbone are:

- Interconnection devices (repeaters/bridges/switches/routers)
- Servers (for the given hierarchical level)
- Network management stations (for the network administrator)

Keeping end-user attachments off the backbone avoids the possibility of user application problems (for example, software faults, misconfiguration, and desktop hardware failures) from affecting multiple users through disruption of a backbone. Imagine an application or device driver gone berserk (or worse, a malicious user!), generating extremely heavy traffic loads, errors, misdirected traffic, and so on, on a campus backbone. Such behavior could potentially disrupt thousands of users. In general, it is good practice to limit backbone connections to the devices listed previously.

14.2.1.1 Desktop Level

The desktop level is the lowest level in the backbone hierarchy. At this level, end-user devices (the "leaves" of the tree) are attached. Depending on the performance level required (and cost constraints), either each switch port may support only a single user (microsegmentation) or small repeaters (typically 4–12 ports) may be used to allow multiple end users to share a single port.

Desktop internetworking devices (typically switches) are usually located in the local wiring closet.[3]

14.2.1.2 Workgroup Level

Sometimes called the *departmental network,* this level is used to provide intercommunication among desktop switches (if any). A workgroup backbone

---

2. It is interesting to note that the level in the hierarchy requiring the highest performance and feature set (enterprise internetworking) has the lowest product volume (total available market). An enormous amount of engineering development is required to compete in the market that produces the fewest sales (albeit at higher prices). This is why there are very few truly high-performance internetworking products and vendors, yet large numbers of options for low-end desktop products, where the required performance and features are less demanding and the potential volumes are orders of magnitude greater.

3. And sometimes on the floor, under the desk of someone who kicks the cables loose as a frustrated response to seeing the message, "Abort, Retry, Fail?" once too often.

will generally be constrained within a single building (typically a single floor). This level provides not only the desktop switch connections, but also attachments for departmental servers (that is, servers owned by and dedicated to the department and providing common application services, printer sharing, and so on), and possibly for a department network administrator. A workgroup switch/router is generally located in a wiring closet within the building in which the department is housed. In many cases, it may be in the same rack of equipment as the desktop switches to which it is connected; there is usually no need for long-distance links.

In the event that desktop switches are not deployed (that is, end users are all on shared LANs) or the department is relatively small, the desktop level can be eliminated and the workgroup level then becomes the bottom of the hierarchy.[4]

14.2.1.3 Campus Level

The campus backbone provides interconnection among workgroups within a single location. Despite its name, in some cases the *campus* may be within a single building containing multiple departments. In the more general case, the backbone connects departments across multiple buildings within a single organization (for example, a corporation or university). The interbuilding links are assumed to be owned and/or controlled by the organization, so common-carrier WAN technologies (with their lower data rates and monthly charges) are not required at the campus level.

A backbone (particularly a campus backbone) may be either *distributed* or *collapsed*. In a distributed backbone (depicted in Figure 14–3), the backbone network itself is brought to the internetworking devices to provide interdepartment interconnectivity. In a collapsed backbone (depicted in Figure 14–4), the backbone consists of a high-performance internetworking device. The workgroup networks must be "brought to" the backbone, often through point-to-point fiber links.

There are advantages and disadvantages to both approaches, as summarized in Table 14–2.

Distributed backbones provide moderate-to-high bandwidth over moderate-to-long distances, albeit at relatively high cost. FDDI, a commonly used campus backbone, provides 100 Mb/s of capacity over a 100-km ring circumference, but it incurs a cost penalty. Typical high-performance FDDI

---

4. This was the typical case in the past, before desktop switching became economically feasible.

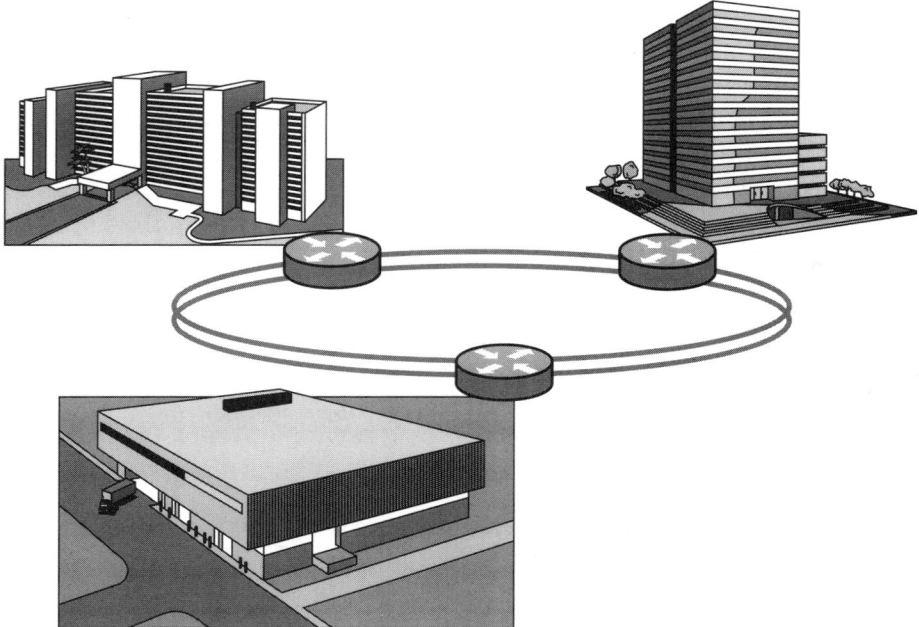

Figure 14–3 Distributed backbone.

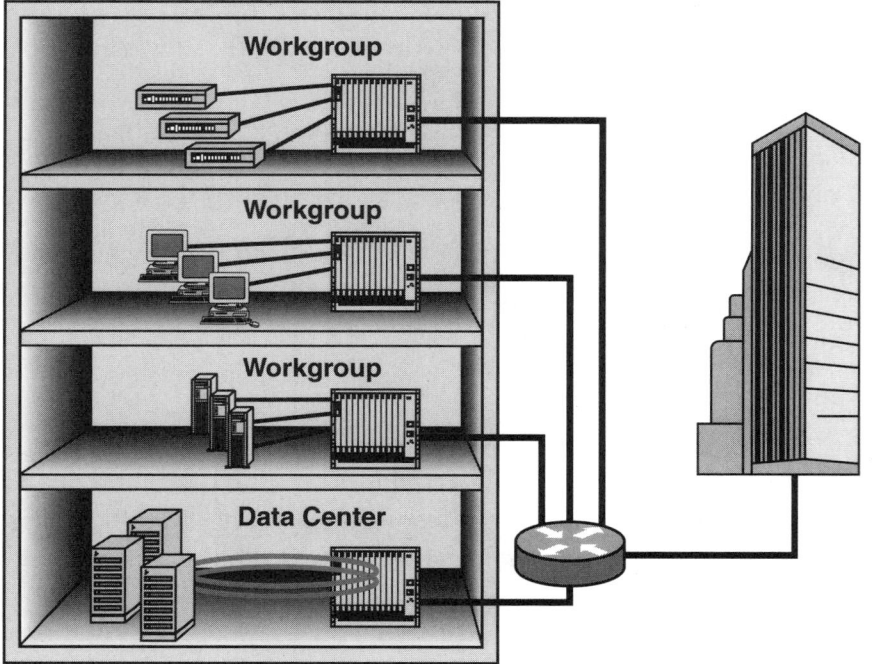

Figure 14–4 Collapsed backbone.

TABLE 14–2 DISTRIBUTED VERSUS COLLAPSED BACKBONE

	Pro	Con
Distributed Backbone	More easily covers large distances	The backbone bandwidth usually achievable is lower.
	Easily expanded	
	Robust (no single points of failure)	
Collapsed Backbone	Has a lower cost per aggregate unit bandwidth	Has a single point of failure
	Offers improved backbone security	Impractical over very long distances (primarily suitable for campus)
	Provides a single point of focus for network management	

interfaces cost thousands of dollars, plus the cost of installing the required fiber ring itself.

A collapsed backbone can provide hundreds or thousands of megabits per second aggregate capacity at lower connect costs than FDDI because the "backbone network" consists of the backplane (or switching fabric) within the internetworking device. By concentrating the internetworking functions into a single device, very high capacity can be provided at lower cost per megabit per second. In addition, the backbone can be made more secure by simply limiting physical access to the collapsed backbone device.

14.2.1.4 Enterprise Level

At the enterprise level, we are interconnecting geographically separated sites, possibly worldwide. Rarely are the links under the ownership or control of the enterprise being interconnected. In general, we must deal with WAN common carriers (long distance telecommunications service providers).

Many of the issues that arise in private enterprise internetworking also apply to Internet backbone design. Indeed, some organizations have begun using the public Internet as their enterprise backbone (occasionally through the use of a Virtual Private Network construct). Thus much of the information presented here relating to enterprise-level internetwork requirements also applies to the requirements for devices being used within the Internet itself. There are some key differences, however:

■ A private enterprise network will likely have many fewer networks within its scope than the Internet. Hence, the size of routing tables in these devices will be lower than for a router being deployed by an Internet Service Provider (ISP).

■ By definition, the Internet is an IP-only backbone. Private enterprise backbones may also support other protocols (for example, IPX, DECnet, and AppleTalk).

■ Private enterprise networks may choose to bridge rather than route some traffic (especially nonroutable protocols such as LAT and NetBIOS). Bridging is not supported across the Internet backbone.

14.2.2 Internetworking Functional Requirements

This section considers some of the key requirements of internetworking devices as a function of the level in the hierarchy at which they are deployed. If you are a user, you can use the information presented here to compare the general set of requirements to your particular needs. If you are a manufacturer, you can use the same information to identify the product requirements in the various market segments.

Of course, the information provided here should be considered general guidelines only. Your particular needs (or product requirements) will vary according to the precise application scenario. In addition, application and product requirements will change as new technologies evolve.

Table 14–3 (at the end of this chapter) provides a complete summary, in matrix form, of the functional requirements relative to the hierarchical interconnection levels. The discussion in the following sections should help you to understand the relevance and interpretation of the data in that table.

14.2.2.1 Numbers of Ports

A port is an interface to a LAN or WAN link. In most devices, there are two types of ports to consider:

1. *Attachment ports* are used to connect to devices at the hierarchical level at which the device is being used; for example, the attachment ports on a desktop switch are those ports connecting to desktop devices.
2. *Uplink ports* are used to connect either to the next tier in the hierarchy or to a high-performance device (for example, a server) at the current level. Uplink ports usually (but not always) operate at a higher level of performance (data rate) than do attachment ports. This is appropriate when attachment traffic is being aggregated to a higher-level backbone or for server connections.

Depending on the level of the hierarchy, there are differing needs for numbers of both attachment and uplink ports. At the desktop and workgroup levels, devices with anywhere from 8 to 24 attachment ports are practical. Fewer than 8 ports results in products with an unacceptable price-per-port; port densities much greater than 24 are rarely needed at this level. Greater port densities are appropriate at the campus and enterprise levels, as there is a need for higher link concentrations.

The number of uplink/server ports required is generally an order of magnitude less than the number of attachment ports. This is due to the typical ratios of clients/servers, as well as to the ratio between the data rates used to aggregate between each level (for example, 10/100/1000 Mb/s).

14.2.2.2 Switching versus Routing

"In the old days," "religious" wars were fought over the issue of bridging (switching) versus routing. [SEIF89, SEIF90, PERL92] Whole corporations came into existence (some subsequently died) on one side or the other of the battlefield. Bridges provided high performance (for a given cost), plug-and-play installation, protocol independence, and automatic configuration. Routers provided additional functionality (for example, IP fragmentation), full mesh topologies with multiple paths, better administrator control, and limited multicast propagation.

Today, few network designers use either technology to the exclusion of the other. Each has its place in the LAN interconnection hierarchy. This is due to several factors.

■ Because of constantly improving technology, the cost/performance trade-off no longer strongly favors bridges. When wire-speed bridges were considered leading-edge technology (pre-1991), wire-speed routers were either virtually unheard of or available only at a severe price penalty. Today, it is possible to build both wire-speed bridges (switches) and routers at reasonable cost.

■ Enterprise networks have grown enormously in extent in recent years such that simplistic approaches (that is, "bridge everything" or "route everything") no longer make sense. The range of application environments is wide enough to require a broad variety of products and technologies.

■ The growth of IP networks, and the Internet in particular, has made routing a necessity. At a minimum, routing is required at the point where the enterprise network connects to the Internet.

- Security concerns have increased the need for firewalls, which are most easily implemented at a router.
- Most vendors do not manufacture either bridges or routers to the exclusion of the other. A company can generate sales regardless of the internetworking method used.[5]

Both technologies are appropriate and necessary. The issue is where to deploy them to achieve the best combination of features, functions, and cost.

It is rarely useful to route *within* a single, logical workgroup. At this level, a flat network makes sense. If internetworking technology is deployed here, it will be in the form of a LAN switch.[6] Thus practical desktop interconnection devices can be implemented as pure switches that have no routing capability.

At the workgroup backbone, there will be a need for both switching (for communications between users and a workgroup server) and routing (for intergroup communications). The bulk of the traffic is likely to be between clients and the local servers, although this may change as organizations move toward Web-style intranetworks with centralized server farms. Since workgroup LANs often incorporate a high mix of equipment types (for example, PCs running NetWare, Macintosh, and UNIX workstations), a router at this level may have to deal with a wide variety of higher-layer protocols. IP is clearly necessary, but there is still a large installed base of NetWare/IPX, AppleTalk, and DECnet Phase 4-based applications.

At the campus level, there is likely to be a high mix of switched and routed traffic, although it should be possible to restrict the number of routed protocols to one or two. IP (for Internet and enterprise intranet use) and IPX (to support the large NetWare installed base) are the most likely candidates for campus-wide internetworking. Other protocols can be either restricted to

---

5. This was not always the case. There used to be companies (for example, Vitalink Communications and Network Application Technology) that built only bridges. There were also companies (for example, cisco Systems and Wellfleet Communications) that focused primarily on routing as the solution for LAN internetworking. These companies all had a vested interest in a particular technology and conducted extensive marketing campaigns in the "bridge versus router" wars, with overall sales dependent on the customers' preference for one style of device over the other. An important lesson can be learned by noting that most of the companies that "bet the farm" on bridging (exclusively) no longer exist.

6. In addition, if a router were used for desktop interconnection, then each user workstation would need to have an IP subnet assigned to it exclusively. (By definition, routers interconnect networks, even if the network has only a single user.) This could easily wreak havoc with a company's subnet allocation and architecture.

the workgroup or tunneled through those protocols that are natively supported (for example, AURP tunneling of AppleTalk through IP. [RFC1504])

Enterprise backbone design (especially for ISPs) leans heavily toward a pure IP-routed environment.

14.2.2.3 Numbers of Switch/Routing Table Entries

Both switches and routers must perform lookup operations (based either on MAC or network-layer addresses) in real time. An important engineering trade-off is the number of entries supported in the lookup table. A device that incorporates a large lookup table can operate in an environment that has a large number of users or networks, but it will impose a cost penalty for being able to execute the more-extensive lookup at wire-speed. Thus it becomes important to properly "tune" the implementation for the target application environment.

Routing protocols usually embody the concept of a *default route*—a path that is chosen when none of the explicitly known paths to given destinations apply as depicted in Figure 14–5. This allows a router to operate in an environment that has large numbers of networks (potentially tens-of-thousands) without having to know about every network explicitly. Thus the number of entries in the routing table is a function only of the number of networks at or below the current hierarchical level. Similarly, a switch can use an uplink port

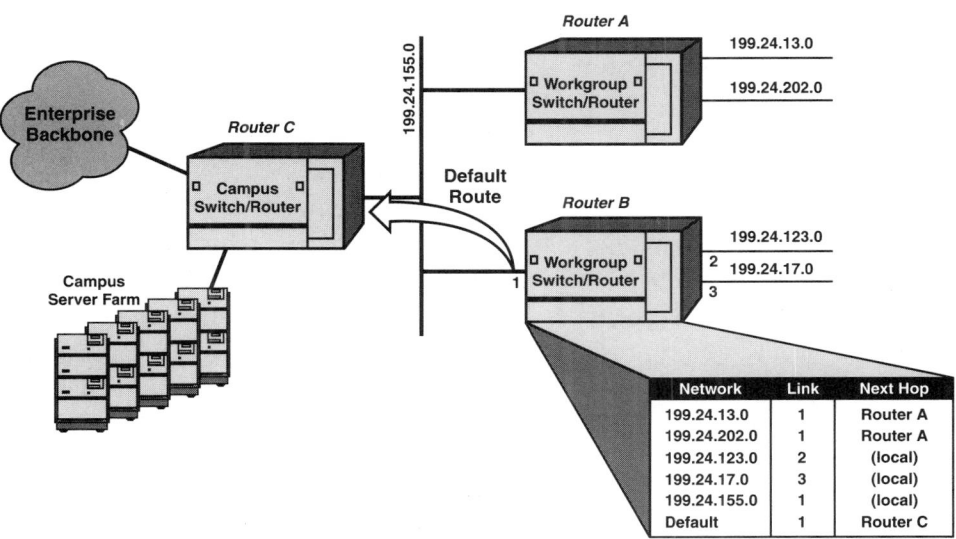

Figure 14–5 Default route.

as a "default route," thereby reducing the lookup table requirement from encompassing every MAC address in the entire switched infrastructure to encompassing only those at or below the current level.

As shown in Table 14–3, desktop switches may be effective supporting only tens of entries in their MAC address tables. As one moves upward in the backbone hierarchy, more and more entries must be supported, reaching tens-of-thousands at the campus level. Similarly, a workgroup router may know of only a small number of directly connected networks, plus a default route to the campus backbone. A router at an ISP may need to support 100,000 routing table entries, or more.

In IP networks, there also is the consideration of ARP caches. Since there can be no implicit mapping of IP addresses to MAC addresses (due to IP's limited address space), there must be an explicit (table-driven) mapping provided. The ARP cache is the data structure that provides the mapping of IP-to-MAC addresses. In general, there must be an entry in the ARP cache for each station that a given device (for example, a router) communicates with directly. This is different from the number of network identifiers (routes) that the router may know about.

Depending on the level in the hierarchy, the size of the required ARP cache will vary, most often in an *inverse* relationship to the number of routing table entries. At the workgroup level, a router may not need to know about very many networks, but it will likely have to know about a large number of directly attached devices (that is, every IP end station in the department). At the other extreme, an Internet backbone router may need to know about a lot of networks, but it has very few directly connected devices (typically the adjacent routers, with few if any end stations).

14.2.2.4 Link Technologies

The technologies deployed also can vary with the position in the hierarchy. At the desktop, there is a huge installed base of Ethernet that must be accommodated. Thus Ethernet-only desktop switches are a reasonable solution for many users. Ethernet appears to be firmly ensconced at the desktop and workgroup levels, and that is not likely to change in the near future. Campus backbones today include a wider mix of technologies, including Ethernet, Token Ring, FDDI, and some ATM. Fast Ethernet and Gigabit Ethernet are strong contenders to become the de facto standards at this level.

At the enterprise level, a router will need to support a wide variety of technologies in the future, from T-carrier (the predominant approach today) to SONET links.

14.2.2.5 Port Data Rates and Aggregate Capacity

Clearly, the data rate of the ports on an interconnection device should corre-spond to the data rate of the devices connecting to those ports. There is no need to provide greater interconnection capability than can be used by the attached devices. The issue thus becomes, "What are the current (and antici-pated future) data rates that are to be found at the various hierarchical levels?"

Desktop attachments today are primarily 10 Mb/s (with over 100 million installed interfaces), but they are moving to 100 Mb/s, if only because the cost of the increased data rate is minimal. Workgroup server ports are already using 100 Mb/s extensively and will likely migrate to 1000 Mb/s as Gigabit Ethernet becomes available. Campus backbone connections are also prime candidates for gigabit technology, as they provide traffic aggregation for thousands of users. Enterprise WAN connections vary from fractional T-1 to SONET links operating at 622 Mb/s or more.

In addition to the data rate of the links, there is the issue of the aggregate capacity of the interconnection device itself. Since the device functions as a collapsed backbone, the aggregate capacity will be a function of the internal architecture and implementation of the device. (See Chapter 11 for a discus-sion of switching architectures.) If the device is touted as being *nonblocking,* the aggregate capacity of the device should be greater than or equal to the sum of the capacities of the individual ports.

It is possible (especially with modular internetworking devices that sup-port very high port data rates) that a device may be nonblocking for certain configurations but not for all possible valid configurations. This does not nec-essarily constitute a problem. Depending on the traffic patterns and offered load distribution, the internal capacity limitation may never manifest itself as a degradation in application performance. Any such problems can be simi-larly avoided by avoiding those configurations that exceed the aggregate capacity of the device.[7]

It is also possible (depending on the architecture and the hardware/soft-ware trade-offs made by the designer) that an internetworking device may operate in a nonblocking manner for certain classes of traffic (for example, switching and IP routing) but not for others (for example, IPX and AppleTalk routing). Whether this is appropriate depends on the traffic levels and proto-cols in use in the target environment.

---

7. For example, just because a device has 12 slots and the manufacturer offers an OC-48 (2.4 Gb/s) interface does not mean that 12 OC-48 ports is a reasonable or nonblocking configuration.

14.2.2.6 Virtual LAN Support

A *virtual LAN* (VLAN) is a logical grouping of users, as opposed to the *physical* grouping imposed by the geography or network topology. VLAN technology is most commonly applied to switched (as opposed to routed) network environments.[8] While a complete treatment of virtual LANs is beyond the scope of this book, one basic differentiation among VLAN-capable switches is the method used by the switch to create the VLAN groupings. As depicted in Figure 14–6, the logical grouping can be:

- **Port-based.** The simplest method of grouping, a port-based switch conveys VLAN membership based solely on the port of attachment. All devices connected through a given port are considered members of the same VLAN, regardless of address, protocol in use, applications, and so on.
- **Address-based.** An address-based VLAN switch can support multiple VLANs on a given port, with the differentiation based on the addresses of the individual devices. This added complexity is useful only when there are multiple devices connected to the same port (that is, not a micro-segmented environment). Such a configuration is more common at the workgroup or campus level and less likely at the desktop, where micro-segmentation is becoming popular.
- **Protocol-based.** A protocol-based VLAN switch allows a single device to be a member of multiple VLANs, thus providing a different logical grouping for IP, IPX, AppleTalk traffic, and so on. When properly implemented, it allows independent Network Layer configurations for each of the supported protocols in a multiprotocol environment. This is especially useful in a campus environment.

A VLAN-aware switch could support one or more of these methods of grouping. The complexity (and therefore the cost) of implementation increases

---

8. It is interesting to note that while there is a great deal of current activity and interest in VLANs from vendors, users, and the standards community, the concepts are not really new. The AppleTalk protocol suite has always included the idea of a logical grouping of users, called an AppleTalk *zone,* that is completely orthogonal to the Network Layer organization (that is, zone identifiers do not correspond to network identifiers). Zone membership allows users to access resources within the zone, regardless of their physical location. The AppleTalk suite includes a number of support protocols to allow seamless operation of zones across an internetwork, including the Zone Information Protocol (ZIP) and the Name Binding Protocol (NBP). [APPL90, SEIF93] In a very real sense, an AppleTalk zone is a Network Layer VLAN.

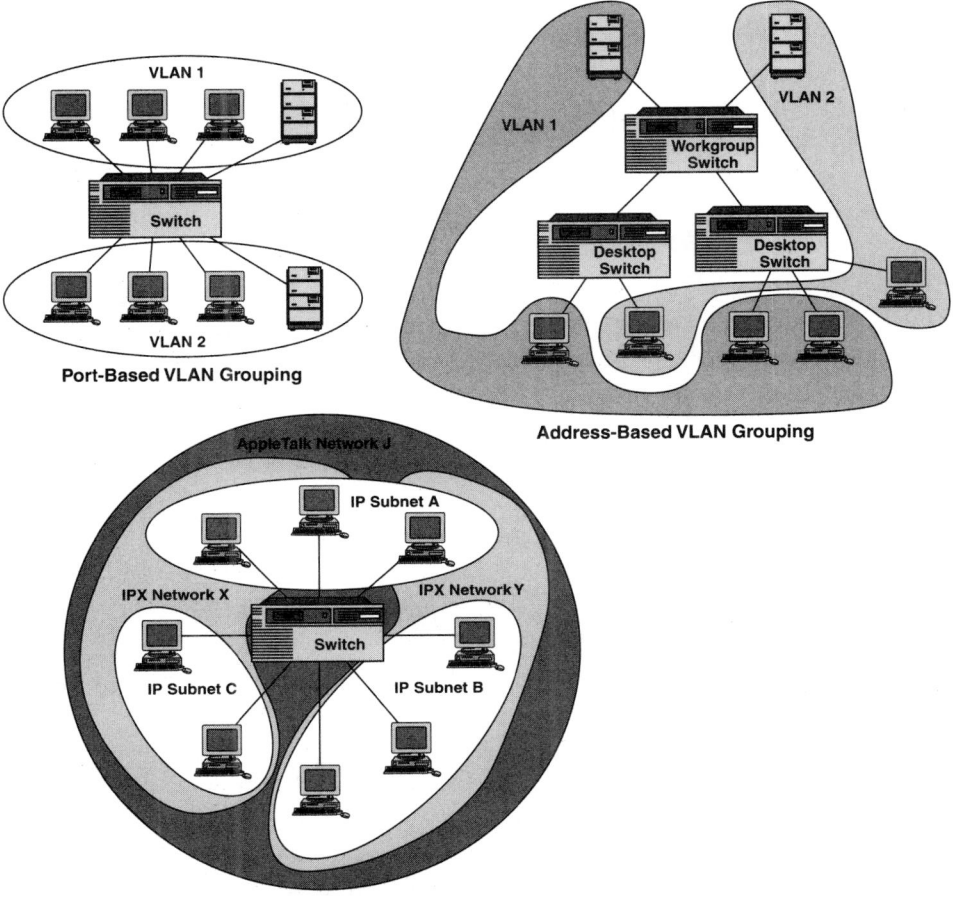

Figure 14–6 Virtual LAN grouping.

as one moves from simple port-based VLANs to address- and protocol-based schemes. Other methods are also possible, for example, grouping based on specific user applications. Future applications (for example, video conferencing) may dynamically create transient VLANs on an as-needed basis, provided support for this capability is available in the switches.

14.2.2.7 Media Support

As one moves from the desktop to the campus, the media of choice changes due to cost, distance requirements, and the need for easy reconfiguration.

TABLE 14–3 LAN INTERCONNECTION PRODUCT CHARACTERISTICS/APPLICATION ENVIRONMENT MATRIX

		Desktop	Workgroup	Campus	Enterprise/ISP
Number of Ports					
	Attachments	8–24	8–24	8–48	16–48
	Uplinks	1–2	2–4	2–8	N/A
Switching versus Routing		Switching only	Primarily switching; some routing for intergroup communications	Primarily routing, some switching for nonroutable protocols	Predominantly routing; some switching for nonroutable protocols (enterprise) Routing only (ISP)
Higher-Layer Protocol Support		N/A	IP, IPX; possibly some AppleTalk and DECnet-4	IP, IPX	IP; possibly IPX (enterprise) IP only (ISP)
Number of Switch Table Entries		32 128 MAC addresses	256 2K MAC addresses	2K 64K MAC addresses	8K 64K MAC addresses (enterprise) N/A (ISP)
Number of Router Table Entries		N/A	16–64 routes 256 2K ARP cache entries	64–1K routes 32–256 ARP cache entries	256 2K routes (enterprise) 10K–100K+ routes (ISP) 16–128 ARP cache entries
Link Technologies					
	Attachments	Ethernet	Ethernet, some legacy Token Ring	Ethernet, some legacy FDDI	FT1/T1/T3 (with/without Frame Relay), ISDN PRI, SONET OC-3/12/48 (with/without ATM)
	Uplinks	Ethernet	Ethernet	WAN technology	N/A
Port Data Rates					
	Attachments	10 Mb/s, migrating to 100 Mb/s	10/100 Mb/s	100/1000 Mb/s	≤1.5–45–155 Mb/s, migrating to 622 Mb/s–2.4 Gb/s+
	Uplinks	100 Mb/s	100 Mb/s migrating to 1000 Mb/s	56 Kb/s–1.5 Mb/s–45 Mb/s, migrating to 155–622 Mb/s	N/A

TABLE 14–3   LAN INTERCONNECTION PRODUCT CHARACTERISTICS/APPLICATION ENVIRONMENT MATRIX (cont.)

	Desktop < 500 Mb/s	Workgroup 500 Mb/s–2 Gb/s	Campus 2–20 Gb/s	Enterprise/ISP >20 Gb/s
Aggregate Capacity				
Virtual LAN Support	Basic, port-based only	Full-featured, port, MAC address-based and protocol-based	Full-featured, port, MAC address-based and protocol-based	Full-featured, port, MAC address-based and protocol-based (if used at all)
Media Support				
Attachments	UTP	UTP	Fiber	FT1/T1/T3 (with/without Frame Relay), ISDN PRI, SONET OC-3/12/48 (with/without ATM)
Uplinks	UTP	Fiber/STP for Gigabit Ethernet connections to workgroup servers and uplinks	WAN media	N/A
Location	Wiring closet or ad-hoc	Wiring closet, server room	Campus central wiring hub or data center	Corporate Data Center, Telco Central Office, ISP Point-of-Presence (POP)
Cost	Critical (cost-driven market)	Moderately important	Not as important as features, performance, and support	Not as important as features, performance, and support
Available Market Size	Tens of millions of ports; millions of devices	Millions of ports; tens to hundreds of thousands of devices	Tens of thousands of devices	Thousands to tens of thousands of devices
Customer	Departmental Network Planner/ Administrator	Departmental Network Planner/Administrator	Facilities Network Planner; Corporate MIS Planner	Corporate MIS Planner; Internet Service Provider

Unshielded twisted-pair cable (UTP) is by far the most popular medium for desktop connections; therefore a desktop interconnection device should be designed with this medium in mind.

A workgroup interconnection device, being similarly restricted in scope to a single floor or building, may also use UTP as its primary attachment medium. Uplink ports from a workgroup device may need to support optical fiber for connection to a campus backbone. Gigabit Ethernet server connections to a workgroup switch could use STP cable (1000BASE-CX), provided the distance restriction of 25 m does not pose a problem.

At the campus backbone level, fiber is the medium of choice, due to the need to support longer distances and to provide electrical isolation for interbuilding connections. Gigabit Ethernet mandates the use of single-mode fiber for the longer distances required at this level.

14.2.2.8 Cost

Clearly, features and performance come at a price. That price may be justified for a workgroup or campus device, for these reasons:

> *Features, Performance, Low Cost—Pick any 2 out of 3!*
> *—Anonymous*

- These environments demand higher feature levels and performance.
- There are relatively few workgroup and/or campus devices deployed within an organization (at least as compared to the number of desktops), so the total cost (price × quantity) is still manageable.

Cost issues become more critical in the desktop market, as the volumes are much greater. Fortunately, the performance and features required at the desktop tend to be lower (for example, data rates, aggregate capacity, and VLAN features).

14.2.3 The LAN Interconnection Product Matrix

Table 14–3 summarizes the product requirements across all of the backbone hierarchical levels.

15 Performance Considerations

Dear Dr. Network:

The network in my office is SO SLOW! We recently upgraded all of our LAN connections from 10 Mb/s to 100 Mb/s, but it didn't make any difference, and now my boss is mad about all the money she spent on new equipment and cabling. Our server is an 80386 with an 8-bit wide ISA bus. We realize that it may be a little out of date, but the network interface card clearly says "100 Mb/s Ethernet" so there really shouldn't be any throughput problem. What should I do?

Confounded by Network Expectations

Dear CNE:

Any time an application communicates across a network, it is often simply *assumed* that the network is the factor limiting the speed of communications. When the environment consists of, for example, downloading detailed graphics images from the Internet using a 28.8 Kb/s modem, this may indeed be the case. However, for the general case of data transfer across an enterprise internetwork (or some portion of it), it is often an invalid assumption.

15.1 End-to-End Communications Paths

Consider the situation depicted in Figure 15–1. The exemplary application is a disk-to-disk file transfer between two machines (for example, a client and a server[1]), each of which is connected through a LAN to an enterprise internet-

---

1. It is important to note that the distinction between a *client* and a *server* is only in the software running on the computers themselves. From the perspective of the network (the NICs, LANs, switches, and so on), there is no difference between a client and a server; they are both simply end stations on the network. The observable behavior of the network protocols (up through at least the Transport Layer) is identical among clients and servers.

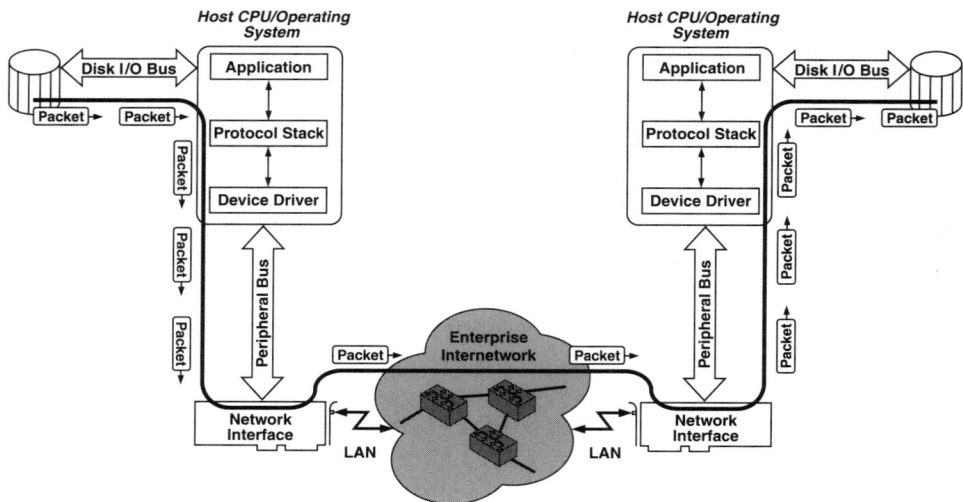

Figure 15–1 End-to-end communications path.

work. This is a very common case; it represents much of the traffic on enterprise computer networks today. The data exchanged could be anything from a short e-mail message to a large file transfer, an application download from a server, or even a disk backup. All of these typically invoke the same mechanisms discussed here.

There are many steps required, many processes invoked, and many technologies employed to complete this "simple" file transfer. In the following sections the limitations of each link in this chain are considered.

15.1.1 Disk Drives

Data (especially bulk file transfer) moving across a network is often originating from (or being transferred to) a magnetic disk at one or both end stations. Disks have a finite, nonzero data access and transfer speed that is a function of the disk technology itself, as well as any associated control circuitry. Even if such slow technologies as floppy disks are ignored, widely used PC-class hard disk drives may be capable of a sustained transfer rate of as low as 3–5 MB/s (24–40 Mb/s). Whether even this relatively low transfer rate can be achieved depends on the physical organization of the data on the disk surface(s); the maximum rate requires that physically contiguous disk sectors be transferred. If head seeks are required between accessing data blocks, interruptions on the order of 10 ms or more can be invoked; 10 ms represents over 1 million byte-times on a Gigabit Ethernet.

Of course, high-performance disk subsystems can be built by using a combination of multiple, interleaved drives, disk caching in RAM, and so on, to achieve higher throughput than could be possible with a single drive. The fact remains, however, that in many data transfer scenarios, the disk itself may be the limiting factor in throughput.[2] Even if the server is equipped with a high-performance disk subsystem, the client likely is not. For a disk-to-disk transfer, the throughput will be limited by the lower-performing end.

15.1.2 Disk I/O Bus

In general, the disk connects to the host processor through an I/O channel (for example, SCSI or IDE). This also imposes a limit on maximum disk transfer throughput. The popular SCSI-2 channel used to connect disks on many personal computers can support a sustained data transfer of 10 MB/s under best-case conditions, assuming an ideal implementation. [ANSI94a] Often, this channel is being shared among many I/O devices, including CD-ROM drives and multiple disks, so the capacity available to a given application is even less than the specified SCSI throughput.[3]

15.1.3 Application Processing

If all we ever wanted to do was move data around, things would be bad enough. However, we are usually moving the data in order to *use it for something practical.* (What a concept!) That is, getting the data there is not sufficient; there is usually some application interpreting and acting on the data. (See Figure 15–2.) This could be, for example, a database application that is extracting significant information from the transferred data and performing calculations on it and/or graphing it or an application that is retrieving remote video streams and rendering them for real-time display. The point is that there may be considerable application processing of the data occurring during the transfer (at least as perceived by the end user).

---

2. An easy way to test whether this is the case is to perform identical data transfers between machines: (1) from disk-to-disk and, (2) from "RAM disk" to "RAM disk," where the RAM disk emulates a disk interface to the host operating system, with the data actually stored in high-speed local RAM. Under controlled network test conditions, a significant improvement in throughput with a RAM disk transfer relative to a real disk transfer indicates that the disk subsystem is a likely bottleneck.

3. The limitations of traditional disk I/O interfaces is a prime reason for the development of technologies such as Fibre Channel and HIPPI, as discussed in Chapter 16.

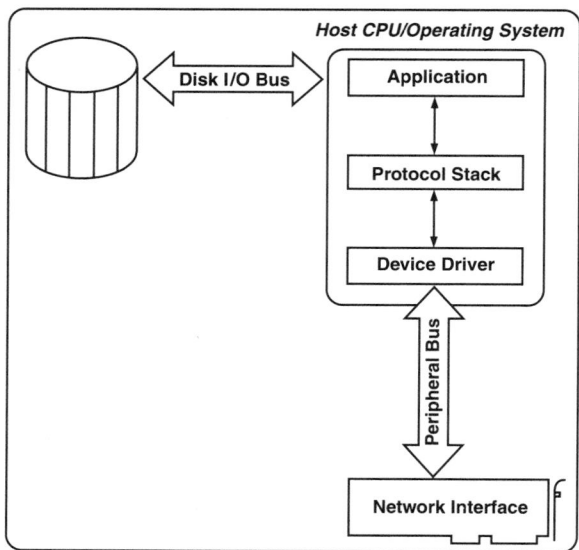

Figure 15–2 End-station network stack.

This application is generally running on a host CPU, and its performance is a function of the CPU processing speed, memory availability, operating system interaction, and so on. In many situations, it is the application processing that is the real limiting factor on throughput, rather than the infrastructure that is moving data between applications.[4]

15.1.4 Protocol Processing

Even if there is no "in-line" application processing required (that is, we are simply moving data without interpreting or acting upon it), there is still CPU intervention required to implement the functions of the higher layers of the protocol stack. Most enterprise internetworks use a protocol suite that provides

---

4. A common example of this phenomenon occurs when popular Web browser software is used on low-end personal computers. Many people assume that the limiting factor in Web access is the speed of their modem connection. To a certain extent this is clearly true, but at some point, increasing the modem transfer rate does not improve user performance significantly. While the new modem (and the computer itself) may be transferring data at a higher rate, the graphics-rendering capability of the browser itself (running on a low-performance computer) becomes the new limiting factor. This can be easily demonstrated by using the browser to load and display images from files that are stored locally, rather than downloaded from the network. The image presentation is often not as instantaneous as one might expect.

connectionless data transfer end-to-end (for example, IP, IPX, AppleTalk, and DECnet). Link Layer communications is usually implemented in hardware (in combination with the device driver, discussed shortly), but the internetwork protocol (for example, IP) will usually be implemented in software executing on the CPU in the communicating end stations. Since many situations require reliable, error-and-flow-controlled data transfer, these functions are performed by higher-layer protocols (for example, TCP), also implemented in host software.

The performance of the protocol stack depends on a number of factors, including:

- **Host CPU performance (processing speed).** Obviously, the faster the CPU can execute instructions, the faster *any* software will execute (including protocol stack implementations).
- **Efficiency of the protocol implementation.** Well-designed protocol implementations use the CPU resources (instructions, memory, and so on) in a manner that allows fast execution of the typical (fast-path) functions required.[5]
- **Operating system design (for example, efficiency of context switching, memory allocation policies, and so on).**
- **Demands of other applications (in multitasking, multithreaded operating systems).**
- **Memory availability.** In many cases, protocol implementations may have relatively high latency (that is, the time to process a given packet or message may be long), but they still achieve high throughput through pipelining. This usually requires that there be sufficient memory to buffer protocol messages for at least the worst-case round trip (end-to-end) network delay. A good example is the use of windows in TCP. Regardless of the latency, TCP will be able to sustain data transfer without artificially

---

5. One of the earliest network-intensive computing systems was the Xerox Alto, best known for being the inspiration for the Apple Macintosh. The Alto employed many of the distributed computing concepts popular today, but it did so decades earlier. Hence, the performance (being limited by the processing and memory capability of its day) was less than satisfying (read: start a program, go get a cup of coffee). This greatly hampered commercial deployment of its direct descendant, the Xerox Star. Dr. Anthony Lauck, a noted network architect at Digital Equipment Corp., who was working with Xerox during the original Ethernet development, approached the developers of the Star with a revelation that he knew how to greatly improve its performance. "I know how you can improve Star performance by 50%," he declared. The Star developers listened intently, hoping to gain some gem that they could use to improve both performance and sales. "Execute 50% fewer instructions!" was his sage advice.

halting the data stream if the TCP window size is at least as great as the bandwidth-delay product (BDP) of the total system. Unfortunately, the converse is also true. That is, the most well-designed TCP implementation will have poor performance if it must restrict itself to small windows due to limited memory availability. This is the equivalent of driving a Ferrari down a city street. The car can move at 300 Kph, but you will be forced to stop at a traffic light on every street corner, thus effectively reducing your *average* speed.

This last issue is especially significant for communications across networks with Gigabit Ethernet connections. Because of Gigabit Ethernet's exceptionally high capacity, there is a much greater likelihood that the BDP will exceed standard window sizes for end stations communicating across Gigabit Ethernet links. To achieve sustained data transfer that approaches the capacity of a Gigabit Ethernet, end stations may need to implement "large window" options (TCP-LW) [RFC1323] to avoid incurring transport flow control, as well as TCP timestamps to protect against sequence number wraparound. The amount of memory allocated for TCP connection buffers will have to increase commensurate with the larger window size.

15.1.5 Device Drivers

The device driver is the software that deals with the implementation specifics of the underlying network interface. It allows the protocol stack to work with a variety of network technologies (or vendor products within a given technology). Similar to the protocols above it, performance can be degraded by an inefficient or memory-constrained driver implementation.[6] The device driver is often more time-constrained than are the higher-layer protocols because it must manipulate NIC configuration parameters (for example, buffer pointers and statistics counters) between individual frames in real time. Thus an efficient implementation is paramount here. While higher-layer protocols and applications may be written in C or other portable languages, the fast-path code in a device driver is almost always written in the assembly language of the target processor in order for maximum performance to be realized.

---

6. This was a common problem with early 10 Mb/s Ethernet interfaces, especially on DOS-based PCs. Under DOS, the device driver and the protocol software often had to permanently reside in system memory space ("low memory"). Since memory was a scarce commodity in early PCs, many implementations sacrificed performance for memory savings. As memory has become less of a limiting factor (and operating systems supported larger memory spaces), device driver limitations have become less of a problem.

15.1.6 Peripheral Bus

Most computers use a standard bus to connect peripheral devices (such as network interfaces) to the host CPU. Examples of peripheral buses include PCI and SBus. Each bus has some inherent maximum data transfer rate. However, in practice, only a fraction of this rate can be achieved. This is because of inherent implementation limitations and statistical access patterns. A 32-bit, 33 MHz PCI bus (a common implementation) is theoretically capable of 1.06 Gb/s data transfer; however, this is under a contrived (single long burst) condition. At the time of this writing, practical PCI implementations can achieve data transfers on the order of 500–600 Mb/s. This should not pose any performance problem for a single 100 Mb/s network interface (even in full-duplex mode), but it clearly would present a bottleneck for a Gigabit Ethernet interface. One must also remember that this bus is often shared among multiple peripherals, possibly including multiple network interfaces.

When PCI is used, the peripheral bus is not likely to be a performance-limiting factor for end stations that have 10 Mb/s or 100 Mb/s interfaces today. This was not always the case; earlier PC-class computers used ISA bus architectures. This peripheral bus could not support even a single 100 Mb/s network interface at full data transfer rate (depending on configuration). In some configurations, it could even be a bottleneck for 10 Mb/s systems.

15.1.7 Network Interfaces[7]

Just because the LAN data rate is 10/100/1000 Mb/s does not mean that a given interface implementation can support sustained data transfer at this rate. There is always a trade-off between performance and cost that must be made in the design of a NIC. While a complete treatment of NIC design is beyond the scope of this book, there are a few important architectural features, discussed next, that merit consideration, especially as NICs strive to support LAN data rates at the gigabit level.

Programmed I/O versus DMA

This was a common trade-off in early 10 Mb/s NICs. For the lowest cost, the NIC would contain (some number of) fixed frame buffers, both for transmit and receive. Upon receipt of a frame, the NIC would interrupt the driver, which would then transfer the contents of the buffer, byte-by-byte, to host

---

7. The term "NIC" is used here to refer to the network interface in a device, whether it is implemented as a physically separate card that plugs into an exposed I/O bus (a traditional NIC) or as an integral part of the host system.

memory. Similarly, the driver would fill transmit buffers on the interface using programmed I/O (byte transfer) and then signal the NIC to transmit the frame. The alternative was to have the NIC itself do the transfer from local memory to host memory, but this required that a DMA channel (or two) be implemented in the NIC, which increased the cost.

This has become less of an issue as the cost of DMA channels has gone down considerably and the performance requirements for 100 Mb/s and 1000 Mb/s LANs make programmed I/O-style interfaces impractical.

NIC Memory

There is always a cost/performance trade-off with respect to the amount of memory locally available to the NIC. Incoming data streams need to be locally buffered, at least to allow for peripheral bus latency and transfer speed differences between the network and the peripheral bus. Figure 15–3 depicts two popular implementations.

In the first case, the NIC has extremely limited memory; there is only a small FIFO in each direction (transmit and receive) that can hold less than a

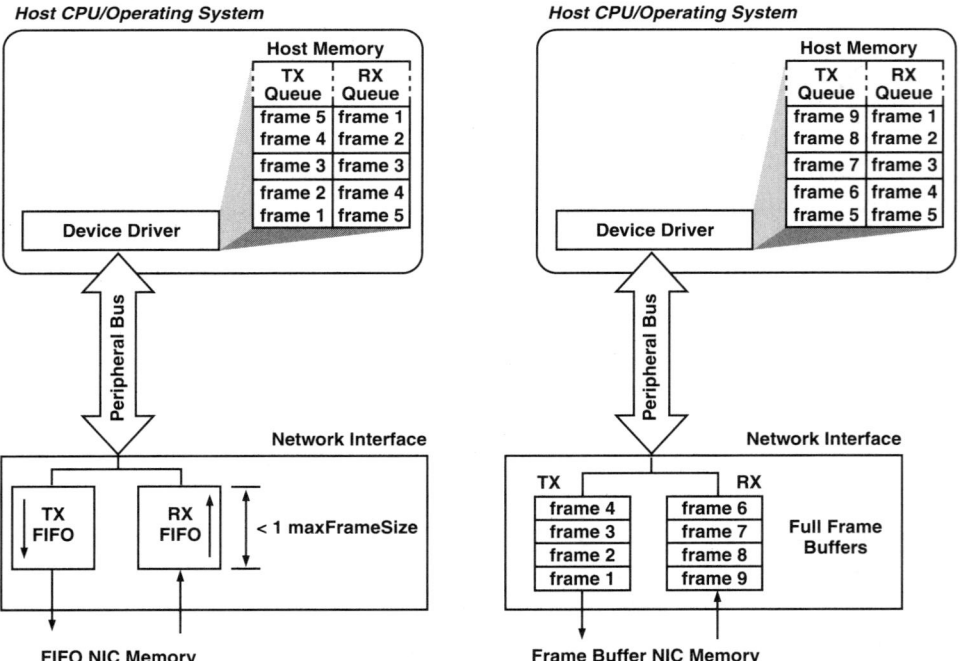

Figure 15–3 NIC memory alternatives.

maximum-length Ethernet frame.[8] When a frame is being received, the NIC starts storing the received data in the FIFO until the complete Destination address has arrived. The NIC then decides whether it needs to continue receiving this frame, based on whether the address matches its unique unicast address or an enabled multicast address. If there is no match, the received data can be flushed from the FIFO in preparation for the next frame. If there is a match, the NIC needs to initiate a DMA operation from the FIFO into host memory across the peripheral bus. The FIFO must have a depth sufficient to allow for the worst-case latency in servicing the DMA request. Otherwise, it can overflow (thereby effectively discarding the frame).

The bus latency is a function of a number of factors, including

- the bus architecture itself,
- the DMA interrupt level of the NIC,
- other processes contending for the bus, and
- the operating system or scheduling kernel running on the host (for example, whether it masks DMA interrupts for extended periods of time).

It is assumed that if the DMA interrupt can be serviced within the FIFO latency allowance, the bus data transfer rate will be sufficient to prevent FIFO overflow. It is not possible to use a FIFO-only interface with a peripheral bus whose data transfer rate does not exceed that of the network itself.

Similarly on transmit, the host transfers (or instructs the NIC DMA engine to transfer) data into the NIC FIFO. When there is sufficient data in the FIFO to accommodate the bus latency, the NIC can arbitrate for the channel and transmit the data. The same types of issues regarding peripheral bus (and host) latency apply in the transmit direction, except that in this direction problems can occur on FIFO underflow, not overflow. The system design must ensure that the FIFO does not underflow during a frame transmission on the network.[9]

---

8. This FIFO is often implemented within the network controller IC itself (either as a true FIFO or as embedded SRAM). Hence, even the need for a separate memory device can be avoided.

9. The result of such an underflow is that a "partial frame" will be transmitted. When the NIC runs out of data to send, it has no recourse but to stop transmission. Depending on the point in the frame when this occurs, the result will appear as either (1) a frame fragment (if less than 64 bytes are transmitted) or (2) a CRC error (if more than 64 bytes are transmitted). It is important that the NIC *not* transmit the contents of the valid CRC when a FIFO underflow occurs. This would cause valid-appearing fragments (undersizePackets, per SNMP [RFC1757]) or valid-appearing truncated frames.

In the second case shown in Figure 15–3, the NIC has sufficient local memory to store multiple frames without intervention from the peripheral bus or incurring overflow. Due to network data rates, NIC frame buffers must generally be implemented in more expensive static SRAM, rather than in the DRAM commonly used for large computer memories. While this increases the cost of the NIC, it relieves the system of much of the concern about peripheral bus and DMA interrupt latency. When a frame buffer architecture is used, it is possible to build a NIC that interfaces a fast network to a slower peripheral bus (for example, a 100 Mb/s Ethernet to an ISA bus). It will not be possible to sustain data transfer in excess of the slower peripheral bus rate, but at least frames can be successfully exchanged.

Interrupt Architecture

The NIC may be able to transfer multiple frames between itself and the host (in either direction) without interrupting host-resident software. Whether it can depends on the amount of memory available to the NIC and the complexity of the driver (and the higher-layer protocol implementations). Until recently, it was almost universal practice to generate an interrupt to the driver for each frame transmitted or received. This makes the design of the driver much simpler (there is no pipelining required) and does not impose a huge burden at relatively low frame transfer rates (for example, on 10 Mb/s networks). As the LAN data rates increase, the burden of frame-by-frame interrupts can become overwhelming. For example, even with *maximum-length* frames (the best case), a wire-speed streaming data transfer at 1000 Mb/s would generate over 81,000 interrupts per second (one every 12 µs)! Clearly, high-speed systems (especially servers) connected to fast LANs need to incorporate NICs that have larger local memories and pipelining drivers to support the higher data transfer rates expected of them.

With some architectures, it may be possible to avoid interrupts altogether. This usually requires extensive memory for both the NIC and the driver, with the driver polling buffers as often as necessary rather than incurring interrupt overhead and latency.

Embedded Memory

Many modern semiconductor processes (including both full-custom and ASIC) allow embedding of SRAM and/or DRAM within the IC. Adding memory to such an IC does not incur any significant additional cost, to the extent that a design is not gate- or power-limited (that is, the IC functionality is limited by the number of pads or IC pins available and there is empty space on the die itself). The embedding of frame buffer RAM is expected to be a common trend in new network controller designs. This approach also offers a number of other advantages:

- On-chip memory is usually faster than conventional packaged RAMs, since there is no high-current signal driver, pin capacitance, or lead inductance to slow down signals.
- On-chip memory can be implemented in nonstandard sizes rather than in the traditional increments of 32K, 64K, and so on. The memory can be perfectly sized for the application.
- On-chip memory can be organized in very wide configurations (for example, 128-bit or even 512 bit-wide, rather than conventional 32-bit widths), since such on-chip widths do not require more IC pins. This allows much more data to be transferred per clock cycle, thus effectively making the RAM faster.

It should be clear by now that there are many reasons why a NIC may or may not actually transfer data at its specified (10/100/1000 Mb/s) rate.

15.1.8 Local Area Networks

Many people *start* thinking about overall network performance at the LAN. That is, they simply assume that the LAN is the bottleneck in network data transfer. This may be the case with slower WAN technologies, but it is often not true for LANs. Nevertheless, many network administrators, when faced with performance problems on their network, assume that a LAN speed upgrade (or changing from a shared to a switched network) will solve their problems. This is due in part to

- the visibility (for example, press coverage) accorded the development of new, higher-speed network technologies, and
- the vendors' desires to sell equipment upgrades.[10]

When Ethernet was first introduced in 1980, the 10 Mb/s data rate far exceeded the data transfer capacity of the equipment typically connected to it. Data transfer (throughput) was invariably limited by one of the other factors discussed previously, rather than by the LAN itself. This is no longer true, and many devices can sustain application data transfer at the full 10 Mb/s rate (and for some devices, at 100 Mb/s). However, whether this means that the LAN is a performance concern depends on the following.

---

10. "What? You're still using that obsolete 10 Mb/s Ethernet? Your network is clearly congested! You need to upgrade to Fast Ethernet, convert your repeater hubs to switches, blah, blah, blah. . . . Here, look at these data sheets!" (Never mind whether the LAN data rate will make any difference in your particular application.)

- **The total data transfer needs of the device over extended periods of time.**
  Even if a device is capable of saturating[11] a LAN, if it needs to transfer
  only a relatively small amount of data, then the LAN is not really causing
  any performance degradation. Consider a workstation/server pair able to
  sustain 100 Mb/s data transfers under test conditions. If the application
  (on average) requires the transfer of 10 MB of data once each hour, then
  (ignoring load from other devices, discussed shortly) the total transfer
  time on a 10 Mb/s LAN will be on the order of 9 seconds, while the transfer time using a 100 Mb/s LAN will be on the order of 0.9 seconds.[12]
  That is, a LAN speed upgrade will save approximately 8 seconds per
  hour, for a 0.2% improvement overall. This hardly seems worth the trou-
  ble. However if the same devices are being used to backup a 40 GB disk
  array over the network (again, assuming that the LAN is truly the bottleneck), the 100 Mb/s LAN will reduce the backup time from 10 hours to 1
  hour, a considerable improvement.

- **The total load offered to the LAN from all attached devices.** In a microsegmented, switched environment, the LAN is dedicated for the exclusive
  use of a single station. With no contention for the channel, there is no
  necessity to consider the needs of others when calculating bandwidth
  requirements. However, if the device is on a shared LAN, the channel
  capacity available to each station is a function of the offered load of the
  other stations as well as its own. As other devices use the channel, that
  time is not available to the instant application. In addition, some channel
  capacity is lost due to the arbitration process itself (that is, the CSMA/CD
  algorithm).[13]

- **The limitations of any other devices in the end-to-end path.** Even if every
  end station is capable of data transfer at a speed higher than that of the

---

11. *Saturation* is defined here as a condition in which the steady-state utilization equals or
approaches the maximum channel capacity.

12. Point-to-point throughput for a TCP client on 10 Mb/s networks with no contention can
be sustained at ~1.1 Mb/s. Similarly, throughput of ~11 Mb/s can be achieved on 100 Mb/s
LANs.

13. Numerous papers have been written about the efficiency of the CSMA/CD algorithm;
[BOGG88] provides an excellent summary. The actual usable capacity is a function of both the
arbitration method and the statistical distribution of the offered load over the
  - number of stations,
  - message lengths,
  - message arrival times (at the various transmit queues), and
  - spatial distribution of the stations.

installed LAN, increasing the speed of that LAN will not improve performance if there is some other device (for example, an internetwork router) in the data path that is not capable of the higher transfer rate. By analogy, a Ferrari may be able to drive much faster than the (currently congested) highway allows. Increasing the capacity of the highway (for example, adding lanes) will not improve travel time if all of the traffic must still cross a bridge (pun intended) that has only one human toll-taker at the entrance.

15.1.9 LAN Interconnection Technologies

This section considers the fate of data transfers that must cross between disjoint LANs. There are two elements involved here:

1. The communication technologies used to provide the LAN-to-LAN links, and
2. The internetworking devices used to provide the interconnection

15.1.9.1 Local Interconnections

For local (that is, within a building or a campus) interconnection, the communications links employed are likely to have capacity equal to, or greater than the LANs to which the end stations are attached (see Figure 15–4). Building and campus backbones often use high-speed LAN technologies (for

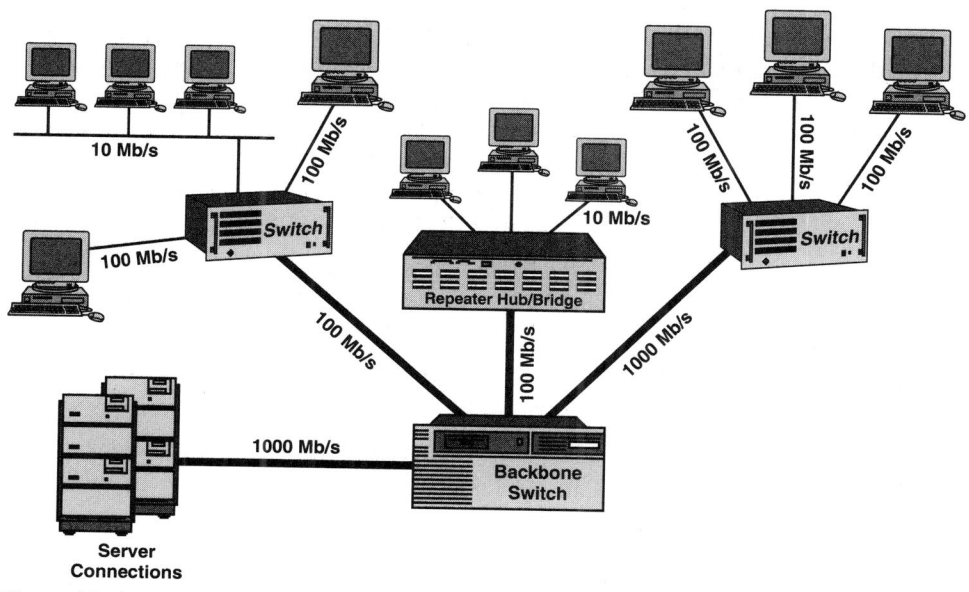

Figure 15–4 Local interconnection links.

example, Gigabit Ethernet) because the cost of bandwidth within the local environment is relatively low. The installation cost for the medium is approximately the same for a 10 Mb/s link as for a 1000 Mb/s link.

While the equipment cost is greater for higher-speed links:

- The cost increment is often less than the capacity increase (that is, a 10:1 capacity improvement may not cost 10 times as much).
- There is no monthly charge for capacity (as with WAN links).

Even though the local backbone connections may have greater capacity than the LANs feeding them, they still can pose a performance bottleneck if traffic is aggregating heavily. While a Gigabit Ethernet can nominally carry the traffic load of ten 100 Mb/s application streams, if there are hundreds of applications simultaneously attempting to move data across that backbone, then it still presents a performance limitation.

Historically, networks were assumed to obey an "80/20 rule" for traffic distribution. That is, at each level in the hierarchy, 80% of the traffic was assumed to be local and 20% of the traffic was assumed to require internetwork forwarding. This was a reasonable assumption when most application services (files, printers, applications, and so on) were provided by a server resident on the users' LAN. The internetwork traffic consisted solely of intergroup communications, which was a small fraction of the total load. In this environment, the backbone capacity was rarely an issue. In some environments the backbone utilization could be such that it would not even require a faster technology than the desktop attachments.[14]

With the recent trends in intranetworking and World Wide Web (WWW)-style computing, the reverse paradigm has emerged. Many common application services are not replicated locally but are provided by centralized servers. Even local communication (such as intragroup mail) may use centralized servers and require capacity on backbone links. In this model, the backbone

---

14. Consider a set of ten workgroup LANs, each with a nominal capacity of 10 Mb/s and an average utilization of 5% over an 8-hour business day, all interconnected by a single backbone. If the 80/20 rule applies, then the average load presented to the backbone by each LAN is

    10 Mb/s × 5% utilization × 20% remote usage = 100 Kb/s/LAN

and the total average backbone utilization over the same period is

    100 Kb/s/LAN × 10 LANs = 1 Mb/s.

Thus the backbone could be implemented with the same 10 Mb/s technology as the workgroup LANs with no significant loss of performance.

traffic increases directly with the number of users and simultaneous applications. This is one of the key driving forces behind the need for high-speed local backbone technologies such as switched Fast Ethernet and Gigabit Ethernet. In some cases, even such high-capacity technologies can become a performance bottleneck due to aggregation of multiple application streams.

15.1.9.2 Wide-Area LAN Interconnection

For traffic that must pass between geographically disjoint sites, the situation becomes graver. Bandwidth is no longer free, as most wide-area links must be leased on a per-month basis (for example, T-carrier links) or per-use basis (for example, dial-up). The cost of usage is generally a function of the distance and the data rate supported. To minimize expense, there is a tendency to use the lowest data rate that is acceptable (albeit frustrating) to the end user. In many (if not most) cases, the real limitation on throughput for remote data transfers is the capacity of the WAN link(s).

Even if high-capacity WAN links are available, the same issues (just discussed) hold regarding aggregation of traffic onto the backbone. A high-speed WAN link is generally shared among multiple simultaneous application streams, so the capacity provided to a given user is some fraction of the total. Indeed, perceived performance (by the end user) could vary greatly over time, as aggregate load varies statistically over minutes or hours. At a time when there are many contending applications, each user gets a correspondingly smaller portion of the available capacity and a lower level of application performance. If an application is lucky enough to request WAN capacity at a time of light aggregate load, the performance may be surprisingly good (at least in comparison to the typical, lousy level)!

15.1.10 Internetworking Devices

Inter-LAN traffic must not only pass through the communications links; it also must be processed by the devices performing that interconnection, typically a set of bridges (switches) and/or routers. As long as the internetworking devices can process data at wire-speed, they should not pose a throughput limitation. This is the desired situation; throughput should be limited by the link capacity rather than the internetworking devices. This is especially true for the wide-area case. It makes little sense to pay for expensive high-speed links when the devices they are connected to cannot take full advantage of their capacity. Fortunately, it is not difficult today to design hardware and software that can drive the most common WAN technologies (for example, T-1 links) at sustained saturation levels. This may change as higher-speed

WAN links become more widely deployed. In particular, OC-12 (622 Mb/s) and OC-48 (2.4 Gb/s) SONET links pose a formidable performance challenge for internetwork designers.

In the local backbone, the links tend to be much higher capacity than in the WAN (for example, 100 Mb/s and 1000 Mb/s) and the internetworking devices may indeed be the limiting factor. This is especially true for devices designed to handle large numbers of high-speed ports, as depicted in Figure 15–5.

The aggregate worst-case demand placed on such a device is the sum of the capacities of all of its ports. This is on the order of tens of gigabits per second in practical products. As 100 Mb/s and 1000 Mb/s Ethernets become more prevalent in the desktop and workgroup application spaces (as opposed to the large current installed base of 10 Mb/s connections), the demands placed on the local backbone switch/router will worsen. It is entirely possible that, in many cases, the campus internetworking device, rather than the backbone link capacity, will become the performance-limiting factor.

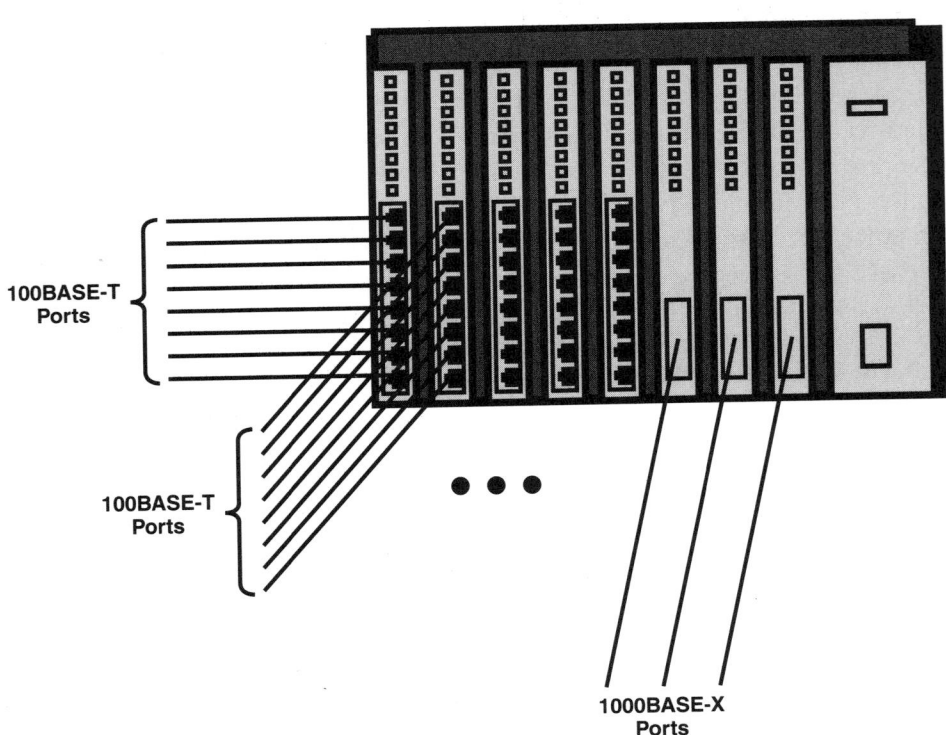

Figure 15–5 Modular campus backbone switch.

15.2 Measuring and Improving Performance

As should be evident from the previous discussion, any of a large number of elements could constitute the performance limitation in a given environment. The symptom, "the network is slow," could result from a performance limitation in any one of the links between the sending and receiving applications, from the disk drives, through the application and protocol processing in the end stations, the NIC and its device driver, *or* the LAN and LAN interconnection infrastructure.

The real issue for our questioning friend (remember him, "Confounded by Network Expectations"?) is how to determine, when network performance is below expectations, where the bottleneck is so that remedial measures can be taken. If the weak link is not identified, then upgrades to LANs, internetworking devices, and such may result in no noticeable difference in performance from the users' perspective. It makes no sense to "improve" the elements of the network that are not limiting performance.

The resources that are being utilized at or near maximum capacity are the candidates for performance upgrade. There is no need to "guess" which element in the system is the weak link. In most cases, direct measurements can be made of utilization. This is true for:

- **Operating systems.** In many operating systems (especially those designed for server applications, such as NetWare, Windows NT, and Solaris), built-in tools are provided for measuring processor utilization and for the allocation of processor resources to various applications, protocol entities, and so on. Measurements of utilization can be made over time to assess both long-term averages and short-term peaks.
- **Network protocol suites.** Many protocol implementations have tools available for test and measurement of throughput and delay (for example, Perform3 for NetWare and ttcp for TCP/IP). A direct measurement of throughput can be made at the interface to the protocol stack. This eliminates variables such as disk drives and disk I/O channels.
- **Network links.** Tools exist both for intrusive test and passive monitoring of network traffic. Rather than its being assumed that a network "must be overloaded," direct measurement of network utilization can easily be accomplished.

15.2.1 Instantaneous versus Average Utilization

A NIC attached to a LAN always transmits and receives data at the rate specified by that LAN. Regardless of whether the interface is capable of high performance, it always transmits and receives at 10/100/1000 Mb/s on a 10/100/1000 Mb/s network, respectively. A Fast Ethernet NIC capable of only 50 Mb/s throughput still transmits and receives data on the channel at 100 Mb/s, not 50 Mb/s.

There are only two possible conditions on an Ethernet channel—either the channel is in use or it is not. The *instantaneous* LAN utilization is therefore either 100% or 0%, and never anything in between. Any measurement that indicates a utilization that is between 0% and 100% must be referring to an *average* over time. For example, a network that is experiencing a 25% utilization over an 8-hour business day is 100-percent busy for 2 hours (not necessarily continuous, of course) and completely idle for 6 hours. Furthermore, it is meaningless to discuss any utilization (other than 0% or 100%) unless you specify the time period over which the averaging is being performed. The complaint, "My network is running at over 50% utilization! I need to upgrade it soon," has no real validity. It is very common for a network to achieve nearly 100% utilization during the period of a stream data transfer between high-performance devices. This may last for a few seconds or longer, depending on the size of the data transfer. Of course, if this condition persists for hours then the user may indeed need to reconfigure their network (especially if other applications are trying to use the same network at the same time). But the key is understanding the time period over which the utilization measurement is being made.

15.2.2 Collision Statistics[15]

A major preoccupation with network administrators these days seems to be monitoring and worrying about the number of collisions on Ethernet networks. There is a great deal of folklore and voodoo concerning what is an "acceptable" collision rate or collision percentage and when the network is "broken" or on the verge of collapse. Except in the most extreme circumstances (all of which are observable through other, better metrics), the number of collisions on a network is an uninteresting and often misleading statistic.

---

15. Gigabit Ethernet is almost exclusively deployed in a full-duplex manner. The discussion of collision statistics in this section and of access delay in the next, while important, apply only to half-duplex (shared) LANs, which are more common at 10 Mb/s and 100 Mb/s. There are no issues related to collision behavior or deferring to other stations' traffic in full-duplex networks.

Perhaps the biggest mistake made in the original Ethernet design was using the term "collision" to describe that (now well-known) event. Since most collisions encountered in everyday life (for example, collisions between trains, cars, and people) are normally to be avoided at all costs, people assume that the same is the case with Ethernet collisions. This is simply not true. A collision is just the mechanism used by Ethernet to control access to the shared medium among all users wishing to transmit data at any given time.

The operation of a half-duplex Ethernet transmitter can be described in an entirely different, but equivalent, manner to that normally used.

- A station with data to transmit first allows transmissions already in progress (at the time they have the frame to transmit) to finish.
- After the completion of any frame-in-progress, a station wishing to transmit must then *arbitrate* (that is, go through a selection system) to determine whether it has permission to transmit.
- The method of arbitration used is to have the station begin transmitting the frame that it wants to send.
- If, while transmitting the frame, the station is *not* informed otherwise, then the station has been granted permission ("won the arbitration"). The station completes the transmission and is finished.
- If more than one station is arbitrating, then they are all informed of their multiple simultaneous arbitration attempts. Being so informed, each station aborts its data transmission and reschedules it.

Described in this manner, a collision clearly is not an event to be avoided. Collisions are not "bad." They are the mechanism Ethernet uses to allocate shared bandwidth among stations wishing to use the channel at the same time.

The key to efficient channel utilization in a shared Ethernet is two-fold.

1. The mechanism used for channel arbitration is the same as that used to send data. There is no time wasted in arbitration if a station is granted the channel. Since this is the typical situation (one station sending at any given time), an Ethernet provides an extremely low delay (essentially zero) for typical channel access.

2. When more than one station wishes to use the channel at the same time (that is, a collision occurs), resolution occurs very quickly. The station almost immediately aborts the transmission, gets off the channel, and reschedules the frame. Very little channel time is wasted for the arbitration as compared to valid data transmission times.

An increase in the number of collisions on an Ethernet is therefore not necessarily indicative of a problem, only that there is more offered load.

Ethernet uses the collision information to quickly redistribute the instantaneous offered load over the available time, thereby maximizing channel utilization and application throughput.

Collisions do not use a large percentage of available channel bandwidth, even under moderate-to-heavy offered load. Thus an increase in observed collision counters is not a problem indication per se. As long as user performance and application throughput are acceptable, collision statistics can be generally ignored. An increase in collision counters while maintaining acceptable user performance is an indication that the Ethernet access control algorithm is properly managing the available channel bandwidth.

15.2.3 Acceptable Channel Utilization

There are many variables to consider when trying to determine what constitutes an acceptable utilization:

- Number of stations on the LAN
- Application behavior
- Traffic patterns
- Frame length distribution

Nonetheless, experience shows that for many common environments, including office automation LANs with tens of stations, the following utilization levels can be used as "rules of thumb"[16] for determining when a shared LAN is approaching excessive load.

- Utilization exceeds 10–20% averaged over an 8-hour work day, or
- Utilization exceeds 20–30% averaged over the worst hour of the day, or
- Utilization exceeds 50% averaged over the worst 15 minutes of the day.

Note that for very short-term periods (seconds, or even tens of seconds), network utilization may be nearly 100% without causing any problems. This might occur during a large file transfer between a pair of high-performance stations on an otherwise quiet network.

Again, these are not hard-and-fast rules, and some application environments may operate well under heavier loads or fail at lighter levels.

Note that a LAN experiencing high utilization over an extended time may cause application performance degradation, not because the LAN cannot

---

16. Before thermometers were invented, brewers would dip a thumb into the mix to find the right temperature for adding yeast. Too cold, and the yeast wouldn't grow; too hot, and the yeast would die. From this technique, we derived the "rule of thumb."

sustain that utilization, but because such high utilization implies that the LAN access delay is most likely much longer than is desirable.

15.2.4 Ethernet Overhead

Ethernets are generally characterized by their raw data rate, that is, 10 Mb/s, 100 Mb/s, or 1000 Mb/s, but what does this figure actually represent? This is the rate at which bits are transmitted and received on the physical channel, from the perspective of the client of that channel (that is, the MAC Sublayer of the Data Link).[17] Every layer in the architecture imposes some overhead on this raw data rate and reduces the available capacity to its higher-layer clients. You can easily see how much of that Ethernet capacity is theoretically available to a given application or protocol entity, using the example depicted in Figure 15–6.

In this example, a TCP client (that is, FTP, the File Transfer Protocol of the TCP/IP suite) is being used to move blocks of data to another device on the network. For the sake of simplicity, assume that the device is operating in full-duplex mode and FTP is transferring back-to-back application data blocks of the maximum length possible (1500 bytes MAC payload; see Chapter 5).[18] This maximum-length message uses 12,304 bits of channel capacity, as shown in the figure.

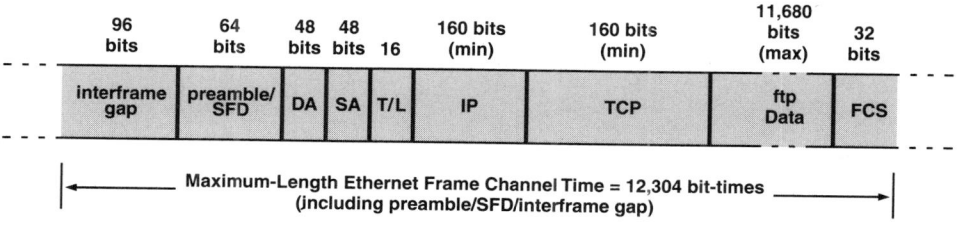

Figure 15–6 Ethernet capacity at various layers.

---

17. The actual signaling rate on the underlying channel may be *greater* than the specified data rate due to block encoding. Thus 100 Mb/s Ethernet is signaled at 125 Mbaud and Gigabit Ethernet is signaled at 1.25 Gbaud.

18. The assumption of full-duplex mode eliminates considerations of capacity loss due to channel arbitration. While in practical networks this reduction in capacity is minimal, the actual performance degradation is a function of the distribution of offered load across multiple stations over time and frame lengths and is therefore hard to quantify. So the example in the text is a *best-case* scenario.

The Ethernet MAC imposes channel overhead due to the following:

Interframe gap	96 bits/frame
Preamble/Start-of-Frame delimiter	64 bits/frame
Destination and Source addresses	96 bits/frame
Type/Length field	16 bits/frame
Frame Check Sequence (CRC)	32 bits/frame

or 304 bits/frame overall. Thus the client of the MAC (IP) has a maximum of

$$\frac{12,304 - 304}{12,304} = 97.5\%$$

of the capacity available. Assuming that no IP or TCP options are in use, these protocols impose an overhead of 160 bits each, or 320 bits total. Thus, in steady-state, FTP can achieve a maximum throughput of

$$\frac{12,304 - 304 - 320}{12,304} = 94.9\%$$

of the channel capacity, corresponding to over 11 Mb/s on a 100 Mb/s Ethernet. (This was the figure used earlier in the discussion of data transfer times on the network.) Such throughput levels are often achieved in practice on uncongested LANs.

16 Technology Alternatives

While the multifarious Gigabit Ethernet start-up companies may wish it weren't so, Gigabit Ethernet is not the only game in town. This chapter discusses alternatives to Gigabit Ethernet. While most 10 Mb/s and 100 Mb/s Ethernets see their widest deployment in desktop/end-user applications, Gigabit Ethernet is most appropriate in the workgroup/campus backbone and for high-speed server attachments. From this perspective, the alternative technology choices include:

- Fast Ethernet (and Switched Fast Ethernet)
- FDDI (and Switched FDDI)
- High-Performance Parallel Interface (HIPPI)
- Fibre Channel
- Asynchronous Transfer Mode (ATM)

For each of these, this chapter considers their advantages and disadvantages relative to Gigabit Ethernet, addressing features, performance, cost, availability, and ease of integration with the rest of the network. However, this chapter is not a tutorial or primer on any of these technologies. Appropriate references are provided for the curious reader.

16.1 Fast Ethernet

While the 100 Mb/s Ethernet is not strictly an alternative *technology*, it clearly is an option relative to Gigabit Ethernet. The issue here is principally that of bandwidth. That is, Gigabit Ethernet provides a higher data rate and lower delay than Fast Ethernet, but at a cost penalty.

16.1.1 Aggregate Capacity versus Throughput

Whether the added capacity of a gigabit link provides any measurable benefit depends on the applications and devices using it and to what it is connected.

For end-station switch attachments (for example, a server connection), a Gigabit Ethernet link provides little benefit if the station is unable to saturate a 100 Mb/s link. That is, it makes sense to increase the link capacity only when the link itself is the limiting factor in communications throughput, as discussed in Chapter 15.

It is more likely that 100 Mb/s Ethernet links may become congested in a switched, collapsed backbone environment, since there can be multiple sources of traffic aggregating on the channel. In this environment, the total load is not limited by the offered load of a single server or application data stream. The use of Gigabit Ethernet reduces delay across the backbone, both by reducing the frame transmission time and by lowering the queuing delay within the backbone switches/routers.

There is an "Ethernet Philosophy" at work here. Underlying much of the design (and success) of Ethernet is the idea that if you make bandwidth "really cheap," then users can afford to over-provision the network, that is, buy more capacity than is actually needed.[1] With excess channel capacity, most or all of the queuing delay can be eliminated when accessing the network from both stations and internetworking devices; queues are emptied ten times faster on a Gigabit Ethernet relative to a 100 Mb/s link. The only delays remaining are signal propagation delays (on the order of a 5–15 µs for backbone links of 1–3 km, independent of data rate) and frame transmission time (12.3 µs for a maximum length frame at 1000 Mb/s).

16.1.2 Distance Restrictions

A minor advantage of Gigabit Ethernet is that, according to the standard, it can operate over 3-km links (using single-mode optical fiber and long wavelength lasers), rather than the standards-based, 2-km limitation of 100 Mb/s Ethernet (using multimode fiber and LEDs). However, there are a number of vendors offering external transceivers that allow standard 100 Mb/s Ethernet interfaces to drive much longer distances than even Gigabit Ethernet. These external transceivers use long wavelength lasers and single-mode fiber at 100 Mb/s and support distances of up to 100 km or more, thereby effectively eliminating any distance advantages of Gigabit Ethernet. (See Figure 16–1. Note, this is not defined in any official standard.)

---

1. This underlies much of the controversy over the need for Quality of Service (see the discussion about ATM later in this chapter).

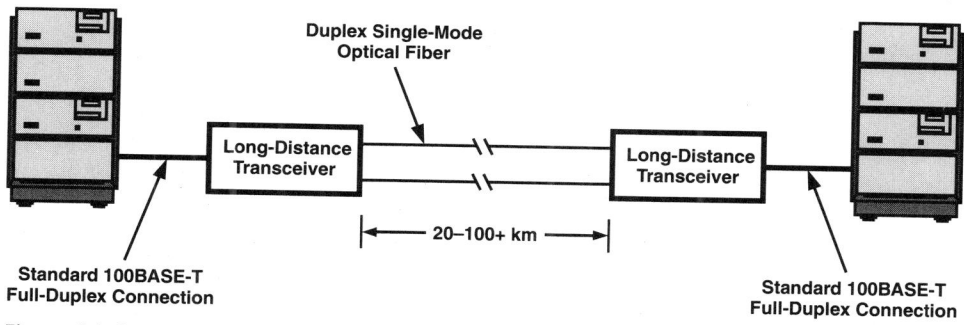

Figure 16–1   Using Fast Ethernet over long distances.

Of course, the transceivers must be used in pairs obtained from the same vendor, as there is no interoperability standard and the link must operate in full-duplex mode. The lengths supported allow the implementation of metropolitan-area, switched 100 Mb/s Ethernet networks.

16.1.3 Switched Fast Ethernet versus Shared Gigabit Ethernet

The debate between switched and shared LANs began with the development of 100 Mb/s Ethernet (switched 10 Mb/s versus shared 100 Mb/s) and continues unabated with the development of gigabit technology. The only difference is that the numbers have increased by an order of magnitude.

There is no single answer to the question of which alternative is best. As always, the issue is a matter of trading off

- aggregate capacity,
- maximum end-to-end throughput, and
- cost.

16.1.4 Aggregate Capacity versus End-to-End Throughput

As depicted in Figure 16–2, a shared Gigabit Ethernet provides an aggregate capacity of 1 Gb/s (or less, depending on frame lengths and traffic patterns). The maximum data stream throughput (for example, for a file transfer between stations on the LAN) is the full 1000 Mb/s data rate. A switched Fast Ethernet provides an aggregate capacity that increases linearly with the number of ports on the switch.[2] Thus a switched 100 Mb/s backbone can

---

2. Full-duplex operation with a nonblocking switch architecture is assumed.

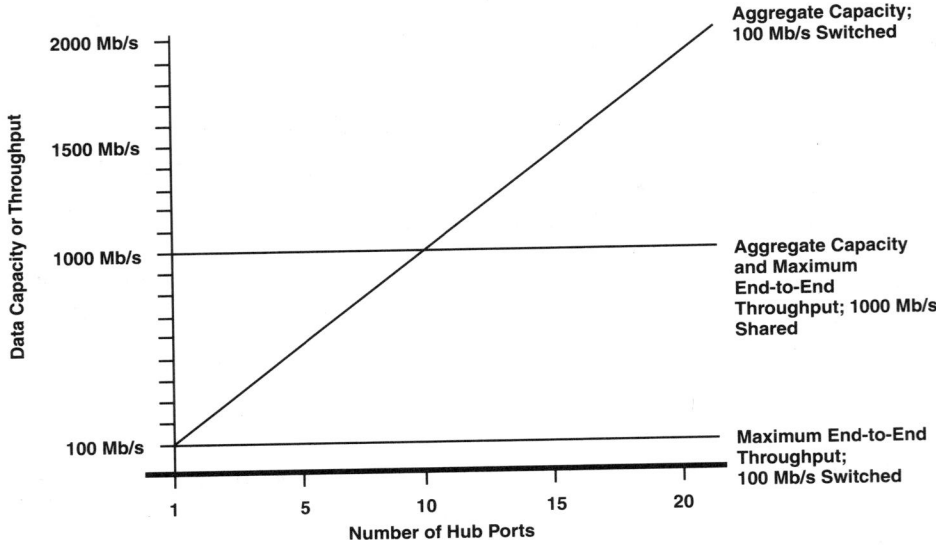

Figure 16–2 Aggregate capacity and maximum throughput.

provide greater capacity than can a shared Gigabit Ethernet for port densities greater than 10. On the other hand, the maximum throughput achievable by any pair of communicating end stations is still only 100 Mb/s.

The system that provides the best performance is therefore dependent on the requirements of the target application. If the LAN is being used for occasional high-speed transfers among devices capable of sustained, greater-than-100 Mb/s throughput (for example, a back-end network among servers), a shared Gigabit Ethernet should provide lower delay than a switched 100 Mb/s system does. If the network is being used to aggregate application data streams from large numbers of low-throughput devices (for example, a workgroup backbone), then a switched 100 Mb/s network will provide the necessary greater capacity.

As discussed in Chapter 11, a Buffered Distributor can provide improved performance over a traditional repeater-based shared LAN. The maximum end-to-end throughput of both systems is identical; both can support single streams of data at the full 1000 Mb/s data rate.[3] However, the aggregate

---

3. Measured at the Physical Layer interface (that is, including all Data Link overhead) and ignoring interframe gap loss. The effect of the interframe gap is quite small, especially for back-to-back maximum length frame transfers, as would be expected in a bulk file transfer application. The loss of unidirectional throughput is only 0.5% of total capacity in this case. (See Section 15.2.4 for calculation details.)

throughput when using a Buffered Distributor can approach the full channel rate (1000 Mb/s) regardless of the distribution of the offered load among various stations and frame lengths. This is because of frame buffering in the Buffered Distributor, and the ability of the Buffered Distributor to instantaneously arbitrate among multiple ports contending for the network. The aggregate capacity of a traditional shared LAN is always less than the maximum. The extent to which this capacity is reduced is a function of the distribution of the offered load among the stations.[4]

16.1.5 Cost and Product Maturity

Cost is also a consideration. (Isn't it always?) One hundred Mb/s ports, both on the attached stations and switching hubs, are already well along their maturity curve; high levels of integration and fierce competition have driven prices down to commodity levels. Gigabit Ethernet ports are much more expensive, at least initially, both at end stations and hubs. In fact, the initial cost penalty may be greater than the performance advantage. That is, a Gigabit Ethernet interface may cost more than ten times that of a Fast Ethernet port, depending on the particular product and vendor. This is a function both of the increased complexity of the system interface required to operate at gigabit rates, as well as the relative immaturity of Gigabit Ethernet products. Assuming that the market is large enough to justify high levels of integration and competition, ultimately you should expect to pay a premium of not more than two to three times for the ten times data rate increase of Gigabit Ethernet. During the "market window," when the cost penalty for the higher-speed interface exceeds the performance gain, aggregating or "trunking" multiple lower-speed interfaces may provide a better price/performance trade-off. This is precisely the idea behind Fast EtherChannel.

16.1.6 Fast EtherChannel

Fast EtherChannel was designed for incremental migration from 100 Mb/s Ethernet to higher speeds. It provides an alternative to Gigabit Ethernet by allowing multiple 100 Mb/s links to be aggregated such that they appear (at

---

4. The performance advantage of a Buffered Distributor over a repeater comes from the fact that in a repeater environment, channel arbitration is being performed by the MAC entities in the end stations. Since these entities are physically separated from each other, it takes some time for the arbitration to occur (for them to detect each other's transmissions) due to propagation delays. In a Buffered Distributor, the head of each station's transmit queue is transferred to the hub where arbitration can take place instantaneously, since they are all within the same device.

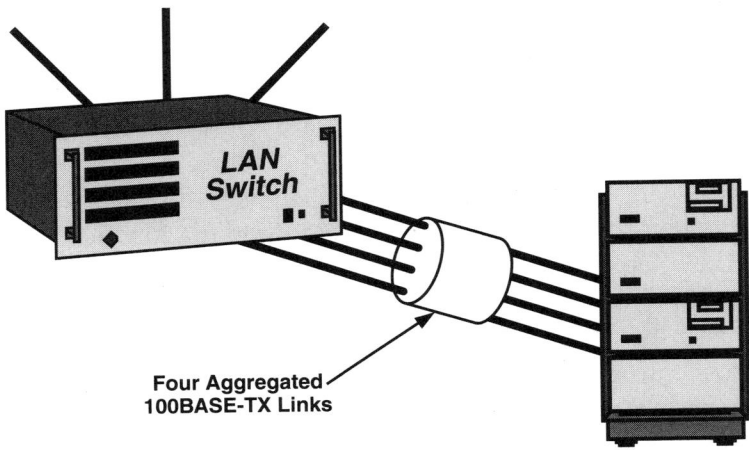

**Four Aggregated
100BASE-TX Links**

Figure 16–3 Fast EtherChannel.

the device driver interface) to be a single, higher-speed link. This is depicted
in Figure 16–3.

Fast EtherChannel was originally developed and promoted by cisco Systems; they are also leading a consortium of vendors to provide interoperable,
multivendor Fast EtherChannel solutions.[5] First shipped in 1997, Fast Ether-
Channel provided a semistandard mechanism for Ethernet operation at
greater-than-100 Mb/s data rates prior to the introduction of standard Gigabit Ethernet products. While the individual links are standard, 100 Mb/s full-
duplex Ethernets, the algorithms for aggregating traffic (and maintaining
proper frame ordering) among the links are currently proprietary. At the time
of this writing, the IEEE 802 committee has approved the formation of a
Study Group to pursue standardization of link trunking technology such as
Fast EtherChannel. This is expected to result in a formal standards activity
and an industry standard.

---

5. Fast EtherChannel is similar to a method of aggregating multiple 10 Mb/s channels developed years earlier by Kalpana Corporation. Prior to the development of 100 Mb/s Ethernet,
Kalpana provided a means for users to connect a single server to multiple 10 Mb/s switch
ports, together with a device driver that made it appear to the network operating system as if
the server had a single, higher-speed interface rather than multiple 10 Mb/s NICs. This avoided
the problem of switch congestion created by the natural aggregation of traffic between clients
and servers. It is not surprising that cisco followed this same path with Fast EtherChannel, as
cisco had previously acquired Kalpana and many of the former Kalpana engineers now work
for cisco.

Fast EtherChannel allows up to 4 full-duplex Fast Ethernet ports to be aggregated. This provides a total of up to 400 Mb/s of link capacity in each direction, in 100 Mb/s increments. The higher-capacity aggregated link can be used only in a point-to-point configuration (a requirement of all full-duplex links, irrespective of aggregation). The primary usage is expected to be for switch-to-switch (or router-to-router) connections and server-to-switch (or router) links, similar to Gigabit Ethernet.

In addition to increasing capacity, Fast EtherChannel allows multiple, parallel Fast Ethernet links to serve as redundant backups for each other, either individually or in groups. This provides a level of fault tolerance in the event of link failure (for example, cable disconnection or interface hardware faults). When Fast EtherChannel is so configured, the redundant links operate purely in a "standby" mode; they do not carry traffic unless the primary link(s) fail. Failure of a primary link can automatically trigger a switchover to the backup link(s) via the spanning-tree method for topology reconfiguration, as implemented in standards-compliant bridges. [IEEE93a]

No hardware changes are required to use Fast EtherChannel. Standard 100 Mb/s server NICs and/or switch interfaces are used, together with the proper device driver and configuration software that make the multiple links appear as one.

It should be noted that unlike Gigabit Ethernet, Fast EtherChannel, when used on a switch-to-switch link, does not increase the maximum station-to-station throughput beyond the 100 Mb/s individual link capacity. This is because for proper frame sequencing to be maintained, any given end-to-end data stream must pass through only one of the aggregated links. The parallel paths are used to increase aggregate capacity, not end-to-end throughput.

16.2 Fiber Distributed Data Interface

The Fiber Distributed Data Interface (FDDI) was developed during the mid-1980s and was the first standard local and metropolitan area network technology capable of operating at 100 Mb/s. For many years (1987–1993), it was the only practical network alternative operating at a data rate in excess of 16 Mb/s. Developed under the auspices of the American National Standards Institute (ANSI), it had (and still has) support from dozens of network equipment manufacturers. FDDI is now an ISO International Standard. [ISO89, ISO89a, ISO90]

While FDDI is not strictly part of the IEEE 802 family of standards, it is fully compatible with it. Architecturally, it provides the same type of service: connectionless frame delivery using 48-bit addressing. Thus it can be bridged to Ethernet without incurring encapsulation overhead or connection setup.[6] FDDI device drivers can be (and are) designed so that standard end-station protocol stacks can communicate over the LAN in the same way that they would with an Ethernet. This is in contrast with Fibre Channel, HIPPI, and ATM, all of which are connection-oriented protocols.

Originally, FDDI was intended for a wide variety of applications:

- Front-end, as a high-speed replacement for desktop LANs (that is, an Ethernet upgrade)
- Back-end, as a processor-to-processor communications system, for server interconnections, multiprocessing systems, and so on
- Backbone, as a means of interconnecting other networks

In practice, FDDI has flourished only in the backbone application environment. This is primarily due to its initial need for fiber media (which effectively eliminates widespread use in the high-volume desktop market) and its high cost.

16.2.1 FDDI Operation

16.2.1.1 FDDI MAC

FDDI was designed around the use of a shared-fiber medium configured in a ring topology, with media arbitration accomplished through token passing (similar to IEEE 802.5 Token Ring MAC). This is depicted in Figure 16–4.

FDDI supports a maximum of 500 stations in the ring. All stations operate at a single, common data rate of 100 Mb/s. A token frame circulates around the ring; when a station wishes to transmit data, it waits for the token to arrive and then substitutes its frame(s) for the token. Following successful transmission of the frame(s) in its transmit queue, the station sends a new token frame, thereby allowing the next station in the ring to similarly send data.[7]

---

6. Explicit support for bridging among IEEE 802 and FDDI LANs is provided in [IEEE93a].

7. This is an extremely simplified description of the FDDI access method. There are numerous details of MAC operation, including restricted token behavior and synchronous bandwidth reservation, that are not presented here because they are not necessary for an understanding of the use of FDDI as an alternative technology to Gigabit Ethernet. Readers interested in the details of the FDDI MAC should refer either to the official standard [ISO89] or to [SHAH93].

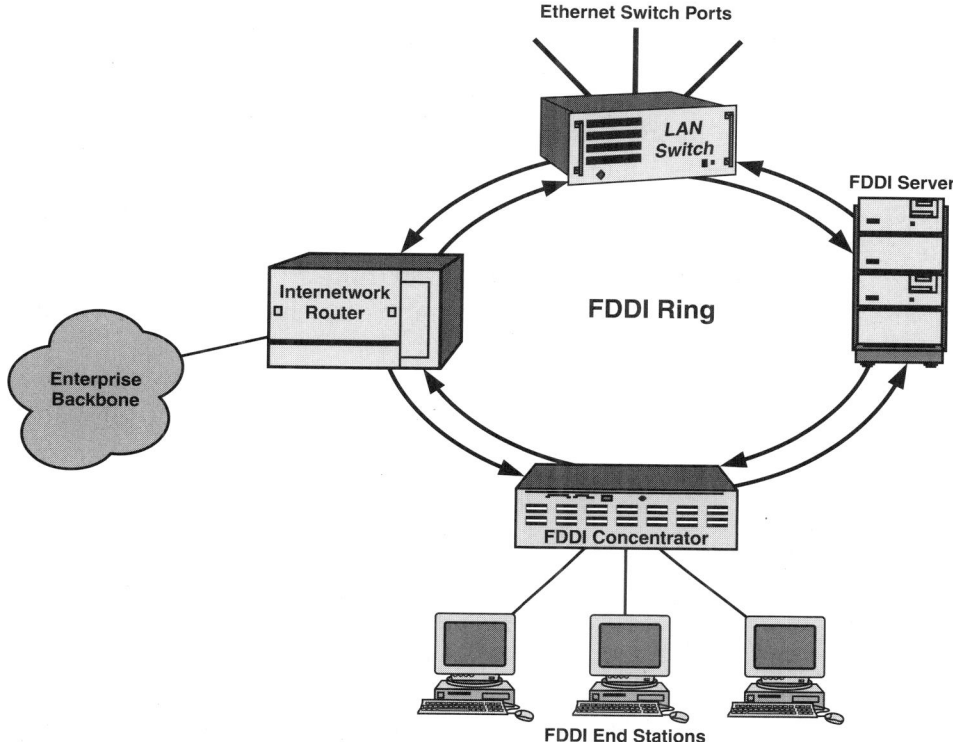

Figure 16–4 FDDI ring.

Frames (as depicted in Figure 16–5) are exchanged among stations. Similar to how Ethernet operates, frames may be sent to individual stations (unicast addresses) or to groups of stations (multicast addresses). FDDI uses the same address space as Ethernet (that is, 48-bit addresses assigned in the same manner and from the same pool as Ethernet addresses).

≥ 2 bytes	1	1	6 bytes	6 bytes	0–4500 bytes	4 bytes	4 bits	≥12 bits
Preamble	SD	FC	Destination Address	Source Address	Data	FCS	ED	FS

SD = Start Delimiter
FC = Frame Control
FCS = Frame Check Sequence (CRC)
ED = End Delimiter
FS = Frame Status

Figure 16–5 FDDI frame.

16.2.1.2 FDDI Topology

Two methods of station interconnection are provided in FDDI. A *dual-ring configuration* uses two, fully redundant rings. One ring acts as the primary communications path. Stations can detect when this primary path fails and automatically "wrap" around the fault, using the second ring, as depicted in Figure 16–6. This provides for highly available networks; this is especially important in backbone and back-end applications. Of course, the cost is higher due to the need for additional physical (optical) interfaces, additional cabling, and logic for the determination and implementation of the fault detection and switchover mechanism.

Where cost is more of an issue, FDDI supports the use of a *single-ring configuration*. Singly attached stations require the use of an FDDI concentrator. Redundant, fail-safe operation is lost, but this is generally less important in desktop (front-end) applications.

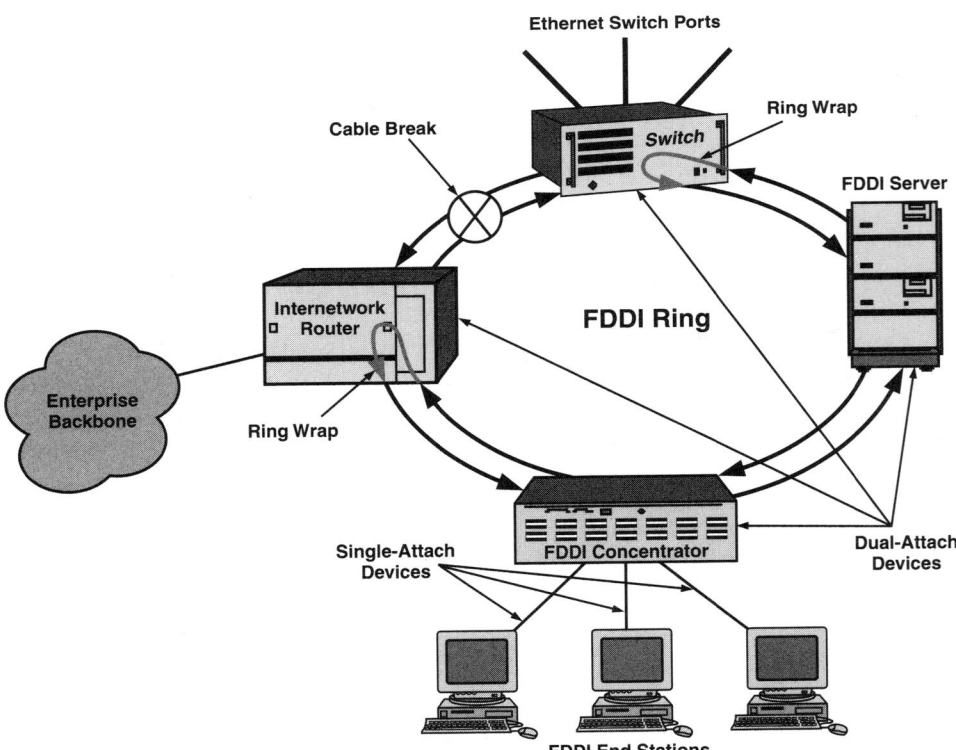

Figure 16–6 FDDI topologies.

16.2.1.3 FDDI Physical Signaling

Obviously from its name, FDDI was originally designed for fiber media (otherwise, it would have been called just DDI). When it was being developed (around 1985), operation at 100 Mb/s over copper media was considered impractical. (At that time, even 10 Mb/s operation over twisted-pair was inconceivable, much less 100 Mb/s operation!) Furthermore, backbone applications require relatively long-distance links (on the order of kilometers); this is impractical even today using low-cost copper media.[8] Thus the original FDDI standard specified the use of multimode optical fiber exclusively. The standard provided for distances of up to 2 km between stations on the ring.[9]

To reduce the signaling rate on the fiber, a block data-encoding scheme was employed. FDDI systems encode 4 bits of data into 5 code bits (4B/5B encoding). This results in a channel signaling rate of 125 Mbaud (100 Mb/s $\times$ ⁵⁄₄). The 4B/5B encoding system was later adopted for use in 100 Mb/s Ethernet systems.[10]

In order to expand the marketplace for FDDI, a system for operating FDDI over twisted-pair copper media was needed, which was developed during the early 1990s. The key technical challenge was to develop a means of signaling at 125 Mbaud in such a way that the signal was still decodable after passing through 100 m of UTP cable and did not violate electromagnetic interference (EMI) regulations. The result was a line-encoding system called

---

8. An exception could be made for CATV-style operation (that is, broadband coaxial cable). However, while the medium itself may be low-cost, transceivers (broadband modems) operating at very high data rates are complex and costly.

9. Both 62.5-μm and 85-μm fibers were supported. Eighty-five-μm optical fiber is virtually unheard-of today.

10. It is interesting to note why FDDI went to a "richer" encoding scheme than Manchester. The optical fiber itself has no difficulty carrying signals of 200 Mb/s or more. The much-simpler Manchester encoding used in Ethernet would not have caused a media problem (unlike its use on twisted-pair at high speeds). At issue were the optical drivers. There are two methods of launching optical power into a fiber: lasers and light-emitting diodes (LEDs). Lasers are capable of operating at much higher speeds than LEDs, but they cost considerably more. At the time FDDI was being developed, low-cost LEDs were not available that could operate at the 200 Mbaud rate required if Manchester encoding was used. Requiring laser drivers would have driven the cost of FDDI systems well above its already-high level. So the encoding was made more complex so that LED technology could be accommodated (125 Mbaud versus 200 Mbaud).

By the time FDDI was widely deployed, LED technology had improved and laser prices had dropped significantly, so the encoding complexity was less important. But the die had been cast. This encoding will be with us for many years as part of Fast Ethernet.

Multi-Level Threshold (MLT-3) that used ternary (three-level) rather than binary signaling to reduce the high-frequency spectrum of the transmissions.[11] FDDI operated over copper media is called either CDDI (Copper Distributed Data Interface, a trade name of cisco Systems) or TP-PMD (Twisted Pair–Physical Medium-Dependent signaling, in ISO terminology). This line-encoding scheme is also used in 100 Mb/s Ethernet.

Today FDDI is supported in standards-compliant devices over multimode optical fiber (2 km, maximum) and both Category 5 UTP and STP (100 m, maximum). Proprietary systems are also available that use single-mode fiber over longer distances.

16.2.2 FDDI Capacity

The basic data rate of FDDI is 100 Mb/s, the same as Fast Ethernet. Because FDDI uses a different MAC algorithm than Ethernet, it has slightly different performance characteristics as a function of offered load. The fact is, however, that both systems can carry a maximum of 100 Mb/s in a shared LAN application.[12]

Similar to Fast Ethernet, FDDI can be used with switching hubs, thereby increasing the aggregate capacity of the network (but similarly retaining the 100 Mb/s maximum end-to-end throughput limit). There is really no difference in data-carrying capacity between a switched 100 Mb/s Ethernet and a switched FDDI system.

There is no industry activity to increase the data rate of FDDI beyond 100 Mb/s.

16.2.3 Advantages of FDDI?

FDDI does not offer users any performance advantage relative to Gigabit Ethernet in any of the common application areas. While there is nothing inherently deficient with the design of FDDI, it is simply an order of magnitude lower in

---

11. While officially MLT stands for Multi-Level Threshold, in reality it is the initials of the founders of the company that developed the technology (Crescendo Communications, later acquired by cisco Systems): Mario Mazzola, Luca Cafiero, and Tazio De Nicolo.

12. FDDI also offers some efficiencies due to its ability to carry longer frames than Ethernet (4500 bytes of payload versus 1500 for Ethernet). This is irrelevant for backbone applications, as the frames will likely originate and terminate on Ethernets. Even with direct FDDI-attached server connections, long frames will probably have to be fragmented in routers that connect the FDDI to Ethernets that comprise desktop LANs (or FDDI frames must be limited to Ethernet maxima). This negates much of the benefit.

data capacity. It does not even support the distances achievable with Gigabit Ethernet (at least not in standards-compliant devices).

Dual-attached FDDI systems do offer some natural redundancy; this may be useful for backbone applications or mission-critical server attachments. However, an equivalent redundancy can be achieved by using multiple Ethernet connections to switches (either at 100 Mb/s or 1000 Mb/s). Automatic switchover capabilities in switches (using the Spanning Tree algorithm) also provide for fault tolerance and automatic switching in the event of failed links or interfaces.

In addition, FDDI interface costs have historically been much higher than for Ethernet attachments. (This is especially true for FDDI interfaces used in high-performance servers and internetworking devices, as opposed to lower-performing end-user NICs.) In 1997, FDDI interfaces for both workstations and internetworking devices were more than double the price of equivalent Fast Ethernet interfaces.[13] In end-station NICs with PCI interfaces, FDDI commanded a price premium of more than 5:1 over Fast Ethernet, at the same data rate.

FDDI was widely deployed from 1988 to 1998 for distributed campus backbone applications. As the needs of the campus increase, Gigabit Ethernet (and to a certain extent, switched Fast Ethernet) is the logical upgrade path for these networks.

16.3 High-Performance Parallel Interface

The High-Performance Parallel Interface (HIPPI) emerged during the late 1980s to support the interconnection of high-speed computers (typically mainframes and supercomputers) and directly attached storage devices (for example, high-speed disk subsystems) at speeds of 800 Mb/s and 1600 Mb/s. While it is still used in these applications, HIPPI's proponents also offer it for use in high-speed local and campus backbone networks. HIPPI has never become a high-volume technology (compared with Ethernet), but it is nonetheless an ANSI standard supported by numerous vendors. [ANSI91, ANSI92, ANSI93] The method for using IP over a HIPPI link is specified by [RFC1374].

HIPPI provides services at the Physical and Data Link Layers of the OSI model. It offers flow-controlled, connection-oriented, point-to-point communications across both copper and optical-fiber media.

---

13. Based on U. S. list pricing from Sun Microsystems and cisco systems for FDDI single-attached versus 100BASE-FX interfaces.

16.3.1 HIPPI Operation

Figure 16–7 depicts a set of devices using HIPPI connections. In its simplest form, HIPPI comprises a point-to-point link between a pair of properly equipped devices. The communications path is 32 bits wide for operation at 800 Mb/s. A 64-bit-wide path is used for 1600 Mb/s operation. HIPPI channels are unidirectional; this greatly simplifies the interface electronics. If bidirectional (dual simplex[14]) communications is required, two HIPPI channels are used (in opposite directions).

When more than two devices are being interconnected, a HIPPI switch is required. HIPPI switches provide circuit-switching among its ports. Connection requests are made to the switch (using out-of-band control signals in the HIPPI cable); the switch creates a temporary physical circuit (not a virtual circuit) between the switch ports. For the duration of the connection, data can be exchanged at the full channel rate. There can be only one connection to (or from) a given port at one time. Additional connection requests are refused by the switch and must wait until the end of the data exchange in progress.

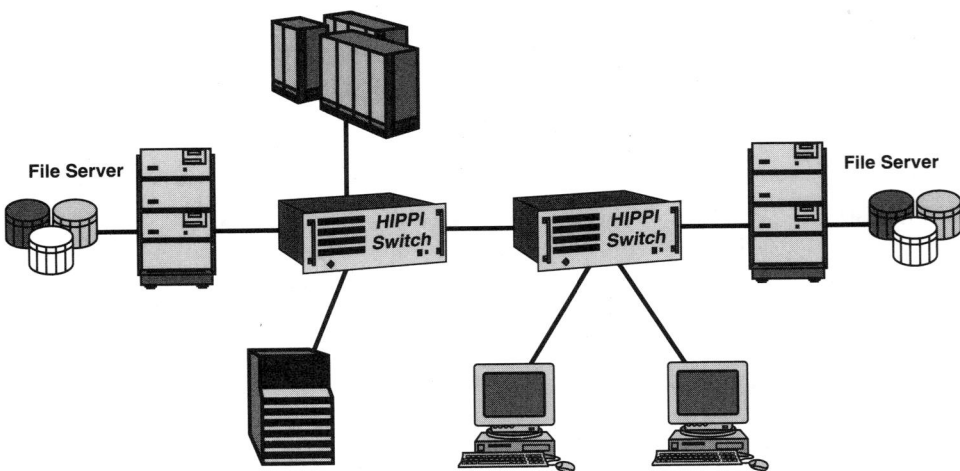

Figure 16–7 HIPPI communications.

---

14. Strictly speaking, it is not full-duplex operation, since it uses two completely independent, uncoordinated unidirectional channels. There is no requirement that the two simplex channels connect between the same pair of devices. That is, device A can transmit data to device B (unidirectionally), while device C is transmitting data to device A (on the other simplex channel connected to A).

Similar to how LANs operate, HIPPI data exchanges provide for Link Layer error detection, but no error correction is built into the system. Since the underlying channel error rate is extremely low, the complexity of forward error correction or an acknowledgment-retransmission algorithm is unjustified. HIPPI provides both byte-parity and a Longitudinal Redundancy Check (LRC) with a length verification. Error recovery, if needed, is provided at higher layers of the architecture.

16.3.2 Flow Control

Since it is possible (in fact, highly likely) that a HIPPI-attached device will be unable to sustain continuous data transfers at the full channel data rate, HIPPI provides an explicit, credit-based flow control mechanism. Receivers signal their ability to receive 256-word (1K or 2K bytes, for 32-bit and 64-bit-wide data paths, respectively) data bursts by pulsing the dedicated *Ready* signal on the interface. The sender keeps count of the number of *Ready* pulses, and never sends more than this many bursts without waiting for additional flow control credits. As receivers process incoming bursts and free up local resources (for example, buffer space), they may issue additional credits

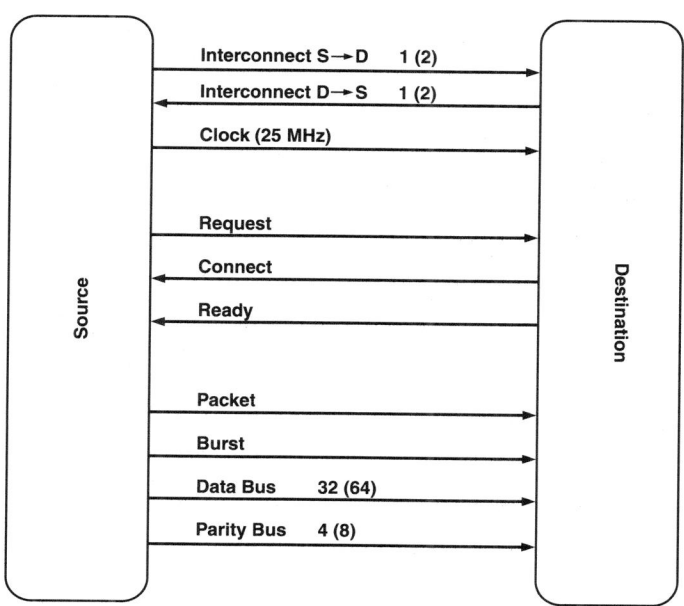

Numbers in parentheses are for 1600 Mb/s operation.

Figure 16–8 HIPPI signals.

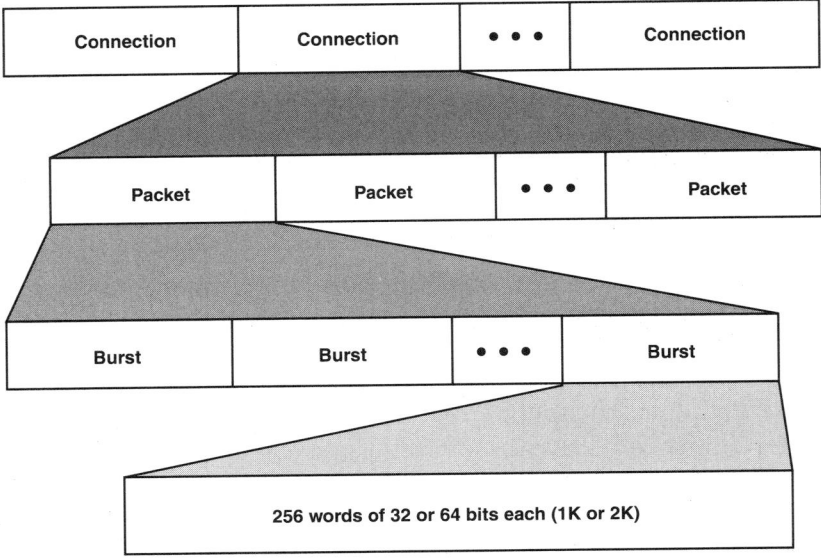

Each connection can contain multiple packets (no limit).
Each packet can contain multiple bursts (no limit).
Each burst contains 256 32-bit words. After each burst, a parity word is sent.

Figure 16-9 HIPPI framing.

while data transmission is in progress, thus sustaining data transfer at the maximum possible rate.

16.3.3 HIPPI Framing

Data is exchanged across a HIPPI using a standardized connection sequence and framing method, as depicted in Figures 16–9 and 16–10.

Before data is exchanged, a connection request is made to the switch. The data source sends an *I-field* (generic Information field) containing (implementation-specific) control information (for example, addresses or priority) and asserts a *Request* signal. If the request is accepted (as indicated by the *Connect* signal), the destination will issue *Ready* pulses to indicate its willingness to accept data bursts, as discussed earlier. The sender sends as many packets as necessary, with each packet composed of data bursts of 256 words or less. When all packets are sent, the sender drops its *Request* signal to terminate the connection.

16.3.4 HIPPI Physical Signaling

The original HIPPI specification supported the use of 50-pair STP cables over distances of up to 25 m, for 800 Mb/s operation. (See Figure 16–8.) Signal

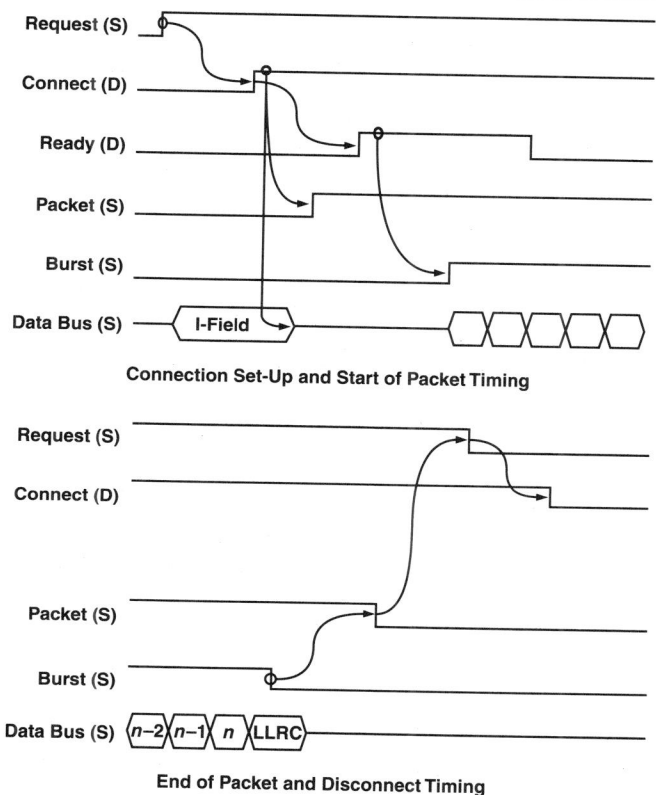

Connection Set-Up and Start of Packet Timing

End of Packet and Disconnect Timing

Figure 16–10 HIPPI timing.

levels use ECL (emitter-coupled logic) voltages; a combination of differential and single-ended signaling is used. The data path is 32 bits wide, with a clock rate of 25MHz (25MHz $\times$ 32 bits = 800 Mb/s).[15] For 1600 Mb/s operation, two cables are required.

While 25-m, 50-pair cables may be acceptable for use within a computer room (for a computer-to-storage subsystem application), it is insufficient for remote system interconnection or LAN backbone applications. To address this concern, Serial HIPPI was developed.[16]

---

15. This is a relatively slow clock rate by today's standards, but it was considered fast in the late 1980s, when HIPPI was being designed.

16. *Serial* High-Performance *Parallel* Interface—talk about an identity crisis!

Serial HIPPI [ANSI97] provides a means for encoding the parallel HIPPI signals into a serial stream. The raw data rate on the fiber is 1.2 Gbaud for 800 Mb/s operation, and includes data, control, and encoding overhead. The system uses two fibers (one in each direction) for a dual-simplex connection; operation at 1600 Mb/s requires four fibers (two in each direction). Table 16–1 indicates the supportable distances as a function of fiber type and optical wavelength.

HIPPI uses duplex SC optical-fiber connectors (the same as 100BASE-FX and 1000BASE-SX/LX). Note the similarity in baud rate, fiber types, connector types, and optical wavelengths employed by Serial HIPPI and Gigabit Ethernet.[17]

16.3.5 HIPPI versus Gigabit Ethernet

On paper, HIPPI and Gigabit Ethernet seem to offer many common capabilities:

- Operation at similar data rates
- Comparable distance limitations, both with copper and serial-optical fiber
- Formal standards in place

At equivalent volume levels, interface costs should not be significantly different; many of the high-cost components (for example, optical interfaces) are identical between the two systems.

TABLE 16–1 SERIAL HIPPI OPTICAL FIBER SUPPORT

	50-μm Multimode	62.5-μm Multimode	10-μm Single-mode
Short-Wavelength Optics (850 nm nominal)	2–500 m	2–200 m	Not supported
Long-Wavelength Optics (1310 nm nominal)	0–1000 m	0–1000 m	0–10,000 m

---

17. In fact, the components used for the two systems are often identical. This leads one to believe (rightfully) that Gigabit Ethernet should be able to operate over longer distances than those specified in the standard. Specifically, systems operating over 10-km distances with single-mode fiber, while not supported by the Gigabit Ethernet standard, are available commercially.

The problem with using HIPPI for computer network applications (as opposed to high-speed storage subsystem applications) is that HIPPI is, at its core, a connection-oriented technology. The system is inherently capable only of point-to-point communications, with only one connection to a device at a given time. Prior to exchanging any data, stations must set up a connection through the HIPPI switches.

HIPPI switches are capable of setting up connections very quickly, on the order of 1 μs or less. In theory, a connection-oriented switch can be made to "appear" connectionless by setting up and tearing down connections extremely quickly. While a 1 μs set-up time may be insignificant overhead for stream data transfers (that is, for connection to a disk subsystem on which the data transfer may take hundreds of microseconds or more), for single-frame exchanges it is the equivalent of increasing the Gigabit Ethernet interframe gap to 1 μs from its current value of 96 ns (a factor of 10 increase).

However, this is just the switch set-up time. HIPPI connections are set up between the communicating end devices (through any switches). The switch set-up time does not include propagation delays incurred in negotiating the connection with the target device. These delays may be low with the original HIPPI design (~500 ns round-trip delay using 25-m cables to a central switch), but they can be quite significant when using Serial HIPPI over 3-km distances, as would be needed for a campus backbone. A 3-km backbone radius around a central switch (6-km diameter) imposes a round-trip delay of approximately 60 μs at a nominal 5 μs/km. The connection establishment time (60 μs) thus dominates over the data transmission time (12 μs for a maximum-length Gigabit Ethernet frame). The maximum frame rate in this application would be on the order of 16,000 frames/second using HIPPI, as opposed to approximately 1.5 million frames/second using Gigabit Ethernet.

In addition, HIPPI has no intrinsic multicast capability. If multicast service is required (for example, for ARP operation within IP), either special multicast channels must be added to the switch or a multicast server (similar to that used in ATM, discussed shortly) must be employed.

HIPPI's use of a connection-oriented architecture makes perfect sense in its intended application: the interconnection of mainframes and supercomputers to intelligent storage subsystems. However, the performance degrades significantly when used in applications that require connectionless frame exchange.

16.4 Fibre Channel

During the late 1980s, Fibre Channel was developed as a method of providing high-speed serial links for processor-to-processor and processor-to-mass storage applications. The most common application was to provide long-distance connections between mainframe computers and intelligent disk subsystems, but it has also been used in computer network applications. Thus its target application environment is not unlike that of HIPPI, except that Fibre Channel is based on serial communications technology rather than HIPPI's parallel data path.

Computer networks based on Fibre Channel have not been very popular due to a combination of technical and marketing factors. Nonetheless, Fibre Channel is an approved ANSI standard and is supported by many vendors. [ANSI94, FCA95]

16.4.1 Fibre Channel Topologies

Fibre Channel supports three topologies, as depicted in Figure 16–11:

1. *Point-to-point links* are dedicated, high-speed serial channels using the Fibre Channel signaling methods and protocols. A point-to-point topology can provide high bandwidth and essentially zero latency (that is, no set-up or arbitration time is required, unlike with the alternative topologies discussed shortly). However, point-to-point links are not widely used or implemented because connectivity is rather limited and their cost is rarely justifiable.

2. *Switching fabrics* are used to provide virtual point-to-point links among a large number of Fibre Channel-equipped stations. Connections are set up through the switches, and data is exchanged (bidirectionally) between pairs of stations. This allows for a high level of connectivity, with full bandwidth available between all ports (assuming nonblocking switch operation). There is a latency penalty, however, because connections must be set up through the switching fabric. Current products can set up connections with latencies on the order of 10 μs. [KESS95]

3. *Arbitrated loops* are the most common implementation for computer networks using Fibre Channel technology. This topology allows the attached stations to share the available channel capacity. Latency can be quite low (just the channel arbitration time), but the total system capacity is limited to that of a single Fibre Channel link that must be shared by all attached stations.

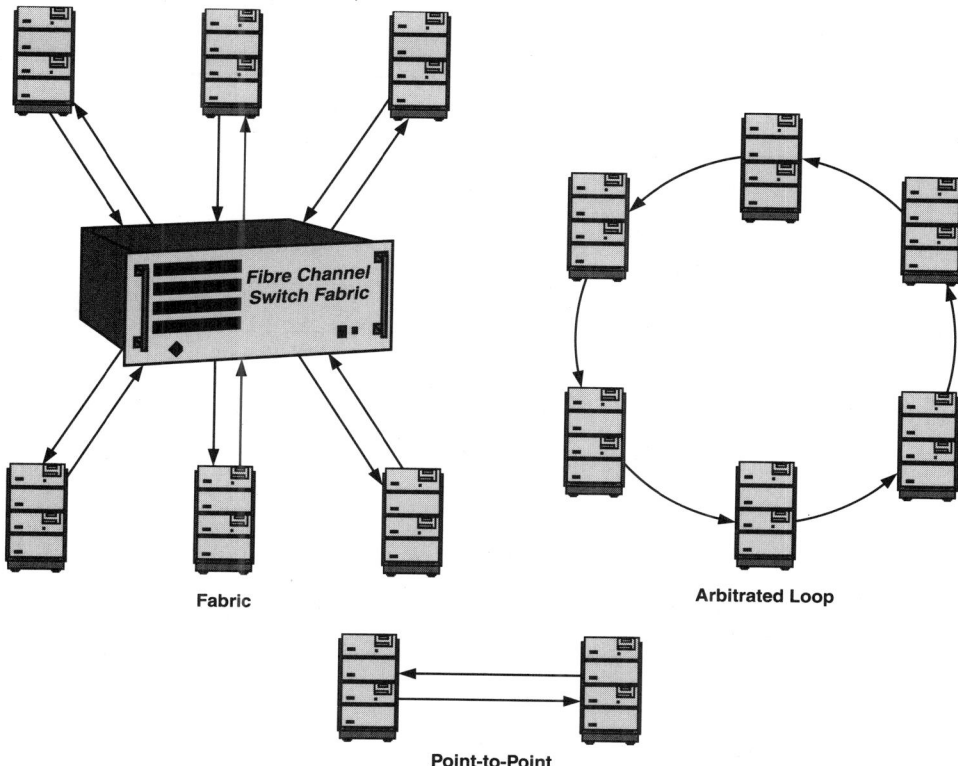

Fabric

Arbitrated Loop

Point-to-Point

Figure 16–11 Fibre Channel topologies.

16.4.2 Fibre Channel Layering and Architecture

Fibre Channel defines a five-layer internal architecture, as depicted in Figure 16–12.

- *FC-0* defines the physical characteristics of the supported links, including transmission speeds, cabling types, and distances.
- *FC-1* defines the block encoding method (8B/10B) used for data and special character transmission.
- *FC-2* specifies how data is exchanged among attached devices, including the frame format, frame sequences, and so on. It also defines three service classes available for use by higher-layer protocols and the algorithms for flow control.
- *FC-3* specifies a set of common services to support higher-layer protocol operation.

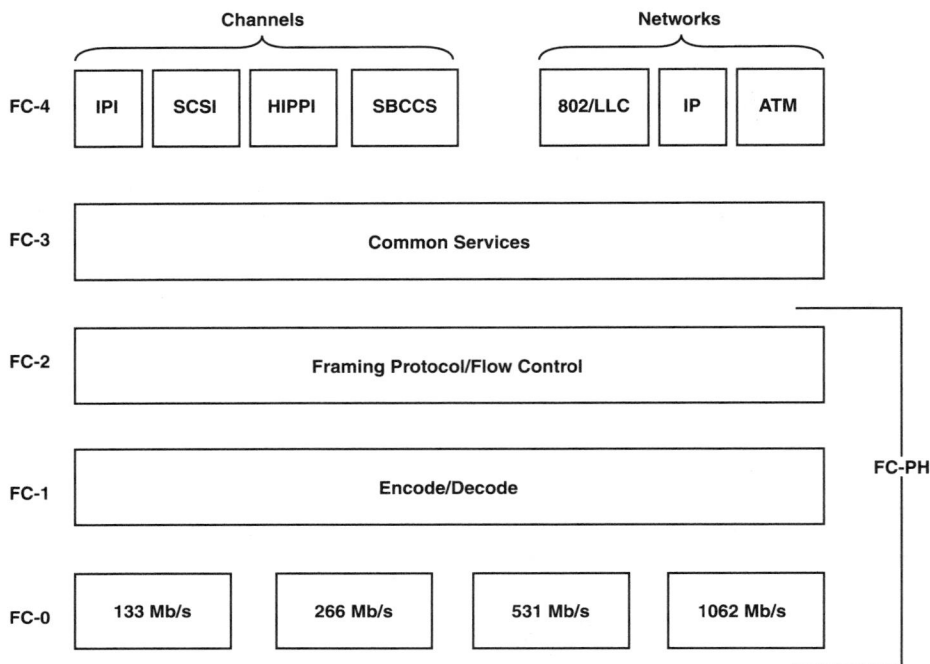

Figure 16–12 Fibre Channel layering.

■ *FC-4* specifies how higher-layer protocols map onto the Fibre Channel services so that they can use Fibre Channel transparently (without changing applications or higher-layer software implementations).

The Gigabit Ethernet Physical Layer is virtually identical to the Fibre Channel FC-0 and FC-1 layers. These technologies were developed for Fibre Channel. Gigabit Ethernet adopted both the encoding and physical link designs, changing only the data rate (increasing it to 1.25 Gbaud).

16.4.2.1 FC-0: Link Characteristics

Fibre Channel links operate at data rates of 100 Mb/s, 200 Mb/s, 400 Mb/s, or 800 Mb/s (unencoded). The corresponding encoded, framed transmission rates are 133 Mbaud, 266 Mbaud, 531 Mbaud, and 1.062 Gbaud. See Chapter 12 for a complete discussion of link signaling and the 8B/10B encoder/decoder.

Fibre Channel supports the same media types as Gigabit Ethernet, including STP copper cable, 50-μm and 62.5-μm multimode fiber, and 10-μm single-mode optical fiber. The maximum distances supported vary with media type and data rate, from 25 m (using STP cable) to as much as 10 km (using single-mode fiber with long-wavelength laser drivers).

16.4.2.2 FC-1: Block Encoding

Fibre Channel uses the same 8B/10B encoding method used in Gigabit Ethernet. Data bytes and control characters are encoded into 10-bit code-words for transmission on the physical link.

16.4.2.3 FC-2: Framing and Service Classes

Fibre Channel exchanges variable-length frames among attached devices. A frame can carry from zero to 2048 bytes of payload. Higher-layer messages greater than 2048 bytes in length are transmitted as a sequence of frames, each containing not more than 2048 bytes. Thus the FC-2 layer can fragment long messages and reassemble them at the receiver while maintaining proper frame order as seen by higher-layer protocols. A standard 32-bit CRC is provided for error detection. The Fibre Channel frame format is depicted in Figure 16–13.

Fibre Channel offers three classes of service

1. **Connection-oriented service.** In this mode, a logical point-to-point link is established between endpoints, using either a true dedicated link or a virtual link through a switching fabric, before any data is exchanged. Full, end-to-end error recovery and flow control is provided, thus ensuring reliable, sequenced delivery. The behavior is similar to that provided by IEEE 802.2 LLC Type 2 service. [IEEE94]
2. **Acknowledged, connectionless service.** In this mode, frames are delivered between endpoints with no error recovery or flow control. However,

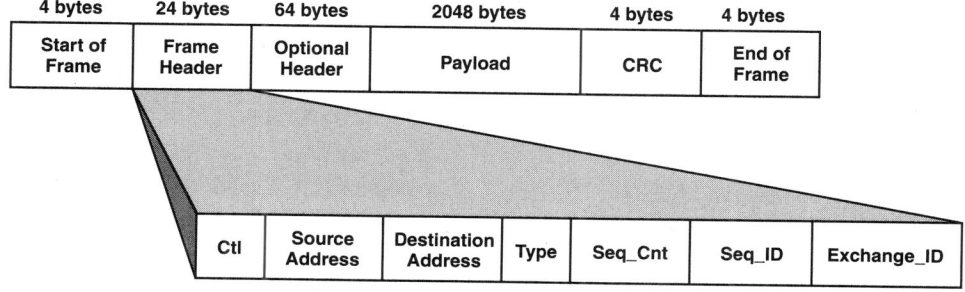

Figure 16–13 Fibre Channel frame.

an indication is provided to the sender that a given frame was properly received. The behavior is similar to that provided by IEEE 802.2 LLC Type 3 service, except that sequenced delivery is not guaranteed.[18]

3. **Unacknowledged connectionless service.** In this mode, frame delivery is neither guaranteed nor acknowledged. This is similar to IEEE 802 LLC Type 1 service and normal Ethernet operation.

Connectionless operation (either acknowledged or unacknowledged) is most effective in an arbitrated loop topology, since there is no need to set up connections through a switch fabric. This avoids the set-up latency for short, connectionless exchanges. Switch fabric topologies are best-suited for applications that require sustained high-throughput, connection-oriented service.

Flow control (both end-to-end and link) is provided in FC-2 by the exchange of buffer credits between receivers and senders.

16.4.2.4 FC-3: Common Services

This layer provides a set of generic services that may be useful to higher-layer protocols or applications, including mechanisms for multicast delivery, "hunt groups" among switch ports, and so on. In practice, very few systems implement FC-3 services.

16.4.2.5 FC-4: Higher-Layer Mapping

FC-4 specifies how various higher-layer protocols can map to Fibre Channel, thus allowing existing applications to use a Fibre Channel without modification. Architecturally, it functions as a *convergence sublayer* by providing the "glue" between existing systems and Fibre Channel. FC-4 mappings are specified (or proposed) both for I/O channel applications such as HIPPI and SCSI and for computer network applications such as IP and ATM. FC-4 is not needed if Fibre Channel services are being used directly (that is, with applications designed to use Fibre Channel in native mode).

16.4.3 Fibre Channel and Gigabit Ethernet

There is no question that Fibre Channel provided the underlying physical technology base for Gigabit Ethernet. Rather than invent a completely new

---

18. Sequenced delivery is a natural behavior for arbitrated loops and single-switch configurations. It is only when a generalized switch fabric is considered (one with multiple available paths between endpoints) that ordering can be lost.

communications system, the developers of Gigabit Ethernet adopted the Fibre Channel FC-0 and FC-1 layers. The data rate was increased from Fibre Channel's maximum of 800 Mb/s to Ethernet's 1000 Mb/s, and the system parameters (for example, maximum distances) were adjusted as a result of a comprehensive analysis of the behavior of the channel in the Gigabit Ethernet environment. Minor changes were also made to the semantics of the 8B/10B encoding scheme to support Ethernet.

In much the same way that Fast Ethernet provided the vehicle for volume deployment of FDDI-over-copper products, Gigabit Ethernet will likely result in greater volume shipments of Fibre Channel physical signaling components than Fibre Channel ever will.[19]

16.4.4 Fibre Channel as an Alternative to Gigabit Ethernet

Virtually all computer network architectures in common use today (for example, TCP/IP, IPX, AppleTalk, and so on) expect connectionless operation at the Data Link layer. Ethernet (and most LAN technologies) provide a best-effort, no-connection-setup-required capability. Alternative technologies that provide only connection-oriented services are very difficult to map to existing computer network architectures.

Fibre Channel can support connectionless operation. However, consider the following available topologies for Fibre Channel networks.

- *Point-to-point links* simply don't provide sufficient connectivity to support a LAN or backbone network.
- Fibre Channel *switch fabrics* can provide adequate connectivity, as well as considerable bandwidth. The capacity is on the order of the number of ports multiplied by the channel data rate. However, Fibre Channel switches are connection-oriented. Before exchanging data, stations must first set up connections through the switch. This can take as much as 10 µs or more.[20] [FCA94] This overhead may be acceptable for bulk data transfer or quasi-static connections, but for small connectionless exchanges, the connection set-up time far exceeds the data transmission time. A connection

---

19. Many of the participants in the Gigabit Ethernet standards development process are the same people that originally developed the technology for Fibre Channel. In some ways, Gigabit Ethernet is seen as the salvation of that earlier effort, that is, as the means to finally achieve the broad commercial success that Fibre Channel never enjoyed.

20. Similar to HIPPI, this does not include propagation delays across the links, which can run to as much as 100 µs or more on a backbone network using switch fabric topology.

set-up time of 10 μs is approximately the same as a maximum-length Ethernet frame at gigabit rates. If a connection needs to be established for each frame (mimicking connectionless behavior), the channel efficiency is reduced by a factor of 50% in the *best case;* for short frames it only gets worse.

■ An *arbitrated loop* allows Fibre Channel to support true connectionless-mode operation; however, this is a *shared network.* It is not possible to achieve the capacity increases offered by switching hubs while using the arbitrated loop topology.

Thus using Fibre Channel as an Ethernet replacement forces one either to accept the performance degradation of using a connection-oriented switch for connectionless communications or to be limited to the capacity of a single link. Gigabit Ethernet allows true connectionless operation in both a switched (high-capacity) or shared environment.

Equally important, Ethernet has been marketed more successfully than Fibre Channel. While Fibre Channel has its proponents, it is still a relatively obscure technology with limited deployment.

16.5 Asynchronous Transfer Mode

Ding! Ding! Ding! Ding! Ding! . . . . Ladee-ee-ees and Gentlemen! Welcome to the Main Event! The knock-down, drag-out heavyweight battle for the Championship of the Campus Backbone! In this corner, from Lannion, France, by way of Morristown, New Jersey, only 10 years old but weighing 622 pounds, wearing gold-plated trunks, the man who finishes every meal in exactly 53 bites, the Asynchronous Transfer Mode Kid! In the opposite corner, from Palo Alto, California, the grandson of the undisputed champion of the desktop for over 15 years, weighing 1000 pounds and wearing a pair of cheap shorts made from leftover Fibre, it's Mr. Gigabit Ethernet!

Seriously, at the time of this writing, most industry observers believe that the only practical alternatives for campus LAN interconnections will be Gigabit Ethernet and ATM. While the other technologies discussed earlier are all feasible (and each has its zealots), ATM and Gigabit Ethernet are clearly attracting the most interest, and have the widest base of products and vendor support. This section looks at the advantages and disadvantages of using ATM, particularly as a campus backbone technology (that is, in the same application space as Gigabit Ethernet). It should not be considered a comprehensive introduction to ATM. Rather, it points out those features and characteristics that provide a contrast to Gigabit Ethernet for high-speed data communications.[21]

16.5.1 Foundations of ATM

ATM is sometimes (naively) thought of as "the answer to everything." DePrycker says, "The ATM concept is now accepted as the ultimate solution for the integrated broadband communications network . . ." [DEPRY93] While it may be overstating the case to say that ATM has already been accepted as the solution (and generally unwise to say that *anything* is an "ultimate" solution!), many people do believe that ATM will eventually replace all existing network technologies, both for data and voice. However, ATM was designed specifically by the telecom industry to solve the problem of achieving efficient, high-speed voice/video communications.[22] This application is characterized by:

- **Sensitivity to absolute delay.** Interactive (real-time) person-to-person communications requires low delay in order to be considered acceptable. Absolute delays in excess of a few hundred milliseconds eliminates the illusion of instantaneous, full-duplex, person-to-person communications. While echo canceling can remove undesirable long-delay echoes (which make normal speech almost impossible to conduct), there is still the long turnaround time between speaking and hearing a response to what was said. This makes the system appear less like a telephone and more like a two-way, single-channel (half-duplex) radio.

- **Sensitivity to delay variance.** Audio and video streams (unlike data streams) must be delivered at the same rate as they were sent; otherwise,

---

21. The focus on *data communications* (exclusively) is important. While it will become obvious that ATM is inappropriate for LAN and data communications use, especially in a localized or campus environment, this by no means detracts from ATM's applicability for voice and video (telecom) applications. Other than a discussion on the integration of voice/video/data networks, the use of ATM for voice/video is not considered in this text.

22. From a communications perspective, the needs of real-time, interactive voice and video applications, other than bandwidth consumed, are virtually identical. Thus, they are treated as a single case in this discussion of ATM. The terms "telecommunications" and "telecom" are used to refer to both voice and video services and are distinguished from *data communications* and *datacom*.

they are not intelligible (audio) or they appear unnatural (video). Thus, the system must provide a smooth flow of information to the receiver. A certain amount of variance (jitter) can be compensated for by having a buffer on the receiver. However, the system still must not jitter more than the buffer can hold (or it may overflow/underflow the buffer). The use of larger buffers increases the absolute delay; ultimately you run into the problem previously discussed.

- **Tolerance of information loss.** Audio and video streams can tolerate the occasional loss (or even corruption) of small amounts of information. If a single sample (or even many samples) of a digitized voice stream are not delivered, the effect to the receiving user will be a slight distortion or "click" in the audio. Similarly, a loss or corruption of portions of a video stream may cause a visual streak or flicker. While these effects are mildly disturbing, they cause no real loss of information content to the receiver, since human voice and visual communications are highly (internally) redundant. The human brain can decode the intended message even in the face of enormous amounts of distortion and interference.

- **A prior knowledge of the communications requirements.** When a call is made, it is known in advance what demands will be placed on the network. The caller knows whether they are making a voice or video connection, the desired quality of sound or picture, and perhaps even the expected duration of the call. Thus the network can allocate resources in advance to ensure that network performance can be sustained at the desired level. A path through the network can be established that remains fixed throughout the duration of the call; this significantly reduces delay variance. Even if the network does not have adequate resources, it can so inform the caller and offer an alternative (for example, lower picture resolution). A negotiation then can take place that results in a known performance demand on the network and set of expectations from the user. The point is that the network can have prior knowledge of future anticipated information streams and allocate resources according to need.

ATM, like the telecommunications applications it was designed to support, is *connection-oriented*. Prior to any exchange of information, a connection must be established across the network. This is identical to how existing telephony systems work, and it makes perfect sense for voice and video applications, which are inherently connection-based. As discussed shortly, this is not the case for data communications applications. Hence adapting ATM to this class of applications is difficult.

Prior to the deployment of ATM, most of the telephony infrastructure used physical circuits (rather than virtual circuits) for the underlying communications. Whether T-carrier (that is, T1 or T3 links) or SONET fiber is used, initiating a call allocates resources not only in the intervening switches, but also in the communications channels themselves. At any given time, a communications link (for example, a channel of a T-carrier trunk) carries signals from a single call. This can be quite inefficient if the *information content* of the communications (that is, bandwidth required for the actual information) is less than the bandwidth allocated. This is typically the case with voice signals, since there is considerable "quiet time" in natural speech. Unfortunately, the excess capacity of the physical-circuit-switched link cannot be used (multiplexed) for other purposes while the line is quiet.

As telephony carriers know well, a significant portion of the cost of providing service is tied up in the capacity of the network. If high-speed links can be used more efficiently, this provides a competitive advantage relative to using the older, circuit-switched technology. The use of packet switching and virtual circuits allows a single physical circuit to multiplex multiple logical streams; the improvement in channel efficiency is well-documented [SCHW87]. The service provider can get maximum use from the available capacity, while maintaining the low delay and variance needed by the (telephony) application.

16.5.2 ATM Technology

Like the popular LAN technologies (for example, Ethernet and Token Ring), ATM operates at the Data Link and Physical Layers of the OSI model [ISO94] (see Figure 16–14). What is not evident from this simple layering equivalence is that ATM is fundamentally different from LAN technologies. Many people equate "fast networking" with ATM, but ATM implies much more than this.

ATM *requires* that connections be established before application (user) communications can proceed. While this has advantages for the network (for example, paths can be established in advance and switch memory and channel bandwidth can be preallocated), it makes the assumption that the application using the service knows its communications requirements in advance; that is, it presupposes a connection-oriented application. This assumption is reasonable for voice/video services, but it fails for most computer network (data communications) protocols as clients of the data link. This is discussed in greater detail in later sections.

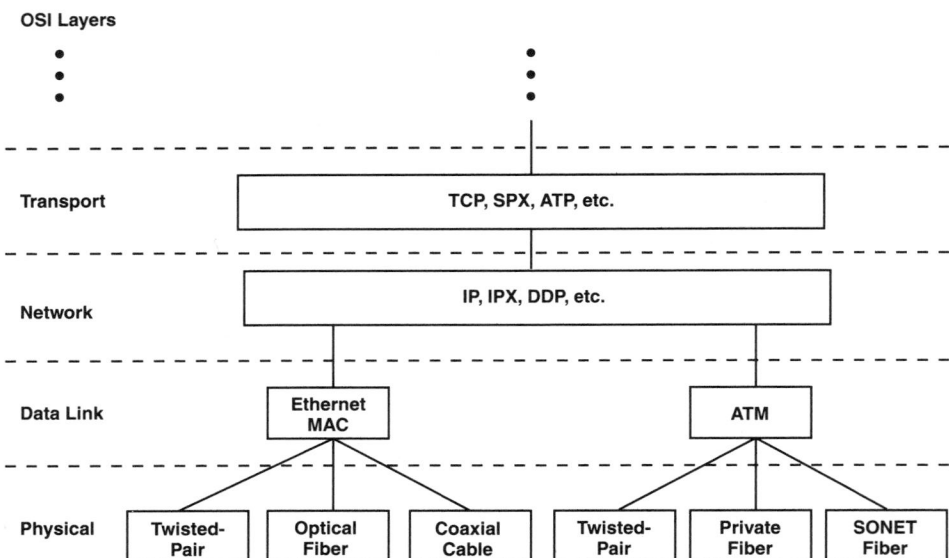

Figure 16–14 ATM and the OSI model.

16.5.2.1 ATM Operation

Simply put, an ATM network provides a connection-oriented, virtual circuit service using fixed-length frames (cells). The network comprises links (of arbitrary capacity) interconnected by ATM switches, as depicted in Figure 16–15. Clients (users) of the ATM service make connection requests. This results in quasi-static[23] virtual circuits being established across the entire network between the endpoints of the connection.

To minimize both the absolute delay and the variance of the delay, the unit of information is kept extremely small (by data communications standards) and of fixed length. While the unit of data at the Data Link Layer is usually called a *frame*, when it is short and of fixed-length it is called a *cell*. Contrary to many industry publications, there is nothing magical about cells; they are simply short, fixed-length frames.

Cell size involves a trade-off. Large cells increase the efficiency of the network:

---

23. Quasi-static connections imply that the path and allocated resources do not vary in time frames that are significant to the application. For the duration of a call, the end-to-end configuration is "static"; the virtual circuits change only during call set-up and tear-down.

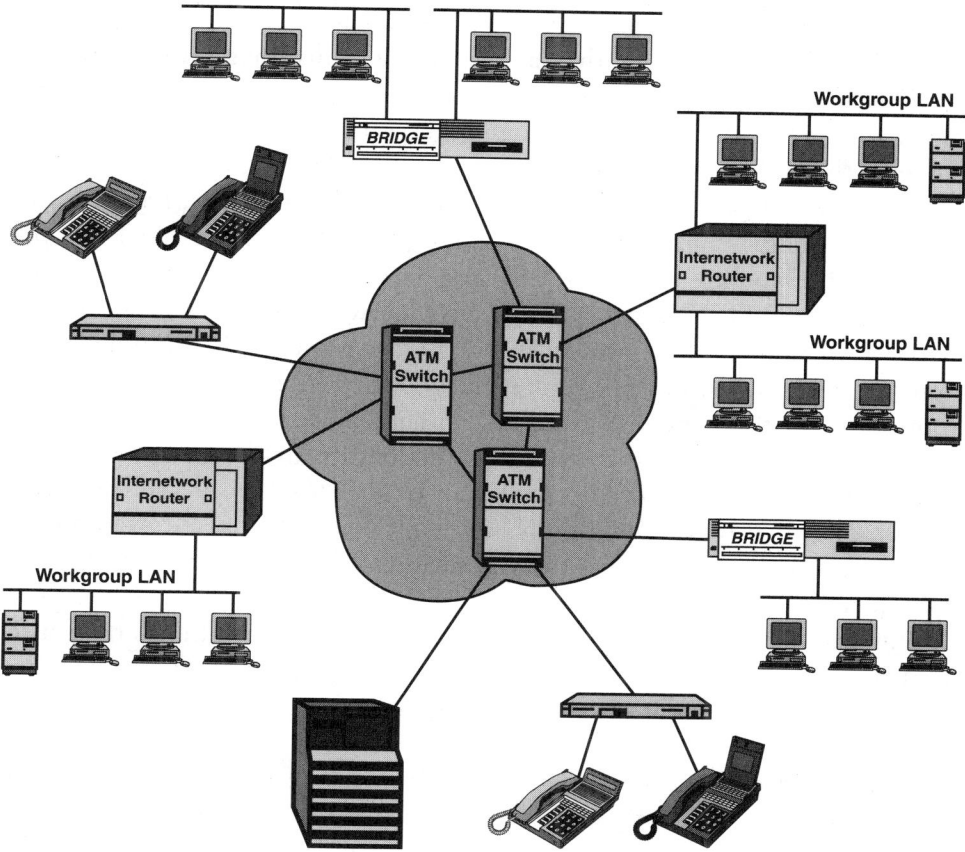

Figure 16–15 ATM network.

- There is more payload per cell. Thus more of the channel bandwidth is used to carry user information as opposed to protocol headers (overhead).
- Fewer cells are needed for a given amount of information. Since each cell must be processed by all of the switches in the circuit path (as well as any ATM-attached end devices), large cells reduce the processing burden and, ultimately, the cost of the network.

Small cells improve the delay characteristics. The smaller the cell, the less time it must wait to be filled (at the originating device). Also, its transmission can be completed sooner (at every switch); that is, it gets out of the way quickly to make room for transmissions from other circuits.

A good analogy is a railroad, with the locomotive being the protocol header and the cars carrying the payload. Long trains (long frames) are very efficient from the perspective of the railroad company (the network). A locomotive (along with an engineer and other railroad personnel) is needed whether the train has one car or one thousand. That is, there is a certain amount of overhead imposed on a per-train (per-frame) basis, regardless of the train's length. Longer trains reduce the percentage of overhead. On the other hand, if you are waiting at a railroad crossing, long trains can impose excessive delay. Short trains (small cells) allow users to cross the tracks (access the channel) more frequently. For a given total number of freight cars (offered network load), the *average* delay getting across the tracks will be approximately the same over time with either short or long trains. (That is, with long trains, most of the time no train blocks your path. But sometimes you must wait a long time for a train to pass). However, if the trains are shorter, the worst-case delay will be less, since you never have to wait a long time for a train to pass. Thus the variance of delay is reduced, even if the average delay is the same.

Further, the use of long trains forces the customer to wait until the entire train is filled before it can move out of the station. This imposes a delay penalty on the user in addition to the delay in waiting for any previous train to pass.

Thus short cells clearly provide the advantage of low worst-case delay and low delay variance; these are important for real-time interactive voice and video. Long frames provide much greater efficiencies when delay and delay variance are less important; they make sense for most data communications applications. ATM's use of short cells is appropriate for its target applications; other applications do not benefit (in fact, their performance is degraded) by the use of short cells. ATM uses a 53-byte cell, with 5 bytes of header and 48 bytes of payload, as depicted in Figure 16–16.[24]

In a LAN environment, a globally unique identifier (48-bit address) is used to distinguish each device in the network. This identifier (actually two of them, one for the sender and one for the receiver) is carried in every frame

---

24. Like the LAN standards world, ATM development also entailed technical and political compromise. Cell size proposals varied from 16 bytes to more than 64 bytes [RTT87]. Very short cells (<32 bytes) allow voice circuits to operate without echo cancellers in almost all cases; very long cells provide greater efficiency in the network. The intermediate cell size chosen (53 bytes) serves neither purpose very well.

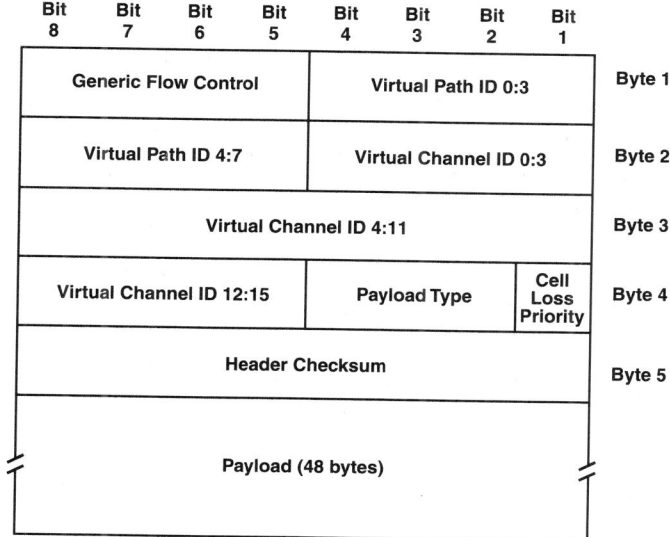

Bit 8	Bit 7	Bit 6	Bit 5	Bit 4	Bit 3	Bit 2	Bit 1	

Figure 16–16 ATM cell.

sent. This is necessary because LANs are connectionless in nature. There is no concept of a virtual circuit (at least not at the Data Link Layer), so each frame must be self-contained and routed (or switched) independently of all others. Each frame therefore must carry all of the information necessary to uniquely identify the sender and receiver of the frame.

ATM networks set up virtual circuits prior to carrying user information. When the circuit is established, a "shorthand" notation for the circuit is generated at call set-up—a *Virtual Channel Identifier* (VCI). This VCI needs to be only as long as the maximum number of circuits supported on a single path through the switch; this differs from LAN addresses, which must be globally unique. Also, the VCI identifies both endpoints of the connection, thereby further enhancing its efficiency. The result is that ATM cells can use a 16-bit VCI rather than two 48-bit addresses, saving 10 bytes per cell.

16.5.2.2 ATM Physical Layer and Data Rates

One advantage of ATM (like any well-designed link technology) is that it is both data rate-independent and Physical Layer-independent. The operation of an ATM end station or switch is the same regardless of the data rate or physical medium in use. There is no change to the cell format, switch algorithms, or allowable topologies as a function of the Physical Layer implementation. This

TABLE 16–2 ATM MEDIA AND DATA RATES

Target Application	Physical Medium	Data Rates	Encoding
LAN	UTP, STP	25 Mb/s	8B/10B[1]
Campus/workgroup backbone	Dedicated (baseband) fiber	100 Mb/s	4B/5B[2]
		155 Mb/s	8B/10B
	Multiplexed (SONET) fiber	155 Mb/s, 622 Mb/s	SONET[3]
WAN	Multiplexed (SONET) fiber	155 Mb/s (OC-3)	SONET
		622 Mb/s (OC-12)	SONET
		2.4 Gb/s (OC-48)	SONET

1. This system is based on the signaling and cabling used for 16 Mb/s Token Ring, except that 8B/10B encoding (as used in Fibre Channel and Gigabit Ethernet) is substituted to achieve a higher effective data rate than the differential Manchester encoding normally used on Token Ring. This is a logical step, as IBM was a prime advocate and developer of Token Ring, ATM LANs, and the 8B/10B code itself.
2. This system is based on the signaling, cabling, and encoding used for FDDI (and Fast Ethernet), except that ATM cells are substituted for FDDI frames.
3. The data rates shown are raw physical channel rates. SONET, ATM cell overhead, AAL overhead, and fragmentation will all reduce the capacity available to higher-layer protocols and applications

is in contrast to Ethernet. In Ethernet, both the allowable topologies and the underlying MAC algorithm has to be changed as the data rate increases from 10 Mb/s to 100 Mb/s to 1000 Mb/s.

While, in theory, an ATM Data Link can operate over any physical technology, a few standards have emerged for the implementation of ATM networks, depending on the application environment. In addition, some "natural" data rates emerge as a function of the underlying physical channel (particularly in WAN applications) and standards committee activities. Three different target applications give rise to a set of popular media and data rates, shown in Table 16–2.

16.5.2.3 Quality of Service

ATM offers applications a choice of various "qualities of service" (QoS). Depending on the needs of the application and the cost the user is willing to bear (higher QoS typically results in a higher cost from a profit-oriented service provider), the network can guarantee the user some combination of bandwidth, delay, and availability. This choice is made at the time of the connection set-up and may comprise a negotiation. The network and the application come to agreement on the level of service before proceeding with end-user communications.

Providing a true guarantee of QoS implies connection orientation. To be assured that the quality assurances are kept, the network must reserve fixed resources (switch memory, channel bandwidth, and so on) in accordance with the stated requirements of the application making the request. Unless the application knows its communications needs in advance, there is no way to reserve resources so that they are not oversubscribed.

Unlike true QoS guarantees, a *priority mechanism* can assure an application only that it will be given preferential treatment in the face of constrained network resources. Priority guarantees that the service provided will be "the best available," but that does not ensure that the service will be above any specified minimum level. However, unlike true QoS, priority mechanisms can be provided in a connectionless environment, including Ethernet. [IEEE97c, PACE96][25] Many LAN technologies have included mechanisms for priority access to the network. [IEEE90a, IEEE95b] Even if end-station MACs do not implement priority, internetworking devices (bridges/switches and routers) can prioritize certain classes of traffic or specific traffic flows between devices. [IEEE97b]

Implementing a priority access mechanism imposes a cost penalty in the devices that implement it, relative to a nonprioritized implementation. This is a key reason why priority was not built into Ethernet in the first place. Priority implies that there are, at a minimum, separate queue structures for priority versus normal traffic, as well as support in the programming interfaces (APIs) to allow access to the priority feature (see Figure 16–17). This adds complexity to the memory interface and possibly increases the memory requirement itself. For priority to be truly effective, it must be implemented in every device through which the prioritized frames pass.[26]

---

25. The IEEE 802.1Q Draft Virtual LAN standard [IEEE97c] provides a mechanism to support carrying priority information in Ethernet frames. It does not specify how those priorities are used or supported in Ethernet devices. There also have been various proprietary mechanisms implemented to give a station priority (unfair) access to an Ethernet, including the use of longer preambles and modified backoff algorithms.

26. There is also a cost, albeit minimal, associated with implementing a protocol to request and arbitrate for fixed network resources with connection-oriented QoS.

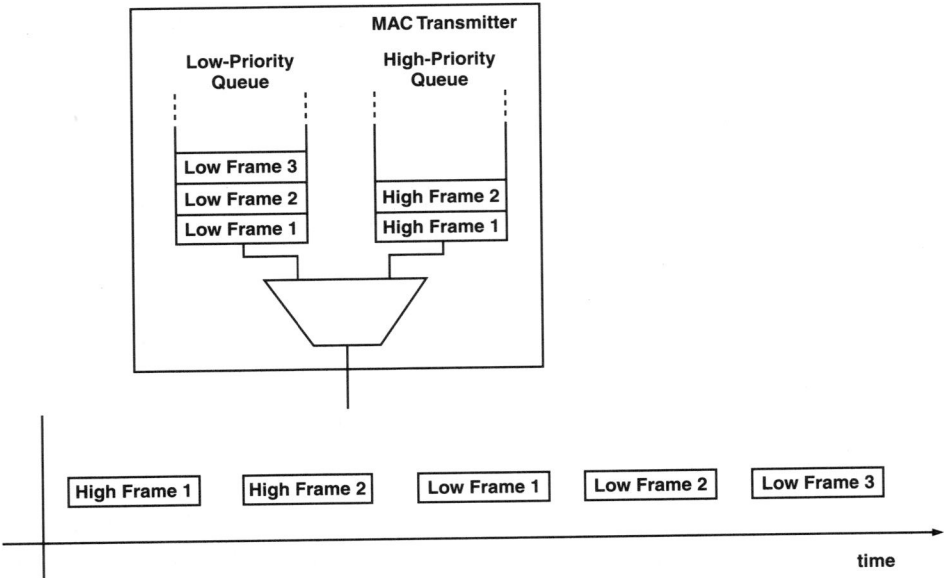

Figure 16–17 Priority queues.

For ATM switches to properly provide independent QoS for each virtual circuit, they must generally implement a separate queue for each virtual circuit (per-VC queuing). While this does not necessarily require more memory, it does increase the complexity of the memory data structures and the hardware required to operate the queues.

16.5.2.4 ATM Application Areas

Notwithstanding claims to the contrary by those who believe that ATM is the "holy grail" and solves all problems for all users, the primary application for ATM is in voice and video telephony. Not surprisingly, this is the application for which it was designed and optimized. Over time, it is possible that ATM technology may appear both in the carrier network and within subscriber telephone systems (that is, ATM PBX equipment). Initial deployment, however, is occurring within the telephony carrier backbone networks, for these reasons:

- Backbone bandwidth is the most expensive and therefore benefits most from ATM technology.
- The high cost of ATM equipment can more easily be justified in the backbone (where it is amortized over many users and years).

The data rates being employed are mostly OC-3 (155 Mb/s), OC-12 (622 Mb/s), and OC-48 (2.4 Gb/s). At the time of this writing, there is some experimental work ongoing at OC-192 (10 Gb/s) [NORT96].

16.5.3 Using ATM for Data Communications

For real-time voice and video telephony applications, ATM provides distinct advantages over both traditional circuit-switched telephony networks (in terms of channel efficiency) and traditional packet-switched data networks (in terms of delay, variance, and QoS guarantees). It is likely that ATM networks will become the basis of the telephony carrier infrastructure over the coming decades. But is there any reason to use an ATM network for data communications?

The requirements of data communications applications are not merely different from those of voice/video applications; they are almost exactly opposite. Consider the applications that constitute the bulk of computer network use:

- File transfer (including upload/download of complex graphics and full-motion video files)
- File/application sharing
- E-mail
- Printer sharing

These applications all have the following characteristics:

- Delay-insensitive (absolute delay is not critical to their operation)
- Delay variance-insensitive (to be effective, the data does not have to be delivered at the same rate as it is sent)
- Asymmetrical (bandwidth is needed in one direction more than in the other)
- Loss-sensitive (data must be delivered completely and error-free)

This is in precise contrast to the design center of ATM. That is, ATM is optimized for exactly those characteristics that are irrelevant for data communications applications.

It is important to note that unlike interactive communications, the transfer of digitally encoded voice/video information across a computer network (for playback through a computer or other device) does not imply the need for low delay or low-delay variance. The difference is that:

- There is no need for the playback to occur while the transfer is occurring. The voice/video information can be stored locally at the destination and played back (at the proper rate) without depending on the network to provide latency or variance guarantees. This greatly reduces the demands placed on the network for applications such as voice/video E-mail, online education/training, and so on.

■ There is no two-way, real-time interaction between the sender and receiver, as there is in a telephony application. This eliminates the requirements for low absolute delay across the network.

16.5.3.1 Connection-Oriented versus Connectionless Operation

The use of ATM for end-station data communications suffers from a fundamental problem. ATM provides its client a connection-oriented data link; a connection *must* be established through the network prior to exchanging any information between end stations. This optimizes resource allocation in the network (primarily switch memory and channel bandwidth), but it presupposes that applications or higher-layer protocols have (or need) the ability to dynamically establish connections at the Data Link Layer. In addition, it is difficult to employ multicast (one-to-many) communications in a connection-oriented data link; ATM does not easily support such a mechanism.

Virtually all computer network architectures in common use today simply do not dynamically establish connections at the Data Link Layer. Indeed, none of them even do so at the Network Layer. If connections are needed at all, they are created at the Transport Layer, as shown in Table 16–3.

In many cases, everything stays connectionless right up to and including the application. Consider the Routing Information Protocol (RIP) and the Simple Network Management Protocol (SNMP), both widely used in data communications networks and depicted in Figure 16–18.

Neither of these protocols ever establishes connections. [RFC1058, RFC1157] RIP maintains routing tables through the use of repeated (every 30–60 seconds) idempotent[27] exchanges. Thus there is no need for reliable data delivery on any given transaction. SNMP management devices regularly poll the management agents throughout the network, in a connectionless

---

27. An *idempotent* transaction is one in which the outcome is the same whether the event occurs once or many times. An instruction to "set a variable to the value x" is idempotent, whereas an instruction to "increment a variable by 3" is nonidempotent. Similarly, if counters are designed to be cumulative and are never reset (as in SNMP), then reading the counter becomes an idempotent transaction. If a protocol is designed around idempotent exchanges, then it is not necessary for any given transaction to occur reliably. Simply repeating the action as often as needed will have the same effect. This allows the use of simpler, connectionless protocols.

TABLE 16–3   CONNECTIONLESS AND CONNECTION-ORIENTED PROTOCOLS

	TCP/IP	**NetWare**	**AppleTalk**	**DECnet**
Transport	Connection-oriented (TCP) Connectionless (UDP)	Connection-oriented (SPX/PEP)	Connectionless (ATP[1])	Connection-oriented (NSP)
Network	Connectionless (IP)	Connectionless (IPX)	Connectionless (DDP)	Connectionless (DRP)
Data Link	Connectionless (Ethernet, Token Ring, FDDI, and so on)			
Physical	Various			

1. The case of AppleTalk Transaction Protocol (ATP) is interesting, especially with regard to its use of "connections." While, at first blush, it appears to be a connection-oriented protocol, a closer look reveals that connections are established for each data-unit being transferred (as opposed to a long-term data stream), with virtually no connection set-up overhead. [APPL90] (The connection set-up is built into the data transfer.) The purpose of such "miniconnections" is simply to provide a reliable delivery mechanism; each data-unit exchange is acknowledged and flow-controlled. ATP should therefore be considered a "reliable connectionless" protocol, rather than truly connection-oriented. The "connection" lasts only as long as the Transport data unit (as little as one packet or as much as eight packets). Even a simple file transfer creates thousands of such short-term "connections," each one transferring just a few kilobytes of data.

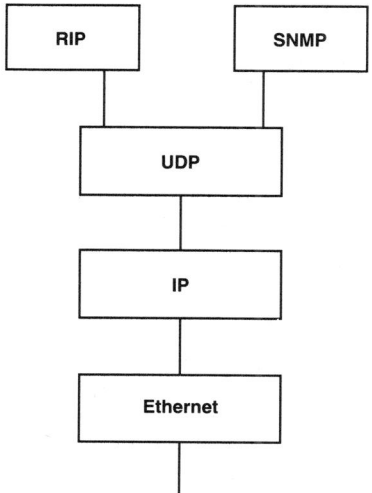

Figure 16–18 Connectionless applications.

manner, to gather information about the ongoing state of the network. The counters and management objects in SNMP are defined such that the exchanges can be idempotent.

In addition, virtually all of the commonly used data communications protocol suites rely heavily on Data Link multicast capability (for service advertisements, address resolution, routing protocols, and so on). This capability is not inherently available in connection-oriented ATM networks.

When one is forced to use a connection-oriented Data Link at end stations in order to move any data (as required by ATM), they are faced with two choices:

1. Make the connection-oriented link *appear* connectionless, thereby allowing the use of existing applications and higher-layer protocols unchanged. In the ATM world, this is called *LAN Emulation;* it is discussed later in the chapter.
2. Change all of the applications and protocols such that they are designed to use connection-oriented links.

Neither choice is attractive. You must either add significant complexity (and therefore cost) to use the connection-oriented link or abandon the huge installed base of applications and protocols.[28]

Now, this presupposes that the connection-oriented link technology must extend all the way to the end stations (that is, ATM to the desk). IP (and other data communications protocol suites) commonly use connection-oriented Data Link technology (for example, Frame Relay and Point-to-Point Protocol [PPP] links). However, these are primarily for *static* connections between routers in geographically separated sites. Connection endpoints

---

28. It can be argued that the failure of ATM to support data communications applications is as much a problem with the development of internet protocols (IP) as it is with ATM. In particular, much of the current design of IP is based on the presumption of (a) an underlying packet-switched medium to transport connectionless datagrams and (b) a medium with IEEE 802 LAN-style intrinsic multicast capability. In spite of claims that IP is technology-independent, it is difficult to overlay on a connection-oriented medium such as ATM. Since its evolution has been closely tied to the evolution of Ethernet and similar LANs, higher-speed Ethernets will naturally be more compatible with IP than will alternative architectures.

However, *if* future LAN applications will require seamless integration with the WAN, as well as the use of reserved data paths within the WAN, then the existing Internet structure of Ethernet-style LANs interconnected by routers might no longer be the best choice (just as it is not now the best choice for voice and video conferencing applications). This is a very large "if."

remain constant over long periods of time. There is no need for the complexity of dynamic call setup and resource allocation as provided by ATM. Is it reasonable to use an ATM link solely as a LAN interconnection mechanism, that is, to interconnect bridges/switches/routers across a backbone, as depicted in Figure 16–19?

Clearly this is possible, and it avoids both of the unattractive choices presented earlier. In fact, this is not really any different from current LAN interconnection methods using T-carrier or other point-to-point link technologies. We have just substituted a virtual circuit for a physical circuit. From the perspective of the LAN internetworking devices, the ATM network is simply a "fat pipe"—a high-speed point-to-point link. Virtual circuits are established at network configuration time and "nailed up" for extended periods (on the order of weeks to months, until new sites are added or the backbone configuration is changed).

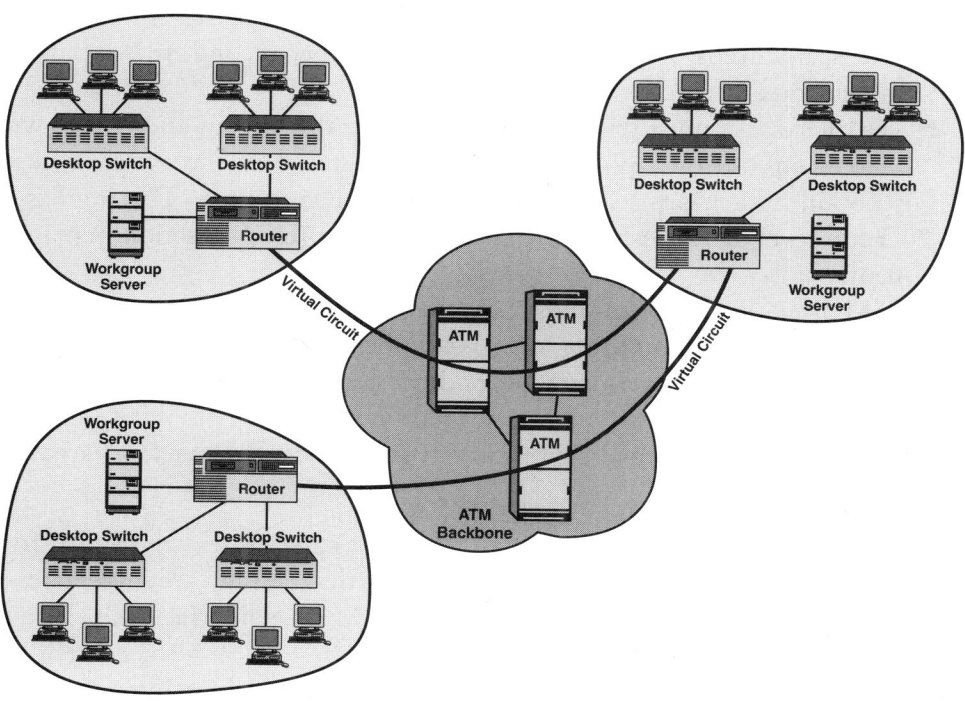

Figure 16–19 ATM backbone.

You can use ATM in this manner, but in so doing you are not leveraging the benefits of ATM, namely:

- Dynamic establishment of virtual circuits
- Low absolute delay and low variance of delay

These features are not needed for backbone data communications applications. You are paying for them (in the implementation of the ATM network) but receiving no benefit. The added complexity of ATM also incurs a potential cost in network downtime due to implementation bugs, product immaturity, and so on.

16.5.3.2 ATM Is More Expensive than Its Alternatives

ATM incurs some unavoidable costs in the devices attaching to the ATM network (for example, an ATM interface on a router) and the ATM switches themselves that are not needed for data communications applications:

- Since ATM networks can exchange *only* 53-byte cells and virtually all data communications exchanges are longer than this, a Segmentation-and-Reassembly (SAR) function (to break longer information units into the 48-byte ATM payload) is required. This must operate at line-speed, that is, hundreds or thousands of megabytes per second. It is typically implemented in silicon.
- ATM networks must provide the means for rapid set-up and tear-down of connections (to support telephony use). In addition, the switches must maintain state information about established connections. This implies a certain level of processing power and memory for connection management.
- ATM attachment devices must be able to map MAC addresses (48 bits, when interconnecting bridges) or Network addresses (different lengths, when interconnecting routers, depending on the Network Layer protocol in use) to the 16-bit Virtual Circuit Identifier (and/or Virtual Path Identifier) for the appropriate ATM circuit, on a packet-by-packet basis, at wire-speed.

These functions are in addition to whatever capabilities are needed for LAN interconnection without the use of ATM; that is, they are incremental requirements. This means that the cost of an ATM LAN interface will always be greater than the cost of either a connectionless LAN interface (such as Gigabit Ethernet) or a traditional connection-oriented link interface (for example, a T1 link using encapsulated Ethernet frames over static circuit connections).

16.5.3.3 Slaying the Quality-of-Service Woozle[29]

Ethernet does not inherently provide for different classes of service. In its "natural form" it provides none of the following:

- *Access priority* (allowing a station to have preferred channel access to a shared LAN, compared with other stations contending for its use)
- *User priority* (allowing applications within a given station to receive preferred service relative to other applications)
- *Service guarantees* (allowing applications or stations to reserve network bandwidth for future use).[30]

The decision not to provide such mechanisms is intentional; it results in a much simpler system design and therefore achieves the lowest possible cost. There are other, standard LANs that do provide such features:

- IEEE 802.5 (Token Ring) [IEEE95b] allows stations to request priority access to the channel through a token priority (and corresponding token reservation) mechanism. The token priority can be adjusted by the station on a frame-by-frame basis across eight priority levels. Proper implementation of access priority in a Token Ring controller greatly increases the complexity of the MAC state machine. As a side effect of priority access, applications requiring bounded delay (an oft-touted feature of Token Ring networks) must use the highest-priority access at all times, since there is no bound on access delay for stations using priorities other than maximum. As a result, virtually every frame ever transmitted on every Token Ring network ever installed has been sent at the highest allowed priority. Few network software vendors are willing to transmit frames using lower priority, since the performance will never be as good as other

---

29. With apologies to A. A. Milne and Mike Padlipsky. [RFC872]

30. There are (nonstandard) implementations of Ethernet that provide access priority. This is typically done through manipulation of access parameters, including preamble lengths, interframe gaps, and backoff times. In addition, there is nothing in Ethernet that prevents a device from providing multiple transmit queues for user priority purposes. The Ethernet MAC algorithm does not need to deal with this case explicitly because the transmit queue(s) is (are) considered to be architecturally above the MAC state machine.

applications using the LAN. If everyone uses the highest priority, there might as well be no priority at all.

- IEEE 802.4 (Token Bus) [IEEE90a] provides for multiple user priorities within a station, up to eight priority levels. A station implementing this feature must generally provide eight transmit queues, which are manipulated by the MAC state machine within the station. Again, this increases the complexity of the state machine, as well as the memory structures. In practice, only four levels of user priority were ever implemented in commercial products, but this does not significantly reduce the complexity.

- FDDI [ISO89] provides for a synchronous service option, where a station can effectively reserve a portion of the channel bandwidth for its exclusive use. In practice, this feature is rarely (if ever) implemented, due to both its complexity and the lack of a compelling need of this feature by data communications applications.

The search for priority, QoS guarantees and the like is really an attempt to answer the question, "When my application wants to use the network, how can I ensure that the performance is acceptable?" Ethernets answer this question without incurring explicit mechanisms to provide service guarantees.

When commercial Ethernets first shipped in the early 1980s, many in the industry were surprised that the network operated at 10 Mb/s. At that time, this data rate far exceeded the capacity of the attached computers to move data.[31] It would be many years before desktop computers could even come close to Ethernet saturation. Many industry observers questioned whether a 10 Mb/s LAN (which was expensive at the time) was really the right choice. A low-cost 1 Mb/s system would have served the needs of the computing world equally well.

While part of the reason for the 10 Mb/s design was to extend the product life, it was equally important that, with such considerable excess capacity, the *delay* as seen by applications was extremely low. The reason for high-speed LANs is not so that they can be used at or near maximum capacity. It is so that the delay (including queuing, access, and transmission times) is acceptable to most applications.

When computers and application demands increased such that a 10 Mb/s channel was no longer overkill, the development of LAN switching and Fast

---

31. Under controlled conditions, a VAX 8600 mainframe (considered a fast computer at the time) could transmit only ~6 Mb/s and receive ~4 Mb/s (measured at the device driver interface) on an Ethernet in 1983. Performance at the Transport Layer under typical conditions produced even lower throughput metrics.

Ethernet served to increase the available capacity such that the delay was again low. As network load increases further (in backbone and server environments), Gigabit Ethernet again increases the capacity such that the delay is acceptable. Ethernet solves the problem of how to reduce delay by increasing bandwidth, rather than increasing complexity.

This approach makes sense when bandwidth is "free," as it is in a local network. While there is a cost for equipment and cabling, there is no ongoing charge for bandwidth usage (as in WANs, where bandwidth is most definitely *not* free!). When the system implicitly provides acceptable service, there simply is no need to provide explicit mechanisms for guaranteed bandwidth or priority.

> **Seifert's Law of Networking #14**
>
> No one needs a QoS guarantee when they have enough bandwidth.

An excellent analogy can be seen in highway systems. A highway has some inherent capacity in terms of cars-per-hour that can be carried at an acceptable delay. If the load (cars) is much less than the capacity of the highway, then everyone is happy. Everyone gets where they want to go within a reasonable time. If the traffic load increases, the delay also increases and ultimately becomes unacceptable. Once this occurs, there are two choices available to handle the increased load:

1. Provide priority access, either for privileged users (carpool lanes) or at a price (toll lanes).[32]
2. Add lanes to the highway.

It is extremely expensive to add lanes to a highway; costs are on the order of millions of dollars per kilometer. So the "Quality of Service" approach is usually taken, at least initially. With LANs, the cost of increased bandwidth is not overwhelming and, in fact, is usually less than the cost of implementing QoS complexity. It is this method that Ethernet has used since its inception to deal with ever-increasing load.

Now, it is possible that there is more-than-adequate bandwidth available most of the time, but at certain peak instances, the network is still congested. During these rare peaks, it may be important to prioritize traffic by class and to provide best performance for the more-important classes. This differs from

---

32. A few highways in California provide reserved lanes that can be used only by paying a fee. Really. While many were skeptical of the idea at first, it has proved to be very popular.

ATM-style QoS and is much easier to implement. A simple traffic prioritization scheme in the internetworking devices may be all that is needed here.[33] [IEEE97b] Connectionless networks can thus provide "quality of service" in a more relaxed manner and with much lower cost and complexity.

16.5.3.4 LAN Emulation over ATM

It is a fairly straightforward matter to use ATM for LAN *interconnection* (that is, point-to-point virtual circuit connections among bridges and routers). No special measures are required other than establishing the required bandwidth and setting up the circuits between the endpoints. If, however, the ATM network is to be used as a replacement for the LAN itself (that is, end stations are attached directly to the ATM network using ATM NICs), then something must be done to make it appear to higher-layer protocols and applications that they are still operating over a connectionless, multicast-capable medium. This is the role of LAN Emulation.

LAN Emulation [ATM95], as the name implies, emulates traditional LAN behavior over ATM circuits. It makes the connection-oriented ATM infrastructure appear connectionless so that existing software can operate (relatively) unchanged. Figure 16–20 depicts an emulated LAN environment. Figure 16–21 shows the architectural layering within:

1. an end station
2. an ATM switch
3. an ATM-to-LAN Bridge
4. a traditional LAN device in an ATM Emulated LAN.

Key to the operation of an emulated LAN are:

- The creation of virtual circuits (as needed) for communication among pairs of devices in the emulated LAN
- The mapping of 48-bit LAN MAC addresses to ATM virtual circuits
- The emulation of LAN multicast services

An Emulated LAN can appear to be either an Ethernet or a Token Ring. A given Emulated LAN is only one or the other. Similar to traditional LANs, it is not possible to mix Ethernet and Token Ring devices on the same logical channel. However, only the frame formats (including frame minima/maxima and internal bit ordering) are emulated. An Emulated LAN does not attempt to mimic the MAC characteristics (for example, CSMA/CD or tokens).

---

33. This is often called "Class of Service" (CoS) to distinguish it from true "Quality of Service" (QoS).

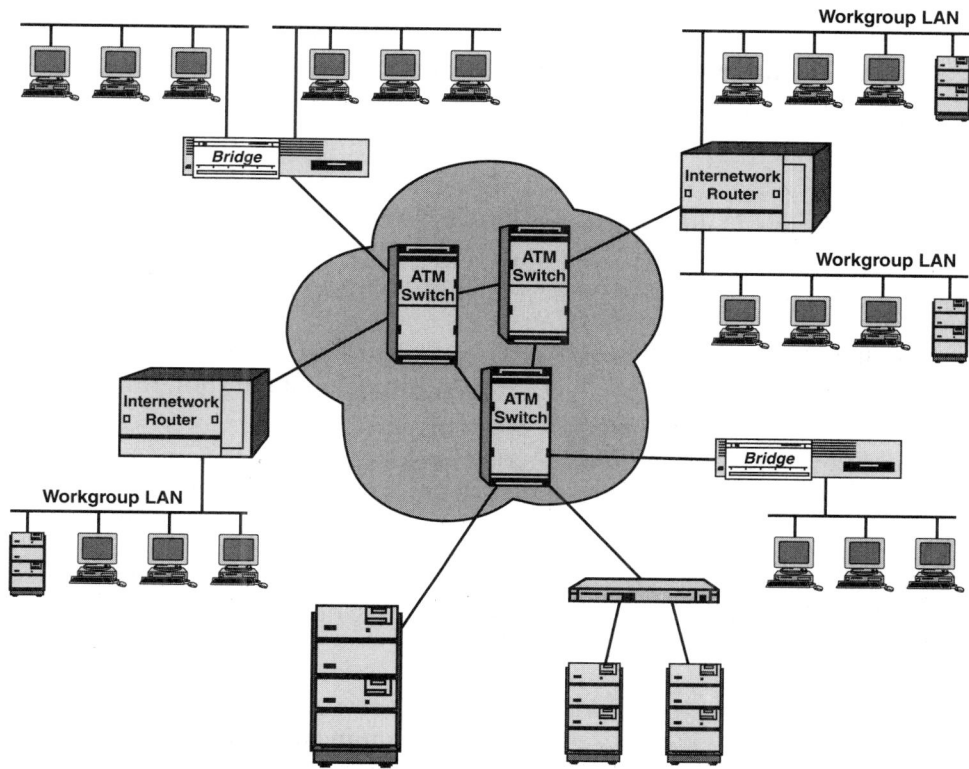

Figure 16–20 Emulated LAN environment.

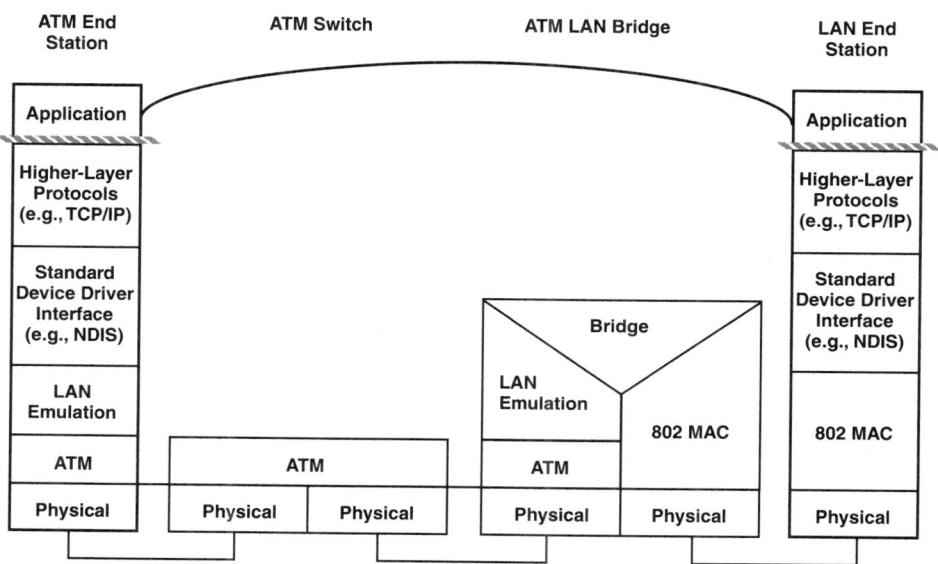

Figure 16–21 LAN Emulation protocol layering.

The use of Emulated LANs requires the existence of three servers:

1. LAN Emulation Configuration Server
2. LAN Emulation Server
3. Broadcast and Unknown Server

LAN Emulation Configuration Server   A LAN Emulation Configuration Server (LECS) is required for all emulated LANs within a given administrative domain, for example, a campus backbone. The LECS provides for:

■ Initialization and configuration of the parameters of each Emulated LAN
■ Assignment of client identifiers and providing configuration information to members of the Emulated LAN
■ Allowing end stations and internetworking devices to join an existing Emulated LAN, and so on.

LAN Emulation Server   A LAN Emulation Server (LES) is required for each Emulated LAN. The LES effectively directs traffic flow on an Emulated LAN. In particular, it:

■ Registers each client's MAC and ATM addresses,
■ Maps MAC to ATM addresses when communication to a specific station is requested by a LAN Emulation client
■ Accepts client requests to hear specific multicast addresses.

Broadcast and Unknown Server (BUS)   A Broadcast and Unknown Server (BUS) is required for each Emulated LAN. The BUS emulates the natural ability of traditional LANs to provide multicast service. All multicast traffic (as well as traffic for as-yet-unknown destinations) is sent to this server. The server "reflects" the traffic individually to every LAN Emulation client that has registered its desire to either:

1. Receive traffic sent to this specific multicast address (typically an end station or router).
2. Receive all multicast traffic (typically a bridge).
3. Hear traffic for all unknown destinations (typically a bridge).
   The efficient use of a BUS requires that each station preregisters its desire to receive particular multicast addresses. While the capability exists to allow stations to request to receive *all* multicasts, the widespread use of this mechanism would significantly reduce performance,

both of the network as well as the BUS itself. Traditional LANs do not require such registration. Each station can "see" all of the multicast traffic naturally and choose to accept or ignore it as necessitated by the applications currently running on that station. LAN Emulation requires an explicit multicast registration protocol.

The LECS and LES can be implemented in either a distributed or centralized manner, at least in theory. The BUS must be implemented in a single centralized device (for a given Emulated LAN). In practice, all of the servers are typically implemented in a centralized manner. This is due to the difficulty of properly implementing distributed servers in a network, the relative immaturity of LAN Emulation, and the fact that there are very few large Emulated LANs requiring the performance and robustness improvements possible from decentralized servers. The servers may be implemented either as dedicated stand-alone servers (with appropriate ATM interfaces) or as nondedicated processes (software) running inside an ATM switch or internetworking device.

LAN Emulation imposes a performance penalty relative to traditional LAN usage. Besides the initialization and configuration required, some of the LAN traffic must pass through either the LES or the BUS. If traffic flows are primarily unicast and quasi-static (that is, large bulk file transfers, client-server sessions, and so on), then the penalty is not huge. Traffic is carried on virtual circuits between the end stations themselves with little intervention from the LES (other than initially assisting to establish the circuit). However, if communications patterns vary considerably over time or involve significant amounts of multicast traffic, then the LES and the BUS can become performance bottlenecks.

The functions performed by the LECS, the LES, and the BUS cannot be implemented in simple state machines. They entail considerable complexity in design, especially when they must support either large numbers of Emulated LANs or large numbers of devices (and their resulting virtual circuits) within those LANs. This complexity results in additional cost for both the servers (LECS, LES, and BUS) as well as the end stations and internetworking devices that implement LAN Emulation.

The problem is that LAN Emulation is attempting to "fit a square peg into a round hole." Existing LAN protocols and applications assume the existence of an underlying connectionless, multicast-capable medium; ATM delivers neither of these. The complexity and cost of LAN Emulation results from its attempt to provide characteristics that are inherently the opposite of

those for which ATM networks were designed. As a result, the use of ATM
LANs and LAN Emulation has not gained much acceptance industry-wide.

Fortunately (for the vendors of ATM network products and services),
LAN Emulation is not needed if the ATM network is being used only for
LAN interconnection; that is, when internetworking devices (bridges and
routers) are the only ATM-attached stations. In an internetworking environment, quasi-static virtual circuits can be established across the ATM network
by human administrators (rather than LAN Emulation servers). Described
earlier, this does not differ fundamentally from existing LAN internetworks
that use T-carrier links.

However, suppose even a single-end station (client or server) has a direct
ATM connection and the ATM network is to be used as a LAN replacement
for that device (that is, existing protocols and applications are being used
above the ATM Data Link). In that case, LAN Emulation is required in every
device directly connected to the ATM network (end stations, bridges, and
routers) that are in the communication path to that end station, as depicted in
Figure 16–22.

It is also interesting (and ironic) to note that the implementation of LAN
Emulation negates the QoS capabilities of ATM. The ATM network emulates
the characteristics of a traditional LAN, which does not include QoS guarantees.

16.5.3.5 Cell Loss

ATM was designed for voice/video telephony. In this environment, the occasional loss of a small amount of information is hardly noticeable. There is
considerable internal redundancy in human voice and video communications;
as long as *most* of the cells are delivered properly, there will be little problem.
As a result, telephony applications do not typically implement any error control mechanisms on an ATM network. There is no need to recover and
retransmit in the face of an occasional corrupted or discarded cell.

This is not true for data communications. File transfers, e-mails, application downloads, and so on all require that 100% of the information is transferred error-free. In the event of an error anywhere in the path between
sender and receiver, higher-layer protocols (typically Transport) must invoke
retransmission mechanisms to ensure that reliable data delivery is assured.

As the error control mechanism is implemented at a high layer in the protocol stack, it is unaware of the cell nature of the underlying Data Link. The
loss of a single cell does not imply the retransmission of only that cell. At a
minimum, a single Network Layer packet will have to be re-sent (typically
tens of cells). Depending on the particular Transport protocol, its implemen-

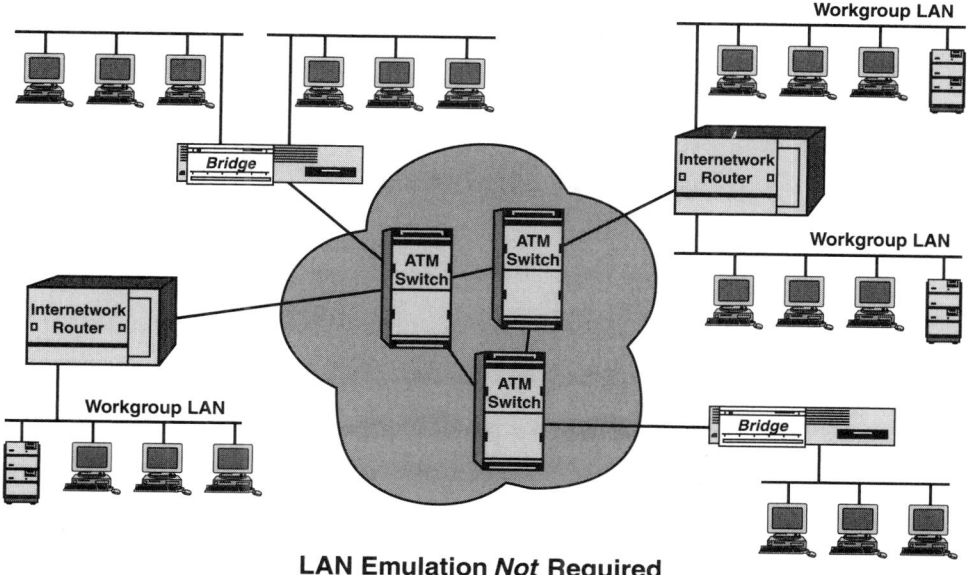

LAN Emulation *Not* Required

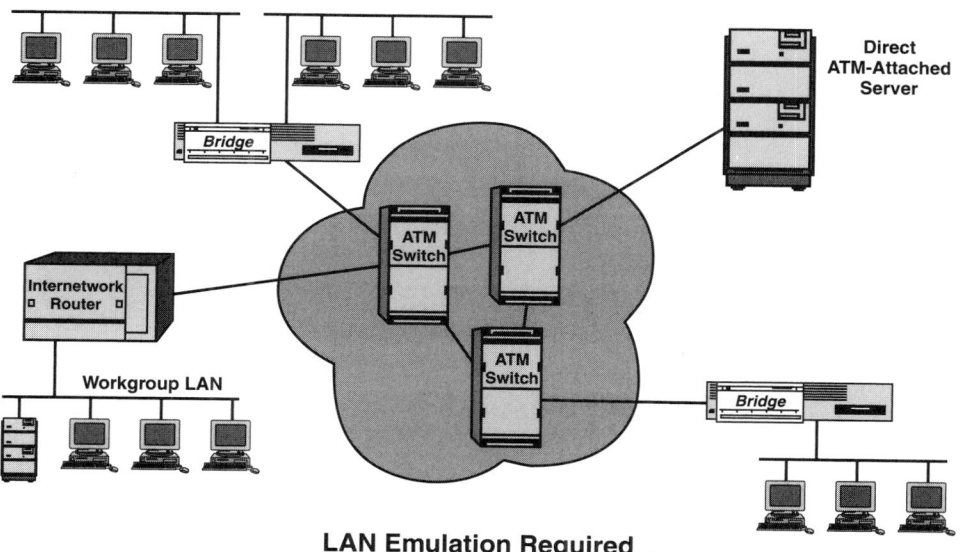

LAN Emulation Required

Figure 16–22 LAN emulation requirement.

tation in the end stations, and the round-trip delay, an entire transport "window" may have to be retransmitted due to a single error event. This can cause many hundreds of cells to be sent twice.

ATM switch design generally allows for the occasional cell to be discarded under congestion conditions. This makes the switch design simpler and causes no problems for telephony applications. However, this can cause severe degradation in performance for data communications applications.

16.5.3.6 LAN versus WAN Usage

One commonly held view is that Ethernet will be used in the LAN and ATM will be used in the WAN. This presupposes that the application requirements are different in a LAN versus a WAN. This simply is not true. The needs of data communications applications are no different when communicating across long distances than when communicating between adjacent offices.

The only significant difference between a LAN and a WAN (from an MIS perspective) is that WAN bandwidth costs more. As a result:

- There is usually less excess bandwidth available for WAN communications.
- Users' expectations of performance must be set lower when using WAN resources.

However, this is true regardless of the WAN technology employed. It holds for T1 circuits as well as ATM connections. While ATM provides efficiencies for bandwidth utilization on the backbone links, these efficiencies generally accrue to the service provider, not to the user.

While users may employ ATM connections as virtual point-to-point links for LAN interconnection among geographically separated sites (as discussed earlier in the chapter), this is due not so much to the need for the inherent features of ATM (for example, low delay variance and QoS guarantees) as to the fact that the WAN carrier may choose to offer only ATM-type service. From the perspective of the user in this case, ATM is just another point-to-point link. There is no real difference in usage relative to T-carrier links, other than the ability to purchase bandwidth in increments other than those of the T-carrier hierarchy.

16.5.4 Integrating Voice, Video, and Data

A common plaint is that users want (or need) to integrate their voice, video, and data networks. It is believed that this will reduce costs and allow integrated applications to thrive. While it may be true that a single physical cabling infrastructure can lower costs (especially in the WAN), it is generally inappropriate to run incongruent applications over the same data link technology.

16.5.4.1 Integrating the Voice/Video and Data Networks at the Link Layer

Most computer users have (at least) two network connections on their desks today: a computer network (probably Ethernet) to support data communications applications and a telephone network to support voice communications. The data network interconnects users, servers, and other equipments, using a combination of repeaters, switches, routers, and similar devices. The voice network interconnects users' telephones both within and outside of the organization by using a PBX switch that has both local and remote trunk connections. There is no "integration" of voice and data networks today.

Why not? It has long been demonstrated that it is technologically feasible to move voice traffic over traditional LANs. [LEWE91] Acceptable levels of performance can be achieved, from the perspectives of delay, bandwidth, and number of calls. Similarly, it is possible to move data across the private telephone network, although the data rates available ($\leq$ 64 Kb/s on a typical digital PBX) are lower than most computer users expect from a LAN. But the fact is, it is feasible to integrate voice and data using today's technology; doing so does not require ATM. So why hasn't there been large-scale deployment of integrated networks?

The reason is that it is simpler and less expensive to keep them separate. The needs of the voice network (connection-oriented, delay-sensitive traffic) and those of the data network (connectionless, delay-insensitive traffic) are fundamentally dichotomous; there is no way to optimize both systems simultaneously. This leaves us with two choices:

1. **Operate the LAN over a connection-oriented Data Link.** This approach optimizes the voice/video network and forces data traffic to make itself "look like" voice/video. Either the computer network applications and protocols must all be changed to use connection-oriented Data Link services (unlikely) or some form of LAN Emulation must be employed to make the connection-oriented link appear connectionless to the applications (unwieldy).

2. **Operate the voice/video network over a connectionless link.** This requires either that accommodations be made in the data link design to support real-time voice/video streams (for example, bandwidth reservation, priorities, and isochronous channels) or that there be so much

available bandwidth that guarantees are not needed (that is, the probability of timely delivery is high enough to support the application).

Both alternatives increase the cost of the overall system. In practice, an integrated voice/video/data system either costs more than separate systems, or leaves one class of users dissatisfied with the level of service. This is why we use, and will probably continue to use, separate systems for telephony and data communications.

The argument is sometimes raised, "Well, what about integrated voice/video/data applications? Don't they need an integrated network?" In reality, unless the application requires extremely tight time synchronization of the voice/video and data streams, then voice, video, and data don't really need to be on the same data link. Time synchronization on the order of tens or hundreds of milliseconds can be easily achieved "out-of-band," by implementing exchange primitives between disjoint networks. The telemarketer needs to see the customer's purchasing information while speaking with the customer, but does not need the information to be synchronized to the microsecond level. In fact, no widely used integrated application today requires synchronization that cannot be achieved out-of-band. Suppose, however, that some future application is developed that absolutely requires tight time synchronization of the voice/video and data streams and provides an irresistible benefit. Then this will be the "killer application" that may demand an integrated network, one that possibly uses ATM. Until then, there is really no need for such integration.

16.5.4.2 Integrating the Voice/Video and Data Networks at the Physical Layer

A valid argument is that it is impractical, especially in the WAN, to have separate *physical networks*. That is, the cost of installing long-distance cables makes it prohibitive to keep telephony and data communications links separated. It makes sense to integrate the networks, at least to the extent that they can share the cable. However, this does not imply that they should use the same data link technology.

The most common WAN technology used today for LAN interconnection is T-carrier. Many organizations use T1 and T3 links to interconnect switches and routers among their geographically separated sites, either directly or through frame relay carriers. T-carrier systems were designed specifically to allow physical multiplexing of voice circuits over a common cable. A T1 circuit can carry 23 voice circuits (plus a control channel)[34]; a T3 circuit can multiplex 28 T1 circuits. The telephone carriers deployed T-carrier technology extensively throughout the 1960s and 1970s, as central office (CO) interconnects. When LAN interconnection became an important market in the 1980s, excess T-carrier capacity was sold for site interconnection.

The reason T-carriers are used for data communications is not because they are an "appropriate" technology from an engineering perspective. In fact, they cause significant problems. This is because the underlying design makes assumptions about the characteristics of the information they carry (such as that signals vary over the short term and that clocks can be synchronized system-wide). Using T-carrier links for LAN interconnection forces us to:

- Use less than the available bandwidth (for example, 56 Kb/s/channel, rather than the 64 Kb/s/channel available) so that data transparency can be maintained.
- Use a link signaling method that forces a minimum number of transitions in a given period (HDLC or PPP with bit-stuffing, [ISO87a, RFC1548]) so that a minimum ones-density is presented.

We do this not because we *want to* but because we *have to* in order to move data across a T-carrier channel. T-carrier is the physical signaling system, and we must accommodate it.

ATM is different. ATM is a data link technology. In the WAN, ATM usually runs on SONET, a Physical Layer technology providing a standardized method of signaling across optical-fiber links. SONET is capable of multiplexing at the Physical Layer; that is, it can support multiple streams simultaneously that come from multiple data link technologies. A SONET link can simultaneously carry ATM virtual circuits, DS circuits (DS-1, DS-3),[35] management circuits, and connectionless datagram traffic (Packet-over-SONET, or POS). This is illustrated in Figure 16–23. It becomes possible to integrate the networks at the Physical Layer without forcing any system (voice/video or data) to accommodate the data-link requirements of the others. This was not possible in the T-carrier network.

In this way, it becomes possible to build a WAN that encompasses ATM voice and connectionless POS data over the same SONET cables. Using a

---

34. This is the North American standard system. The European standard system, E1, carries 30 × 64 Kb/s channels.

35. Digital Signaling (DS) is the logical signal carried by a T-carrier. DS-1 is the signaling for a T1 link, DS-3 for a T3 link, and so on.

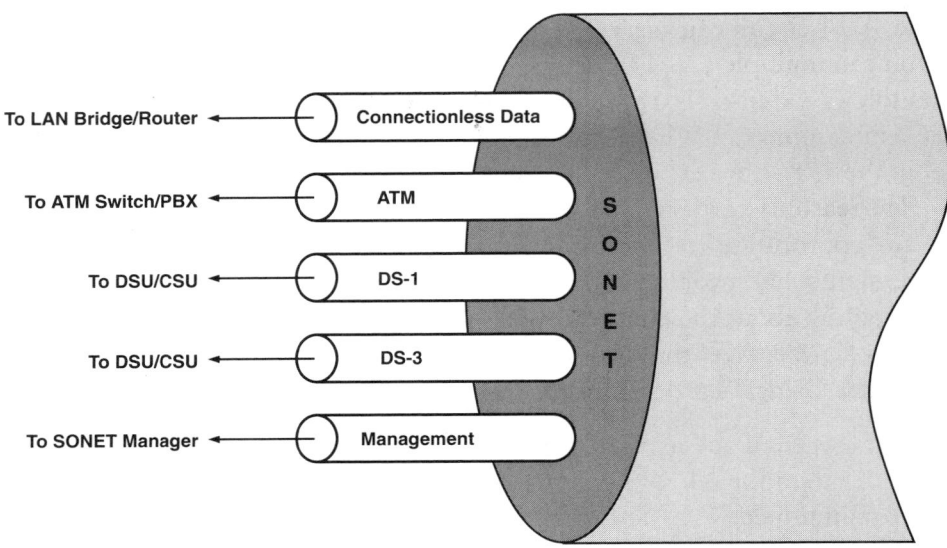

Figure 16–23 SONET multiplexing.

SONET multiplexer, the ATM voice/video circuits are directed to ATM switches and the POS data is directed to internetwork switches or routers, as appropriate for the application. Conventional DS circuits also can be accommodated to allow migration from an existing T-carrier network. SONET bandwidth can be allocated among the various services as appropriate to the user organization.

The same business model that makes Frame Relay attractive today (that is, amortizing the cost of the WAN data-carrying capacity among large numbers of users) remains attractive. However, now the network can be implemented at data rates far in excess of T1 speeds.

The connectionless data traffic can travel from desktop to desktop through the LAN, campus, and WAN backbones without incurring any penalty in connection-oriented call set-up, LAN Emulation, frame disassembly/reassembly into ATM cells, or frame format conversions. Similarly, voice/video traffic is not forced onto any LANs; this eliminates the need for LAN QoS or isochronicity. Both the data and voice/video networks can be seamless, end-to-end.

16.5.5 ATM: The Wave of the Future?

ATM is often touted as the ultimate solution for all communications needs; any alternative is expected to be short-lived. Sooner or later, proponents say, everything will be ATM, whether you like it or not, so you better get on the bandwagon before you are left behind.

There have been a number of such "ultimate solutions" in the past.

- In the mid-1980s, Manufacturing Automation Protocols (MAP) were assured to be the basis for the future of all factory and process-control systems. [VALEN92] General Motors led the development of these systems, and invested heavily in MAP technology. Hundreds of suppliers made commitments to the technology, and there were regular trade-show-like MAP User's Group meetings that extended for years.

- In the late 1980s and early 1990s, it was generally accepted that the ISO protocol suite [ISO84, ISO87b] would replace all of the proprietary (and open) protocol suites in use at the time. TCP/IP was considered a "steppingstone to OSI." Virtually every vendor embraced the ISO protocol suite and offered a migration path for their customers.

None of these "ultimate solutions" ever happened. The majority of factory automation systems are built using Ethernet technology, and TCP/IP is clearly the protocol of choice for multivendor interoperable systems. Even the U. S. government dropped its long-standing requirement that their systems support ISO protocols [GOSIP91].

The reason for these "solutions" not taking off is that there was no "killer application" that offered a compelling reason to move to the proposed alternative technology. There was nothing that could be done in the new systems (for example, MAP or ISO) that could not be done with existing technologies (Ethernet and TCP/IP). Granted, the new technologies may have had features that would make system development easier or more elegant, but they provided no capability that could not be achieved (albeit perhaps with greater effort) using the mature, lower-cost, existing technology. The same is true of ATM—it is *different*, but it provides no practical benefit for traditional data communications applications. While telecom equipment suppliers may hope for the addition of new customers from the data communications world, there is no driving force that is making this happen, at least not today.

16.5.6 Advantages and Disadvantages of ATM

ATM offers a number of features and capabilities beyond those offered by Ethernet (as well as most connectionless LAN systems):

- Low delay variance
- QoS guarantees
- Integration of voice/video and data at the Data Link Layer

Whether these features are *advantages* depends on whether they are important to the application and if they are needed in the target environment. While real-time interactive voice and video applications generally require bandwidth guarantees (at least to a high degree of probability) and low variance of delay, these features accrue no real benefit to data communications applications. The integration of voice/video and data communications at the Data Link Layer seems to be an unnecessary complication, offering no benefit for current applications.

The disadvantages of ATM for data communications, particularly in a LAN or campus environment are obvious:

- Higher cost
- Connection-oriented architecture
- Significant complexity in the transformation from Ethernet frames to ATM cells and back, which is needed solely to accommodate the requirements of ATM

ATM offers the lure of high-speed communications, but so does Gigabit Ethernet, and without the added complexity and cost. In addition, the use of Ethernet (at 10 Mb/s, 100 Mb/s, and 1000 Mb/s) allows much more seamless integration among desktop, workgroup, and campus interconnections.

Appendix
8B/10B Code Tables

TABLE A-1 VALID DATA CODES

Name	Byte Value	8 Bits		10B Code Word (RD −)		10B Code Word (RD +)		New RD
		HGF	EDCBA	abcdei	fghj	abcdei	fghj	
/D0.0/	00	000	00000	100111	0100	011000	1011	same
/D1.0/	01	000	00001	011101	0100	100010	1011	same
/D2.0/	02	000	00010	101101	0100	010010	1011	same
/D3.0/	03	000	00011	110001	1011	110001	0100	flip
/D4.0/	04	000	00100	110101	0100	001010	1011	same
/D5.0/	05	000	00101	101001	1011	101001	0100	flip
/D6.0/	06	000	00110	011001	1011	011001	0100	flip
/D7.0/	07	000	00111	111000	1011	000111	0100	flip
/D8.0/	08	000	01000	111001	0100	000110	1011	same
/D9.0/	09	000	01001	100101	1011	100101	0100	flip
/D10.0/	0A	000	01010	010101	1011	010101	0100	flip
/D11.0/	0B	000	01011	110100	1011	110100	0100	flip
/D12.0/	0C	000	01100	001101	1011	001101	0100	flip
/D13.0/	0D	000	01101	101100	1011	101100	0100	flip
/D14.0/	0E	000	01110	011100	1011	011100	0100	flip
/D15.0/	0F	000	01111	010111	0100	101000	1011	same
/D16.0/	10	000	10000	011011	0100	100100	1011	same
/D17.0/	11	000	10001	100011	1011	100011	0100	flip
/D18.0/	12	000	10010	010011	1011	010011	0100	flip
/D19.0/	13	000	10011	110010	1011	110010	0100	flip
/D20.0/	14	000	10100	001011	1011	001011	0100	flip
/D21.0/	15	000	10101	101010	1011	101010	0100	flip
/D22.0/	16	000	10110	011010	1011	011010	0100	flip
/D23.0/	17	000	10111	111010	0100	000101	1011	same

TABLE A–1 VALID DATA CODES (*cont.*)

Name	Byte Value	8 Bits		10B Code Word (RD –)		10B Code Word (RD +)		New RD
		HGF	EDCBA	abcdei	fghj	abcdei	fghj	
/D24.0/	18	000	11000	110011	0100	001100	1011	same
/D25.0/	19	000	11001	100110	1011	100110	0100	flip
/D26.0/	1A	000	11010	010110	1011	010110	0100	flip
/D27.0/	1B	000	11011	110110	0100	001001	1011	same
/D28.0/	1C	000	11100	001110	1011	001110	0100	flip
/D29.0/	1D	000	11101	101110	0100	010001	1011	same
/D30.0/	1E	000	11110	011110	0100	100001	1011	same
/D31.0/	1F	000	11111	101011	0100	010100	1011	same
/D0.1/	20	001	00000	100111	1001	011000	1001	flip
/D1.1/	21	001	00001	011101	1001	100010	1001	flip
/D2.1/	22	001	00010	101101	1001	010010	1001	flip
/D3.1/	23	001	00011	110001	1001	110001	1001	same
/D4.1/	24	001	00100	110101	1001	001010	1001	flip
/D5.1/	25	001	00101	101001	1001	101001	1001	same
/D6.1/	26	001	00110	011001	1001	011001	1001	same
/D7.1/	27	001	00111	111000	1001	000111	1001	same
/D8.1/	28	001	01000	111001	1001	000110	1001	flip
/D9.1/	29	001	01001	100101	1001	100101	1001	same
/D10.1/	2A	001	01010	010101	1001	010101	1001	same
/D11.1/	2B	001	01011	110100	1001	110100	1001	same
/D12.1/	2C	001	01100	001101	1001	001101	1001	same
/D13.1/	2D	001	01101	101100	1001	101100	1001	same
/D14.1/	2E	001	01110	011100	1001	011100	1001	same
/D15.1/	2F	001	01111	010111	1001	101000	1001	flip
/D16.1/	30	001	10000	011011	1001	100100	1001	flip
/D17.1/	31	001	10001	100011	1001	100011	1001	same
/D18.1/	32	001	10010	010011	1001	010011	1001	same
/D19.1/	33	001	10011	110010	1001	110010	1001	same
/D20.1/	34	001	10100	001011	1001	001011	1001	same
/D21.1/	35	001	10101	101010	1001	101010	1001	same
/D22.1/	36	001	10110	011010	1001	011010	1001	same
/D23.1/	37	001	10111	111010	1001	000101	1001	flip
/D24.1/	38	001	11000	110011	1001	001100	1001	flip
/D25.1/	39	001	11001	100110	1001	100110	1001	same
/D26.1/	3A	001	11010	010110	1001	010110	1001	same

TABLE A–1 VALID DATA CODES (*cont.*)

Name	Byte Value	8 Bits HGF	8 Bits EDCBA	10B Code Word (RD –) abcdei	10B Code Word (RD –) fghj	10B Code Word (RD +) abcdei	10B Code Word (RD +) fghj	New RD
/D27.1/	3B	001	11011	110110	1001	001001	1001	flip
/D28.1/	3C	001	11100	001110	1001	001110	1001	same
/D29.1/	3D	001	11101	101110	1001	010001	1001	flip
/D30.1/	3E	001	11110	011110	1001	100001	1001	flip
/D31.1/	3F	001	11111	101011	1001	010100	1001	flip
/D0.2/	40	010	00000	100111	0101	011000	0101	flip
/D1.2/	41	010	00001	011101	0101	100010	0101	flip
/D2.2/	42	010	00010	101101	0101	010010	0101	flip
/D3.2/	43	010	00011	110001	0101	110001	0101	same
/D4.2/	44	010	00100	110101	0101	001010	0101	flip
/D5.2/	45	010	00101	101001	0101	101001	0101	same
/D6.2/	46	010	00110	011001	0101	011001	0101	same
/D7.2/	47	010	00111	111000	0101	000111	0101	same
/D8.2/	48	010	01000	111001	0101	000110	0101	flip
/D9.2/	49	010	01001	100101	0101	100101	0101	same
/D10.2/	4A	010	01010	010101	0101	010101	0101	same
/D11.2/	4B	010	01011	110100	0101	110100	0101	same
/D12.2/	4C	010	01100	001101	0101	001101	0101	same
/D13.2/	4D	010	01101	101100	0101	101100	0101	same
/D14.2/	4E	010	01110	011100	0101	011100	0101	same
/D15.2/	4F	010	01111	010111	0101	101000	0101	flip
/D16.2/	50	010	10000	011011	0101	100100	0101	flip
/D17.2/	51	010	10001	100011	0101	100011	0101	same
/D18.2/	52	010	10010	010011	0101	010011	0101	same
/D19.2/	53	010	10011	110010	0101	110010	0101	same
/D20.2/	54	010	10100	001011	0101	001011	0101	same
/D21.2/	55	010	10101	101010	0101	101010	0101	same
/D22.2/	56	010	10110	011010	0101	011010	0101	same
/D23.2/	57	010	10111	111010	0101	000101	0101	flip
/D24.2/	58	010	11000	110011	0101	001100	0101	flip
/D25.2/	59	010	11001	100110	0101	100110	0101	same
/D26.2/	5A	010	11010	010110	0101	010110	0101	same
/D27.2/	5B	010	11011	110110	0101	001001	0101	flip
/D28.2/	5C	010	11100	001110	0101	001110	0101	same
/D29.2/	5D	010	11101	101110	0101	010001	0101	flip

TABLE A–1 VALID DATA CODES (*cont.*)

Name	Byte Value	8 Bits HGF	8 Bits EDCBA	10B Code Word (RD −) abcdei	fghj	10B Code Word (RD +) abcdei	fghj	New RD
/D30.2/	5E	010	11110	011110	0101	100001	0101	flip
/D31.2/	5F	010	11111	101011	0101	010100	0101	flip
/D0.3/	60	011	00000	100111	0011	011000	1100	flip
/D1.3/	61	011	00001	011101	0011	100010	1100	flip
/D2.3/	62	011	00010	101101	0011	010010	1100	flip
/D3.3/	63	011	00011	110001	1100	110001	0011	same
/D4.3/	64	011	00100	110101	0011	001010	1100	flip
/D5.3/	65	011	00101	101001	1100	101001	0011	same
/D6.3/	66	011	00110	011001	1100	011001	0011	same
/D7.3/	67	011	00111	111000	1100	000111	0011	same
/D8.3/	68	011	01000	111001	0011	000110	1100	flip
/D9.3/	69	011	01001	100101	1100	100101	0011	same
/D10.3/	6A	011	01010	010101	1100	010101	0011	same
/D11.3/	6B	011	01011	110100	1100	110100	0011	same
/D12.3/	6C	011	01100	001101	1100	001101	0011	same
/D13.3/	6D	011	01101	101100	1100	101100	0011	same
/D14.3/	6E	011	01110	011100	1100	011100	0011	same
/D15.3/	6F	011	01111	010111	0011	101000	1100	flip
/D16.3/	70	011	10000	011011	0011	100100	1100	flip
/D17.3/	71	011	10001	100011	1100	100011	0011	same
/D18.3/	72	011	10010	010011	1100	010011	0011	same
/D19.3/	73	011	10011	110010	1100	110010	0011	same
/D20.3/	74	011	10100	001011	1100	001011	0011	same
/D21.3/	75	011	10101	101010	1100	101010	0011	same
/D22.3/	76	011	10110	011010	1100	011010	0011	same
/D23.3/	77	011	10111	111010	0011	000101	1100	flip
/D24.3/	78	011	11000	110011	0011	001100	1100	flip
/D25.3/	79	011	11001	100110	1100	100110	0011	same
/D26.3/	7A	011	11010	010110	1100	010110	0011	same
/D27.3/	7B	011	11011	110110	0011	001001	1100	flip
/D28.3/	7C	011	11100	001110	1100	001110	0011	same
/D29.3/	7D	011	11101	101110	0011	010001	1100	flip
/D30.3/	7E	011	11110	011110	0011	100001	1100	flip
/D31.3/	7F	011	11111	101011	0011	010100	1100	flip
/D0.4/	80	100	00000	100111	0010	011000	1101	same

TABLE A–1 VALID DATA CODES (*cont.*)

Name	Byte Value	8 Bits HGF	8 Bits EDCBA	10B Code Word (RD –) abcdei	10B Code Word (RD –) fghj	10B Code Word (RD +) abcdei	10B Code Word (RD +) fghj	New RD
/D1.4/	81	100	00001	011101	0010	100010	1101	same
/D2.4/	82	100	00010	101101	0010	010010	1101	same
/D3.4/	83	100	00011	110001	1101	110001	0010	flip
/D4.4/	84	100	00100	110101	0010	001010	1101	same
/D5.4/	85	100	00101	101001	1101	101001	0010	flip
/D6.4/	86	100	00110	011001	1101	011001	0010	flip
/D7.4/	87	100	00111	111000	1101	000111	0010	flip
/D8.4/	88	100	01000	111001	0010	000110	1101	same
/D9.4/	89	100	01001	100101	1101	100101	0010	flip
/D10.4/	8A	100	01010	010101	1101	010101	0010	flip
/D11.4/	8B	100	01011	110100	1101	110100	0010	flip
/D12.4/	8C	100	01100	001101	1101	001101	0010	flip
/D13.4/	8D	100	01101	101100	1101	101100	0010	flip
/D14.4/	8E	100	01110	011100	1101	011100	0010	flip
/D15.4/	8F	100	01111	010111	0010	101000	1101	same
/D16.4/	90	100	10000	011011	0010	100100	1101	same
/D17.4/	91	100	10001	100011	1101	100011	0010	flip
/D18.4/	92	100	10010	010011	1101	010011	0010	flip
/D19.4/	93	100	10011	110010	1101	110010	0010	flip
/D20.4/	94	100	10100	001011	1101	001011	0010	flip
/D21.4/	95	100	10101	101010	1101	101010	0010	flip
/D22.4/	96	100	10110	011010	1101	011010	0010	flip
/D23.4/	97	100	10111	111010	0010	000101	1101	same
/D24.4/	98	100	11000	110011	0010	001100	1101	same
/D25.4/	99	100	11001	100110	1101	100110	0010	flip
/D26.4/	9A	100	11010	010110	1101	010110	0010	flip
/D27.4/	9B	100	11011	110110	0010	001001	1101	same
/D28.4/	9C	100	11100	001110	1101	001110	0010	flip
/D29.4/	9D	100	11101	101110	0010	010001	1101	same
/D30.4/	9E	100	11110	011110	0010	100001	1101	same
/D31.4/	9F	100	11111	101011	0010	010100	1101	same
/D0.5/	A0	101	00000	100111	1010	011000	1010	flip
/D1.5/	A1	101	00001	011101	1010	100010	1010	flip
/D2.5/	A2	101	00010	101101	1010	010010	1010	flip
/D3.5/	A3	101	00011	110001	1010	110001	1010	same

TABLE A–1   VALID DATA CODES (*cont.*)

Name	Byte Value	8 Bits HGF	8 Bits EDCBA	10B Code Word (RD –) abcdei	10B Code Word (RD –) fghj	10B Code Word (RD +) abcdei	10B Code Word (RD +) fghj	New RD
/D4.5/	A4	101	00100	110101	1010	001010	1010	flip
/D5.5/	A5	101	00101	101001	1010	101001	1010	same
/D6.5/	A6	101	00110	011001	1010	011001	1010	same
/D7.5/	A7	101	00111	111000	1010	000111	1010	same
/D8.5/	A8	101	01000	111001	1010	000110	1010	flip
/D9.5/	A9	101	01001	100101	1010	100101	1010	same
/D10.5/	AA	101	01010	010101	1010	010101	1010	same
/D11.5/	AB	101	01011	110100	1010	110100	1010	same
/D12.5/	AC	101	01100	001101	1010	001101	1010	same
/D13.5/	AD	101	01101	101100	1010	101100	1010	same
/D14.5/	AE	101	01110	011100	1010	011100	1010	same
/D15.5/	AF	101	01111	010111	1010	101000	1010	flip
/D16.5/	B0	101	10000	011011	1010	100100	1010	flip
/D17.5/	B1	101	10001	100011	1010	100011	1010	same
/D18.5/	B2	101	10010	010011	1010	010011	1010	same
/D19.5/	B3	101	10011	110010	1010	110010	1010	same
/D20.5/	B4	101	10100	001011	1010	001011	1010	same
/D21.5/	B5	101	10101	101010	1010	101010	1010	same
/D22.5/	B6	101	10110	011010	1010	011010	1010	same
/D23.5/	B7	101	10111	111010	1010	000101	1010	flip
/D24.5/	B8	101	11000	110011	1010	001100	1010	flip
/D25.5/	B9	101	11001	100110	1010	100110	1010	same
/D26.5/	BA	101	11010	010110	1010	010110	1010	same
/D27.5/	BB	101	11011	110110	1010	001001	1010	flip
/D28.5/	BC	101	11100	001110	1010	001110	1010	same
/D29.5/	BD	101	11101	101110	1010	010001	1010	flip
/D30.5/	BE	101	11110	011110	1010	100001	1010	flip
/D31.5/	BF	101	11111	101011	1010	010100	1010	flip
/D0.6/	C0	110	00000	100111	0110	011000	0110	flip
/D1.6/	C1	110	00001	011101	0110	100010	0110	flip
/D2.6/	C2	110	00010	101101	0110	010010	0110	flip
/D3.6/	C3	110	00011	110001	0110	110001	0110	same
/D4.6/	C4	110	00100	110101	0110	001010	0110	flip
/D5.6/	C5	110	00101	101001	0110	101001	0110	same
/D6.6/	C6	110	00110	011001	0110	011001	0110	same

TABLE A–1 VALID DATA CODES (*cont.*)

Name	Byte Value	8 Bits		10B Code Word (RD –)		10B Code Word (RD +)		New RD
		HGF	EDCBA	abcdei	fghj	abcdei	fghj	
/D7.6/	C7	110	00111	111000	0110	000111	0110	same
/D8.6/	C8	110	01000	111001	0110	000110	0110	flip
/D9.6/	C9	110	01001	100101	0110	100101	0110	same
/D10.6/	CA	110	01010	010101	0110	010101	0110	same
/D11.6/	CB	110	01011	110100	0110	110100	0110	same
/D12.6/	CC	110	01100	001101	0110	001101	0110	same
/D13.6/	CD	110	01101	101100	0110	101100	0110	same
/D14.6/	CE	110	01110	011100	0110	011100	0110	same
/D15.6/	CF	110	01111	010111	0110	101000	0110	flip
/D16.6/	D0	110	10000	011011	0110	100100	0110	flip
/D17.6/	D1	110	10001	100011	0110	100011	0110	same
/D18.6/	D2	110	10010	010011	0110	010011	0110	same
/D19.6/	D3	110	10011	110010	0110	110010	0110	same
/D20.6/	D4	110	10100	001011	0110	001011	0110	same
/D21.6/	D5	110	10101	101010	0110	101010	0110	same
/D22.6/	D6	110	10110	011010	0110	011010	0110	same
/D23.6/	D7	110	10111	111010	0110	000101	0110	flip
/D24.6/	D8	110	11000	110011	0110	001100	0110	flip
/D25.6/	D9	110	11001	100110	0110	100110	0110	same
/D26.6/	DA	110	11010	010110	0110	010110	0110	same
/D27.6/	DB	110	11011	110110	0110	001001	0110	flip
/D28.6/	DC	110	11100	001110	0110	001110	0110	same
/D29.6/	DD	110	11101	101110	0110	010001	0110	flip
/D30.6/	DE	110	11110	011110	0110	100001	0110	flip
/D31.6/	DF	110	11111	101011	0110	010100	0110	flip
/D0.7/	E0	111	00000	100111	0001	011000	1110	same
/D1.7/	E1	111	00001	011101	0001	100010	1110	same
/D2.7/	E2	111	00010	101101	0001	010010	1110	same
/D3.7/	E3	111	00011	110001	1110	110001	0001	flip
/D4.7/	E4	111	00100	110101	0001	001010	1110	same
/D5.7/	E5	111	00101	101001	1110	101001	0001	flip
/D6.7/	E6	111	00110	011001	1110	011001	0001	flip
/D7.7/	E7	111	00111	111000	1110	000111	0001	flip
/D8.7/	E8	111	01000	111001	0001	000110	1110	same
/D9.7/	E9	111	01001	100101	1110	100101	0001	flip

TABLE A–1 VALID DATA CODES (*cont.*)

Name	Byte Value	8 Bits HGF	8 Bits EDCBA	10B Code Word (RD –) abcdei	10B Code Word (RD –) fghj	10B Code Word (RD +) abcdei	10B Code Word (RD +) fghj	New RD
/D10.7/	EA	111	01010	010101	1110	010101	0001	flip
/D11.7/	EB	111	01011	110100	1110	110100	1000	flip
/D12.7/	EC	111	01100	001101	1110	001101	0001	flip
/D13.7/	ED	111	01101	101100	1110	101100	1000	flip
/D14.7/	EE	111	01110	011100	1110	011100	1000	flip
/D15.7/	EF	111	01111	010111	0001	101000	1110	same
/D16.7/	F0	111	10000	011011	0001	100100	1110	same
/D17.7/	F1	111	10001	100011	0111	100011	0001	flip
/D18.7/	F2	111	10010	010011	0111	010011	0001	flip
/D19.7/	F3	111	10011	110010	1110	110010	0001	flip
/D20.7/	F4	111	10100	001011	0111	001011	0001	flip
/D21.7/	F5	111	10101	101010	1110	101010	0001	flip
/D22.7/	F6	111	10110	011010	1110	011010	0001	flip
/D23.7/	F7	111	10111	111010	0001	000101	1110	same
/D24.7/	F8	111	11000	110011	0001	001100	1110	same
/D25.7/	F9	111	11001	100110	1110	100110	0001	flip
/D26.7/	FA	111	11010	010110	1110	010110	0001	flip
/D27.7/	FB	111	11011	110110	0001	001001	1110	same
/D28.7/	FC	111	11100	001110	1110	001110	0001	flip
/D29.7/	FD	111	11101	101110	0001	010001	1110	same
/D30.7/	FE	111	11110	011110	0001	100001	1110	same
/D31.7/	FF	111	11111	101011	0001	010100	1110	same

TABLE A–2 VALID SPECIAL CODES

Name	Byte Value	8 Bits HGF	8 Bits EDCBA	10B Code Word (RD −) abcdei	fghj	10B Code Word (RD +) abcdei	fghj	New RD
/K28.0/	1C	000	11100	001111	0100	110000	1011	same
/K28.1/	3C	001	11100	001111	1001	110000	0110	flip
/K28.2/	5C	010	11100	001111	0101	110000	1010	flip
/K28.3/	7C	011	11100	001111	0011	110000	1100	flip
/K28.4/	9C	100	11100	001111	0010	110000	1101	same
/K28.5/	BC	101	11100	001111	1010	110000	0101	flip
/K28.6/	DC	110	11100	001111	0110	110000	1001	flip
/K28.7/	FC	111	11100	001111	1000	110000	0111	same
/K23.7/	F7	111	10111	111010	1000	000101	0111	same
/K27.7/	FB	111	11011	110110	1000	001001	0111	same
/K29.7/	FD	111	11101	101110	1000	010001	0111	same
/K30.7/	FE	111	11110	011110	1000	100001	0111	same

References

[ABRA85]   Abramson, N., "Development of the ALOHANET," *IEEE Transactions on Information Theory*, Vol. IT-31, March 1985.

[AMD96]   Kalkunte, Mohan and Jayant Kadambi, Performance Simulations of 1 Gb/s Networks, presented to IEEE 802.3z Task Force, May 1996.

[ANSI91]   ANSI Standard X3.183, High-performance Parallel Interface, Mechanical, Electrical and Signaling Protocol Specification (HIPPI-PH), 1991.

[ANSI92]   ANSI Standard X3.210, Information Systems–High-performance Parallel Interface, Framing Protocol Specification (HIPPI-FP), 1992.

[ANSI93]   ANSI Standard X3.222, Information Systems–High-performance Parallel Interface, Switch Control Specification (HIPPI-SC), 1993.

[ANSI94]   ANSI Standard X3.230, Information Technology—Fibre Channel—Physical and Signaling Interface (FC-PH), 1994.

[ANSI94a]   ANSI Standard X3.131, Information Systems—Small Computer Systems Interface-2 (SCSI-2), 1994.

[ANSI96]   ANSI Standard X3.287, Information Technology—Fibre Channel—Link Encapsulation, 1996.

[ANSI97]   ANSI Standard X3.300, Information Technology—High-Performance Parallel Interface—Serial Specification, 1997.

[APPL90]   Sidhu, Gursharan S., Richard F. Andrews, and Alan B. Oppenheimer, *Inside AppleTalk*, 2nd ed., Addison-Wesley, 1990.

[ATM95]   ATM Forum Technical Committee, LAN Emulation over ATM, Version 1.0, January 1995.

[BARR96]   Barry, Dave, *Dave Barry in Cyberspace*, Crown Publishers, 1996.

[BOGG78]   Boggs, David R., and Robert M. Metcalfe, Communications network repeater, U.S. Patent 4,099,024, assigned to Xerox Corporation.

[BOGG88]   Boggs, D. R., J. C. Mogul, and C. A. Kent, "Measured Capacity of an Ethernet: Myths and Reality," *Proceedings of SIGCOMM '88*, ACM SIGCOMM, 1988, pp. 222–234.

[CCITT92] CCITT Recommendation G.707, Synchronous Digital Hierarchy Bit Rates, June 1992.

[CHES91]   Chesson, G., "The Evolution of XTP," *Proceedings of the Third International Conference on High Speed Networking*, North-Holland, Amsterdam, 1991.

[CISCO97] cisco Systems, Inc., "Fast EtherChannel," *White Paper*, 1997.

[COME95]   Comer, Douglas E., *Internetworking with TCP/IP, Volume 1: Principles, Protocols, and Architecture*, Prentice-Hall, 1995.

[CUNN97]   Cunningham, David, Modal Bandwidth Investigation: Examination of the Fundamentals of Multimode Fiber Behavior with Laser Sources, presented to IEEE 802.3z, November 1997.

[DEPRY93] De Prycker, Martin, *Asynchronous Transfer Mode*, 2nd ed., Ellis Horwood, Ltd., 1993.

[DALA81]   Dalal, Yogen K., and Robert S. Printis, "48-bit Absolute Internet and Ethernet Host Numbers," *Proceedings of the Seventh Data Communications Symposium*, 1981.

[DIX80]   Digital Equipment Corp., Intel Corp., and Xerox Corp., The Ethernet: A Local Area Network, Data Link Layer and Physical Layer Specifications, Version 1.0, September, 1980.

[DIX82]   Digital Equipment Corp., Intel Corp., and Xerox Corp., The Ethernet: A Local Area Network, Data Link Layer and Physical Layer Specifications, Version 2.0, November, 1982.

[EIA69]   EIA Standard RS-232-C, Interface Between Data Terminal Equipment and Data Communications Equipment Employing Serial Binary Data Interchange, October 1969, reaffirmed June 1981.

[EIA91]   EIA/TIA Standard 568, Commercial Building Telecommunications Wiring Standard, July 1991.

[EIA91a]   EIA/TIA Bulletin TSB-36, Additional Cable Specifications for Unshielded Pair Cables, November 1991.

[FCA94]   Fibre Channel Association, *Fibre Channel: Connection to the Future,* 1994.

[FRAN84]   Franaszek, Peter A., and Albert X. Widmer, Byte oriented DC-balanced (0,4) 8B/10B partitioned block transmission code, U.S. Patent 4,486,739 assigned to International Business Machines Corp.

[FRAZ97]   Frazier, Howard, Results of Field Measurements of Optical Fibers, presented to IEEE 802.3z, November 1997.

[GLEI87]   Gleick, James, *Chaos: Making a New Science,* Viking Penguin Press, 1987.

[GOSIP91]   National Institute of Standards and Technology, Government Open Systems Interconnection Profile, Version 2, October 1991.

[HAMM75] Hammond, J. L., J. E. Brown, and S. S. Liu, "Development of a Transmission Error Model and an Error Control Model," *Technical Report RADC-TR-75-138,* Rome Air Development Center, 1975.

[IEEE90]   IEEE Standard 802, Overview and Architecture, 1990.

[IEEE90a]   ISO/IEC Standard 8802-4, Token-passing bus access method and physical layer specifications [ISO publication of IEEE Standard 802.4], 1990.

[IEEE93]   IEEE Standard 802.3j, now published as [IEEE96], Clauses 15–18, 1993.

[IEEE93a]   ISO/IEC Standard 10038, Media Access Control (MAC) Bridges [ISO publication of IEEE Standard 802.1D], 1993.

[IEEE94]   ISO/IEC Standard 8802-2, Logical Link Control [ISO publication of IEEE Standard 802.2], 1994.

[IEEE94a]   ISO/IEC Standard 8802-9, Integrated Services (IS) LAN Interface at the Medium Access Control (MAC) and Physical (PHY) Layers [ISO publication of IEEE Standard 802.9], 1994.

[IEEE95]   IEEE Standard 802.3u, Media Access Control (MAC) Parameters, Physical Layer, Medium Attachment Units, and Repeater for 100 Mb/s Operation, Type 100BASE-T, 1995.

[IEEE95a]   IEEE Standard 802.12, Demand Priority Access Method, Physical Layer and Repeater Specification for 100 Mb/s Operation, 1995.

[IEEE95b]   ISO/IEC Standard 8802-5, Token ring access method and physical layer specifications [ISO publication of IEEE Standard 802.5], 1995.

[IEEE96]   ISO/IEC Standard 8802-3, Carrier sense multiple access with collision detection (CSMA/CD) access method and physical layer specifications [ISO publication of IEEE Standard 802.3], 1996.

[IEEE96a]   IEEE 802.3, Gigabit Ethernet Project Authorization Request, July 1996.

[IEEE97]   IEEE Standard 802.3x, Specification for 802.3 Full Duplex Operation, 1997.

[IEEE97a]   IEEE Standard 802.3y, Physical Layer Specification for 100 Mb/s Operation on Two Pairs of Category 3 or Better Balanced Twisted Pair Cable (100BASE-T2), 1997.

[IEEE97b]   Draft Standard IEEE 802.1p, Revision to IEEE 802.1D (MAC Bridges): Traffic Class Expediting and Dynamic Multicast Filtering, 1997 (not approved at the time of this writing).

[IEEE97c]   Draft Standard IEEE 802.1Q, Virtual Bridged Local Area Networks, 1997 (not approved at the time of this writing).

[IEEE97d]   Draft Standard IEEE 802.3ac, Frame Extensions for Virtual Bridged Local Area Networks (VLAN) Tagging on 802.3 Networks, 1997 (not approved at the time of this writing).

[IEEE98]   Draft Standard IEEE 802.3z, Media Access Control (MAC) Parameters, Physical Layer, Repeater and Management Parameters for 1000 Mb/s Operation, 1998 (not approved at the time of this writing).

[ISO84]   ISO/IEC Standard 8073: 1984, Information Technology—Open System Interconnection—Connection Oriented Transport Protocol Specification, 1984.

[ISO87]   ISO/IEC Standard 8824, Information Technology—Open System Interconnection—Specification of Abstract Syntax Notation One (ASN.1), 1987.

[ISO87a]   ISO Standard 4335, Information Processing Systems—Data Communications—High-level Data Link Control Elements of Procedures, 1987.

[ISO87b]   ISO Standard 8473, Information Processing Systems—Data Communications—Protocol for providing the connectionless-mode network service, 1987.

[ISO89]   ISO/IEC Standard 9314–2, Information Processing Systems—Fibre Distributed Data Interface—Part 2: FDDI Token Ring Media Access Control (MAC), 1989.

[ISO89a] ISO/IEC Standard 9314-1, Information Processing Systems—Fibre Distributed Data Interface—Part 1: FDDI Token Ring Physical Layer Protocol (PHY), 1989.

[ISO89b] ISO/IEC Standard 9596, Information Technology—Open Systems Interconnection—Common Management Information Protocol Specification (CMIP), 1989.

[ISO90] ISO/IEC Standard 9314-3, Information Processing Systems—Fibre Distributed Data Interface—Part 3: FDDI Token Ring Physical Layer Medium Dependent (PMD), 1990.

[ISO94] ISO/IEC Standard 7498-1, Information Technology—Open System Interconnection—Basic Reference Model: The Basic Model: 1994.

[KESS95] Kessler, G., and W. Goralski, *Fibre Channel: Standards, Applications, and Products*, December 1995.

[KLEIN75] Kleinrock, L., and F. Tobagi, "Random Access Techniques for Data Transmission over Packet-Switched Radio Channels," *Proceedings of the National Computer Conference*, 1975.

[LEWE91] Lewen, Ronald C., et. al, Communication network integrating voice data and video with distributed call processing, United States Patent 5,341,374, assigned to TriLAN Systems Corporation.

[MALA90] Malamud, Carl, *Analyzing Novell Networks*, Van Nostrand Reinhold, 1990.

[METC76] Metcalfe, R. M., and D. R. Boggs, "Ethernet: Distributed Packet Switching for Local Computer Networks," *Communications of the ACM 19-7*, July 1976.

[METC77] Metcalfe, Robert M., David R. Boggs, Charles P. Thacker, Butler W. Lampson, Multipoint data communication system with collision detection, U. S. Patent 4,063,220, assigned to Xerox Corporation.

[NORT96] Northern Telecom, *S/DMS TransportNode OC-192 Product Portfolio*, 1996.

[PACE96] Christensen, D., and D. Flynn, "Scaling Workgroup Performance (Switched Ethernet and Fast Ethernet)," *3Com Technical Journal*, May 1996.

[PADL85] Padlipsky, Michael A., *The Elements of Networking Style*, Prentice-Hall, 1985.

[PCI95]   Peripheral Component Specification, Revision 2.1S, PCI Special
             Interest Group, 1995.

[PERL92]   Perlman, Radia, *Interconnections: Bridges and Routers,* Addison-
             Wesley, 1992.

[PETER72]   Peterson, W. W., and T. J. Weldon, *Error Correcting Codes,* 2nd
             ed., MIT Press, 1972.

[RFC791]   Postel, John, Request for Comments 791: Internet Protocol, Sep-
             tember, 1981.

[RFC872]   Padlipsky, M. A., Request for Comments 872: TCP-on-a-LAN,
             September, 1982.

[RFC1058]   Hedrick, C. L., Request for Comments 1058: Routing Informa-
             tion Protocol, June 1988.

[RFC1094]   Sun Microsystems, Request for Comments 1094: NFS-Network
             File System Protocol specification, March 1989.

[RFC1157]   Case, J. D., M. Fedor, M. L. Schoffstall, and C. Davin, Request
             for Comments 1157: Simple Network Management Protocol
             (SNMP), May 1990.

[RFC1242]   Bradner, S., Request for Comments 1242: Benchmarking termi-
             nology for network interconnection devices, July 1991.

[RFC1374]   Renwick, J., and A. Nicholson, Request for Comments 1374: IP
             and ARP on HIPPI, October 1992.

[RFC1504]   Oppenheimer, Alan, Appletalk Update—Based Routing Proto-
             col: Enhanced AppleTalk Routing, August 1993.

[RFC1516]   McMaster, D., and K. McCloghrie, 802.3 Repeater MIB, Sep-
             tember 1993.

[RFC1548]   Simpson, W., Request for Comments 1548: The Point-to-Point
             Protocol (PPP), December 1993.

[RFC1757]   Waldbusser, S., Remote Network Monitoring Management
             Information Base, February 1995.

[RFC1944]   Bradner, S., and J. McQuaid, Benchmarking Methodology for
             Network Interconnect Devices, May 1996.

[RFC2108]   de Graaf, K., D. Romascanu, D. McMaster, and K. McCloghrie,
             Definitions of Managed Objects for IEEE 802.3 Repeater
             Devices using SMIv2, February 1997.

[ROSE96]   Rose, Marshall T., *The Simple Book—An Introduction to Net-
             working Management,* 2nd ed., Prentice-Hall, 1996.

[RTT87]   RTT Belgium, "ATM Considerations about the Cell Size," *CEPT/NA5*, Stuttgart, June 1987.

[SCHW87]   Schwartz, Mischa, *Telecommunication Networks*, Addison-Wesley, 1987.

[SEIF83]   Seifert, Rich, Introduction to Ethernet, presentation at Digital Equipment Corporation User's Society (DECUS), Spring 1983.

[SEIF89]   Seifert, Rich, *Choosing Between Bridges and Routers*, Infonetics Research Institute, 1989 (2nd ed., 1990; 3rd ed., 1991).

[SEIF90]   Seifert, Rich, Have Remote Bridge Vendors Made a Big Blunder?, *Data Communications*, April 1990.

[SEIF91]   Seifert, Rich, "Ethernet: 10 Years After," *BYTE*, January 1991.

[SEIF93]   Seifert, Rich, *The Design and Planning of Enterprise-Wide AppleTalk Internetworks*, Apple Computer, 1993.

[SEIF96]   Seifert, Rich, "The Use of Backpressure for Congestion Control in Half Duplex CSMA/CD LANs," *Networks and Communications Consulting*, 1996, available by anonymous ftp at:

             ftp://ftp.netcom.com/pub/se/seifert/TechRept15.pdf

[SHAH93]   Shah, Amit, and G. Ramakrishnan, *FDDI: A High Speed Network*, Prentice-Hall, 1993.

[SPUR96]   Spurgeon, Charles, *Ethernet Configuration Guidelines: A Quick Reference Guide to the Official Ethernet (IEEE 802.3) Configuration Rules*, Peer-to-Peer Communications, 1996.

[STEV94]   Stevens, W. Richard, *TCP/IP Illustrated, Volume 1: The Protocols*, Addison-Wesley, 1994.

[TANEN88]   Tanenbaum, Andrew S., *Computer Networks*, Prentice-Hall, 1988.

[TIA96]   Telecommunications Industry Association, Minutes of the TIA meeting, Ottawa, Ontario, Canada, Sept 9–13, 1996.

[VALEN92]   Valenzano, A., C. Demartini, and L. Ciminiera, *MAP and TOP Communications*, Addison-Wesley, 1992.

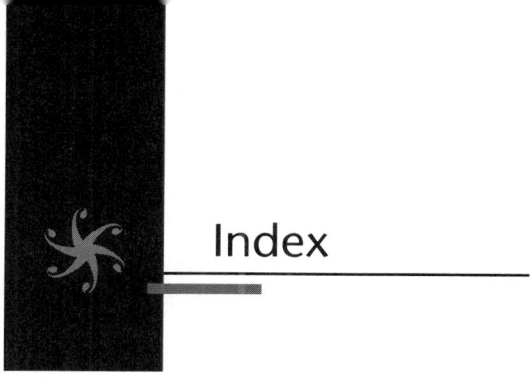

Index

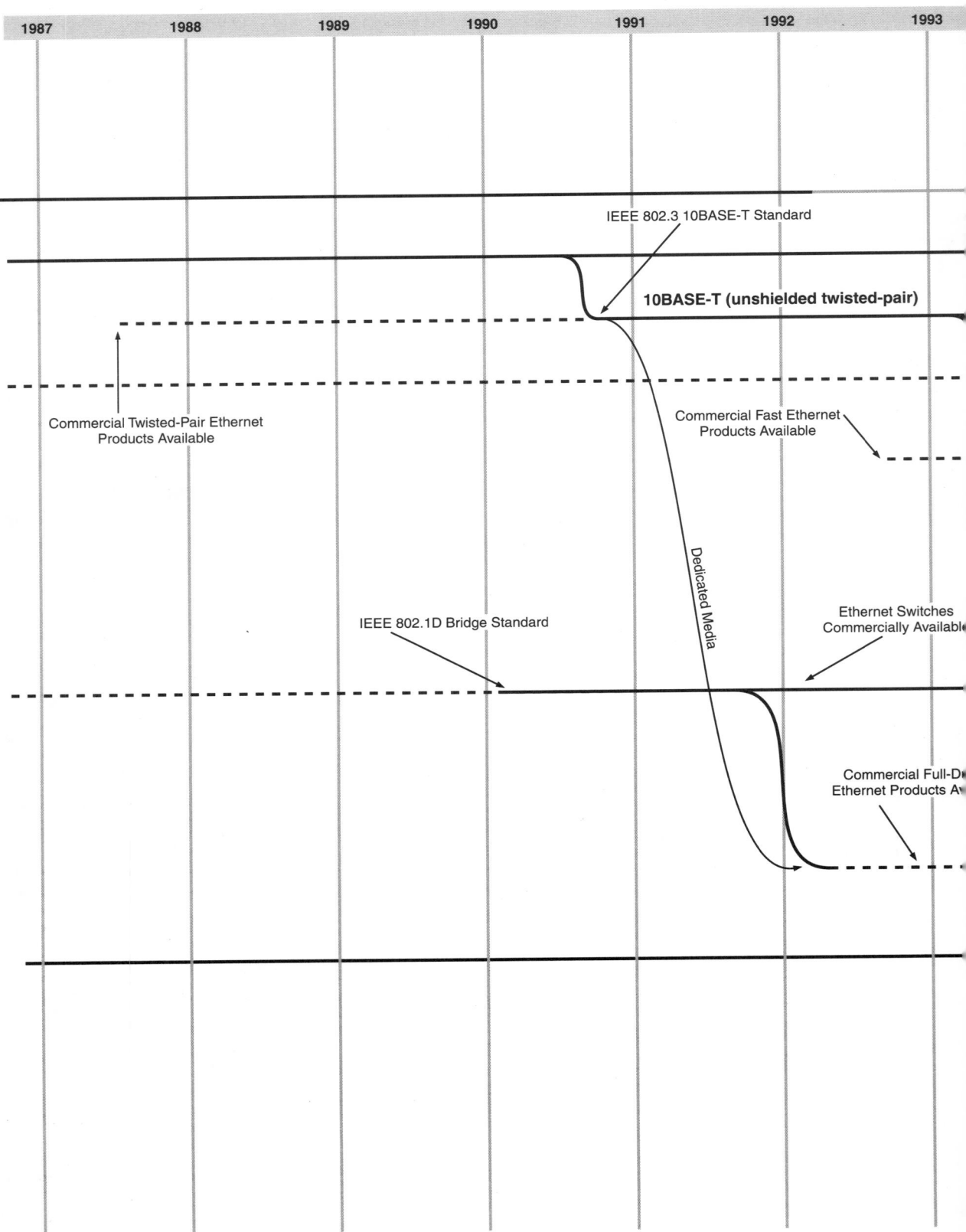

| 1987 | 1988 | 1989 | 1990 | 1991 | 1992 | 1993 |

IEEE 802.3 10BASE-T Standard

10BASE-T (unshielded twisted-pair)

Commercial Twisted-Pair Ethernet
Products Available

Commercial Fast Ethernet
Products Available

Dedicated Media

IEEE 802.1D Bridge Standard

Ethernet Switches
Commercially Available

Commercial Full-D
Ethernet Products A